Lou Dempsey

THE HOUSE OF

Also by Russell Miller:

Bunny: The Real Story of Playboy

THE HOUSE OF

Russell Miller

HENRY HOLT AND COMPANY

NEW YORK

First published in the United States in 1986 by Henry Holt and Company,
521 Fifth Avenue, New York, New York, 10175.
Published simultaneously in Canada.

Library of Congress Cataloging in Publication Data
Miller, Russell.
The house of Getty.
Includes index.
1. Getty, J. Paul (Jean Paul) 1892–1976.   2. Getty
family.   3. Businessmen—United States—Biography.
4. Millionaires—United States—Biography.   5. Petroleum
industry and trade—United States.   I. Title.
HD9570.G4M55   1986   332′.092′4   [B]   85-30540
ISBN 0-8050-0023-2

Printed in the United States of America
10   9   8   7   6   5   4   3   2

ISBN 0-8050-0023-2

To my family,
with heartfelt thanks
that our name is not Getty

Contents

List of Illustrations

THE HOUSE OF
GETTY

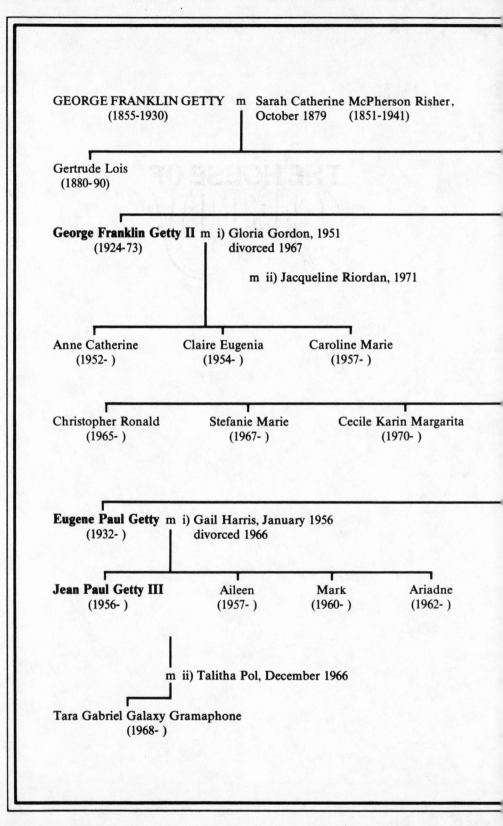

GEORGE FRANKLIN GETTY m Sarah Catherine McPherson Risher,
(1855-1930)   October 1879   (1851-1941)

Gertrude Lois
(1880-90)

George Franklin Getty II m i) Gloria Gordon, 1951
(1924-73)   divorced 1967

                                    m ii) Jacqueline Riordan, 1971

Anne Catherine   Claire Eugenia   Caroline Marie
(1952-)   (1954-)   (1957-)

Christopher Ronald   Stefanie Marie   Cecile Karin Margarita
(1965-)   (1967-)   (1970-)

Eugene Paul Getty m i) Gail Harris, January 1956
(1932-)   divorced 1966

Jean Paul Getty III   Aileen   Mark   Ariadne
(1956-)   (1957-)   (1960-)   (1962-)

                          m ii) Talitha Pol, December 1966

Tara Gabriel Galaxy Gramaphone
(1968-)

GETTY FAMILY TREE

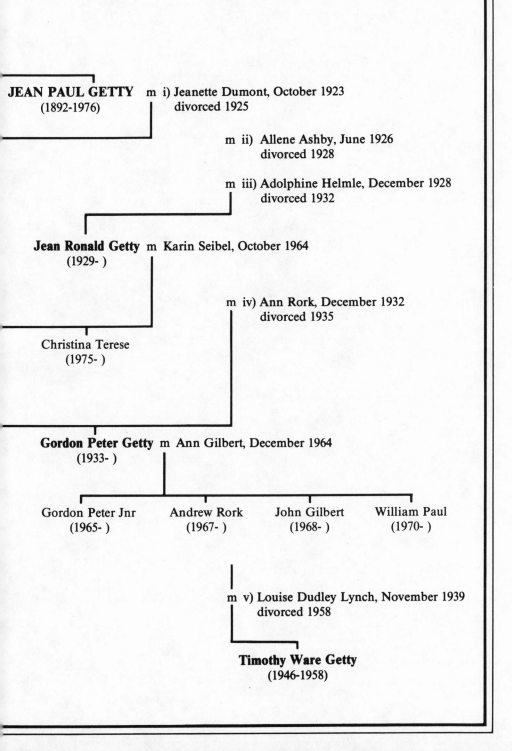

JEAN PAUL GETTY m i) Jeanette Dumont, October 1923
(1892-1976)   divorced 1925

m ii) Allene Ashby, June 1926
       divorced 1928

m iii) Adolphine Helmle, December 1928
        divorced 1932

Jean Ronald Getty m Karin Seibel, October 1964
(1929-)

m iv) Ann Rork, December 1932
       divorced 1935

Christina Terese
(1975-)

Gordon Peter Getty m Ann Gilbert, December 1964
(1933-)

Gordon Peter Jnr   Andrew Rork   John Gilbert   William Paul
(1965-)   (1967-)   (1968-)   (1970-)

m v) Louise Dudley Lynch, November 1939
      divorced 1958

Timothy Ware Getty
(1946-1958)

Prologue

The Midas contagion

In the grounds of a white-painted hacienda overlooking the Pacific at Santa Monica there is a simple marble mausoleum, forlornly unvisited. Three names, companionable in death as never in life, are engraved on the facade: J. Paul Getty 1892-1976, George F. Getty II 1924-1973, Timothy Getty 1946-1958.

Paul Getty, once said to be the richest man in the world, last saw this place more than thirty-five years ago, when it was a tranquil oasis of lawns, eucalyptus trees and lemon groves, tucked into the lower flanks of the Santa Monica mountains. Today, traffic roars day and night along a nearby six-lane highway lined with gimcrack motels and junk-food joints. Where the mountains were once covered with chaparral, they are now covered with condominiums. Where there was once the sweet smell of the ocean, there is now the noxious stench of exhaust fumes, hamburgers and pizzas.

Even in death, the Gettys can find no peace.

The old man shares the mausoleum with the oldest and youngest of his five sons. First to die was little Timmy who, like his famous namesake Tiny Tim, was marked out from the start by the angelic nature – even saintliness – that so often characterises the chronically sick child. His father adored him, but saw him infrequently, since Timmy lived in New York and Getty lived in hotel suites in Europe. A few weeks before Timmy was twelve, Getty telephoned to ask the boy what he would like for his birthday. He replied: 'I want your love, Daddy, and I want to see you.' He died in hospital a few weeks later, without seeing his father. Getty was devastated.

But there was still George, big, bluff George – the only Getty of his generation to show any interest in the family business. To their father's despair, Ronnie, Paul and Gordon were all hopeless businessmen and, one by one, they dropped out of Getty Oil. It was George who was groomed to take over, George who would ensure that a Getty remained at the helm of the business founded by his grandfather and built into an empire by his father. Then George killed himself.

With his cherished hopes of a dynasty crushed, the old man looked to his museum for a lasting memorial, a monument to his success, and he

1

made it into the most richly endowed foundation in the world. But money tainted his philanthropy, just as surely as it rotted the enigmatic bonds that normally bind families together. The J. Paul Getty Museum became feared for its fabulous wealth and the threat it represented to the stability of the art market. Its power became universally known as 'the Getty factor'. Instead of a monument, the old man begat an epithet.

The museum is not far from its creator's last resting place, just a short walk along a gravel path which winds through thickets of lustrous evergreen shrubs. It is a rich man's folly, just as ludicrous and wonderful as San Simeon: a full-scale replica, here in Malibu, California, of a Roman villa which was buried by the eruption of Vesuvius in 79 AD. Getty never saw it, but was hurt when critics derided it as being like something out of Cecil B. De Mille.

The eldest of the old man's three surviving sons, Ronald, lives close by the museum. Just outside the gates, turn left along the Pacific Coast Highway, left again into Sunset Boulevard, then left through the wrought iron portals of Bel Air. Some of the most high-profile personalities in the world live here. Ronald Getty is not one of them. He is a failed film producer and sometime real-estate developer, a large, surly man with the appearance and demeanour of a dour bank manager, who is rarely seen in public except when he is required to make an appearance in court.

The Gettys are ferocious litigants. In the chaotic records office at Los Angeles Superior Court, entire shelves are occupied by volume after volume of yellowing documents chronicling the Getty family squabbles. Most of the time, the Gettys fight about money – divided by the very stuff that was to have proved their making – although Ronald's mother once filed a suit to evict her son from his house on South Beverly Glen Boulevard so that she could live there alone. Ronald professed himself to be 'distressed' that she had chosen to air family problems in public – nevertheless, when the time came, he did not shrink from nursing his own vendettas through legal channels too.

A recent long-running courtroom drama centred around payments made by a family trust to J. Paul Getty's heirs. Ronald was aggrieved, for some reason, that he received only $3000 a year from the trust, whereas his half-brothers, Paul and Gordon, did rather better, collecting around $120 million a year *each*. His attempts, through the courts, to obtain an equal share of the family fortune were naturally vigorously opposed by his loving brothers, who took the view that Ronald's miserly share was Ronald's bad luck. Actually, the explanation is rooted in the murky past. Fifty years ago Getty, angered by the amount he had to pay to divorce Ronald's mother, took his revenge by virtually disinheriting their son – a wholly arbitrary act that

2

effectively ensured the present feud between Ronald and his brothers.

But Ronald's suit was no more than a passing tiff when compared to the fury recently directed at the cherubic head of Gordon Getty, who was sole trustee of the $4-billion family fortune and was named in 1984 as the richest man in America. Gordon, an enthusiastic amateur composer and singer, affects the distracted mien of an absent-minded, slightly dotty, but thoroughly endearing professor. He is liable to wear odd socks, for example, or forget where he has left his car, or close his eyes during a dinner party to 'study opera scores'. Tall and curly-haired, he lives with his wife Ann and four sons in a three-storey mansion in San Francisco with a wonderful view across the bay to the Golden Gate bridge. For a multi-millionaire, his lifestyle is unostentatious: he likes camping with his kids and watching football on television, particularly if his home-town team, the San Francisco 49-ers, is playing.

Being of a musical and artistic bent, Gordon was perhaps doubly unwelcome when he began to take an interest in Getty Oil, to the exasperation of the directors who viewed him as something of an eccentric. Irritation turned to alarm when Gordon became enamoured of the idea of following in his father's footsteps as an oil tycoon and taking over control of the company. 'I didn't want to go into the office every day,' he said, 'but I would like to have been able to call the shots.'

He was never to get the chance, though. If the company directors were alarmed, his relatives were outraged at the prospect of dreamy Gordon running Getty Oil and rushed to their lawyers. Gordon was positively deluged with lawsuits: even his fifteen-year-old nephew, the exotically named Tara Gabriel Galaxy Gramaphone Getty, issued a writ. Most of the suits were aimed at clipping Gordon's wings by getting a co-trustee appointed, but George Getty's three daughters (known in the family, unaffectionately, as 'the Georgettes') filed a suit to have Gordon declared unsuitable as a trustee and thrown out.

When it dawned on Gordon that he was not going to be able to take over the reins of Getty Oil, he declared his second preference was to sell the company. This naturally prompted further writs, but he was not to be thwarted: out of the melée there emerged the biggest corporate takeover in US history – a $9.9 billion dollar deal to sell the family business to Texaco. Afterwards, one of the Georgettes fired off a bitter and angry letter to Gordon. 'I hope you are satisfied,' she wrote, 'now that Getty Oil is gone.'

Gordon's older brother, Paul, took no part in these proceedings, not out of any respect for his brother or revulsion at the spectacle his family was making of itself but because he wanted to avoid having to appear as a witness in an American court. Paul was a heroin addict, which made travelling difficult. He lived until recently as a recluse in a large, gloomy house in Cheyne Walk, Chelsea, with only a manservant for company. In London, he was known as a lover of antiquarian books – his collection is worth well over a million dollars – but he never appears at parties or social functions. For nearly fifteen years Paul has been mourning his second wife, the beautiful Talitha, who died of a heroin overdose in Rome. He blames himself for the tragedy and believes he could have saved her life, had he not been stupefied by drugs at the time. To help him forget, he drinks a bottle of rum a day.

But it is Paul's oldest son, J. Paul Getty III, who is the most striking casualty of the Getty millions. Kidnapped in Rome in 1973, his ear was cut off before his grandfather could be persuaded to pay a ransom for his release. Young Paul never really recovered from the ordeal. Restless, disturbed and apparently bent on self-destruction, he virtually lived on drink and drugs until, at the age of twenty-four, he suffered a stroke in Los Angeles. His father, trapped in his own misery in Cheyne Walk, refused to pay the boy's medical bills until obliged to do so by a court.

J. Paul Getty III is today blind, quadriplegic and unable to speak. He lives in San Francisco and is looked after by nurses round the clock and loved by his young wife, Martine, who clings movingly to the belief that Paul will one day get better. No doctor encourages her in this belief.

In 1976, the year J. Paul Getty died, his autobiography was published posthumously. 'Despite anything and everything,' he wrote, 'be it wealth, divorce, tragedy or any of the other myriad conditions and tribulations of life, the Getty family *is* a family and will continue to be one. That is not a boast. It is a statement of fact made with no little pride.'

PART ONE

THE MAKING OF AN OILMAN
1903-23

1. *'Set another place for breakfast'*

Oil Creek was a shallow, malodorous stream which wound through dark-forested hills of pine and hemlock in north-west Pennsylvania two hundred years ago. The Seneca and Cornplanter Indians who lived along the banks of the creek floated blankets on the water to collect the iridescent scum smearing the surface and squeezed the greasy residue into earthenware pots, using it as a liniment or cure-all medicine for aches and pains.

Not long after the War of Independence, General Benjamin Lincoln was conducting a government survey in the area and considered the curative properties of Oil Creek to be worthy of note.

In the northern part of Pennsylvania, [he reported in 1785] there is a creek called Oil Creek, which empties itself into the Allegheny, on top of which floats an oil, similar to what is called Barbadoes tar, and from which may be collected, by one man, several gallons in a day. The troops, in marching that way, halted at the spring, collected the oil, and bathed their joints in it. This gave them great relief, and freed them immediately from the rheumatic complaints with which many of them were affected.

Although land bordering the creek was rich and fertile, white settlers were initially deterred by the noxious stench rising from the water. But news of the miraculous properties of 'Seneca oil' soon spread and before the turn of the century an enterprising young man by the name of Nathaniel Carey was in business selling it for twenty dollars a barrel to a druggist in Pittsburgh. Carey, one of the first settlers willing to tolerate Oil Creek's fetid fumes, bribed the Seneca Indians to take him upstream in their canoes to show him where the oil seeped from a spring. He promptly staked a claim to a tract of the surrounding river bank and began collecting the oil in kegs, using a flat wooden paddle to scrape it from the surface of the water. When he had filled a couple of kegs, he rode the eighty miles to Pittsburgh, where the druggist purified it and sold it in bottles to the pioneer settlers who regularly stopped in the town to stock up with supplies before setting out into the unknown.

Apart from its dubious value as a patent medicine, the oil which oozed from the ground in so many American states was generally regarded as a pollutant and a damned nuisance, particularly by the men

7

who earned their living drilling for salt. Time and again, holes laboriously bored with an iron chisel bit, worked by a man jumping on a hinged plank, were abandoned when the bit came up dripping with oil. Salt-well drillers referred to oil, with disgust, as the 'devil's tar'. In 1829 two men drilling for brine near Burkesville, Kentucky, hit a pocket of oil instead and so unleashed America's first 'gusher'. With barely a warning rumble, a mighty column of oil and gas shot high into the air, demolishing the derrick. The drillers fled for their lives and within minutes the gusher belched into a terrifying inferno, setting fire to the surrounding woodland and destroying hundreds of acres of forest, further convincing salt-well drillers of oil's pernicious nature.

In 1850 a new wonder cure, Kier's Rock Oil, appeared on the patent medicine market, lauded by a lyrical little verse:

> The healthful balm, from Nature's secret spring,
> The bloom of health and life to man will bring;
> As from her depths the magic fluid flows,
> To calm our sufferings and assuage our woes.

Samuel Kier was a colourful character with a successful business operating canal boats between Pittsburgh and Philadelphia. He also had an interest in his father's salt well at Tarentum, to the north of Pittsburgh, and when he learned that oil oozing up through the well was drained off and allowed to run into the ground to prevent it con-taminating the brine, he resolved to put it to better use. Before long, the rank black fluid was being peddled around the country, in half-pint bottles, as 'Nature's Remedy from Four Hundred Feet below the Earth's surface'. A born showman, Mr Kier did not hesitate to make astonishing claims for Kier's Rock Oil, not least that the lame were made to walk and 'several who were blind have been made to see' with nothing more than the recommended dose of three teaspoonsful three times a day. 'Cases that were pronounced hopeless and abandoned by Physicians of unquestioned celebrity,' an advertising leaflet promised, 'have been made to exclaim "This is the most wonderful remedy ever discovered".'

Kier's Rock Oil suffered, however, from a major marketing flaw: it smelled disgusting, even to white settlers to whom personal hygiene was a low priority, and tasted even worse. In an attempt to rid the stuff of its powerful stench, Kier asked a local chemist to purify the oil in a still, a process that caused an even worse stink and so infuriated his neighbours on Seventh Avenue in Pittsburgh that they lodged a formal complaint before a magistrate. In the unlikely event of them not being asphyxiated by the smell, they said, they certainly expected Kier's experiments to result in an explosion that would dispatch the entire neighbourhood to kingdom come. The magistrate was sympathetic and obliged Kier to move his refinery to a site outside the city limits.

As production of oil at Tarentum far exceeded Mr Kier's most fervent attempts to sell it at fifty cents a bottle, he looked around for other uses for the stuff. Even in its refined state it still smelled just as bad, but Kier discovered to his delight that the processed product would burn with a bright light, and without smoking, in a modified camphene lamp. Not only that, but he could undercut the price of whale oil by at least one dollar a gallon. Kier was soon in business selling 'carbon oil illuminant' at a dollar fifty the gallon.

Whale oil had been the primary source of feeble illumination in log cabins across America for decades, as well as lubricating the spindles and bearings in early machinery. But the whaling grounds were being worked out and the great whaling fleets operating from New Bedford and Nantucket were finding it increasingly difficult to meet the rising demand. As railroads struck out towards the west and the first steamships chugged the coastal waters and factories were built to accommodate burgeoning new industries, the search for alternative sources of oil was stepped up, both in Europe and America.

Oil was extracted from other animal fats, vegetables, coal, shale and bitumen, with varying degrees of success, but the oil in the ground was largely ignored (it was thought it could only be collected in small quantities) until the autumn of 1853 when a consortium of businessmen, perhaps attracted by the success of the indefatigable Samuel Kier, set up the Pennsylvania Rock Oil Company. They leased a hundred-acre farm on the banks of Oil Creek where, they had been told, oil would fill any trench dug in the spongy soil. But the amount that could be collected from ground seepage proved disappointingly small and the company did not prosper. It was thus in a spirit of desperation rather than adventurous speculation that the directors decided, in 1859, to drill a well.

No one had ever tried to drill for oil before, and in the nearby township of Titusville the notion was widely ridiculed, as was the man put in charge of the drilling – Edwin L. Drake. Born on a dirt farm in the Catskills and barely educated, Drake was thirty-nine years old, a drifter with a career only remarkable for its relentless mediocrity. He had been a clerk on a Lake Erie passenger boat, a farm labourer, a hotel clerk in Michigan, an assistant in a dry goods store in New York and finally a railroad conductor before he arrived in Titusville and got a job with the ailing rock oil company as an agent at $20 a week. In order to bolster his status in the town, the company addressed letters to him at the American Hotel as 'Colonel Drake', an appellation he did not find in the least disagreeable and which would stay with him for the rest of his life.

When 'the Colonel', resplendent in top hat, frock coat and stove-pipe trousers, began supervising the construction of a rickety wooden drilling rig on the banks of Oil Creek and let it be known he was after oil, locals dubbed the structure Drake's Folly. Undeterred by this hurtful sobriquet, Drake engaged William Smith, a blacksmith from Tarentum with experience of sinking salt wells, to make a 'string' of tools and to take charge on site. Smith, known to everyone as 'Uncle Willy', enlisted the help of his two sons. They began drilling in June 1859, and soon ran into trouble when the ground kept caving in. To solve this problem Drake suggested lining the top of the hole with a cast-iron pipe and lowering the drill into it on a cable – a technique which would eventually be adopted throughout the oil industry. With a steam engine slowly lifting and dropping the drill string, it pounded through bedrock at a rate of about three feet a day. After two months of apparently fruitless work, the directors lost heart and dispatched a note to Titusville instructing Drake to cease operations and abandon the well. Fortunately, the mail coach took some time to arrive.

By 27 August Uncle Willy and his boys had reached a depth of sixty-nine feet. Just before they finished work that day, the drill bit suddenly dropped at least six inches into some kind of crevice underground. Next morning, a Sunday, Willy strolled over to the rig and observed something strange about the water in the hole. He plugged one end of a tin tube and scooped up a cupful of the liquid. It was oil – America's first oil well.

The almost unbelievable news that the Colonel had struck oil spread rapidly and brought crowds of farmers and lumbermen out on to the single dusty street of Titusville to celebrate. By the following morning, the first prospectors and speculators had arrived in town to start buying up leases on all the land around Drake's Folly. The price of a lease on a promising site doubled and quadrupled overnight and farmers scarcely able to scratch a living from the unforgiving soil suddenly found that they were rich. William Barnsdall, a tanner from England who drilled the next well, made sixteen thousand dollars in just five months; another Titusville storekeeper would eventually clear one and a half million dollars from a strike on Oil Creek. (Sadly Edwin Drake was not so lucky. The man who drilled the world's first producing oil well soon returned to accustomed obscurity, contrived to lose all his money in oil and land speculation and died penniless in Bethlehem, Pennsylvania, in 1881.)

Drake's Well triggered the birth of the American oil industry. Within a few years, oil seemed fundamental to daily life, as the author of *Petroleum and Petroleum Wells* wrote in 1866:

From Maine to California it lights our dwellings, lubricates our machinery, and is indispensable in numerous departments of arts, manufacture and domestic life. To be deprived of it now would be setting us back a whole cycle of civilisation. To doubt the increased sphere of its usefulness would be to lack faith in the progress of the world.

Before the end of the century, oilfields had been discovered in fourteen states from California to New York and from Wyoming to Texas. Wildcatters – prospecting in every state, eternally hopeful – told fabulous stories of oil literally bursting from the ground. In October 1884 a field correspondent of the *Oil City Derrick* wrote a vivid description of a strike near Thorn Creek, Pennsylvania:

When the barren rock, as if smitten by the rod of Moses, poured forth its torrent of oil, it was such a magnificent and awful spectacle that ... men familiar with the wonderful sights of the oil country were struck dumb with astonishment as they gazed upon this mighty display of nature's forces. With a mighty roar the gas burst forth. The noise was deafening. It was like the loosing of a thunderbolt. For a moment the cloud of gas hid the derrick from sight, and then as it cleared away a solid golden column, half a foot in diameter, shot from the derrick floor eighty feet through the air. For over an hour that grand column of oil, rushing swifter than any torrent, and straight as a mountain pine, united derrick floor and top.

The quest for oil inevitably led wildcatters into Indian Territory, that shameful dumping ground west of the Mississippi where more than sixty Indian tribes had been forced to settle after being displaced from their traditional hunting grounds to accommodate the white man's lust for land. Cherokee, Creek, Choctaw, Chickasaw and Seminole had joined the trek along a 'trail of tears' from the land of their fathers, bitterly complaining they were being sent into a wasteland to starve and little realising that under Oklahoma's red earth were undreamed riches.

Some tribes illuminated their camps by pushing a tube or gun barrel into the ground and lighting the gas escaping from the top. But the first white man to strike oil in Indian Territory was Michael Cudahy, a former meat packer from Omaha who had obtained a dubious blanket lease from the Creek tribe and began drilling at Muskogee in 1894. Cudahy had no luck until he was contacted by George Keeler, the manager of a general store on the bank of the Caney River across from Jacob Bartles's trading post. Keeler had heard of an oil strike not far away in Kansas and recalled that when he was a cowboy, twenty years earlier, his horse always refused to drink water from nearby Sand Creek because of the scum on the surface. He bought a lease from the Cherokees on a tract five miles square around the store and asked Cudahy to sink a prospecting hole.

Neither man was in the slightest deterred by protests from the Secretary of the Interior in Washington that the Cherokees were not empowered to grant leases, nor by the fact that the lease had not even been signed by Little Star, the Cherokee chief. Fourteen teams were needed to drag a drill string from Tulsa, fifty miles distant, to Bartles's trading post before Cudahy could start work. Then he had to sink a hole to 1300 feet before he struck oil. But the well came in flowing at the prolific rate of 150 barrels a day, making both Keeler and Cudahy rich men. Within a few years a thriving settlement, with a hotel, grist mill, blacksmith's shop and livery stable, had mushroomed around the trading post and drilling rigs sprouted everywhere as far as the eye could see. By 1899, when the Sante Fe railroad reached the area, Bartlesville was a thriving oil town.

In August 1903 a prosperous middle-aged lawyer from Minneapolis checked into the Rightway Hotel in Bartlesville prior to a meeting with a client the following day. His name was George Franklin Getty.

The Gettys were, if not quite Pilgrim Fathers, then the next best thing. Of unimpeachable Western European stock, they had come over in good time to count themselves amongst America's pioneers. James Getty was the first to emigrate from County Londonderry, Ireland, in 1780 and it was he who placed the family name firmly on the map of America by supposedly buying, from the heirs of William Penn, the land on which Gettysburg now stands. Ten years later, his cousins John and William followed. John Getty arrived in New York with his younger brother William in 1790. William headed south, wrote his brother a single letter from Kentucky, and was never heard from again. John, who had served as a mercenary in Europe before setting out for the New World, became one of the first settlers in Allegany County, Maryland. He married a girl called Nelly in Cresaptown and eventually prospered as a farmer.

Nelly bore John three children, James, Polly and Joseph, but died shortly after Joseph's birth. Burdened by the responsibility of bringing up three young children alone, John Getty took to drink. In a half-hearted attempt to keep the family intact, he remarried, but chose as his wife a young girl with a local reputation for being 'fast'. She was hardly the perfect stepmother and none of the children received any education. Blearily incapable most of the day, Getty neglected the farm and in 1817 he sold out and opened a ramshackle, two-storey tavern in Grantsville, where he could more conveniently squander his remaining savings on the demon drink. In the winter of 1830, when he was seventy, he fell off his horse, presumably drunk, and froze to death.

John Getty's offspring somehow contrived to rise above the unfavourable circumstances of their upbringing and all three of them made successful marriages, despite being left penniless by their father. Polly went to Ohio and married a farmer and while visiting his sister there, Joseph met his future wife. James, the eldest, married a Jennie McKenzie in Grantsville in 1823 and moved to a hard-scrabble farm five miles away in Piney Grove, Maryland, where Jennie gave birth to three sons who would considerably improve the status of the family.

Joseph, born in 1828, became a successful businessman in eastern Ohio, a minister of the United Brethren Church and a zealous temperance lecturer.

> It was a terrible battle to rise above ignorance and low estate [he wrote in a letter dated 1890]. Sometimes it seemed that fate was against me; but I took fresh courage, and thank God that although not far advanced myself, I have done what I could to lift my children out of this mire of ignorance and shame in which my Grand-Father and my Father left me on account of the Demon Drink, and oh to think how near it came to getting me makes me tremble; but thank God I am free, yes free, indeed, no strong Drink or Tobacco in any form for me.

Joseph's younger brother, William, born in 1832, was involved in an accident on the farm when he was only eleven years old which confined him to bed for three years and left him permanently disabled. But he refused to allow this misfortune to hold him back and at the age of fifteen he left home for Pennsylvania where, according to local records, 'by labor and strict economy he succeeded in saving sufficient means to enable him to attend a select school.' Failing health obliged him to leave school after three years, whereupon he embarked on a career in merchandising, in the lumber business, with considerable success. In 1859, already a pillar of the community, he was elected Justice of the Peace and subsequently held many public offices, becoming the first senator of Garrett County in 1872.

The *Biographical Cyclopaedia of Representative Men of Maryland and District of Columbia,* published in 1878, gave him a glowing testimonial:

> By strict economy, indomitable perseverance, and unimpeachable integrity in every pursuit of his life, he has not only risen to financial independence but, what is far better, he has secured and enjoys the unlimited confidence and esteem of those who know him best. He is kind and generous in his disposition, and one in

whom the worthy poor always find a friend. His fellow citizens delight to honour him, because they take pride in his past record and know that he will not betray the confidence reposed in him.

The youngest of James Getty's sons, John, was born in 1835 and was perhaps somewhat overwhelmed by his ambitious and determined older brothers – John wanted nothing more than to be a farmer. At the age of nineteen he married Martha Ann Wily, daughter of the local schoolteacher and preacher, and within a year their first child, George Franklin Getty, was born. That same year, 1855, they moved across the Maryland border to the Buckeye state, settling on a small farm near New Philadelphia, in Tuscarawas County. Three more children followed in rapid succession, but in 1861 disaster struck the family – John, twenty-six years old, died of malignant diphtheria. Martha was left alone and impoverished, with four children under the age of six.

For George Franklin Getty, the loss of his father was compounded by the family's severely straitened circumstances. Although he was only six, he immediately went to work in the fields to help keep the farm going. For several years he laboured on the farm through spring and summer and was only able to resume his place in the country school during the winter months, when frost made the ground unworkable. Salvation arrived, when George was twelve, in the shape of his Uncle Joseph who offered to provide the boy with an education in Ohio at his own expense. George enrolled in the grammar school at Canal Dover, Ohio, looked to be a promising scholar and later went from there to the Ohio Normal university to study science.

Five feet ten inches tall, broad-shouldered, blue-eyed and curly-haired, George was an unusually serious young man with high ideals, deeply imbued with the idea of self-improvement. He abhorred drink, revered education and was determined, after a childhood of poverty, never to be poor. To pay for his studies at university he taught during the winter term, but he also found time to start dating Sarah Catherine McPherson Risher, a pretty girl three years his senior, who was at the same university. In July 1879 George graduated with honours and three months later, on 30 October 1879, he and Sarah married despite feeble opposition from both sets of parents. In November 1880 Sarah gave birth to a daughter, Gertrude Lois.

It was George Getty's intention to make a career as a teacher, but Sarah had other plans. Sarah was a young woman with delicate health and an iron will: she wanted to be married to a lawyer, not a teacher. Lawyers enjoyed a social standing far above that of teachers and, besides, they made more money. Even while they were courting, Sarah was always gently suggesting that George should consider studying law and he always promised he would think about it, but when he was offered a job as a teacher at his old school at Canal Dover, he did not hesitate to accept. Sarah was by no means beaten and when George began to express some small disillusionment with teaching – the children, he felt, took education too much for granted – she returned to her old theme, even offering him a dowry of one hundred dollars to clear his debts so that he could start at law school with no financial worries. George at last succumbed to her genteel pressure and enrolled in the law department at Michigan University. In March 1882 he was called to the bar, one of only four students in a class of seventeen to pass the examinations, and went into practice with a leading attorney in Caro, Tuscola County. To Sarah's enormous gratification, her husband proved to be a brilliant young lawyer and in the fall of 1882, although only twenty-seven years old, he was elected Circuit Court Commissioner for Tuscola County.

In 1884 the Gettys upped sticks and continued their intermittent journey westward, making for the rapidly-growing city of Minneapolis, as Sarah complained that the damp in Michigan was worsening her already poor health. George now set up in practice on his own account, specialising in the lucrative field of insurance and corporation law. His personal bank balance very soon exceeded a hundred thousand dollars and he became, quite rapidly, a figure of some prominence. He was appointed general counsel to several large corporations, among them the National Benevolent Association and the Railway Building and Loan Association. He was an eloquent advocate in the Supreme Court, a member of the Commercial Club of Minneapolis and the Board of Trade, and a regular worshipper in the Methodist Episcopal Church.

Influenced by his Uncle Joseph and family horror stories about how his great-grandfather nearly brought ruin down upon them all, in 1886 George Getty inaugurated a lively anti-liquor campaign throughout the state of Minnesota, temporarily forsaking his allegiance to the Republican party, believing the temperance cause was better advanced by the Democrats. For two years he was chief editor of *The Review*, the official state prohibition newspaper, but became discouraged by lack of support, abandoned active politics and quietly returned to the Republicans.

Successful, respected and well-liked, Sarah and George had every reason to be happy with their lot. But just when it seemed everything was going so well for them, they were devastated by the worst conceivable tragedy. In 1890 a typhoid epidemic swept through Minneapolis, which had grown in population from 47,000, only ten years earlier, to 165,000. Sarah was first to be brought down by the disease and for weeks she clung to life by what seemed the slimmest of threads. Just when it seemed she was beginning to recover, Gertrude came home from school complaining of a headache and quickly fell into a fever. She died on 9 October, just a few weeks before her tenth birthday. It was as if the light had gone out of their lives.

The loss of their adored only child was a blow from which neither of them expected they would ever recover. Sarah grieved openly for more than a year and George turned to the church for solace and to spiritualism to seek a meaning for their loss. Not long after Gertrude's death, he became a Christian Scientist.

In 1892, George merited a substantial entry in the *Biographical Dictionary of Representative Men of Chicago and Minnesota Cities* which was sufficiently up to date to note that Gertrude, 'a lovely child aged nine years and the sunbeam of the household', had passed away. After describing his career and achievements in fulsome prose, the entry concluded:

> Again, in the subject of this sketch, do we find another illustration of what a boy of this great and grand commonwealth may become. His family ancestors may be humble or hidden in obscurity, his birthplace be unknown, his early years full of hardships and reverses, influential friends may not be his, strangers may surround him, but the ladder of success, pointing upwards into the mystic clouds of the future, stands with its bottom round at his feet, and if he will but mount it, patiently, industriously and with perseverance, he will and must obtain success.

In the spring of that same year, something quite unexpected happened: Sarah found herself pregnant, at the age of thirty-nine. Ten days before Christmas 1892, she gave birth to a lusty baby boy. It was nine o'clock in the morning when the nurse came out of Sarah's bedroom and broke the news to George, who was pacing the corridor outside, that he had a son. He reacted with uncharacteristic levity, marched into the kitchen and exultantly boomed at the maid: 'Set another place for breakfast!' The baby was named Jean Paul Getty.

When George Franklin Getty stepped off the Atcheson, Topeka and Santa Fe Railroad at Bartlesville in Indian Territory in August 1903, he was amazed to find the place in the throes of a roaring oil boom. He had expected a sleepy little frontier settlement of raw-pine shacks; instead here was a bustling modern town with several brick buildings. As he walked to his hotel, he passed no less than three banks, a sure sign of prosperity. Heavily-laden supply wagons pulled by horses or mules jolted along the corrugated ruts of the sun-baked single street, the drivers cursing and cracking their whips. More wagons were being loaded outside the American Well and Prospecting Company on one side of the street and the Oil Well Supply Company on the other. On the dusty sidewalks of sagging wooden duckboard oil men of all kinds – roustabouts and roughnecks, toolies and prospectors, teamsters and lease brokers – mingled with fashionably gowned women, farmers and a few mystified Indians in tattered remnants of tribal dress. Getty noted with distaste that the town had already attracted a number of gamblers and gaudy good-time girls, gathered to the honey pot to separate the newly-rich from their riches.

The population of Bartlesville had doubled to two thousand in the previous twelve months, an influx picturesquely described by the editor of the *Bartlesville Weekly Examiner*:

> Here the representatives of nearly every civilized nation on the globe may be found – the sturdy Norseman from the 'Land of the Midnight Sun', the industrious German, the Englishman who has had his eye teeth cut, the excitable Frenchman, the 'Wild Irishman', the carefree son of Italy, the Greek. All are here animated by a common desire – to capture and sequester the Great American Dollar. The Eastern capitalist thinks nothing of lighting his fifteen-cent cigar from the stump of a cowboy's proffered 'two-fer'. All sorts and conditions of humanity are to be found here, but in spite of this heterogeneous mass, the people get along well together and in the main are peaceable and law-abiding.

By 1903 Getty considered himself, with every justification, to be a man of substance. He had accumulated a considerable personal fortune of around $250,000 by dint of hard work, probity and prudence. He was well-known and respected in the community. He lived in the best part of Minneapolis, in a large and comfortable apartment on Hennepin Avenue, kept staff, owned two horses, and had his sixty-five-dollar suits made by Pease, the finest tailor in town. A severe attack of typhoid fever in 1896 had forced him into semi-retirement for some time, but he had recovered his health completely and at the age of forty-seven was contentedly set in his ways, conducting a leisurely business settling claims and lawsuits on behalf of the Northwestern National Life Insurance Company, of which he was a director, secretary and treasurer. He was, perhaps, one of the least likely of all men to be smitten by the get-rich-quick lure of the rowdy oil business.

It was Northwestern National Life Insurance business which brought Getty to Bartlesville, a trifling matter of a claim for $2500 which he was able to settle, the day after his arrival, for $1500. With time on his hands and his curiosity thoroughly aroused by the rumours of new oil strikes which seemed to ripple through the town every hour, he began chatting with the various oil-smeared adventurers who hung around the lobby of the Rightway Hotel at all hours of the day and night or gathered in the adjoining 'Smoke House' – a combined magazine, tobacco and soft drink store. Although oil production in the entire Indian Territory only amounted to about five hundred barrels a day, a well in the nearby Osage Nation had just been brought in at fifty barrels a day and there was an air of expectation in the town, as if everyone knew that at any moment the Bartlesville sand would give forth its black, sticky treasure.

Getty knew nothing about the oil business but was convinced, unlike many of his friends, that the gasoline automobile was the transport of the future. Most people at that time believed that once the celebrated inventor Thomas Edison had perfected the battery, electric cars would render obsolete the dirty gasoline-powered automobiles which had trundled uncertainly on to the American scene at the turn of the century. Although more than three thousand of the first Öldsmobile model, with a distinctive curved dashboard like the front of a sleigh, had been sold, the gasoline engine was thought to be unreliable and noisy compared to electricity. This was not a view shared by Getty nor a man called Henry Ford, who had incorporated the Ford Motor Company in Detroit only a matter of weeks before Getty arrived in Bartlesville.

Compared with the sophistication of Minneapolis, Bartlesville was another world, but it was one that Getty found rather amenable. He enjoyed talking to the oilmen and liked their company, but had little thought of entering the business until he met the Carter brothers. Will and Bud Carter were veteran wildcatters who had been in the oil business since the days of Oil Creek and could tell stories of every oil rush since. Will, the older of the two, was the driller and Bud the smooth-talking fixer, always immaculately dressed, who arranged finance and bought the leases. A career of wildly fluctuating fortunes had left them philosophical about the vagaries of the oil business and when they met Getty they were looking for an opportunity to off-load Lot 50, a lease on 1100 acres in the Osage Nation. It was miles from the nearest producing well and the brothers wanted to move on to pastures new. They offered it to Getty, who was clearly worth a dollar or two, for five hundred dollars and, somewhat to their surprise, he accepted.

Five hundred dollars was hardly a dangerous gamble for a man in his position, but Getty did not like to think he might lose his money and so he wasted no time, on his return to Minneapolis, in offsetting the risk. As he was 'very fond' of Doctor John Bell, the family doctor who had treated him during his typhoid attack, he offered to cut him in on the deal. The terms were hardly generous. Getty offered Dr Bell a two-sevenths interest in Lot 50 for a thousand dollars. The good doctor accepted one-seventh for five hundred which, although it did not provide Getty with an instant profit, neatly erased his original investment. Drilling began on Lot 50 in October.

Jean Paul Getty was by this time eleven years old and a pupil at Emerson Grammar School in Minneapolis. He was a sturdy lad with a round face, his mother's downturned mouth and his father's long nose. Mightily thankful that his mother had at last agreed to cut his curls, he brushed his wiry hair into a neat side parting, but it still stuck out from under the trilby he was obliged to wear on family outings. Keen on swimming, boxing and all outdoor pursuits, his few indoor interests revolved mainly around his stamp collection and Ruth Hill, the 'dream girl' who was in his class at Emerson and sat across the aisle from him.

He had not the slightest interest in his father's business affairs, except inasmuch as his father had been in Indian Territory, which the boy imagined to be populated by Red Indians either constantly at war with cowboys or being pursued by the US Cavalry. When his father incorporated the Minnehoma Oil Company and suggested that Jean Paul should invest five dollars of his savings and subscribe for a hundred shares at five cents each, he meekly complied without really knowing or caring what it was all about. His father signed the stock certificates and presented them to the boy with a proud flourish, saying 'There! Now you're part of the company for which I work. You're one of my bosses.' Jean Paul Getty smiled and said nothing; sometimes his father said the strangest things.

In December 1903 the Minnehoma Oil Company (named 'Minne' for Minnesota and 'homa' for Oklahoma) struck oil on Lot 50 at 1400 feet. The well came in as a gusher and settled down to the steady production of one hundred barrels a day, making George Getty an instant oil magnate. He was, naturally, delighted and decided to take his wife and son to Bartlesville in the New Year so that they could watch the second well being drilled.

Young Paul could scarcely contain his excitement when his father told him about the projected visit to Indian Territory. Every day he asked when they would be leaving and in the classroom at Emerson he sat daydreaming for hours about the Wild West, oblivious of lessons. Even playing games of cowboys and Indians with his friends seemed faintly pointless when, as he told them, he would soon be rubbing shoulders with *real* cowboys and *real* Indians. On New Year's Day 1904 Paul made a resolution to start a diary and penned the first entry in a childish hand: 'Fine day for New Year. Read in the morning and went out to dinner. Ate two big plates of turkey, olives and a lot more. Went out playing in the afternoon.'

Saturday 2 January, he reported, was fourteen degrees below zero. 'I went out and hitched my sled on a sleigh. The guy wouldn't let me so I got as far back as I could. He tried to hit me with his whip, but couldn't.'

Sunday 3 January: 'Got up late. Went to Sunday School at twelve o'clock and stayed till one in the afternoon. Me and William went out coasting till it was dark. Had some supper and read till bedtime.'
Monday 4 January: 'School began today after the holidays. After school me and some other boys went coasting till it was dark. Played in the evening with games.'
Tuesday 5 January: 'Fine day, after school went riding. After that we went coasting. Broke the board to my sled and will have to fix it. I am too lazy to do it.'

Paul kept a journal right through 1904 and most of 1905. It was a laconic narrative of a secure, happy and entirely conventional childhood of play, mischief, Sunday School, piano practice, boxing lessons, tests at school, riding out in the buggy with Dexter, the family horse, and trying to sell copies of the *Saturday Evening Post* door to door to earn pocket money. Papa's comings and goings on business were faithfully chronicled ('Papa went away last night to Bartlesville') but Mama remained a constant, and sometimes generous presence ('After school, Mama gave me twenty cents for doing an errand').

He had a voracious appetite for reading, particularly the novels of G. A. Henty ('In the afternoon I read *The Dash for Khartoum* by G. A. Henty. It was fine.'), and was always running down to the library for another book.

Unrecorded in the diary was Paul's mounting excitement at the prospect of visiting Indian Territory. On Sunday 17 January, he noted simply: 'Snowing today. Went to Sunday School in the morning. In the afternoon Papa gave me ten cents to go down to the post office with a letter. After that I read. We are going away to Indian Territory Tuesday night.' First leg of the long-awaited journey was on the night train for Kansas City which left Minneapolis, its bell ringing, at 8.30 in the evening on 19 January. Paul went to bed soon after their departure and woke up to find it snowing hard as the train clattered south through Iowa and Missouri. They stayed overnight Wednesday at the Midland Hotel in Kansas City ('This is one of the largest hotels', Paul wrote. 'The waiters are all negroes. I ate a big dinner.'), and caught the train for Bartlesville at 12.25 next day.

As they headed towards Indian Territory, Paul later remembered his father talked all the time about the oil industry, while his mother listened patiently and he sat glued to the window of their Pullman coach, waiting for his first glimpse of war-painted braves riding bareback across the prairie. 'I haven't seen any Indians yet,' he complained after about an hour of fruitlessly scanning the horizons rolling by.

'Don't worry, son,' his father replied. 'You'll be able to see quite a few round Bartlesville.'

'Are they dangerous?' Paul asked hopefully. 'Will we have to fight them off?'

George Getty laughed. 'No, they're not dangerous,' he said. 'They're rather quiet and peaceful. The only Indians we may have to fight off are the ones who sell pottery and blankets outside the railroad station.'

Paul slumped back in his seat with a frown, but soon resumed his vigil at the window, not entirely giving up hope of a comic strip coming to life before his eyes. It was dark when the train pulled into Bartlesville and the Gettys went directly to the Rightway Hotel. Paul sleepily glimpsed a few shadowy figures on the street and concluded, with a shiver of excitement, that if they were not sheriffs or gun-slinging cowboys, then they must certainly be outlaws.

He could not have been more disappointed when he woke the following morning. In the harsh grey light of a cold January dawn, Paul discovered that Bartlesville was nothing more than a dreary oil town. Some of the men he saw on the street carried Colts strapped to their belts, but they were clearly oilfield workers, not cowboys. And the few Indians about were a sorry lot, mainly half-breeds, far from the noble savages of his imagination and dressed, he noted with disgust, in 'store clothes'. In his peaked cap, knee breeches and button boots he walked to the end of the main street, past the rickety clapboard structures filling the gaps between the town's first brick and stone buildings, in the hope of finding a stockade or perhaps even a fort. He found instead a cluster of crude shacks, an oil boom shanty town. Beyond, as far as he could see, was a sparse, flat landscape prickled with derricks.

Barely able to conceal his boredom he wrote in his diary: 'The sun shone for the first time in three days. In the morning I took a walk into the woods, about four miles and back. In the afternoon I walked over to a high hill about three miles away. I went to bed about 7.30.' Next day his spirits rose a little when he found some boys of his own age to play with. 'We had a fine time riding,' he noted, 'and throwing the lasso.' On Sunday he was further cheered by the arrival at the Rightway Hotel of ten Indian chiefs wearing feathered headdresses and wrapped in blankets. His father told him they were on their way to see President Theodore Roosevelt and he was thrilled to observe that one of them, named Two Keys, had two little gold keys in each ear lobe.

Paul's first spark of interest in the oil business was kindled when his father took him out to the lease for the first time and he caught a whiff of the glamour and excitement of drilling for oil. Lot 50 was about nine miles from Bartlesville, a two-hour drive with a team and buggy along a rough winding track and across a difficult ford at Sand Creek. On their first trip Getty let his son take the reins there and back, an unforgettable experience for an eleven-year-old, particularly as he nearly upset the buggy twice on the return. But it was the drilling site itself which made the biggest impression on the boy. He was fascinated by the clanking, noisy mechanics of the drill and by the crew who operated it. Cowboys suddenly paled as heroes, compared to these muscular desperadoes struggling to wrest oil from the recalcitrant rock. They lived in tents around the derrick, cooked on open fires and invariably brawled on pay-nights: it seemed a fine and romantic life to a small boy.

The drilling supervisor who showed Paul round pointed out one of the crew as Henry Starr, a notorious former outlaw whose features had appeared on countless 'Wanted – Dead or Alive' posters throughout Indian Territory. Starr, it was said, had held up Jake Bartles, the founder of Bartlesville, three times, but had never netted more than a couple of dollars. After the third hold-up, the exasperated Starr was said to have bellowed: 'Jake, I'm tired of being made a monkey. You go down to the bank tomorrow and get five thousand dollars in cash and carry it with you in future. The next time I hold you up and you ain't got five thousand dollars, I'm a-going to kill you.' Bartles always carried the cash about with him thereafter, allegedly explaining 'Starr may be a low-down no-good thieving skunk, but he's a man of his word.'

Young Paul listened to this unlikely tale with wide eyes and never forgot it. He was also deeply impressed when, on another visit to the site, he asked one of the roustabouts how old he was and the man scratched his head and replied 'Well, I dunno. I guess I must be about thirty-five or forty.' Paul thought it was extraordinary that he should be so unconcerned.

After that first visit, the boy never missed an opportunity to ride out with his father to the lease and he was soon familiar with oilfield jargon. By constantly asking precocious questions, he got to know a great deal about oil and oil wells; nothing pleased him more than being able to sit with the crew around a fire and listen to the tales they told of strikes and fires and dry holes. Back in Bartlesville, he spent much of his time with a yellow mongrel dog which had attached itself to him and which he named Jip. He liked to walk out along the railroad track with Jip, jumping from tie to tie on the bridge across the Caney river. The dog figured prominently in his diary.

Monday 1 February: 'Fine day. In the morning I saw the funniest thing. A lot of burros came along with four cowboys driving them. I set Jip on them and soon a dozen dogs were barking and snapping at their heels. Then the cowboys began to swear and lasso the burros.'

Monday 8 February: 'Fine day. In the morning I walked over to the river. Jip swam across. In the afternoon I walked four miles out into the country. Jip followed me and nearly got a rabbit. In the evening I read some magazines I got from the cook.'

Jip was allowed to sleep in the corridor outside Paul's room in the Rightway Hotel. The consequences of trying to smuggle the dog into his room were reported in the entry for 17 February: 'Papa gave me a whipping for saying he was a doggoned fool and the chambermaid had better go soak her head in Jip's mouth.'

Still the diary gave no hint of Paul's youthful infatuation with the oil business. Wednesday 24 February 1904: 'Cloudy today. In the morning I and Edward went down the river to see them shoot an oil well. The explosion was just hard thunder. In the afternoon I played marbles.' Even when he drove out to the lease with his parents at the beginning of March to watch the second well being brought in, an experience he would later describe as a 'unique thrill', he only wrote: 'Fine day. We all went out to see the well come in. It came in at 1426 feet below the surface. I got a stone that was once on the seashore. It is perfectly oblong.'

The second well matched the production of the first. Together they were disgorging about two thousand five hundred barrels a month at a time when the price stood at eighty-eight cents a barrel. George Getty, very pleased with himself, told his crew where he wanted the next hole sunk on Lot 50 and decided it was time his family returned to Minneapolis.

Paul arrived back at Emerson after a six-week break, full of his adventures in Indian Territory. Summer passed uneventfully, skinning marbles off his friend Harry, counting his stamps, fighting and playing jokes.

1 April: 'I fooled people and rang doorbells.'
26 April: 'At midnight I yelled "Fire, Fire" everybody screamed.'

In May he joined the school baseball team, the Imperial Sluggers.

Tuesday 17 May: 'We are going to play the Tigers tomorrow at 4 o'clock. They have a good team.'
Wednesday 18 May: 'In the afternoon we played the Tigers on their grounds. We had to stop though because a boy was sick.'

To boost his pocket money, he set up a lemonade stand outside his house, but got so bored waiting for customers that he invariably drank the pitcher himself. He was no more successful trying to sell subscriptions to the *Saturday Evening Post*, door to door. Only when trading marbles or automobile catalogues with his friends did he display any indication of the keen competitiveness of a future businessman.

In October the family made a second brief trip to Bartlesville, stopping on the way to visit the World's Fair in St Louis. Paul, enterprising boy, made a special note in his diary that he found a catalogue in the Palace of Fine Arts and was able to sell it to another visitor for fifteen cents. He was also deeply impressed by Jin Key, a horse that was able to spell Minneapolis, change money and count up to thirty. After a week's sightseeing in St Louis, they continued their journey and checked into the new brick-built annex of the Rightway Hotel in Bartlesville on 16 October. Paul wasted no time renewing his acquaintanceship with Jip, whom he had left with a friend, and was gratified by the tail-wagging enthusiasm of his reception.

Next day they went out to the lease.

> Monday 17 October: 'Fine day. In the morning we got up at six o'clock, took breakfast and all started for the lease, including Jip. We got there at ten o'clock and walked around to see the four oil wells all good. No. 3, the poorest of the lot, was shot last night at 10.15 with a hundred quarts of nitroglycerine. We saw the column of oil from the drilling shoot a hundred feet into the air and keep it up for five minutes. We had lunch at a tent. It was not very good. In the afternoon Papa located another well.'

On the way home to Minneapolis a week later, they stopped again at St Louis, where Paul and his mother had a ride on a moving staircase in the May Company store, and in Chicago, where they visited Marshall Field, one of the largest stores in the world. In the book department Paul bought two books by Horatio Alger – *Risen from the Ranks* and *Born to Rise*.

2. *'You'll have to start at the bottom'*

By May 1905 six producing wells had been drilled on Lot 50, all of them located by George Getty. His success led him to believe, in uncharacteristically fanciful moments, that he perhaps had a 'sixth sense' about where oil could be found underground, although he never claimed, like some of his contemporaries, that he could walk a lease, sniff the air and 'smell crude'. Production on Lot 50 was running at about a hundred thousand barrels a month, but Getty was worried because the price per barrel had dropped to fifty-two cents and looked like falling even further.

Two huge oil strikes – one near Tulsa and another at the Glenn Pool, further south in Indian Territory – had created a glut, despite increasing demand. There were more automobiles on the road than ever, factories everywhere were using oil to fire industrial plant and steamship companies and railways were rapidly converting to oil: the Southern Pacific Railroad, operating in Texas and Louisiana, alone consumed 2,640,000 barrels in 1905. Yet there was still more oil being pumped from under the ground than was being used above it. The early days were over, along with that first fine careless rapture. The oil industry had come of age, and it was time for a little business acumen – which suited George Getty fine. When Minnehoma found itself unable to get even fifty cents a barrel, he put a brake on drilling operations and built five 1600 barrel wooden tanks to store production until the price improved. George Franklin Getty was not a man to sell cheap.

Around this time Getty decided to move his family to southern California. Although oil had been discovered in the 'Golden State' in 1901, it was not this fact that necessarily prompted the move. Sarah had relatives in Los Angeles and San Diego whom they had visited in February 1905. The climate and environment seemed so much more congenial than Minnesota and they realised on their return to the Midwest that there would be nothing to keep them in Minneapolis once Paul had graduated from Emerson school. Most of Getty's business interests were now rooted in Indian Territory, which was as accessible from California as it was from Minnesota and while they had been perfectly happy during their twenty years in Minneapolis, both George and Sarah were attracted to the idea of a new life in the sunshine. Paul, too, was delighted by the prospect.

They first considered San Diego, which at that time promised to be the metropolis of southern California, but Sarah thought it was too small and sleepy, so they decided on Los Angeles instead. Paul was glad they had been able to spend some time in San Diego, for his father bought him a black greyhound pup for thirty dollars from an old Irishman who lived on North Island in San Diego Bay. The dog, named Prince, became his friend and inseparable companion, although he never, Paul noted, 'quite took the place of my beloved Jip'.

In the summer of 1906 the Gettys moved into a comfortable rented apartment in the Frontenac on South Grand Avenue in Los Angeles and Paul was enrolled, to his disgust, as a day student at the Harvard Military Academy on the corner of Crenshaw and Venice Boulevards. George and Sarah thought the discipline of a military school would be good for the boy; Paul, by then thirteen, fundamentally disagreed. He hated the place from the first day, bridled at what he considered to be a ridiculous regime and openly resented the hours spent on 'bull', polishing buttons and boots. He could never see the point of it and constantly outraged the 'upper-classmen' by his sloppy appearance. Most evenings he could be found on the square between the school's two yellow-stucco buildings, wearily drilling with a knapsack on his back as a punishment for some petty sartorial lapse. Once he paraded for a school photograph in white tennis shoes, instead of the regulation black boots; inexplicably, his footwear was not noticed until the photograph was developed. The whole school had to parade again for another picture and Paul found himself extremely unpopular for a while.

One small consolation was that the academic curriculum concentrated on the classics, which suited Paul perfectly. He took readily to Latin and ancient Greek and continued to read voraciously in his spare time, alternating Henty or Dickens with Plato and Pliny. He was so often to be found with his nose in a book that his classmates called him 'Dictionary Getty'.

Although he learned to accommodate the requirements of military discipline after a couple of terms, he was never indoctrinated by it and always considered it to be a complete waste of time. As far as Paul was concerned, the rules were there to be thwarted. Once he and a friend 'went AWOL' in order to keep an assignation with two girls they had met the previous week at a heavily chaperoned dance. Paul was only fourteen but was considered by his classmates to be 'girl crazy' and after this adventure it was widely surmised, from his heavy hints, that he had contrived to lose his virginity. Certainly Paul never disabused anyone from believing he had reached that enviable state.

Towards the end of 1907 the Gettys moved into their first real home in Los Angeles – 647 South Kingsley Drive, a substantial frame-and-stucco mansion built in an English style, surrounded by eucalyptus trees and meadows, just off an unpaved road known as Wilshire Boulevard. Well outside the built-up area of the city (street cars only ran as far as Sixth Avenue and Vermont, about a mile away), the corner lot cost just $8000. George Getty had been looking for a suitable site on which to build ever since they arrived in California; one realtor had offered him Santa Catalina Island for $250,000 but he had rejected it out of hand. Later, when it was developed into a multi-million dollar resort, George liked to joke that he had 'missed the boat by passing up an island'. It was a boat he never regretted missing, for both George and Sarah felt they had made the right decision with their new house, which had light, airy rooms furnished in fashionable velvet and hung with tapestries. One of only two houses on Wilshire between Vermont and Western Avenue, it adequately reflected their status without being ostentatious, something they both abhorred, and cost, Getty noted with pride, less than $30,000, including the expense of piping a water supply to the site from the Hollywood Water Company.

Paul, still chafing at the strictures of military discipline, eventually persuaded his parents that he would be better placed in the less formal academic environment of the local Polytechnic High School, to which he transferred in the autumn of 1908. He had vague ideas of wanting to become a vet, but after graduating from high school in June 1909, he asked his father if he could have a vacation job working for Minnehoma in the oilfields. 'It's all right with me,' his father replied gruffly, trying not to show his pleasure, 'if you're willing to start at the bottom.' Getty carefully explained to Paul that he could expect no special treatment, there would be no favouritism. He would have to start as a roustabout, the name for a general labourer on an oil rig. Roustabouts tackled the heaviest and dirtiest work and were paid three dollars a day for a twelve-hour shift. Although Paul was only sixteen years old, his father said, he would be expected to do a man's share of the work.

Paul agreed to all these conditions and departed happily for Bartlesville, glad to be free from school and heading back to a place of such fond boyhood memories. He had no doubt of his ability to handle the work. He was big for his age – nearly six feet tall and 160 pounds – and was very strong, having recently developed an interest in weight-lifting. Even so, life on a drilling rig came as a shock after the comfort and privilege of being the only son in an extremely wealthy family. He was immediately put to work with the other roustabouts constructing a seventy-four-foot derrick out of heavy, rough-hewn timbers which had to be nailed together by hand. At the end of his first shift, he ached so much he could hardly drag himself to his cot in the bunkhouse. At the end of a week, the palms of his hands were a bloody pulp of blisters. He uttered not a word of complaint, not even when he suspected that he was being given a particularly hard time just because he was the boss's son and he became completely accustomed to being addressed by everyone as simply 'Hey, you!' It was as if he had neither a name nor an identity as one of the crew.

The blisters were turning to calluses and he was just beginning to earn some grudging respect as a hard worker when he received a message from his father, which came as a signal from another world. He was to join his parents, he was informed, on a trip to Europe. He was to stop work at the rig immediately, take a train to Philadelphia and pick up a new six-cylinder Chadwick tourer which his father had ordered from the factory at Pottstown. He was to accompany it with a chauffeur to New York and meet his parents there in time to sail on the White Star liner, *Baltic,* on 14 July. Paul left Bartlesville with mixed feelings. It was hard not to be excited about the trip to Europe which had materialised completely out of the blue, but at the same time he felt he was leaving the rig just as he was beginning to be accepted by the other men.

It is possible, although unlikely, that George Getty organised the automobile trip to Europe in the summer of 1909 in order to spare his son the rigours of working on Lot 50 for the whole vacation. It is more plausible, given his unbending Victorian values, that he decided it was time to take Sarah on a holiday and that their enjoyment of Europe would be increased by having Paul along. There was no question that they could afford it: George and Sarah Getty owned more than seventy per cent of the Minnehoma Oil Company which, despite continuing low prices for crude, still managed to report handsome profits every year. (By 1915, Lot 50 had produced a clear profit of $326,000.)

Whatever the reason, the trip was an enormous success. The Chadwick, a fine ninety horsepower machine with four comfortable seats, was unloaded from the *Baltic* in Liverpool after an exceptionally smooth Atlantic crossing. Getty hired a chauffeur, a Liverpudlian with an accent so thick they could not at first understand a word he said, and over the next three months the family toured England, France, Switzerland, Holland and the Rhine Valley in Germany. They returned to the United States in October on the *Rotterdam* of the Holland-America Line. This time the North Atlantic was less kind, but the three of them proved to be good sailors and rough seas did not prevent them enjoying the pampered luxury of first-class travel on a great ocean liner.

Back in Los Angeles, Paul enrolled at the University of Southern California to study political science and economics. He continued to live at home, but contrived a clandestine social life to relieve the urgent stirrings in his seventeen-year-old loins. Central to the organisation of what he liked to describe as his 'love life' was the Chadwick, which had been shipped back from Europe.

George Getty allowed his son to drive the Chadwick during the day when he was not using it, but at nights it was always tucked away in a garage at the back of the house. Paul, who was not the most handsome boy in town, quickly discovered that an automobile was an almost irresistible attraction to a potential 'date' and casually got into the habit of stealing the Chadwick after his mother and father had gone to bed, which was usually mercifully early.

He would sneak out of the house when he judged the coast to be clear, silently open the garage doors, push the Chadwick out on to the street and roll it down a slight, but convenient gradient until he was far enough away to start the engine without waking his parents. Then he was off, king of the road, to rendezvous with a friend and their two girls for the evening – 'double dating' was the popularly accepted convention at that time, since parents believed their daughters were safer in foursomes. They reckoned without the ingenuity and lust of young men like Paul Getty. The Chadwick would spend hours parked in a suitably secluded spot, rocking and creaking gently while Paul and his friend each sweatily discovered the joys of 'heavy petting'. At the end of the evening, Paul returned the Chadwick to its garage, coasting the last few yards with the engine switched off, and meticulously wound back the odometer to its original mileage.

He was always careful to replace the petrol he had used, but there was nothing he could do to prevent his nocturnal jaunts causing excessive wear on the tyres. His father, a stickler for value, complained irritably to the tyre supplier who checked the alignment of the wheels, found no fault and professed himself to be mystified that after only a thousand miles they were showing such signs of wear. Since he had not been discovered, Paul did not see any reason why he should not continue using the car and a couple of nights later he borrowed the Chadwick again for an important 'double heavy double date'. They drove to a nightclub in downtown Los Angeles, thinking themselves the gayest of blades, and left with a half-finished bottle of red wine to drink during the ritual petting session.

It was a mistake. While passing the bottle round, one of the girls spilled the contents over the seat covers. Paul was horrified. They did their best to clean it up, but a telltale dark red stain remained as damning evidence of his deceit. Paul returned the Chadwick to the garage with a heavy heart and all next day he waited for the dreaded summons from his father. When his father said nothing, he began to think he might perhaps get away with it. Maybe the stain was not as obvious as it had seemed the night before; maybe it had dried out. By the evening he was convinced that he was in the clear and after his parents had gone to bed, he crept out to the garage as usual, opened the doors and discovered the wheels of the Chadwick firmly chained to the concrete floor.

Nothing was ever said, to Paul's great relief, about this new arrangement but it was some months before he could muster the courage to raise with his father an idea that had hatched soon after the Chadwick's chains appeared. Paul had little doubt that if he was to ask his father for a car he would be refused, but he thought there was a chance his father might come up with the money if he suggested building his own car. He was right: it was the kind of initiative George Getty appreciated, particularly in his son, and he agreed to finance the project.

Paul rented space in a repair shop not far from his home and ordered all the mechanical parts for the hot-rod racer he had in mind. He designed a low-slung two-seater body, welded it together himself and assembled the entire contraption with only minimal help from a mechanic. He called it the 'Plaza Milano', because it sounded suitably exotic, and proudly invited his father to be the first passenger to be taken for a spin. This turned out to be a somewhat literal invitation, since Paul discovered the Plaza Milano displayed an alarming tendency to pirouette viciously in the wet; nevertheless both father and son were pleased with the result.

By this time Paul was regularly dating a girl called Edith McNair, the daughter of a family who lived nearby. Edith was ten years older than Paul, had travelled extensively abroad, could speak fluent French and was considered to be 'sophisticated'. None of this mattered to Paul so much as the revelation, to his astonishment and delight, that Edith not only permitted him to have sexual intercourse with her, but actually encouraged it and apparently enjoyed it. He was thrilled to be escorting an older woman, but an older woman who ... well, it defied the imagination.

Paul wasted no time calling for Edith in his Plaza Milano, but on their first trip he threw the car into a tight spin and Edith was violently ejected on to the sidewalk, where she rolled over several times, ruining her lambskin coat. She was badly bruised by the staunch boned corset worn by all ladies of fashion at that time and after this incident Edith's parents forbade her from riding in Paul's car. The ban was temporarily lifted on New Year's Eve 1910, when Paul drove Edith to a party at the Ship café in Venice, a coastal resort southwest of Los Angeles. On the way home in the early hours of the morning, Paul was driving too fast, missed a bend and careered off the road, across a ditch into a ploughed field. The luckless Edith was once more summarily ejected, again sustaining no more than bruises from her corset stays. But when she arrived home with her clothes torn and covered in mud, she was again forbidden to drive with Paul, this time forever. Fortunately, Edith's parents remained blissfully unaware that their daughter ran a far greater risk of a 'fate worse than death' than she ever did of being mangled in his car.

At university, Paul was not happy. He was a somewhat strait-laced student anxious to learn and acquire the best education he could find, having inherited his father's inordinate respect for learning. He disliked the rah-rah playground atmosphere of the campus. He resented being treated like a child, being closely supervised and checked in and out of class; and he despised his fellow students for acting like children, with their crass college humour and juvenile politics. Most of all, he hated the snobbishness of the fraternities and sororities, which he considered to be a pernicious contradiction of America's democratic principles. Paul took little or no part in campus activities and concentrated on his studies, earning good grades although he complained that the political science and economics course was insular and chauvinistic. 'I was disappointed and bored,' he recalled, 'and felt I was getting nowhere.'

Throughout the summer vacations in 1910 and 1911, Paul cheerfully worked for his father in the Oklahoma oilfields, where he graduated from roustabout to tool-dresser with the help of a veteran 'toolie' by the name of Grizzle. The tool-dresser had to sharpen and maintain the drilling tools and was considered to be the second most important man on a rig, after the driller. Grizzle, who had no other name for all Paul knew, took a liking to the lad and offered to teach him the toolie's trade, retempering the bits on a portable forge, repairing broken equipment and making spare parts. He was a hard man to please: Paul would sweat and toil over his work before presenting the result to Grizzle for inspection, who would squirt a stream of rancid tobacco juice into the sizzling forge, snarl 'Dammit, I could chew rock faster than I could drill it with the edges on this!' and send Paul away to try again.

Pay-nights were invariably spent in Bartlesville getting drunk on throat-scorching bootleg whisky and brawling with crews from rival rigs. During his summer stint in 1911 Grizzle grudgingly conceded that Paul had passed his apprenticeship and, on the older man's recommendation, he was given a job as a toolie. He also noticed around this time that instead of being addressed constantly as 'Hey, you!', the other men took to calling him 'Red' because of the colour of his hair, or sometimes even 'Paul', and he knew then he was at last accepted.

When he returned to the West Coast, he decided to transfer to the University of California at Berkeley, near San Francisco, in the hope of finding a more constructive and congenial atmosphere. To his disappointment, he found it no better than his previous university in Los Angeles and in April 1911 he resigned from the course without graduating, after convincing his parents that the only place he could find the education he wanted was abroad, probably at Oxford – which they had visited during their trip to Europe two years previously. He was by this time seriously considering a career in the diplomatic service, an ambition about which George Getty wisely said nothing.

Before going to Oxford, Paul persuaded his father to finance a trip to the Far East so that he could 'broaden his experience of the world'. In May he left for a two-month tour of Japan and China, where he was greatly impressed by Oriental art and bought two Chinese bronzes and several small pieces of carved ivory, all for less than fifty dollars, the first modest items of his art collection. He returned to America in July for another backbreaking three-month stint in the oilfields and in November he sailed for England, leaving the Plaza Milano in the care of his father who had offered to drive it 'now and then'.

For the next two years while his son was away in Europe, George Franklin Getty, then nearly sixty years old, could be found jauntily driving to his office every day, to the astonishment of his colleagues, at the wheel of the Plaza Milano.

Paul liked Oxford, liked to feel a part of the glittering elite in caps and gowns lodged among the dreaming spires. He arrived with a letter of introduction addressed to Herbert Warren, the president of Magdalen College, and signed by the President of the United States, William Howard Taft, who was a useful friend of his father. Warren invited the young man to tea for a 'chat', using the occasion to probe the state of his knowledge, and a few days later Paul learned to his delight that he had been accepted as a non-collegiate student. He found lodgings above an antique shop in the High and settled contentedly into the sedate pace of life in Edwardian England, with a two-hundred-dollar-a-month allowance to ensure an adequate supply of its comforts.

As an American, Paul was considered to be something of an oddity at Oxford, but his engaging personality and unusual reserve soon won him many friends, among them the Prince of Wales, a fellow student with a place at Magdalen. (They would still be friends, still on Christian name terms, when the prince briefly became the King of England before renouncing the throne for the love of Mrs Wallis Simpson.) Paul was a frequent guest at weekend house parties, at a time when the families owning English country houses could still afford to assign every guest a personal servant and serve the finest champagne. On weekday evenings he and his friends often took the train to London in white tie and tails to attend a ball or the theatre. England was, he wrote home to his parents, so exceptionally *civilised*, perhaps prompting them to wonder what was so uncivilised about Los Angeles.

Oxford was also infinitely preferable, in Paul's eyes, to any of the

American universities. He was enormously impressed by the way students were treated as mature adults with minds of their own and by the absence of supervision; after experiencing the strict discipline at the University of Southern California, he could hardly believe his ears when he learned that attendance at lectures was entirely voluntary. 'If you are brilliant enough', his tutor told him at their first meeting, 'to pass your examinations without attending a single lecture, that's fine by me. In fact it's even better than fine, since no one has managed it before.' Paul could not help but laugh. He also appreciated being free to enjoy his favourite sports – still swimming, boxing and weightlifting – without pressure to join the college team and participate for the glory of the university.

Paul sat for a non-collegiate diploma in economics and political science in June 1913, and passed. More than ever determined to pursue a career in the diplomatic service, he wrote to inform his father of his plans to make a long overland trip across Europe into Russia, visiting the great political and industrial centres to acquire first-hand experience of how the theories he had learned in university worked in practice. George Getty approved and told his son he would arrange for a two-hundred-dollar banker's draft to be dispatched each month to the nearest American Express office on his route.

The expedition was not as worthy, or as educational, as Paul had led his father to believe. His first stop was Berlin, where the nightlife was quite as much an attraction as his observations of Germany's military preparedness under the Kaiser. From Berlin he went to Denmark and Sweden, then crossed the Gulf of Bothnia to Finland and Russia. He stayed at St Petersburg for a while to learn the rudiments of Russian, writing long letters home about the 'brooding fatalism' of the Russians under the Tsarist regime. One of the friends he made in St Petersburg was a young aristocrat who offered to accompany him on a steamer trip down the Volga to Baku, during which Paul experienced the remarkable generosity of ordinary Russian people: every time they put ashore at one of the ports along the great river, he was invariably invited into someone's home for a meal and innumerable glasses of vodka. On the steamer, he passed the time enjoyably by learning a repertoire of traditional Russian songs.

In Budapest Paul was invited to dine with a party of Hussar officers and 'several lovely young ladies', whose company he particularly enjoyed. He recalled an exchange which typified the carefree atmosphere of the evening when one of the girls suddenly asked her escort: 'What would you do in a war, Laszlo?' Laszlo feigned great surprise and replied with a grin: 'War? Why, that would ruin everything for everyone!'

Paul spent his twenty-first birthday – 15 December 1913 – halfway across the Mediterranean on board a battered Rumanian steamer bound for Alexandria and wallowing in a gale of such ferocity that all its lifeboats were torn away. He was convinced the ship was close to foundering several times and was immensely relieved when the coast of Egypt at last hove into view. Two months were fully occupied sightseeing around the pyramids and the ancient temples along the Nile and then he booked a passage for Gibraltar on a new Cunard liner, the *Franconia*, having vowed never again to travel on old steamers. From Gibraltar he crossed into Spain, which was a complete surprise. Classroom memories of the evils of the Inquisition and the extermination of the Aztecs, combined with the virulent anti-Spanish propaganda prevalent in the United States for years after the Spanish-American war in 1898, prepared the young man to dislike Spain; instead he fell instantly in love with the country and its people. He wrote home expressing his surprise, and his conviction that the dignity, pride and honour of the Spanish probably made them closer lineal descendants of the ancient Romans than any of the other Mediterranean races.

In April Paul arrived in Paris, took one look round that glorious city on a spring day and decided there and then that his serious sociological research would require him to stay for some time. Parisian social life and Parisian girls might also have had some influence on this decision. At that time the city, and indeed most of France, was obsessed with the delicious scandal of *l'affaire Caillaux*: the wife of a leading politician, Joseph Caillaux, had shot and killed the editor of *Le Figaro* after he had threatened to publish love letters Caillaux had written to his wife when she was his mistress. No drama could have been better designed to capture the imagination of the French public and Paul thoroughly enjoyed the gossip and the endless speculation about the fate of Madame Caillaux, who was then awaiting trial. 'Even the weather was the best in any Frenchman's memory,' he recalled. 'I readily succumbed to the general euphoria, savouring all I could of Parisian life.'

While he was thus occupied, Paul heard from his mother and father that they were planning another trip to Europe; they had booked a cabin on the biggest passenger ship in the world, the *Vaterland* of the Hamburg-America Line, departing New York on 16 June. Paul was to meet them when the ship arrived in Hamburg, accompany them on a tour of Berlin, Paris and London and return with them to the United States. Paul never indicated what he felt about these arrangements but his deep affection for his parents was never in doubt, so he would presumably have been pleased to see them, if a little saddened that his pleasant sojourn in Europe was being brought to an end.

George Getty kept a diary of this trip, his second to Europe, and the impending war loomed large in its pages. The most exciting event in

Berlin, he recorded, was the daily appearance of the Zeppelin. He was also full of admiration for the Kaiser, who was 'the most beloved man in Germany'. On 28 June 1914 he wrote: 'A horrible thing has occurred. The Crown Prince Archduke Franz Ferdinand and the Archduchess was shot and killed in an automobile in which they were riding in a street in Sarajevo ...' The full significance of this event was yet to be understood and five days later Getty hopefully noted: 'By the way, the name "Goethe" is pronounced here as I pronounce my name and indicates the roots of my name may reach back to the name of Germany's most illustrious poet.'

In Paris the Gettys enjoyed being shown around by their son, visited art galleries, museums and the opera, took a box at the races in the Bois de Boulogne and did their best to ignore the talk of war. *L'affaire Caillaux* still occupied the headlines and when at the races they saw uniformed *gendarmes* hurry with a message to the nearby box of Raymond Poincaré, the president of France, they immediately assumed that it was news of some sensational development in the Caillaux case, rather than news of war. 'There was', Getty wrote in his diary, 'not the slightest intimation of the approach of a European war.'

His views changed rapidly when they left for London towards the end of July and arrived 'amidst the greatest war excitement'. Within a few days, World War One had made its inexorable and terrible debut. The Gettys were booked to return to America with the Hamburg-America Line, an impossibility now that Britain and Germany were at war. It was not easy, Getty soon discovered, to arrange an alternative passage since many liners were being commandeered as troop transports and hundreds of Americans were similarly marooned. He was eventually able to book accommodation on the *Lusitania*, departing Liverpool on 12 September. Apart from the small difficulty of finding a ship, Getty had little real appreciation, like most other people, of the awful reality of what was happening to the world. 23 August 1914: 'Paul and I yesterday visited the National Gallery and had a very interesting time there ...' However in Liverpool he remarked 'the martial spirit is as active here as anywhere in the Empire. On Friday night a long procession of recruits, getting ready for active service, marched by our hotel.'

The return voyage on the *Lusitania* was cramped but uneventful: several months would pass before she was sunk by a German U-boat with the loss of 1189 lives, eventually provoking the entry of the United States into the war. In New York, and on the journey back across America by train to Los Angeles, the Gettys were surprised to observe that the war in Europe had no apparent effect on life in America. They had been on its doorstep, but for most Americans it was too far away to worry about overmuch.

At home at last, George Getty put to his son the question that had been uppermost in his mind, but unspoken, for the previous four months. 'What,' he asked, 'do you intend to do now?'

3. 'Congratulations, Paul, it's making thirty barrels'

George Getty desperately wanted his son, his only child, to follow him into the oil business. The Minnehoma Oil Company had expanded considerably since its foundation in 1903. Nearly forty wells had been drilled on Lot 50, only one of them a dry hole, and in 1911 Minnehoma bought seven more leases near Cleveland, Oklahoma, some of which were already showing signs of being more profitable than the whole of Lot 50. Yet despite its size and success, Getty always thought of the Minnehoma Oil Company as a family business and there was only one man he wanted to run the company when he was ready to hand over control – his son, J. Paul Getty.

Paul had other ideas, lots of them. He wanted to travel more, partly for the sheer pleasure of it and partly to equip himself further for a career as a diplomat. He also had a vague ambition to be a writer and imagined he could probably combine writing with a post in the diplomatic service, thereby satisfying both intellectual and artistic inclinations. He had absolutely no desire to become a businessman like his father, and had little interest in oil outside the machismo glamour of the drilling rigs. Though he had enjoyed working on site during his college vacations, he had no intention of going in for such backbreaking toil as a career.

But Getty was a man accustomed to having his own way. When he laid out all the compelling arguments why Paul should go into the oil business, Getty presented his case in a reasonable, logical manner, as if perfectly ready to listen to any sensible counter-arguments. He had alwas entertained the hope, he said, that Minnehoma would remain a family business. It was a company worth millions of dollars, he was nearly sixty and would soon be thinking of retiring; Paul was his only son and the logical choice to carry on the business he had built. While he respected Paul's inclination towards a career as a diplomat, he was convinced that Paul would soon become frustrated by bureaucracy; did he realise how long he would have to wait to climb each rung of the ladder? Finally, he said, Paul had virtually grown up in the oil business, knew as much about it, if not more, than many of the men already successfully making fortunes out of oil.

All he asked, Getty continued with quiet insistence, was for Paul to spend a year in the business. If at the end of that period he still wanted to

37

be a diplomat, he could go with his father's blessing. At worst he would simply have wasted a year which, at the age of twenty-two, would not be a great setback. Getty offered his son a deal: he would pay one-hundred-dollars-a-month living expenses while Paul scouted Oklahoma for low-cost leases, and provide the capital for exploratory drilling. If they found oil, any profits would be shared – seventy per cent to Getty Senior, thirty per cent to Paul.

It was an offer Paul felt he could not, in all conscience, refuse. But then Paul could not refuse 'Daddy' anything. He adored his father, admired him above all other men, and frequently quoted his favourite aphorisms, like 'No man's opinion is better than his information' or 'Moral responsibility must on no account be sidetracked'.

In September 1914, less than two weeks after returning from Europe, Paul checked into the Cordova Hotel in Tulsa, Oklahoma, and prepared to set himself up in business as a wildcatter. Tulsa had become the focus of Oklahoma oil operations in the spring of 1912 when a huge new oilfield was discovered not far distant at Cushing, in Creek County, a few miles to the west. Thomas Slick and Charles Shaffer, the two wildcatters who opened the field, were canny operators: when they struck oil at 2319 feet on a farm near Cushing, they hired all the livery rigs in town and locked them in their stables to try and prevent the news leaking out in the hope that they might fend off the lease brokers while they tied up the surrounding acres for themselves. They might have saved themselves the trouble, for word spread rapidly from mouth to mouth, unleashing yet another rabble-rousing oil rush.

For a few brief and inglorious months the Cushing field was the greatest light-oil pool in the world. The surrounding farmland rapidly sprouted a forest of derricks and huge black gushers leapt into the Oklahoma sky with astonishing frequency. Caution was thrown to the wind by greed, wildcat rigs regularly exploded in terrifying balls of fire, and the quiet town of Cushing itself was transformed into a roistering madhouse. The main street, churned into a quagmire by iron-wheeled wagons, was lined with pine-shack brothels and gambling saloons with their doors flung open to reveal tables piled high with money – and pistol-packing guards sitting on balconies overlooking the tables. Hordes of prostitutes, gamblers, gangsters and confidence tricksters flooded into the town to fleece the unwary; gunfights, murder and robberies were common.

Accommodation was so scarce that the owner of Cushing's pool hall made a tidy profit renting tables as beds, squeezing up to three men on each table. The whole territory became a lawless jungle: the dirt track, fourteen miles long, which connected the railroad at Cushing to the oilfield, was passable only by horse or mule, or in a determined Model T Ford and travellers were held up by armed gangs so frequently that it became known as the 'road to Jericho'.

Many of the leases were owned by the Osage, Cherokee and Comanche tribes; suddenly rich beyond their dreams, they were mercilessly preyed upon by crooks and swindlers of all kinds. Some Osage families had incomes in excess of sixty-five thousand dollars a year and they became notorious for buying new Cadillacs or Pierce Arrows, driving them until they broke down and abandoning them at the roadside. Ornate decorated hearses were also very popular, and it was not unusual to see a hearse careering across the prairie with an Indian at the wheel and his family cheerfully bouncing in the coffin compartment at the rear.

Four towns mushroomed around the Cushing oilfield – Drumright, Dropright, Allright and Damright – but the real business was conducted in Tulsa, fifty miles away. The population of Tulsa tripled in the three years following the discovery of the Cushing pool. Once just a ford across the Arkansas River, by 1914 Tulsa boasted 11 hotels, 8 jewellers, 84 law firms and 126 oil prospecting companies, among them the Minnehoma Oil Company, which opened a small field office in Rooms 1016 and 1017 in the R. T. Daniel Building, one of several new office blocks in the town.

The lobby of the ten-storey Tulsa Hotel was where the oilmen gathered and the deals were done. Drillers in muddy boots and oily pants sprawled in the leather armchairs, lease brokers huddled with wildcatters over maps and deeds, noisy groups swapped outrageous stories over bottles of bootleg whisky, cigar smoke hung heavy in the air and tobacco juice puddled round the spittoons. Martin Moran, podgy president of a pipeline company, could be found sitting at the poker table most nights with his eyes closed and if anyone said 'Mart's asleep' he would open one eye and grunt 'No, he ain't!' Will Rogers, already famous as a rope-throwing cowboy in vaudeville shows, often dropped by and another regular was Bill Roeser, who had made and lost several fortunes before he was thirty and once strolled through Tulsa sporting a ten-thousand-dollar bill as a boutonnière. Will and Bud Carter, the brothers who sold George Getty the lease on Lot 50, hung around the lobby frequently as did Colonel Wood, oil reporter for the *Tulsa World*, for it was not only the best source of stories but also the first place to hear of a new strike.

The fresh-faced young man who shyly sauntered into the lobby of the Tulsa Hotel in September 1914, was unquestionably the least colourful of all the characters present. He was tall, well-built and soberly dressed in a high-button tweed suit and starched collar, his auburn hair neatly parted in the middle and smarmed down to control the curls. Paul Getty looked around and knew, instinctively, that he had come to the right place to start out as a wildcatter.

Paul had taken a small room at the Cordova Hotel for six dollars a week and arranged to have his meals at a boarding house nearby for another six dollars, leaving him a little more than fifty dollars spending money each month, which he considered to be ample. He had bought a third-hand Model T Ford for transport and was offered the use of Minnehoma's office facilities in the Daniel Building, even though he was to operate quite separately from Minnehoma.

He felt he was pretty well set up, until he first got into casual conversation with a couple of oilmen at the Tulsa Hotel and learned that lease prices had skyrocketed in the wake of the Cushing boom. Property owners, increasingly aware of the value of oil, were beginning to demand – and receive – ludicrous sums for drilling rights far beyond the reach of smaller operators. The war in Europe was stimulating the demand for oil and crude prices were rising again, prompting the bigger and more prosperous companies to pay the inflated lease prices.

Paul knew his father well enough to be quite sure he would never sanction paying over the odds for a lease, but he still had hopes of finding, somewhere, a promising parcel of land with oil potential at a not too unreasonable price. Over the next few months, when he was not out scouring the countryside in his battered Model T, Paul made it his business to spend as much time as possible at the Tulsa Hotel, getting to know the regulars and listening to the gossip. Some of the old-timers knew his father and referred to him as 'Getty's boy', but he was soon accepted on his own account once he had proved that he knew what he was talking about when the conversation turned, as it always did, to sinking holes in the ground to find oil.

Some of the men with whom he shared a dining table at the boarding house were also aspiring wildcatters and several became lifelong friends. There was Harold Breene, a tall strapping youth whose uncle was one of his father's partners on a lease at Cleveland; O. O. Owens, a young lease broker who worked every day from six o'clock in the morning until midnight; Josh Cosden, who started his own company with five hundred dollars when he was twenty-six years old and was a multi-millionaire before he was thirty; little Joe Ardizonne, who was killed on a derrick by a bursting pipe on the brink of making his fortune; John Markham, who bought a lease very cheaply at the north end of the Cushing field and developed it into the most profitable lease in Oklahoma; and Bill Skelly, soon to found the Skelly Oil Company. Over dinner they liked to speculate which of them would be first to succeed or which of them would be first to make a million.

Rarely did any of them give voice to doubts about their ability to become millionaires, but Paul must have wondered, as he set out each day on yet another fruitless expedition, if he was ever going to be able to find a lease at a price his father would approve. Christmas 1914 came and went, the Ford Motor Company announced the production of its millionth car, a Stutz set a world automobile speed record of an astounding 102.6 miles an hour, the first motorised taxis appeared on the streets of New York and still Paul, grimly determined to succeed, slewed and slithered along the muddy tracks crisscrossing the Oklahoma oilfields at the wheel of his Model T. Every time he got stuck, he would walk across the fields to find the nearest farmer and hire a team to pull him out; every time the farmer would chortle and offer the same advice: 'Why don't you get yourself a horse, son?' In the lobby of the Tulsa Hotel, Paul kept himself posted and got a reputation among the habitués for being able to trade useful information. But he still seemed as far away as ever from finding a lease and was often on the verge of giving up the whole infuriating project. Only the encouragement and support of his friends kept him going.

Adding to his frustration was the continuing, apparently effortless success of his father's Minnehoma Oil Company. Getty, typically far-sighted, was one of the first oilmen to be convinced that the science of geology could make a vital contribution to locating the presence of oil underground and from the beginning of 1915 Minnehoma employed a full-time geologist to assist with prospecting. The first lease Minnehoma acquired on geological advice was a forty-acre plot in Creek County, north of the Cushing pool and some miles from the nearest producing wells. Most oilmen believed the land was dry, but the geologist told Getty that it was the north end of the Cushing anticline, with an extremely favourable structure for oil. Getty bought a five-eighths interest in the lease for $21,875 then, lucky as always, sold one eighth to John Milliken, president of the Milliken Oil Company, for $17,500. Minnehoma started drilling five wells on the lease in April and found five gushers. Before the end of the year, Getty had been offered $250,000 for his half-interest.

While his father seemed to be able to pull off such lucrative deals one after another, Paul felt his chances to be slipping away. One day in the summer of 1915, sensational news circulated in the lobby of the Tulsa Hotel: Gunsburg and Forman, a partnership widely known in the oil business as 'G & F', had bought a small, undrilled lease near Drumright for $120,000 cash. It was considered by many old-timers to be a preposterous price, complete folly. Paul knew one of the partners, George Forman, and casually asked him if he thought G & F might have paid too much. 'I would like to buy a similar lease,' Forman replied confidently, 'at the same price every day.' It was a daunting reply to a young man hoping to find a lease for considerably less than one tenth of that price.

September 1915, the anniversary of his arrival in Tulsa, passed without finding him any closer to making a start in the oil business. He could, perhaps, have legitimately confronted his father and pointed out that he had kept his side of the bargain: he had wasted a year trying to be an oilman, now he wanted to follow his own inclinations and become a writer and diplomat. But that would have meant admitting failure and he was not ready for that.

In November Paul heard a whisper going round the Tulsa Hotel lobby that a promising lease would soon be coming up for auction in Muskogee County. It was a half-interest in 160 acres, known as the Nancy Taylor Allotment, at Stone Bluff. Paul knew the area quite well but drove out early next morning for a closer inspection of the property and felt an 'immediate positive reaction'. Back in Tulsa, it did not take him long to discover there was considerable interest in the lease and the price was expected to be high. Anders, Cory and Associates, a successful and well-established lease broker, already owned half the lease and had declared their intention to acquire the other half. It seemed to Paul that he would be beaten even before he got to the starting gate.

That night he lay awake in bed in his room at the Cordova Hotel, turning over in his mind different ways in which he could thwart the competition. By morning, he had a plan. Two days later he cranked the Model T (it would only start with violent cranking and only stop when both brake and reverse gear pedals were pressed) and drove out to Muskogee, where he had an appointment with the vice-president of the town bank, a man he could claim as an acquaintance. Paul laid his cards on the table. He wanted to bid for the lease on the Nancy Taylor Allotment, but did not stand a chance because everyone present would know that the funds available from his father were strictly limited. 'I want you to attend the sale on my behalf,' he said, 'and bid for me, but please don't let on that you are acting for me.'

The plan, such as it was, represented Paul's only hope. He reasoned that if a prominent local banker attended the sale and bid strongly at the beginning, the other bidders might, just might, assume the bank was acting for a major oil company with unlimited funds and drop out early. It was not a particularly original idea and often did not work, but it was the best he could come up with.

Paul could not bear to attend the auction in Muskogee, a week later, but waited impatiently outside. After what seemed an eternity, the banker emerged with a broad smile on his face and said: 'It's yours.' The ploy had worked even better than Paul dared hope: it transpired the minute the banker opened his mouth to bid, the others all lost heart. J. Paul Getty had bought his first lease, for the unbelievable sum of five hundred dollars. It was, by an odd coincidence, exactly what George Franklin Getty had paid for *his* first lease, nearly thirteen years earlier.

Paul telegraphed the good news to his father in Los Angeles and contacted a lawyer to set up a company to take over the lease and finance the drilling of a test well; he called it, on the spur of the moment, the Lorena Oil Company, after Lorena Carbutt, one of his girlfriends. In the weeks leading up to Christmas 1915 Paul was busy in Tulsa hiring the best drilling crew he could find and on New Year's Day 1916 they began to build the derrick and install the rig. Paul spent every day at the site, driving out to Stone Bluff early in the morning in an old Dodge he had bought to replace the Model T Ford, and returning late at night. He would sit and watch the drill sink deeper and deeper into the ground – 'heading for China', the oilmen called it – with palpable excitement; sometimes he could hardly bear to drag himself away.

On the morning of 2 February, the drill hit oil sand. Paul was watching as the bailer, a device which cleared waste rock from the drillhole, suddenly began turning up the mushy sand. He knew its significance – if there was oil down there, the drill would almost certainly reach it within twenty-four hours. He found the tension almost unbearable and his obvious jitters began to grind on the nerves of the crew until one of them snapped in exasperation: 'Be a good boy, boss. Get the hell out of here before you have a fit, or make us have one.' Paul was irritated at being addressed as 'boy', but recognised the wisdom of the advice and reluctantly climbed into his Dodge, leaving his fate in their hands.

In Tulsa Paul went first to the Cordova Hotel, but he could not sit down for more than a minute at a stretch and so he walked over to Minnehoma's office in the Daniel Building to get on the nerves of the man in charge there, his uncle J. Carl Smith. A former building superintendent from Denver, Smith was a large, ruddy-faced man with an easy-going temperament whom George Getty had first employed in 1903 to supervise the development of Lot 50. In the intervening years he had learned a great deal about the oil business and he knew how young Paul was feeling – even for a veteran oilman, waiting to learn whether you owned an oil well or a dry hole was a time of great stress. With Paul pacing the office like a caged tiger, Smith guessed he was not going to get much work done and he offered to go out and supervise the last few hours of the drilling. Paul accepted gratefully and Smith left on the next train for Stone Bluff, promising to return on the last train the following day – there was only a single telephone line between Stone Bluff and Tulsa and it was so rarely working that neither of them considered attempting to get the news back by telephone.

In his hotel room that night, Paul tossed and turned in bed, unable to sleep. Thursday 3 February 1916 dawned grey, cold and bleak. Paul got up at first light, feeling terrible, took a shower and plodded over to the boarding house where he usually ate breakfast. He had no appetite for ham and eggs, but drank several cups of black coffee in a fruitless effort

43

to get into shape to face the day. No mail arrived for him at the Cordova Hotel and he walked to the Daniel Building to pass the time with Martha Cornelius, the stenographer who had been left in charge of the office.

Years later, he recalled that day in graphic detail:

> For hours I did little but fidget and glance repeatedly at my watch. A hundred times or more I decided to drive out to the drilling site – and a hundred times or more rejected the idea. Somehow I managed to wait the day through, but I was at the Tulsa railroad depot, anxiously pacing the passenger platform, more than an hour before the late train from Stone Bluff was due to arrive. It was already dark. A chill, dust-laden prairie wind swept the platform in raw gusts that stung my face and seemed to slice right through my overcoat. But I was aware of neither cold nor wind as I did my sentry-go up and down the deserted platform. Every now and then I would stop, either to check the time shown by the large clock that clung to the depot's soot-grimed facade, or to peer along the railroad track in futile hopes the train might come in ahead of schedule.

When at last he could hear the train's mournful bell and its single light appeared out of the gloom, Paul felt his heart thumping in his chest. As the train pulled into the station, several oilmen jumped out of the carriages and one of them, who knew Paul, shouted: 'Heard a rumour your well came in. It's a good one!' He was gone before Paul could question him further, but then Paul spotted J. Carl Smith stepping down from the last coach. Paul hurried to meet him and saw he was smiling.

'Congratulations, Paul,' Smith said. 'We brought in your well this afternoon. It's making thirty barrels.'

Paul stopped in his tracks, suddenly overwhelmed with disappointment. Thirty barrels a day! That was virtually *nothing*; hardly worth being called a well.

Smith laughed heartily, and reached out to shake Paul's hand. 'Yes sir! It was making thirty barrels an hour when I left.'

Thirty barrels an *hour* – that was more like it. 'When I heard that,' Paul said, 'I felt Oklahoma had a new oil producer.'

It was an exhilarating, unforgettable moment. From that day on, J. Paul Getty would never again entertain the idea of making a career as a writer or a diplomat. He had become an oilman.

Paul celebrated his success, and his overnight elevation in status, by trading in his Dodge for a 1916 Cadillac V-8 Roadster, which he bought

44

for $2800 from D. D. Wertzberger, a rig builder who doubled as the Cadillac agent in Tulsa. This rakish new automobile, in which the young oil-well owner felt he cut quite a dash, marked the beginning of his lifelong affection for Cadillacs. But it was his single extravagance – he continued to live in his six-dollar-a-week room at the Cordova Hotel and continued to eat at the boarding house.

Production at the well at Stone Bluff declined rapidly in its first few days of operation from around seven hundred barrels a day to two hundred barrels a day. This was by no means unusual, but Paul's inclination was to sell out for a quick profit and invest the proceeds in further leases; his father agreed. On 12 February Paul negotiated the sale of the Getty interests in the Stone Bluff lease to the Cosden Oil and Gas Company for $40,000. Under the agreement with his father, he received 30% of the net profit – $11,850.

During the next three months Paul ran a hectic and highly successful business as a lease broker, swiftly buying and selling and almost always turning a profit by relying on a combination of instinct and luck. He even managed to make a small profit out of drilling a dry hole on a lease in Creek County, by judiciously selling interests in the test drilling. It seemed he had suddenly acquired a golden touch; he was involved in so many deals that he did not have time to stop and count how much money he was making. Riding high, he even found oil where everyone knew no oil existed – in the Oklahoma red beds.

There was no good reason for the popular belief that this barren tract of reddish sandstone and shale was dry. It was just accepted wisdom – a collective hunch. Paul decided to employ a geologist to check it out. Most veteran oilmen were suspicious of geologists, referring to them derisively as 'doodlebugs' and openly sneering at the idea of 'some damned bookworm' being able to find oil; prospecting was thus largely a question of playing hunches, guesswork, superstition and luck. Paul believed in playing hunches, too, but he also believed, like his father, that the infant science of petroleum geology had more to offer than the alleged facility of veteran oilmen to 'sniff crude' three thousand feet under the ground. In April 1916 Paul's faith was rewarded when, on the recommendation of a highly favourable report from Doctor Edward Bloesch, a leading geologist, and in the teeth of dire warnings of folly and a fair amount of ridicule from other wildcatters, he secured several leases in the red beds and brought in three wells in quick succession.

Spurning the use of Minnehoma's office in Tulsa, Paul preferred to do business in the field, using the front seat of his Cadillac as an office – and the back seat as a bedroom, when the drilling of a new well reached a critical stage. Dozens of leases and contracts were signed on the hood of the Cadillac and witnessed by the scrawled signature of the nearest

45

roustabout. It was a point of pride to Paul that he was a working boss, able to tackle any job on a rig from 'riding a hook' while setting up a derrick to sharpening a dull drill bit, but because he was so young he constantly had to *prove* he was the boss. One day on a rig a surly roustabout baldly announced that he was going to take it easy that day because he had a terrible hangover after a payday spree the previous night. Acutely aware the rest of the crew were watching him to see how he would react, Paul said: 'OK, I'll make a deal with you. I was out last night, too, but I can still work. To prove it, I'll give you a ten-second start and if you can race me up the rig you can have the day off.' 'You're on,' said the roustabout. Paul stripped off his jacket and gave his watch to the driller. The roustabout jumped on to the rig and began climbing; ten seconds later Paul followed, up the other side. Cheered from below, both men heaved themselves from spar to spar, panting for breath; Paul slowly gained on the roustabout and just got his hand on the crown block, at the top of the rig, first. 'All right,' he said when he came down, 'let's get back to work.'

On 25 May Paul and his father formalised their partnership by incorporating, in Oklahoma, the Getty Oil Company. Getty was president and treasurer of the fledgling corporation and his son was secretary; the total assets comprised no less than 55 leases acquired by Paul for a total of $25,000 and having an estimated market value of $100,000. A thousand stock shares were issued, 700 to Getty and 300 to Paul. They resolved to continue sharing profits on a 70/30 ratio for any joint ventures undertaken by the Getty Oil Company, but agreed that both would continue independent operations. When Paul could finance a wildcat hole from his own resources, his father would not share any profit; conversely, Paul would only profit from those of his father's activities in which he chose to invest his own money. It was a sensible, business-like arrangement which they both considered to be eminently fair, if perhaps a little unusual for a father and son.

Not long after the incorporation of the Getty Oil Company, Paul discovered, to his faint surprise and unmitigated delight, that he had become a dollar millionaire at the age of twenty-three. It dawned upon him that as there was really no need for him to make any more money, he might just as well devote his time to enjoying it. He had proved himself as an oilman, both to his own satisfaction and that of his father. What more could anyone ask? Thus justified, he began to make arrangements to return to California, muttering something to his friends in the boarding house about the probability of America becoming involved in the war in Europe and the need to 'do his bit', a noble resolve that was not the whole story by any means. What Paul really wanted to do was to have some fun with his money and get his hands on the beautiful Californian girls who figured so frequently in his restless dreams. 'I fear the realisation that I was a millionaire,' he said, 'went to my head.'

In June 1916 he packed a trunk and two suitcases and prepared to leave Tulsa. Rather than face the rigours of the roads across country to the West Coast, he decided to ship the Cadillac roadster home by train. Going the rounds to say goodbye to his friends, he learned that Bill Roeser, of the $10,000-boutonnière fame, was also planning to put his car on the same train. When they found they could save freight charges by shipping the two cars together, Roeser suggested shooting dice to decide who would pay. Although he was always ready to take a gamble on an oil well, Paul did not like to gamble for its own sake but thought it would be churlish to refuse his friend.

He rolled the dice and won, of course.

Sarah and George Getty were far from pleased when their son arrived home and calmly announced his precocious intention to retire from the oil business. His father was appalled by such indolence, and not at all placated by Paul's rationalisation that since America would soon be in the war – he had already put his name down either for the Air Service or the Coast Artillery – he wanted to have some fun before he was called up.

George Getty, who would never forget the grinding poverty of his childhood on a dirt farm, believed that wealth begat responsibility, that it was the businessman's moral duty to make money work, to invest and re-invest to build businesses and create jobs and wealth for others. And he practised what he preached: although he was worth well over a million dollars, his bank account at that time stood at only $28,518. Getty pleaded with his son to reconsider. 'Your wealth,' he said, 'represents a better life for a great many people besides yourself.'

Paul was not of a mind to listen to arguments about moral responsibilities. He had just spent nigh on two years in the Oklahoma oilfields, chilled to the bone in the winter and spitting dust in the summer; he firmly believed his retirement to be richly deserved and would not be dissuaded. George Getty was dismayed, shocked almost, to realise that he was not able to bend his son to his wishes.

Within a few months of his return to California, the name of J. Paul Getty could frequently be found in the society columns among those attending the biggest charity balls, the best parties, the most fashionable nightclubs and the latest Hollywood premieres. Paul liked the movie community and considered there to be an affinity between the oil business and the film business, inasmuch as they were both high-risk enterprises capable of creating overnight millionaires.

'It was a camaraderie,' he insisted, 'of people who were willing to gamble everything on the next thousand feet of drilling or the next thousand feet of film.' He would number among his friends people like Douglas Fairbanks, Cary Grant, Sam Goldwyn, Cecil B. De Mille, Rudy Vallee, Jean Harlow, Gloria Swanson and Clara Bow. He had frequent arguments with Charlie Chaplin over girls, particularly when Chaplin suspected his leading lady, Edna Purviance, was taking more interest in Paul than she was in him. One of Paul's regular companions was a shy young man who earned fifty dollars a week as a dancer in a nightclub floor show. At parties Paul always had to prod him to get him to talk to a girl and he could never get over the fact that Rudolph Valentino soon became the world's greatest screen lover.

At home, Paul made little pretence that he was interested in anything but leisure. While his father left early each morning for his office in the Union Oil Building downtown, Paul languished in bed in a part of the house he had conveniently converted into a self-contained bachelor suite. It comprised a large room on the ground floor with its own entrance, a sleeping alcove and a bathroom. The walls were still covered with the gold brocade Sarah Getty had chosen years before, but it was barely visible behind Paul's pictures and he furnished the room according to his own taste, with a simple iron bed, a sprung divan and an oak desk. Books were stacked on every available shelf and all the flat surfaces were littered with gadgets, souvenirs and bric-a-brac of all kinds. Paul had his own keys, kept the door firmly locked when he was out and would allow none of the domestic staff to clean up lest they disturb the chaos with which he was cheerfully familiar. From his room there was direct access to the basement which he had fitted out as a gymnasium with weights, parallel bars, punch bags and a steam bath.

Most mornings Paul spent an hour working out in the gymnasium before taking a shower and carefully dressing for the day, usually in a smart suit of fashionable cut with a silk handkerchief tucked into the top pocket. About midday he would be at the wheel of the Cadillac roadster, often with a pretty girl at his side, heading for the Beach Club at Santa Monica, where the day could be happily frittered away in sunbathing, swimming, playing tennis and flexing his muscles with other wealthy young men who liked to describe themselves, with their tongues firmly in their cheeks, as 'beach bums'. Paul was extremely fit and powerfully built: he could lift a 50-lb barbell disc by holding it between the fingers of one hand and he was never beaten at broomstick wrestling (twisting a broomstick at one end from the grip of an opponent at the other). In his one-piece singlet bathing suit with the Beach Club emblem embroidered on the front, he liked to throw out his chest the better to display his fine physique when he was being photographed.

Evenings were invariably spent on the nightclub circuit or at parties, popping champagne corks, tackling the foxtrot and the Charleston with verve and listening to a foot-stomping, vibrant new sound that was sweeping the United States – jazz. Girls smoked cigarettes, wore bobbed hair and lipstick and dresses with V necks, which were considered dangerous to both health and morals. It was a fine time for a libidinous young man with money to be alive: Paul rarely returned home before dawn, usually having stopped on the way to canoodle with his latest lady friend in a suitably secluded spot.

Sometimes Paul entertained at home, earning frequent sniffs of disapproval from his mother who made no secret of the fact that she considered her son's friends to be 'riff-raff'. Among his regular visitors was a young professional boxer who fought under the name of Kid Blackie but was better known to his friends as Jack Dempsey. Paul used to spar every week with Dempsey in the basement gymnasium three years before he became world heavyweight boxing champion. Dempsey always said that Paul was good enough to turn professional had he wanted and a rumour circulated that Paul was the only man ever to have knocked Dempsey out. It was not true. The story went that they had a fight over a girl and Paul laid Dempsey out with a left uppercut. What actually happened was that Paul visited Dempsey's training camp at Saratoga Lakes to find out if he could really box. 'I think I'm pretty good, Jack,' he said. 'I want you to do the best you can against me and I'm going to do the best I can. When it's over we're still going to be friends, but I'm going to try and knock you out.' He quickly discovered he was not as good as he thought he was. 'We shook hands,' said Dempsey, 'and I knocked him down a couple of times and bloodied his nose. I didn't try to kill him or anything like that, just to show him he couldn't fight.'

Paul did not neglect the oil business entirely – he somehow managed to find the time, for example, to attend the annual meeting of Minnehoma stockholders in December 1916 – but he refused to take any active part in the operations either of Minnehoma or the Getty Oil Company. He was neither asked for an opinion nor expressed one when his father decided, that same month, to sell Minnehoma's first lease – Lot 50 at Bartlesville – for $125,000 in cash. Getty had made around $200,000 from the wells on Lot 50, but production was falling and he decided it was time to get out, a decision he would later regret when Oklahoma crude prices soared from 58¢ a barrel in 1915 to $1.73 in 1917. In fact the sale nearly fell through because Getty insisted on excluding a fine team of draught horses named Pat and Madge. Although he was not normally a softhearted man, he had become very fond of Pat and Madge, who would come to his call on his visits to the lease and nuzzle him while he rubbed their ears. At first the purchaser of

Lot 50 insisted that the team be included as part of the lock-stock-and-barrel deal, but Getty uncharacteristically put sentiment before business and said he would not part with the lease unless the horses were excluded. Pat and Madge went into retirement with Getty's blessing, unlike his son, Paul.

In April 1917 the United States entered what President Woodrow Wilson optimistically described as 'the war to end all wars'. Paul did not subscribe to the view held by many Americans that the war in Europe was 'none of our business'. Many of the friends he made during his year at Oxford had already sacrificed their lives in the trenches and he thought it was high time America got involved. On the other hand he was not too disappointed to learn that his application to join the newly-formed Air Service of the US Army could not yet be accepted because of insufficient training facilities and aircraft. While he was attracted to the glamorous idea of becoming an Army flier, the postponement meant he was free to continue enjoying himself with an entirely clear conscience. He never did get called up and was amused after the war to receive a letter signed by the Secretary of War thanking him for his 'outstanding display of patriotism' and regretting that 'exigencies of military service' had prevented him from being called for active duty.

Some time during the early summer of 1918, Paul tired of his role as playboy millionaire. He never really explained why. Perhaps he simply got bored, or it might have had something to do with the oil rush developing on his doorstep in southern California – maybe he could not bear not to be a part of it. Perhaps, as he sometimes liked to say, oil was already in his veins and the oil fever that had affected him in Oklahoma was only lying dormant.

Whatever the reason, the minutes of a special meeting of the board of directors of the Getty Oil Company, held on 22 August 1918 at the Union Oil building in Los Angeles, provided clear evidence that Paul had re-entered the business.

> J. Paul Getty reported the sale of two leases recently made, one of the Webber in Township 12, Range 8 East, Oklahoma, for $2400 and the other near Garber, Oklahoma, for $2000. The subject of a dividend was then considered, and J. Paul Getty, Director, moved that $5000 of the Company's funds on hand be distributed to the stockholders as a dividend; and it was therefore ordered that a dividend of 5% on the outstanding stock of the Getty Oil Company, as of record at this date, be declared and paid at once.

'Congratulations, Paul, it's making thirty barrels'

George Getty welcomed his son back into the business, drily expressed himself pleased that Paul had decided to end his 'post-adolescent hibernation' and never mentioned it again.

4. 'This is oil land!'

After his brief – but thoroughly enjoyable – retirement, Paul returned to work with gusto, resuming his responsibilities as a born-again director of both the Minnehoma Oil Company and the Getty Oil Company. At the same time he renewed operations as an independent wildcatter, scouting for promising leases where he could drill wells with his own money. There followed an eventful few years, both for the Getty companies and for Paul himself – a period that marked the end of his dilettante phase and saw him firmly indentured to the oil business.

His time out as a playboy impinged only once on his business affairs: one day when he was supervising the drilling of a well at Long Beach, a convoy of limousines pulled up alongside the rig. Clara Bow, the 'It girl' then at the height of her fame, stepped out of the first car, followed by Pauline Frederick, John Gilbert, Dorothy Gish, David Mdivani and other Hollywood luminaries, all of them Paul's friends. Miss Bow announced that they thought it would be fun to pay Paul a surprise visit and so they had come for 'a picnic'.

While the drilling crew stood and gaped, liveried chauffeurs set up a table, covered it with an immaculate white cloth and began unpacking hampers. Once the table had been set, the visitors invited Paul and the crew to join them for a champagne lunch. Afterwards the awed oilmen produced greasy scraps of paper to collect autographs and one of them shyly asked Clara Bow if she would autograph his car.

'Gladly,' she said, 'but won't it wash off in the rain?'

'No ma'am, it won't,' he replied. 'I want you to do it with this.' He produced a chisel from behind his back and asked her to scratch her name in the paintwork on the hood, close to the windshield so that he could see it when he was driving. Miss Bow obliged and Paul heard later that the man had the scratched signature electroplated to protect it from rust.

Apart from this incident, Paul rarely allowed pleasure to interfere with business now that he was back at work and his reputation as a sharp and successful oilman spread. In October 1919 he was approached by a consortium of bankers and financiers in Los Angeles who were anxious, with crude prices edging up to three dollars a barrel, to get into the oil business. Paul was attracted by the idea of the financial backing they could provide, but concerned that the consortium was expecting quick profits. His warnings that oil was a high-risk business were brushed aside and, despite his misgivings, he was persuaded to take charge of a new company, capitalised at five million dollars to prospect for oil in Oklahoma and California.

Paul quickly regretted his involvement with the consortium. Before a single lease had been purchased, there was a dispute about stock rights which was only settled by going to court. Almost before the new company had time to sink test holes, his fellow directors were badgering him to produce profits. Then they were up in arms when he drilled a couple of dry holes. 'I considered my job to be the production of oil,' he noted with disgust, 'not the operation of a kindergarten for starch-collared financiers harbouring get-rich-quick hopes.'

The company was eventually dissolved. Paul was glad to be rid of it and free to return to wildcatting on his own account, in between his duties as a director of the Minnehoma and Getty oil companies. The experience taught him a valuable lesson he was never to forget: thereafter he would be his own boss.

1920 was ushered in by the Oklahoma field's most dramatic spectacle to date. On New Year's Eve the Minnehoma Oil Company was drilling a routine hole on a lease at Lookout Hill in Osage territory. As the winter sun dipped below the horizon, Harley Robinson, the driller, scrawled in the log that the drill had penetrated fifty feet into Mississippi lime, struck at 2295 feet. Oil was already seeping up out of the hole at each turn of the screw and Robinson reckoned the well looked good for two hundred barrels a day, if not more. Suddenly the pitch of the drilling engine changed noticeably and the wire rope leading into the hole slackened. 'Throw on the tug ropes, Roy,' Harley shouted. 'Something has broke loose down in this hole.'

Roy McCunn, the toolie, set the bull wheels turning to withdraw the drill string, but the wire rope began kinking out of the hole. Robinson knew what was happening – pressure from somewhere under the earth was pushing up the drill. He leapt across the rig and jammed open the throttle of the engine, running it at full speed in an attempt to take up the slack. Still the wire rope coiled out of the hole, forming loops on the derrick floor, and an ominous rumble could be heard above the roaring of the engine and the screaming bull wheels. Robinson realised the well was going to blow out and there was nothing he could do to stop it. 'Let's get out of here,' he shouted to McCunn. Both men dropped their tools and ran for their lives.

They were still running when the heavy iron drill shot out of the hole like a rocket, demolished the crown block at the top of the rig and arched through the air, falling to the ground with such force that it burrowed fifteen feet into the earth. It was followed by a terrible demonic roar as a mighty column of oil leapt into the night sky. Panting for breath, Robinson and McCunn stood at a safe distance, gazing awestruck at their handiwork with the oil spattering onto their heads. Robinson, who had worked on plenty of big wells, believed he was looking at the biggest well in Oklahoma and estimated it was blowing out at the rate of around fifteen thousand barrels a day.

At dawn the great geyser was still spouting with undiminished force and an extraordinary, hellish scene was revealed by the first rays of daylight. A huge cloud of black mist swirled around the remains of the derrick and the roaring fountain of oil. The prairie had turned a dirty brown colour as far as the eye could see and a small frame house in a copse not far from the well was obliterated from view by oil dripping from the trees. Black rivulets flowed down gulleys in the flanks of Lookout Hill, forming pools which overflowed allowing the oil to creep inexorably across the prairie floor. Here and there, small gangs of blackened figures toiled with scrapers and shovels to build earth dams in a desperate attempt to contain some of the overflow.

At midday the first sightseers arrived, driving out across the prairie from the nearby towns of Pawhuska and Personia to gape at this burst artery in the earth's crust. A correspondent noted in the *Oil and Gas Journal:*

> To report that the gusher caused excitement in the region round and about Pawhuska is a mild saying. All trails leading to the well soon became beaten paths. The Midland Valley railroad traverses the prairie a mile distant from the well and the big spouter was gazed upon by hundreds of eyes as the passengers crowded the windows of the up and down trains. If there was a city, town or hamlet within a radius of fifty miles of the well that was not represented by delegations, I failed to learn. To ensure safety, the crowds were kept back in the safety zone for fear some unthinking person would strike a match which might cause a disastrous fire and probably the loss of life.

During the afternoon on New Year's Day, J. Carl Smith arrived from Tulsa to take charge of the operations. Every available man in Pawhuska was recruited to help dig sumps and dams to capture the escaping oil. Smith negotiated a deal with two pipeline companies, Prairie and Gulf, to lay three-inch lines to the well without delay. By the evening overflowing oil had reached Middle Bird Creek, three miles from the gusher, where it congealed on the frozen surface of the creek and began forming a huge pool. A boom was thrown across the creek to contain the pool and squads of labourers worked through the night with horse teams to excavate a huge sump on the right bank of the creek.

At the rig itself Minnehoma's most experienced men, clad in rubber suits, struggled to bring the spouting oil under control, bellowing at each other to make themselves heard above the roar of gusher. By the early morning of Friday 2 January, it was clear to J. Carl Smith that they were fighting a losing battle. Only two 250-barrel storage tanks had been completed, the pipelines were still miles away, the crude sumps built with earth dams were all overflowing and still the gusher poured forth, with no signs of abating. It was no surprise to Smith when officials of the Osage Indian Agency arrived on the site and ordered the well to be capped before the local rivers were polluted, affecting the water supply to surrounding towns. Harley Robinson and his crew, working in appalling conditions, rigged up a tackle alongside the gusher to lift a two-ton high-pressure gate valve onto the hole. At 3.30 in the afternoon, the valve was dropped into place and the gusher was brought down. It was, Robinson said as he left the rig, a 'real humdinger'.

The *Oil and Gas Journal* chose to pay its lavish tribute for the success of the operation to Minnehoma's founder.

George F. Getty of Los Angeles is the man who tamed the oil wildcat in its native lair in several Oklahoma districts. He has a record of having drilled forty wells in succession without pulling a blank in the entire list. His energy and good luck are what put the 'Get' in Getty, and in the course of events he drilled a hole in the scenery over in the Osage country which on New Year's Day started off at the rollicking rate of something like twenty thousand barrels daily. The rush of oil and gas from the depths tossed the tools out of the hole and turned loose a deluge of petroleum ... And Brother Getty has been receiving congratulations by wire and otherwise, wishing him many happy returns of the day. Anybody who can figure oil at $2.75 a barrel can readily ascertain just what the said returns amount to, approximately.

This report was somewhat premature. Having been capped, the well was reluctant to flow again. It was not an unusual phenomenon in the oil business, but in this case it proved unusually difficult to get the well back into production. At first it would produce nothing but water, then a mixture of water and oil and eventually it offered up a miserable trickle of oil amounting to no more than sixty barrels a day.

Inquests in Pawhuska into what had gone wrong were reported by the *Kansas City Star* on 12 January:

Oilmen are a clannish lot and will stick to each other through thick

and thin, but there are those here who say that had the representatives of the Minnehoma company used a little more headwork
when Minnehoma started gushing, and a little more finesse, she
might still be gushing. They say that the night of 31 December,
when the well was pouring oil all over the countryside, an oil
'expert' spent hours of precious time trying to telegraph the good
news to the company's president in Los Angeles, instead of getting
teams and workmen and exerting his last effort to dam Bird Creek
and save the oil.

Offset wells were drilled all round the gusher in the hope of another big
strike, but little was found. 'Where it disappeared to,' Paul Getty said,
'is a mystery.'

In September that year George Getty, then sixty-five, fulfilled a long-
held ambition to drive the 1500 miles from Los Angeles to Tulsa. He set
out in a Cadillac roadster with Arch Hyden, Minnehoma's office
manager, sitting alongside him in the front seat and Mabel McCreery,
his secretary, in the back. (Sarah declined her husband's invitation to
join the adventure.) Many of the roads across Arizona and New Mexico
were still unpaved, but they completed the journey in just five and a half
days, miraculously without a single puncture.

Minnehoma had moved into bigger offices in Tulsa and the payroll
now included a scout as well as a staff geologist. Getty could afford
to pay good wages, and he did – J. Carl Smith was on three hundred
dollars a month and Martha Cornelius, the woman who answered the
telephone and did the typing, earned one hundred dollars a month, a
fabulous sum for a secretary in those days. By then Minnehoma was
operating something like seventy-five producing wells in Oklahoma
alone and the high price of crude was bringing in profits in excess of a
million dollars a year.

Getty did not expect it to last, neither did Paul. From its earliest days
the oil industry had been vulnerable to wild fluctuations in the price of
crude oil, as surplus followed shortfall. In the autumn of 1920, with top-
grade crude at an inflated premium of $5.25 a barrel, father and son
agreed that all the pointers were indicating another imminent price
break. (Paul had even warned the consortium of 'starch-collared
financiers' that a slump in crude prices was likely, but they were not of
a mind to listen.)

Demand for oil had risen sharply during World War One, greatly
stimulating prices. When the Armistice, in November 1918, brought the
carnage in Europe to an end, crude prices did not fall as expected:
Russia was in the agonised throes of a revolution and a bitter civil war,
depriving the West of output from the vast Baku oilfields, which had
once supplied more than fifty per cent of the world's oil. In addition,

domestic demand for oil was increasing rapidly – automobile production in the United States doubled between 1915 and 1919, when seven million new cars took proudly to the highways.

It might have seemed, superficially, that the oil industry was all set for a bonanza, but Getty was worried that high prices would lead inevitably to over-production by an ever-increasing number of oil companies anxious to cash in on the boom. Huge new oilfields had already been discovered in Texas and there was news of fresh strikes almost every day. Prospecting in Wyoming and Arkansas had opened up further new fields, production in Oklahoma was snowballing and California promised enormous reserves. This seemingly limitless flood of oil spurred fears of a surplus and led, inexorably, to the price break that both Gettys had feared was in the offing.

It happened on 24 January 1921. Oklahoma crude plunged overnight, without warning, from $3.50 a barrel to $1.75. On 10 February Getty convened an emergency meeting of the directors of the Minnehoma Company – Paul, his mother, Sarah, and Mabel McCreery who had been elected as a director in 1916. In a sombre atmosphere, Getty asked for their agreement to withhold the usual dividend to stockholders in order to help the company ride the price-break crisis. This was agreed, but soon proved inadequate, even though Minnehoma was a company with assets valued in excess of two million dollars.

On 21 March Getty told his wife and son at another formally minuted directors' meeting that there was only a small amount of cash left in the Minnehoma coffers, hardly enough to meet the company's operating expenses for more than a few days. Although it was anathema to the Gettys to borrow money, there was no alternative – fifty thousand dollars was borrowed from the Security Trust and Savings Bank at 6.5% to tide them over for ninety days. At the same time, they agreed to make rigorous operating economies wherever possible.

By the beginning of June the company was in even deeper water, as indicated by the minutes of a directors' meeting held on 9 June:

The meeting reported that the price of oil had again been reduced in the mid-continent field 25¢ per barrel, making the base price $1.25 per barrel...This price, considering the price of materials and labor, is so low we are having difficulty to keep sufficient money in the bank to meet our expenses and have already had to borrow at the bank to meet disbursements; that at the present time our lifting cost of oil on nine of our properties exceeds $1.25 a barrel and on fourteen of our properties lifting cost exceeds $1.00 per barrel. In order, therefore, to continue in business, it is necessary for all officers and employees in the company to bear a portion of the burden. On motion duly seconded, it was unanimously ordered that the salaries of all officers and employees of the company in the Los Angeles, California and Tulsa, Oklahoma offices be reduced 20%, taking effect 1 June 1921.

Throughout this period Minnehoma was involved in expensive litigation to protect a valuable lease – the Lete Kolvin – in the north of the Cushing field. Seven lawsuits had been filed contesting ownership, and the case degenerated into a rollicking courtroom slinging match gleefully reported at length by the local newspapers. Soon after the first hearing in the District Court of Creek County, Oklahoma, the judge was accused of taking bribes. Judge Lucien B. Wright vigorously denied the allegation, only to be then accused of being a drunk. A report in the *Tulsa Tribune* on 23 August 1921 nicely reflected the tenor of the proceedings under the headline BOOZE PLAYS A BIG PART IN WRIGHT TRIAL:

> A local bootlegger by the name of Andy Higgins testified that the Judge had bought whiskey from him and was often drunk. 'I met Judge Wright in his room at the motel the night before the trial started and gave him a bottle of whiskey which he had requested,' said Higgins. 'About a week after the trial started I took another quart up to the France hotel to him. I had to take him home in a cab that night.'
> 'Why?' asked Judge Harve Maxey, representing the Minnehoma Oil Company.
> 'Because he was drunk,' retorted Higgins.
> 'Higgins, what is your business?' asked Attorney Lytle, for the defence.
> 'Farming a little and handling a little stock,' answered Higgins.
> 'You handle a little whiskey too, don't you?' persisted Lytle.
> 'Yes, I handle a little when I drink, like when me and you drank together yesterday morning,' Higgins flashed back. Lytle quickly dismissed the witness from the stand.

Minnehoma eventually won the case and established its title to the lease, but it cost the company $135,000 in legal fees at a time when it could ill afford such additional expense.

However the economies introduced by Getty enabled the company to survive the crisis of 1921. All the employees accepted the twenty per cent salary cut imposed in June; indeed, some of them even offered to loan the company their life savings to help tide it over the slump. Getty was touched by their loyalty and at the end of the year, when prices had picked up, he did not delay restoring salaries to their previous level. Thereafter the Minnehoma Oil Company ticked over with its existing leases, producing reasonable profits year after year. It acquired very few additional leases, since the Gettys rather lost interest in Oklahoma after Paul at last convinced his father, in November 1921, to turn his formidable attention to California.

Oil had been discovered in California soon after the gold rush, but it remained a back-lot business for decades. The first wildcatters, former goldminers like Ed Doheny and Charlie Canfield, dug their wells with picks and shovels. In the 1890s there were three hundred producers in and around Los Angeles, averaging less than seven barrels each a day. Wells were drilled so closely together on city lots that there were stories of drill strings being lost down one hole and fished out of another nearby. Most of the wildcatters were good friends and hung around together at weekends at the old St Elmo Hotel on north Main Street where the proprietor, a German Jew known as 'Daddy Ikey' Eichenhoffer, always gave credit to the lads on hard times.

In 1910 Charlie 'Dry Hole' Woods drilled a well which entirely changed the nature of the Californian oil business. Charlie, a veteran driller, was known as 'Dry Hole' because he had a reputation for being able to do anything with a well, except find oil. He lost his nickname when he was brought in by the Lake View Oil Company to straighten a twisted hole drilled in the foothills north of Maricopa and hit a gusher that became for a time the biggest producing well in the United States. With a roar that could be heard miles away, the Lake View well came in at eighteen thousand barrels a day and increased to a prodigious eighty thousand at peak production. Walls twenty feet high and fifty feet long were built to dam nearby canyons as sumps. An awed spectator said after a visit to the well: 'It's hell. Literally hell. It roars like hell. It mounts, surges and sweeps like hell. It is as uncontrollable as hell. It is black and hot as hell.'

So much oil was produced by the Lake View well that crude prices plummeted from fifty cents a barrel to less than thirty cents, making it something of a mixed blessing as the *Mining and Scientific Press* of San Francisco reported on 23 July 1910:

> The phenomenal and diabolical production of the Lake View gusher continues. It has ceased to be a novelty, but its output is so tremendous and its effect on the oil industry so demoralising that it cannot be forgotten. When the well first came in, it was looked upon with favour by most oilmen. It would call the attention of the world to California oil, and show how lavish with her mineral wealth Mother Nature had been to us. The well was expected to flow for a few hours or days, until all eyes had been attracted and

would then accommodatingly sand up until its production was needed. The Lake View had no such intention. Its program has never varied, except in degree, from day to day. It has produced in a steady torrential stream. Its daily output has been more than the total daily production of any other field except Coalinga. It has entirely changed the outlook of the industry.

After Lake View the Californian oil industry was dominated not by the guys who met at weekends at Daddy Ikey's place, but by grey-suited executives of corporations with smart downtown office blocks. In 1919 Santa Fe Springs, the first of three big pools in the Los Angeles basin, was opened up for the Union Oil Company by William W. Orcott, California's top geologist. The Huntington Beach field was discovered in the following year by Standard Oil and the Shell Oil Company opened Long Beach, the biggest of the three, the year after that. A few years previously Orcott had drilled a dry hole on Signal Hill at Long Beach and when he heard that Shell was prospecting the area, he snorted: 'I'll drink all the oil there is at Long Beach!' It turned out to be around seven million barrels.

Twenty-six-year-old J. Paul Getty made his first moves to get a foothold in the California oil industry even before the Sante Fe Springs pool started producing. It was entirely typical of him that he was not in the slightest daunted either by the fact that the major oil companies ruled the roost nor by the fiasco of his first venture. Using his own money, he acquired a lease on a property called the Didier Ranch near Puente, California, but because of his commitments in Oklahoma he decided to employ a drilling contractor rather than supervise the work himself. In October 1919 a test well was spudded in on the ranch.

Paul did not follow its progress too closely. He was shuttling regularly between Tulsa and Los Angeles and was already involved in the ill-fated venture with the bankers' consortium and while thus occupied he had little time to check on his investment at the Didier Ranch well. When he did, seven months after drilling had begun, he was disconcerted to discover that the hole had only reached a depth of two thousand feet and that more than ninety thousand dollars had been paid out in fees to the drilling contractor. The time-cost-depth ratio was a record low, he noted bitterly. He halted the drilling operations immediately, fired the contractor and relinquished the lease to the owner of the property.

This unpromising start did nothing to shake his own conviction that there was money to be made in California, but it was some time before he could persuade his father to consider the opportunities on his own doorstep. Although he lived in Los Angeles virtually surrounded by oilfields, George Getty had avoided prospecting for oil in California because drilling costs were much more expensive than in Oklahoma and the major oil companies were so much in control. But when, on 3 November 1921, the Union Oil Company brought in a well at Santa Fe Springs with an initial production of 2500 barrels a day, Paul at last prevailed on his father to drive out and inspect the site which was only about fifteen miles from their home off Wilshire Boulevard.

Two days after Union Oil's strike, Paul was at the wheel of his father's Cadillac heading for Santa Fe Springs. George Getty sat stolidly in the front passenger seat and Emil Kluth, the Minnehoma geologist, was in the back. They found the Union Oil well just off Telegraph Road without difficulty and began driving slowly around the area, peering out of the windows of the Cadillac at the topography of the ground. Kluth, perhaps sensing Getty Senior's doubts, declared himself unimpressed. 'I'd say there were much better possibilities elsewhere in southern California,' he said. 'This doesn't look like very promising oil land to me.' If there was a pool of any size in Santa Fe Springs, he added, he thought it would be to the east of the Union Oil well but it was his general opinion that the field was probably very limited.

As the geologist spoke, Getty was watching a long freight train puffing across the scrubland towards a crossing at Telegraph Road, south of the Union well. Although the terrain appeared to be perfectly flat, the locomotive was toiling perceptibly until it crossed the road when the driver eased off the power and the train began to pick up speed.

'Did you notice that train, Paul?' Getty asked with an unaccustomed hint of excitement in his voice.

Paul nodded, instantly aware of its significance.

'This *is* oil land!' Getty said. 'Now I'm sure of it. The top of the structure – the dome – is right here on Telegraph Road!'

Next day Getty discovered most experts agreed with Kluth that more oil was most likely to be found to the east of the Union well – there had been a scramble for leases in that area. No one was interested in the flat scrub to the south and Getty was able to buy a lease on four plots fronting Telegraph Road, each measuring 50 feet by 145 feet and known as the Nordstrom Lease, for only $693. Extremely pleased with himself for picking up such a bargain, a few weeks later he bought further leases at Huntington Beach and Long Beach. 'From then on,' Paul noted, 'the name of Getty would be associated to an ever-increasing extent with California.'

The Gettys' first producing well in California – Synoground No. 1 at Long Beach – was brought in on 16 April 1922 for 2375 barrels a day. Ten days later Nordstrom No. 1 at Santa Fe Springs was brought in for 2300 barrels a day. During 1922 father and son invested more than $600,000 drilling sixteen wells in California, all of them producers. The

Nordstrom Lease would eventually prove to be the best investment of George Getty's career – during the next seventeen years it would produce a profit of $6,387,946.65. Paul, who liked to quote the figure, noted that it was 'more than 9200 times the original $693 cost of the lease.'

By the beginning of 1923 George Getty had amassed a fortune of around fifteen million dollars and his son was worth about three million, most of it invested in the oil business as operating capital – a further thirty California wells were either in the process of being spudded or were planned, and a gasoline plant was being built at Santa Fe Springs to process the prolific output.

At the age of sixty-seven Getty still personally managed and directed all his business affairs and the explosive growth of his operations in California inevitably exacted a heavy toll on his time, energy and ultimately his health. On the afternoon of Saturday 10 March 1923 he was enjoying a round of golf with friends at the Brentwood Country Club in Los Angeles when he suffered a severe stroke. Paul heard the news by telephone at home and drove immediately to the hospital with his mother to be at his father's bedside. 'His doctors grimly warned me that he was desperately ill,' Paul said. 'I did what I could to comfort my mother, who was herself near collapse from shock and worry.'

For several days, Getty's life hung in the balance. When the doctors said that the immediate crisis was past, they told Paul that his recovery would be very slow and he was likely to be permanently crippled for the rest of his life. In the meantime he was to be shielded from worry – neither Paul nor his mother was to mention business during visits.

Paul felt it was both his right and his duty to take charge of his father's business affairs. He moved swiftly to establish his authority and soon found himself in conflict with some of the old-timers who considered they worked for George F. Getty, not his upstart son. For some time Paul had been concerned by what he considered to be sloppy and inefficient working practices on the Getty rigs, but he had maintained a discreet silence on the matter out of respect for his father. Now, with his father safely out of the way in hospital, he warned all the drilling crews that he intended to tighten up field operations and he would expect new standards of efficiency. He made it clear that only his wish not to usurp his father's authority prevented him from sacking some of the crews.

Somewhat to his surprise, Paul found he was deeply resented. His instructions were carried out with an obvious reluctance which he found deeply galling and there was much muttering behind his back about waiting for the 'real boss' to return. His position was not helped when a well on the Nordstrom Lease blew out and caught fire, melting the steel rig like butter. Paul was on site when it happened and was worried that the fire might spread to adjacent wells and storage tanks, endangering the Santa Fe Railroad, which ran within a thousand yards of the well. He telephoned the traffic superintendent in Los Angeles, said his name was Paul Getty and asked for all trains along the line to be halted until the fire was under control. To his intense embarrassment, his warning was ignored and the traffic superintendent insisted on sending out a man to see the fire for himself before taking any action. The incident did nothing for Paul's status.

Towards the end of May Getty recovered sufficiently to take an interest in his business again and he was not pleased to be told about his son's high-handed assumption of power. There was no shortage of 'loyal' employees ready to poison his mind against Paul and the old man grimly directed a reorganisation of his business to keep his son at arm's length in the future. A new company, George F. Getty Incorporated, was set up to oversee his various interests. 'From now on my affairs will be conducted by *my* organisation,' he brusquely informed his son.

Paul was deeply hurt, but forbore to complain or defend himself for fear of further upsetting his father and endangering his recovery. Getty was greatly enfeebled by the stroke – his right arm and right leg remained partially paralysed and he could only walk for short distances with the help of a cane. Although his mind was still as astute as ever, he had difficulty in speaking and drooled at the mouth. Paul was shocked by his condition: 'Before the stroke, he had been an active, vigorous man, looking and acting ten years younger than his age. When he returned to his office in August, he was an old man.'

Sarah, characteristically grim-faced, supported her husband in his attitude towards their son and for a time the atmosphere at South Kingsley Drive became strained even though Paul did his best to behave like a loving and dutiful son.

The tension between Paul and his unforgiving, Victorian parents was soon to heighten dramatically. Two months before his thirty-first birthday, Paul returned home from a trip to Ventura and announced to his astonished mother and father that he had got married!

PART TWO

THE WAYWARD
HUSBAND
1924-48

5. 'Who was that girl with Paul?'

Paul had been thinking of getting married for some time. He was, after all, of an age to settle down and a man of entirely 'normal appetites' which was the popular euphemism applied at that time to describe the enjoyment of heterosexual sex. Paul loved the oil business, loved to make money, but after that he loved women. He simply could not resist them. In an age when female chastity was valued among the highest of virtues and young women expected to go chaste to their marriage beds, Paul devoted a great deal of his time and energy to sex, tirelessly seeking out those few girls who had already sacrificed their virginity, or were willing to do so with a little persuasion.

For a man not blessed with rugged good looks, he had more than his fair share of success. He was, of course, rich (which indisputably helped) but he was also charming, polite and always immaculately dressed, had a sharp sense of humour and a gift for mimicry. He could usually break the ice with a girl by making her laugh and thereafter sheer persistence, on the leather seats of his Cadillac roadster, often paid dividends.

Throughout his twenties he continued to live at home, apparently without ever giving much thought to finding a place of his own, which would have undoubtedly made seduction simpler. But he had become accustomed to sneaking girls in and out of his own quarters within his parents' house and the provision of elementary home comforts made him disinclined to leave.

Paul always described his relationship with his parents as close and loving, although there was little real evidence that either George or Sarah showed Paul much overt affection. George tended to belittle his son's business achievements, perhaps to disguise his pride; Sarah was stern and aloof, a woman not given to displays of emotion. Unquestionably both of them disapproved of the company their son chose to keep and disapproved, in particular, of the girls he chose to date, partly because he made little effort to introduce them to his parents. He brought them home in hopeful anticipation of sex, not to meet his folks.

Paul first considered marriage when he was twenty-nine. He had been dating a sweet girl three years his junior for some time and was actually on the brink of proposing when an apparently insignificant little incident turned him off the whole idea. They were driving to a nightclub one evening in Paul's Cadillac and the car suddenly hit a pothole in the road, jolting the girl forward so that she bumped her head lightly on the windscreen. 'Why don't you look where you're going?' she snapped. 'You might have killed me!' Paul was astonished at her outburst; suddenly she did not seem so sweet any more and he dropped her soon afterwards.

In August 1923 George and Sarah Getty caught a first tantalising glimpse of the girl who was to be their future daughter-in-law. The Gettys had agreed to pay for a swimming pool for the drilling crews at Santa Fe Springs if the men collected enough money for a diving board and the opening ceremony was in August. Paul arrived a little late accompanied by a beautiful young brunette and stayed only five minutes, leaving the tongues to wag after his departure. 'Who was that girl with Paul?' Sarah asked of anyone who might possibly know, but no one had ever seen her before.

The next time they set eyes on her was in October when Paul sheepishly introduced her as his wife. Jeanette Dumont was eighteen years old and only a few months out of school. Born in California of Polish parents, she had lustrous dark eyes, creamy skin, a vibrant personality and intelligence. Paul was as captivated by her as she was flattered by the attention of an eligible older man and when he proposed they decided, on the mad spur of that romantic moment, to elope. They married in Ventura, California, on 1 October 1923 without telling a soul.

Sarah and George Getty took the news badly. They were angry and disappointed at Paul's furtive 'hole-in-the-corner' behaviour; the least he could have done was give them some warning or allow them to meet the girl before he took such a step. Paul tried to explain, but could not. He and Jeanette moved into a comfortable rented house on Wilshire Boulevard, not far from his parents, and seven weeks later Jeanette was pregnant. This development melted Sarah's initial coldness towards her daughter-in-law and it was not long before Jeanette's beauty, charm and obvious devotion to Paul won over both his parents.

Single-minded as ever, Paul had no intention of allowing marriage to interfere with business. Virtually excluded from George F. Getty Inc., he was bent on showing his father that he could succeed as a lone wild-catter and in May 1924 he bought two leases in the Athens field, in the southern suburbs of Los Angeles, for around twelve thousand dollars each. After the Didier Ranch debacle, Paul vowed he would always act as his own drilling superintendent whenever possible and so when he was not out scouting for new leases, most of his time was spent in the field, working alongside his drilling crews.

At first Jeanette was sympathetic to Paul's need to spend so much time away from home; he was often not back in time for dinner and sometimes, when a new well was being spudded in, he would be out all night. Once he spent seventy-two hours at a stretch without sleep on a rig and arrived home in a state of complete exhaustion. On the evenings he was home, it was not unusual for him to shut himself away to finish some paperwork, leaving Jeanette to sit alone with her sewing in another room.

Eighteen years old and pregnant, Jeanette's patience was finite. 'I never see you any more,' she complained one night when Paul arrived home late. 'We might just as well not be married if this is the way we're going to live. I want to enjoy myself with you, not sit here alone or go places by myself. I hate your wretched business. I married you, not your oil wells.' Paul loathed any kind of scene and half-heartedly promised to mend his ways.

He tried taking Jeanette out to the Brown Derby and the Coconut Grove, the nightclubs he had frequented as a bachelor, but only succeeded in aggravating the problem. As often as not, the places were full of girls he knew and Jeanette, feeling ugly, vulnerable and unloved with her thickening girth, was jealous. 'How could you say hello to that little slut?' she would hiss as Paul smiled at one of his erstwhile girl friends. She imagined, sometimes correctly, that she was surrounded by her husband's former lovers and would demand confessions from him: 'You had an affair with that blonde bitch you waved to, didn't you?'

Paul quickly tired of this behaviour and took to going the rounds of the nightclubs alone, whenever he had a free evening. On 9 July 1924 Jeanette gave birth to a son, who was christened George Franklin Getty II in honour of his grandfather. Paul professed himself 'overjoyed', but the baby was unable to repair the cracks in their marriage. Two months later Jeanette informed Paul that her life with him had become intolerable and she was leaving. She returned to her parents with the baby; Paul went back to his parents' house. Sarah and George were angry and upset. They blamed their son for not being able to make the marriage 'work' and were scandalised, as devout Christian Scientists, by the prospect of a divorce. 'That boy deserves a spanking,' George Getty grunted about his thirty-one-year-old son.

On 15 February 1925 Jeanette was granted a divorce by the California court on grounds of extreme mental cruelty, harsh words and infidelity. She accused her husband of 'carrying on' with other women, calling her lazy, calling the child a 'brat' and saying he was 'sick and tired' of their marriage.

Paul was supervising the final drilling stage of a new well at Athens at the time of the divorce and if he felt any sadness, it was forgotten the following day when his well came in at 4350 feet with an initial yield of 1500 barrels a day. He was particularly pleased as the well confirmed his theory that there was an upper zone of rich oil in the Athens field, well above the deep zone to which most operators were drilling.

For the remainder of the year Paul was happily occupied as a full-time wildcatter and drilling superintendent, spending most of his time in the oilfields in a pair of greasy overalls and a battered safety hat. He rented desk space from the offices of George F. Getty Inc. in the A. G. Bartlett building in downtown Los Angeles and employed a girl as a part-time bookkeeper and stenographer, but was otherwise a lone operator. Like most wildcatters, his primary interest was in finding oil – once he had brought in a producing well, he sold 'an interest' to a company which would market the oil, leaving him free to move on to the next hole.

Being a working boss, he believed, paid handsome dividends. 'When a boss proved he knew his way round a rig,' he said, 'it didn't matter if he was worth one million, or one hundred million, dollars – he was accepted as an "honest-to-Gawd" oilman. The men felt they were partners with the boss in a mutual effort, rather than merely employees of some corporation run by executives they never saw and who had probably never set foot on a drilling platform in their lives. Morale – and production – soared as a result.'

Paul prided himself on being able to recruit the best drillers in the business – men like Wally Phillips and 'Spot' McMurdo – and he was enormously gratified one day when a roughneck from a nearby rig owned by a major oil company asked him for a job. The rig looked like a model for the industry. It was approached by a neatly trimmed gravel drive and equipped with all the latest drilling equipment, as well as hot showers and a laundry for the crew. Paul was mystified. His own outfit could not compete. Why would a man give up such home comforts?

'I've been on that rig for four months,' the roughneck replied, 'and we've only gotten down four thousand feet!' His tone made his contempt quite clear.

'How long do you think it'll take me to get down that far?' Paul asked.

'From the looks of you, about ten days,' the other man said. 'That's why I'd rather work for you than that cream-puff outfit over there.'

Paul gave him a job on the spot.

In March 1926 all drilling had finished on the two Athens leases – one was a rich producer, the other was dry – and Paul decided to take a look at the prospects in Mexico, combining the trip with a holiday in a country he had wanted to visit ever since the pleasant surprise of his student trip through Spain. He packed his bags into the back of a racy new Duesenberg which he had recently acquired to replace his Cadillac roadster, and drove alone across the southern California border to Mexico City – a journey of some 1500 miles.

Although he found the red tape, procrastination and deep-rooted suspicion of *gringos* very nearly impenetrable, he fell in love with the country, just as he had with Spain. After herculean efforts, he managed to acquire an oil concession at Laguna de Champayan, near Tampico, from the Mexican government which he was then able to assign to the Mexican Gulf Oil Company at a five per cent royalty. But this transaction was so protracted and frustrating that he decided he could more usefully employ his time studying Mexican history and Spanish on a summer course at the National University in Mexico City.

He would never be able to satisfactorily explain the lunacy of the next few months. Among his fellow students were two sisters, Allene and Belene Ashby, the daughters of a wealthy Texas rancher. They were young, pretty and vivacious and Paul was irresistibly drawn to their company. They went out together in a threesome in his Duesenberg, visiting the sights, taking photographs of each other in front of crumbling monuments, laughing a lot, soaking up the sun and the heady ambience of Mexico. Both sisters were expert horsewomen and Belene took a photograph of her grinning sister, in a spotless white riding habit, pretending to pull Paul up on to her horse while he stared into the camera, unsmiling as always, holding a trilby in one hand. He claimed they often went riding together, but that day he was hardly dressed for equestrian pursuits in a single-breasted suit and a bow tie.

Other people who knew them at the time thought that Paul might have fallen for Belle (Belene), who was the older of the two and slightly more glamorous. But one hot summer morning in June, Paul and Allene drove secretly to Cuernavaca and were married. He was thirty-three; she was seventeen.

'Perhaps I was on what is commonly called the rebound,' he said later, 'from my failed marriage to Jeanette. Perhaps we were influenced by the romantic atmosphere of Mexico. She being young and inexperienced and I being much too enchanted by her, neither of us recognised an essentially summer romance for what it was.'

They discovered within weeks that they knew nothing about each other and had almost nothing in common. They both agreed they had made a terrible mistake and as the end of the holiday loomed, they agonised about what to do. Paul had no desire to take his bride back home to Los Angeles and his new bride had no desire to go anywhere but home to Texas. They decided to try and forget the marriage had ever happened. Allene swore her sister Belle to secrecy and promised to seek a divorce as soon as she could. Paul said he would make it as easy as possible and would pay the lawyer's bills. Maybe, they thought, if they all kept quiet, no one need ever know.

71

Paul drove back to Los Angeles in September and was relieved to find his parents greeted him quite normally; they obviously knew nothing about Allene. Much of the time he had been away his father had been in Boston on a Christian Science study course but George Getty, even though a semi-invalid as a result of the stroke in 1923, was neither stupid, nor out of touch. He still went into the office every day, even if only for an hour or so, and he made it his business to know what his son was doing; it was not long before Getty got wind of what had happened. It was, he thought, almost unbelievable that his son could have been so stupid. Sick at heart, the old man altered his will with a shaking hand, leaving the bulk of his estate, and control of his business, to his wife. (This recourse to his will, as a way of exerting his rightful authority as Victorian-style paterfamilias, was to set a pattern which would become unhappily familiar to future generations of Gettys.)

Paul, who was certainly expecting to take over the company when his father died, had no idea he was to be virtually disinherited as a punishment for his failed marriages. Getty told no one that he had changed his will, not to protect his son's sensibilities, but to shield Sarah.

Perhaps to avoid too many conversations at South Kingsley Drive about what he had been doing with himself in Mexico, Paul wasted no time getting back to work. A drilling boom had started at Huntington Beach and he had only been back a few days when he clinched a six-thousand-dollar deal with Bill Bohen, a lease broker, to sublease five lots. The first of five wells was spudded on 10 October and was producing at the rate of 2200 barrels a day by 28 November.

This time Paul broke his own rule and employed a drilling superintendent so that he would have more time to look for other leases. He also rented his own office – Room 903 in the Bartlett building – and took on a full-time secretary, Lillian Marvin, at $130 a month. On 15 October he met a lease broker who was looking for a quick profit on an unproven property, less than an acre in size, at Alamitos Heights. Known as the Cleaver lease, the broker had bought it a few days previously for four thousand dollars. Paul was familiar with the property and knew that the Petroleum Securities Company was drilling only four hundred feet away – if this well came in, there was a very good chance that oil would also be found on the Cleaver lease. If he could get the lease, the Petroleum Securities Company would virtually be drilling a test well for him, free of charge.

'How much do you want for it?' he asked the broker.

'I'm a great believer in doubling my money,' the other man replied. 'I paid four thousand for it. I'll take eight thousand.'

'You've just made yourself a deal,' Paul said. He took out a cheque-book from his jacket pocket, unscrewed his pen and wrote out a cheque for eight thousand dollars on the spot. (It was a moment he would often look back on with nostalgic pleasure, as the lease eventually produced a clear profit of eight hundred thousand dollars.) The Petroleum Securities Company struck oil at 4757 feet on 20 February 1927 – Paul began drilling on the Cleaver lease the following day and brought in the first of four wells at the end of March for an impressive 5100 barrels a day.

By April Paul had five producing wells at Huntington Beach and four at Alamitos Heights, but he was also in trouble. Almost overnight, his market disappeared. He suddenly found that none of the major oil companies wanted to buy his oil. At the same time, he began receiving telephone calls from brokers offering to buy up his leases at ludicrously low prices. 'Who are you acting for?' he demanded angrily. 'Who's behind this?' None of them would say.

Paul had been in the oil business long enough to know that he was clamped in the jaws of a well-organised squeeze. It had happened before, often enough. If an independent operator grew to be a little too successful, the big guys got together and squeezed him out. Nothing could be simpler – no wildcatter could stay in business for long if he was unable to sell his production. Paul was in a double dilemma since drilling nine wells in quick succession had strained his finances to the limit and he badly needed the injection of funds which selling his oil would produce.

Whoever thought young Paul Getty would submit to a squeeze was a fool. Absolutely determined not to shut down any of his wells, he began to look around for storage facilities. At first he was unable to find big enough tanks anywhere within the Los Angeles basin, but after several anxious days he found a bankrupt refining company with two large empty storage tanks, one for eighty thousand barrels, the other for fifty-five thousand, about ten miles from the Cleaver lease. He wrote out a cheque for $675 for the first month's rental and hired a trucking contractor to transport his production at ten cents a barrel.

This arrangement bought him precious time, but did nothing to solve the original problem – and it was not long before the first of the two tanks was full. With the second filling rapidly, Paul realised he had only a few days left before he would be forced to start shutting down his wells and he was ready to try anything. When he heard that Sir George Legh-Jones, the English president of Shell Oil, was visiting Los Angeles, he asked for an interview and was told, to his surprise, that Sir George would be happy to see him.

Paul arrived at the Shell Building at three o'clock in the afternoon and was promptly shown into Sir George's office. Initially nervous that Shell might be party to the squeeze, he was greatly comforted by Sir George's outraged reaction to his story. At four o'clock a full English tea was served, to Paul's barely concealed amusement, and by the end of the afternoon he had been assured of Shell's help. Sir George was genuinely shocked by such disreputable business tactics and offered to buy the next 1,750,000 barrels produced at Alamitos Heights and lay pipelines to the lease to shift it. The effect of Shell's involvement was remarkable – the secret boycott was immediately lifted and Paul was able to sell the entire contents of both storage tanks not long afterwards at the posted price of ninety-two cents a barrel. He was never squeezed again.

In May George and Sarah Getty invited Paul to join them on another visit to Europe. Paul was deeply moved by their invitation. He felt they were telling him he had been forgiven for the divorce (he was reasonably confident they knew nothing of the fair Allene) and realised it would almost certainly be their last trip abroad together. Both his parents were over seventy and his father was clearly never going to make a complete recovery. Although he was left in no doubt that they strongly disapproved of his lifestyle and most of his friends, Paul's love and respect for his parents never wavered. He always referred to Sarah as 'my darling mother' and George was 'dearest father'. Even at the age of thirty-four, he was not in the slightest self-conscious about expressing his adoration for them.

They left by train for Chicago and New York at the beginning of June accompanied only by Frank Komai, Getty's Japanese valet who had been with him for some twenty years. Looking out of the Pullman's windows as the train rattled north across the vast landscape of America, they fell to talking about the sweeping changes that had taken place since their first trip together from Minneapolis to Oklahoma twenty-three years earlier, when the only oil the family had needed was a drop or two to lubricate the axles of their horse-drawn carriage. 'Do you remember,' Sarah suddenly asked, 'how much you hoped to see wild Indians on that first trip to Bartlesville?' 'Yes, I do, momma,' Paul replied. To his surprise and embarrassment, he found tears in his eyes.

They sailed from New York aboard the SS *Resolute* on 7 June, arriving in Southampton eight days later after a pleasant and calm Atlantic crossing. Two weeks were spent in London at the Savoy Hotel followed by a week at the Grand in Paris. Then they took a train to Strasbourg and Baden Baden before hiring a seven-passenger Hoch landaulet for the long drive over the Dolomites to Venice via Munich. Near the top of the Brenner Pass the Hoch broke down and refused to restart for an hour, but they arrived safely in Venice despite having been without a reverse gear for the last part of the journey. Paul recorded few details of how they passed their time on this holiday, other than to note the names of the hotels in which they stayed. It may not have been much fun trailing around with two elderly parents, since a high point seems to have been Frank Komai's reaction to boarding the gondola which was to take them to the Danieli Hotel. 'I thinking this very funny place,' he apparently said, 'nothing like same in Japan.'

George and Sarah Getty returned to America in August on the *SS Olympic*, leaving Paul in London. It was their idea that he should stay a little longer in Europe and he welcomed a chance to spend some time on his own. Girls did not occupy all his attention during his four weeks in London, as he wanted to seek out the Camberwell Weightlifting Club, where he had been told he would find William A. Pullum, the author of *Weightlifting Made Easy and Interesting,* one of his favourite books. In a letter to *Health and Strength* magazine he wrote:

> I must admit that the few weeks I have spent over here have made an Englishman of me. In England, if you meet a lifter or physical-culture enthusiast, you forget you are in a foreign country and step right into a friendly circle ... It was with great interest that I approached the Camberwell Weightlifting Club, 5 Church Street, for the first time ... When I announced myself as an American come over to take a look at British weightlifting, W.A.P. gave me a warm welcome. I was introduced to Herman Gorner ('the gorilla man from Africa') and for me to sit and chat with these two was just as a movie fan having tea with Chaplin and Fairbanks.

From London he took the boat train for Paris, where he rented a *petit meuble* at 12 rue St Didier. 'It served perfectly as a twice-divorced bachelor's pad,' he said, 'a term which describes the uses to which the apartment was put.' At the end of October Paul made preparations to return to the United States and booked a passage for himself on the SS *Majestic*, sailing from Cherbourg.

> The *Majestic* was too big to dock at Cherbourg for the new docks capable of accommodating the largest steamers were not built yet. The boat train arrived early in the afternoon, but the *Majestic* was late and did not arrive until ten in the evening. Passengers went to meet it in a tug and when we drew alongside the mighty steamer it seemed to me that the ship's great height above the water might make her top-heavy in a storm. The *Majestic* had a magnificent smoking room forward on the promenade deck. There were large windows and comfortable chairs in it facing the bow. In the late afternoons the ship's course seemed directed towards the sinking sun. The weather was fine and I reposed in one of these chairs and enjoyed each beautiful sunset.

Back in Los Angeles Paul was concerned to learn that George F. Getty

Inc. was not participating in a promising new development at Long Beach where a number of companies were drilling to find the untapped zones of oil sand which were believed to lie under the pay-zones reached by existing wells. Getty's field management executives told Paul that leases were too difficult to obtain at Long Beach and in any case they had little faith in deeper drilling. Paul disagreed on both counts.

In Paul's view, George F. Getty Inc. was suffering from his elderly father's infirmity and inability to run the company in the way he once did. Getty usually arrived at the office at around eleven o'clock in the morning, spent an hour or so conferring with his managers, and left for home at about twelve-thirty or one o'clock. Before his stroke he had been bursting with energy and ideas, ready to take risks and very much in charge of the whole show; no important decisions were made without his knowledge and assent. Now he left day-to-day operations in the hands of salaried employees and Paul had little time for most of them. The company was spending an alarming amount of money on unproductive leases and dry holes and was neglecting the real opportunities that offered a worthwhile chance of profits.

Paul drove out to Long Beach in his Duesenberg to see how the land lay. From records in the county clerk's office and from his contacts among lease brokers, he was able to draw up a short list of available properties in or near producing fields. He checked out each one personally. After rejecting those he felt to be overpriced and a couple with dubious titles, he made successful bids for five leases and, with his father's agreement, transferred a fifty-per-cent interest to George F. Getty Inc. This was not entirely altruistic since he needed to spread both the risk and the cost of drilling test wells, but he could have made a deal with any number of companies. Obviously, though, it was in his own long-term interests to help along the profitability of the company he naturally assumed he would one day inherit.

Deep-drilling on all five leases resulted in producing wells and good profits, both for Paul and George F. Getty Inc. Not long after spudding the first Getty well at Long Beach, he got a call from one of his crews at Santa Fe Springs, where he was still drilling on his own behalf, to tell him that they had a 'twist-off': the rotary drilling bit had broken from the drill string and become jammed in the bottom of the hole. It was worrying news: no further progress could be made until the bit had been removed, which meant blindly 'fishing' for it with crude clamps and hooks. This could take weeks; nor was there any guarantee of success.

Paul hurried to Santa Fe Springs and discovered the bit was stuck nearly four thousand feet below the ground. The crew had fishing tools lowered into the hole, but the foreman warned Paul it looked like it might be a long job. Acutely aware that he would be paying wages for the whole crew while most of them sat around doing nothing until the bit had been recovered, Paul cast about for a quicker method of clearing the hole and decided to risk drastic measures. He drove to a stonemason's yard adjoining a cemetery in Los Angeles and poked about among the gravestones until he found what he was looking for – a six-foot column of solid marble. He told the stonemason he wanted to buy it but that he wanted one end cut into a point. 'What inscription do you want?' the mason asked. 'Don't bother with an inscription,' Paul replied. 'Just cut the point and help me carry it to my car.'

When Paul's Duesenberg arrived back at the rig, creaking distressingly under the weight of a marble pillar sticking out of the back, the men exchanged puzzled glances and wondered what was coming next. 'Get your fishing tools clear,' said Paul, lugging the marble out of his car, 'then throw this down the hole.' They stared at each other for a moment, shrugged in bewilderment and did as they were told. The pointed missile slipped down the hole like a torpedo and smashed the drill bit clear so that drilling could resume again, with a new bit, immediately. It was a technique soon widely employed throughout the oilfields to deal with 'twist-offs'. Granite was used instead of graveyard marble, carved into whipstocks known as 'Paul Getty Specials'.

Similar ingenuity was required when Paul was offered a lease on a minuscule plot of land surrounded by oil wells at Seal Beach, south of Los Angeles. No bigger than the floor area of a small house, it was too small to accommodate a drilling rig, some distance from the nearest road and for all practical purposes inaccessible – the only approach was along a right of way less than four feet wide. Most wildcatters rejected the lease as unworkable, but not Paul. He got together his most experienced men and they all drove out together to look over the property. Paul parked at the nearest point on the road and they walked the last few hundred feet along the right of way. After pacing out the lease, one of the drillers squatted down, scratched the soil with a stick and said: 'I guess we could drill with an undersized rig. If you could find someone to design and build it, we could sure set it up and get it operating. But I can't figure out how we're going to bring everything we need in from the road.'

Paul pondered the problem for a while, turning over in his mind the idea of building a miniature rig. It was the word 'miniature' which provided him with the solution. If he built a miniature rig, why not set it up with the help of a miniature railway? That was how they did it. At the risk of making themselves a laughing stock, they laid a narrow-gauge track along the right of way from the road and used two small flatcars, pushed by hand, to shift the miniature rig in sections to the drilling site. Several months later, they struck oil. The well was never a great producer, but Paul was delighted with it since it represented a triumph over everyone who said the site was impractical. After he sold the lease to Shell, who owned an adjoining property, he had the track cut up and used a section as a commemorative paperweight.

In the summer of 1928, while his parents were on holiday in Honolulu, Paul returned to Europe alone to attend the Olympic Games in Amsterdam. After watching the sensational Paavo Nurmi from Finland win his sixth gold medal in the ten thousand metres, he decided to spend a few days in Vienna. He checked into the Grand Hotel and once again found himself caught up, at the age of thirty-five, in a whirlwind romance with a beautiful young woman.

Adolphine Helmle, known to her friends as Fini, was eighteen years old – a tall, ravishing, flaxen-haired blonde from Karlsruhe. She was staying at the Grand with a girlfriend and her parents while her father, Dr Otto Helmle, head of the Badenwerk industrial complex, attended a technical conference in Vienna. Paul first saw her when she walked into the hotel restaurant where he was having dinner alone and sat at a nearby table with her friend and her parents. Paul could not take his eyes off her. He gaped from behind the cover of a newspaper until the four of them got up from their table, walked out to the elevators and the doors closed behind them. 'She was not only beautiful,' he said, 'but her lively face and every movement radiated vitality and vivacity.' Paul tipped the waiter to find out her name and room number.

Two nights later, Fini and her friend were sitting in the bedroom they shared, gossiping together after an early dinner, when there was a gentle knock at the door. A waiter stood outside holding a visiting card. A Mr J. Paul Getty, he said, would like to invite the young ladies to join him downstairs in the writing room. The two girls were *thrilled*. Both eighteen and on their first grown-up trip abroad, it was just the kind of adventure they had been longing for. Fini went into her parents' room and told her mother that they both had headaches and were going to lie down. Then they sneaked out and went downstairs.

Paul jumped to his feet as soon as the girls walked into the writing room and introduced himself in halting German. He would like, he said, to invite them to dinner. Fini accepted before her friend had a chance to open her mouth and say that they had just eaten. 'He ordered the most expensive meal and wine,' she said, 'and by the time I got through it, I really did have a headache. He was the most correct host and talked interestingly about his oil business, but I just wanted to go to bed.'

After dinner both girls politely thanked Paul and retired, feeling bloated and distinctly sick. No sooner had they got safely back to their room, thankfully without being observed by Fini's parents, than there was another knock on the door. At first they thought Paul might have followed them, but agreed he was too much of a gentleman. Fini called out to ask who was there. 'It's the waiter,' said a voice. She opened the door and the waiter held out a piece of paper. 'Pardon Fräulein, here is your bill,' he said. Her mouth dropped open with surprise and anger. 'My God!' she said, 'What a nerve!' It was a big bill, but she had just enough to pay it as her parents had given her money earlier in the day to buy a new pair of shoes. 'How am I going to explain what has happened to it?' she wailed to her friend after the waiter had gone. They thought they had been duped and agreed never to speak a word to Paul should he have the effrontery to approach them again.

'When Paul tried to speak to me in the lobby the next afternoon,' Fini said, 'I refused to listen to him. I thought he was a crook. Then he discovered the waiter had made a colossal blunder by bringing the bill to me. Actually, it had also been added to his hotel account, as he told the head waiter to do. The amount was refunded to me by the hotel with the manager's profuse apologies. Once the muddle was straightened out, I thought it hilariously funny.'

Thereafter, Paul spent his time with Fini whenever she was able to steal away without raising the suspicion of her parents. She thought it was too soon to introduce Paul, correctly suspecting that her father would not be too pleased at his daughter's interest in an American nearly twice her age. At the end of Dr Helmle's conference, the family returned to Karlsruhe. Fini managed to contrive a furtive and tearful farewell, gave Paul her post office box number and asked him to write.

There followed a madcap few weeks during which Paul, besotted by Fini, followed the family backwards and forwards across Europe. Fini had only been home for a few days when she called at the post office in Karlsruhe, hoping to find a letter. The clerk told her that a man had been in several times that day inquiring about her – at the same moment she felt her hand being gently squeezed and spun round to find Paul standing behind her. They met secretly every day, sometimes driving out to the Herren Alp, an inn on the edge of the Black Forest, or walking along the banks of the Rhine, or sitting in a quiet café over steaming coffee and cakes piled with cream. A few weeks later the Helmles boarded a train for Venice, where they planned to take their annual holiday. Paul followed by car and resumed clandestine trysts with Fini among the palaces and canals of that romantic city. It was while sightseeing together in Venice that Paul asked Fini to marry him; she said yes and Paul kissed her for the first time. They immediately went off to find her parents and break the good news.

Paul's introduction to Fini's parents was not a happy occasion. Dr Otto Helmle was deeply unimpressed with J. Paul Getty as a potential son-in-law, particularly when he discovered that Paul was thirty-five years old and had been married before (Paul somehow neglected to mention Allene.) His daughter was too young and inexperienced, he said, to consider marriage to a man 'twice her age'. Furthermore, he did not want her to marry an American and leave Germany. Fini wept and pleaded with her parents to reconsider but while her mother rather liked Paul, the Herr Doktor remained resolutely opposed to the match.

The matter was still unresolved when the Helmles returned to Karlsruhe. This time Paul wisely chose not to follow them and made his way to Paris, whence he wrote every day to Fini. She kept up a relentless pressure on her father, reproaching him with tears in her eyes whenever the subject of Paul cropped up and at last she succeeded in obtaining his reluctant consent, on the sole condition that Paul's parents gave their blessing. It was Dr Helmle's fervent wish that the Gettys would be as loath to have a German daughter-in-law as he was to have an American son-in-law.

Fini persuaded her mother to chaperone her on a brief visit to Paris to say goodbye to Paul before he returned to the United States. They spent a few happy days together, with mother always present, of course. On the day before Paul was due to catch the boat train to Cherbourg, Fini and her mother went home. Two days later, Paul showed up in Karlsruhe. He could not bear to say goodbye so soon, he said, so instead of catching the boat train he had got in his car and driven to Karlsruhe. It was the kind of sweet, impulsive and romantic gesture that Fini adored; it even moistened her mother's eyes.

Paul might have stayed longer in Europe had he not received a cable from his father offering him a one-third interest in George F. Getty Inc. Getty was seventy-three years old and tired. He could see that his business was failing, but no longer had the energy to set it right. For all his faults, Paul had proved himself to be an excellent oilman and Getty wanted a rapprochement with his son, even though he still had no intention of allowing Paul to inherit the business. Once he was dead, sensible Sarah would wield the power and curb Paul's excesses, if necessary. Paul arrived home at the end of October and formally asked his parents' permission to marry the wonderful girl he had met in Vienna. George and Sarah were pleased by Paul's rather more conventional approach to matrimony and felt he was adopting a more mature attitude than on the previous occasion. Sarah wrote a friendly letter to Fini and her parents, saying she would be welcome as a daughter-in-law.

In her frequent and loving letters, Fini began gently hinting that it was time for Paul to name the day and she became upset and worried when Paul prevaricated. The problem was that Paul was not yet divorced from Allene, about whom Fini knew nothing. While writing reassuring letters to Fini in Karlsruhe, he was also frantically writing and telephoning Allene in Texas to get a move on with the divorce. At the same time, he was negotiating terms with his father to buy ten thousand shares. (Typically he was only being offered an opportunity to *buy* his way in, not a straight gift.) They concluded the deal on 5 December 1928. The price was $1,000,000. Paul paid $250,000 in cash and $750,000 in promissory notes.

Not long afterwards he heard that his divorce had come through and he cabled Fini to meet him in Havana, Cuba, where they had chosen to marry. There was a slight hiccup when the marriage papers revealed Allene's existence to the surprise, and distress, of the bride. 'Why didn't you tell me?' Fini asked, tears welling in her eyes. 'If I had said I had been married *twice* before,' Paul replied pragmatically, 'you would never have married me.' Even his parents did not know, he said. 'At least,' he added thoughtfully, 'my mother doesn't.'

They soon made it up – Paul, said Fini, had 'the sweetest way of wooing' – and were married a few days before Christmas 1928. During a leisurely honeymoon in Palm Beach, Florida, Paul took the opportunity to brush up his German, repeating words over and over again with Fini's help until his accent was perfect. But they had a lot of fun too, and when they went out together Paul liked to make Fini laugh by suddenly affecting a ludicrous Charlie Chaplin waddle at an inappropriate moment. It was a marvellously relaxed and happy time for them both and they drove back across country to California, arriving in Los Angeles at the beginning of March 1929, full of hope for the future.

It had been decided that because Fini was a stranger to America and could speak very little English, she and Paul would move in with his parents rather than find a place of their own. The idea was that Paul's mother would be company for her, show her around and introduce her to society. But Sarah Getty was seventy-seven years old, suffering from rheumatism and increasingly hard of hearing. The Gettys, both George and Sarah, did their best to welcome their new daughter-in-law whom they thought was charming, but it was almost inevitable that Fini would be lonely and homesick in a large, strange house in a strange country. Only one person was really able to help her, and he was otherwise preoccupied.

Now that he was a shareholder in his father's company, Paul was determined not to allow George F. Getty Inc. to decline any further. The company had performed poorly in 1928, producing a profit of only $397,848 on an income of more than $3.6 million. Nearly $1,000,000 had been spent in the previous four years on unproductive leases ($276,000 went on 179 worthless leases in Kern County alone) and rather more had gone on drilling dry holes. The company had also been hit by a disastrous blowout and fire on the Nordstrom Lease at Santa Fe Springs, which burned for six weeks before it could be brought under control – and this at a cost of some $300,000, not counting the lost oil.

On 11 March, only a few days after his arrival in Los Angeles with Fini, Paul was elected a director of George F. Getty Inc. and from that moment on took an active role in the management of its affairs. 'As I looked more and more closely into its operations,' he said, 'I found many examples of unduly large or unnecessary overhead expenses which could have been prevented by tighter management and closer supervision. It was plain to me that effort and money were being expended in the wrong places, at the wrong times and on the wrong ventures.'

As had happened before, he quickly found himself in conflict with some of the old-timers who had worked for his father for years. 'My views and opinion,' he noted sourly, 'were at wide variance with the incumbent field management.' But this time George Getty supported his son and Paul was able to stand his ground, demanding new procedures in the field, where the waste was most evident. On 1 July the field superintendent and his assistant resigned, declaring they were unable to work with Paul. Getty was alarmed at losing two such key personnel at a time when the company was engaged in a heavy drilling programme, but Paul replaced them with his own men and production improved noticeably.

Finally convinced of his son's ability, George Getty resigned as general manager of the company on 1 August and appointed Paul to succeed him. Paul was also re-elected as a director of Minnehoma, having been dropped in 1926 following his divorce from Jeanette Dumont.

Completely engrossed in the business, Paul virtually ignored his young wife. He left the house early every day, returned late and often spent the evening discussing business with his father. 'I worked,' he admitted, 'almost literally round the clock to achieve the aims and goals I had set.' Fini felt herself to be neglected and was desperately lonely. In May she broke the news to Paul that she was pregnant, expecting perhaps that he would show her a little more attention. She was to be disappointed. Her troubles were exacerbated by a deluge of letters from home. Her parents were constantly writing to tell her how much she was missed, how much they longed to see her again. When she told them about the baby, they began pleading with her to return home so that their first grandchild would be born in Germany.

In September Fini asked Paul if they could both go back to Karlsruhe for a while, at least until the baby was born. Paul said the business was in a crucial state; he could not possibly leave. They argued and in the end he agreed, reluctantly, to allow her to return home alone and promised to follow as soon as he was able. Fini packed her bags and caught the first train east, her sadness at leaving Paul outweighed by her happiness at returning home to Germany.

*   *   *

By the middle of October 1929, the affairs of George F. Getty Inc. were running smoothly and sufficiently to Paul's satisfaction for him to feel he could afford to take time off to be with Fini in Germany when the baby was born. He had booked a transatlantic passage and was making preparations to join her when the stock market crashed.

The first tremor of panic ran through Wall Street on the morning of 24 October. Rumour fed rumour on the floor of the New York Stock Exchange. For nearly two years there had been much rash speculation in securities and now, gripped by a sudden fear, investors wanted their money out. Millions of shares changed hands and after five frenetic days of selling, the market collapsed on 'Black Tuesday', 29 October, ushering in the Great Depression. New Yorkers were soon to witness the horror of ruined bankers hurling themselves from the uppermost windows of Manhattan's famous skyscrapers. 'It was borrowed time anyway,' wrote F. Scott Fitzgerald, 'the whole upper tenth of a nation living with the insouciance of a *grand duc* and the casualness of chorus girls.'

Although none of the Getty companies was quoted on the stock exchange, Paul felt an irresistible desire to see for himself what was going on in New York and so he cancelled his passage across the Atlantic, cabled Fini that he had been unavoidably detained and caught a train for New York. 'It might well seem to have been a foolish, or at best unnecessary, change of plan,' he noted later. 'But I felt that what was happening on Wall Street would have extremely far-reaching effects. I sensed that the stock-market collapse and its ramifications would set the course of the nation's overall economy for several years to come. I thought it important to be on the spot to look and listen and, above all, learn. I made regular visits to the New York Stock Exchange during those hectic, chaotic days and watched the debacle at first hand. I talked to brokers, bankers, businessmen, financiers, investors and speculators and what I saw during the fortnight I remained in New York proved invaluable to me in the years that followed. I learned much about the perils and pitfalls of speculation, and realised that I was an eyewitness to the violent death of an era.'

Paul eventually sailed for Europe on 13 November, on board the SS *Berengaria*. He took a train from Cherbourg to Karlsruhe and found, on his arrival at the Helmles' house, that the atmosphere was pointedly frosty. Fini, heavily pregnant, had regaled her parents with stories of how she had been neglected by Paul in America, how lonely and homesick she had been, and the Helmles were not in a forgiving mood. Dr Helmle took Paul into his study and told him he thought Fini's best interests would be served by obtaining a divorce after the birth of the baby; she was only nineteen and had time to make a fresh start. Paul protested vigorously and tried to explain the vicissitudes of the oil business. He had had to cope with a crisis and thus had devoted an inordinate amount of time to the business, but that did not mean he did not love Fini. A red-eyed Fini was brought into the discussion and, prompted by her father, told Paul that she was not prepared to be abandoned in America again and that she wanted her child to be brought up in Germany. She wanted to stay married to Paul, but it would have to be in Germany.

It was clear to Paul he was not welcome at the Helmles'. Fini was due to have the baby at a hospital in Berlin and he went there to look for a place where they could be together, away from her parents. He found a lavish apartment ('one of the finest in Berlin', he was told) off the Herkulesbrucke and moved in a few days before Fini went into hospital. The baby, a boy christened Jean Ronald, was born on 19 December. 'Paul was sweet when Ronnie was born,' said Fini. 'He sat looking at the baby for hours and I had to force him to go home for meals. I thought the baby was an ugly little thing, but Paul adored him.'

Paul's hopes that they might be able to set up home together in Berlin for a while were short-lived. When the time came for Fini to leave the hospital on the day before Christmas Eve, instead of going to the apartment off the Herkulesbrucke where Paul was waiting, she was collected by her parents and driven home to Karlsruhe. Paul was left to spend Christmas alone in Berlin. He remained in Europe for four months, fending off Dr Helmle's persistent demands for a divorce, staying in touch with his business in America by telegram and letter and consoling himself with the company of Hildegard Kuhn, a pert little office clerk, twenty-three years old, he met at a dance hall in Berlin. Hildegard had at first refused Paul's request for a date, but he had wheedled her telephone number from her friend and his usual perseverance paid off.

Hildegard took some time off from work to accompany Paul on a little excursion round Europe and he was in Montreux, Switzerland, on 22 April 1930 when he got a telephone call from Rush Blodget, a director of George F. Getty Inc. and a close friend of his father's. Over a faint and crackling transatlantic line, Blodget broke the news to Paul that his father had suffered a second stroke and was not expected to live. Paul left the same day for Cherbourg and found a passage on the first liner leaving for the United States. In New York a telegram was waiting for him – 'HURRY,' it said, 'LEST YOUR FATHER'S FIGHT TO SEE HIS SON AGAIN BE LOST.' He had hoped to be able to charter an aeroplane for the journey to the West Coast, but bad weather had grounded all flights. Travelling across the continent by train, he arrived home nine days after receiving the telephone call in Montreux.

Paul could see that his father was dying. 'No words can portray', he wrote in his diary, 'my mental anguish and feeling of helplessness.' He did what he could to comfort his distraught mother and together they kept vigil at the deathbed for thirty days while the old man slowly lost his grip on life. He died on 31 May aged seventy-five, and his ashes were placed in a bronze casket at Forest Lawn Memorial Park.

At the next meeting of the directors of George F. Getty Inc., the following resolution was passed:

> Whereas, George Franklin Getty, Founder and President of this Corporation, departed this life at his home in Los Angeles, California, on the 31st day of May in the year of our Lord, nineteen hundred thirty: and
>
> Whereas, the Board of Directors of George F. Getty Incorporated, in meeting assembled, desire to record upon the minutes of the Company a tribute to his memory, that all who may later benefit from the industry so ably founded and builded by him, may pause in later years and learn a lesson from his life: and
>
> Whereas, George Franklin Getty was born in Grantsville, Maryland, in 1855, and commenced the battle of life in comparative poverty, armed only with his honest heart, his keen mind and his willing hands:
>
> He was self-educated, paying his own way through college, later generously rewarding that college for its gifts to him, from the bounty of his own successes:
>
> He was devout, always acknowledging his debt to his Saviour, and always walking in the paths of rectitude:
>
> He was industrious, toiling ceaselessly that his industries might succeed and bring prosperity to all who labored with him and for him:
>
> He was honest, always paying his just obligations, not only in money when money was due, but in kindly appreciation when others had done him a service:
>
> He was loyal, always adhering faithfully to his friends and employees through the vicissitudes of life:
>
> Now therefore be it resolved; That the members of this Board of Directors, on behalf of the stockholders and employees of this Company, hereby record their tribute to the character and attainments of George Franklin Getty, and their sorrow at his demise; and extend to his bereaved family their heartfelt sympathy.

6. *'He should dress you in sable'*

'It is never easy,' Paul lamented, 'for the son of a successful business-man to step into his father's shoes. In my own case, it was made doubly difficult owing to the provisions of my father's will.'

Paul was stunned when the will was read. He learned he was to receive nothing but five hundred thousand dollars, money he neither needed nor wanted. What he wanted, what he had expected, was control of the business. He had devoted considerable amounts of time, money and energy to the management of his father's companies, often at the expense of his own enterprises, on the implicit understanding that he would take over the reins on his father's death. Now his adored Papa had denied him what he considered to be his rightful inheritance. He could hardly believe it.

Even Sarah, grieving pitifully, admitted that she was surprised. She knew that when her husband made the will he had been angry and deeply distressed by Paul's divorce from Jeanette Dumont, but she had always assumed that Paul had been forgiven and reinstated in later years. Her husband told her often enough that he had come to realise Paul was not entirely to blame for the divorce; and he had certainly been grateful at the time to be able to stand down as general manager of the business and hand over to his son. Casting around for comfort, Sarah suggested to her dismayed son that the only explanation was that his father had simply forgotten to alter his will, tearfully pointing out as further evidence that while he had provided for his eldest grandson, George, baby Ronnie did not get so much as a mention.

It was of little comfort to Paul to be told he had forfeited control of George F. Getty Inc. because of a moment's absent-mindedness on his father's part (although years later he liked to quip 'When Daddy had a change of heart, he forgot to have a change of will'). But the only other explanation was that his father had not forgiven him for the divorce and considered he had disqualified himself as a suitable heir. Paul was not prepared to accept either story. He revered and admired his father and needed to be able to eulogise his memory. 'His loving kindness and great heart,' he wrote, 'combined with a charming simplicity of manner, made him the idol of all who knew him. His mental ability was out-standing to the last. I, his son and successor, can only strive to carry on to the best of my ability the life work of an abler man.'

Jean Paul Getty I, 'the richest man in the world'.

PETROLEUM, OR ROCK OIL.

A NATURAL REMEDY!

PROCURED FROM A WELL IN ALLEGHENY COUNTY, PA.

Four hundred feet below the Earth's Surface!

PUT UP AND SOLD BY

SAMUEL M. KIER,

CANAL BASIN, SEVENTH STREET, PITTSBURGH, PA.

The healthful balm from Nature's secret spring,
The bloom of health, and life, to man will bring;
As from her depths the magic liquid flows,
To calm our sufferings, and assuage our woes.

CAUTION.—As many persons are now going about and vending an article of a spurious character, calling it Petroleum, or Rock Oil, we would caution the public against all preparations bearing that name not having the name of S. M. KIER written on the label of the bottle.

PETROLEUM.—It is necessary, upon the introduction of a new medicine to the notice of the public, that something be said in relation to its powers in healing disease, and the manner in which it acts. Man's organization is a complicated one; and to understand the functions of each organ, requires the study of years. But to understand that certain remedies produce certain impressions upon these organs, may be learned by experience in a short time. It is by observation in watching the effects of various medicines, that we are enabled to increase the number of curative agents; and when we have discovered a new medicine and attested its merits, it is our duty to bring it before the public, so that the benefits to be derived from it may be more generally diffused, but have no right to hold back a remedy whose powers are calculated to remove pain and to alleviate human suffering and disease. THE PETROLEUM HAS BEEN FULLY TESTED! About one year ago, it was placed before the public as A REMEDY OF WONDERFUL EFFICACY. Every one not acquainted with its virtues, doubted its healing properties. The cry of humbug was raised against it. It had some friends;—those that were cured through its wonderful agency. These spoke out in its favor. The lame, through its instrumentality, were made to walk—the blind, to see. Those who had suffered for years under the torturing pains of RHEUMATISM, GOUT and NEURALGIA, were restored to health and usefulness. Several who were blind have been made to see, the evidence of which will be placed before you. If you still have doubts, go and ask those who have been cured! Some of them live in our midst, and can answer for themselves. In writing about a medicine, we are aware that we should write TRUTH—that we should make no statements that cannot be proved. We have the witnesses—crowds of them, who will testify in terms stronger than we can write them to the efficacy of this Remedy, who will testify that the PETROLEUM has done for them what no medicine ever could before—cases that were pronounced hopeless, and beyond the reach of remediate means—cases abandoned by Physicians of unquestioned celebrity, have been made to exclaim, "THIS IS THE MOST WONDERFUL REMEDY EVER DISCOVERED!" We will lay before you the certificates of some of the most remarkable cases; to give them all, would require more space than would be allowed by this circular. Since the introduction of the Petroleum, about one year ago, many Physicians have been convinced of its efficacy, and now recommend it in their practice; and we have no doubt that in another year it will stand at the head of the list of valuable Remedies. If the Physicians do not recommend it, the people will have it of themselves—for its transcendent power to heal, will and must become known and appreciated—when the voices of the cured speak out; when the cures themselves stand out in bold relief, and when he who for years has suffered with the tortures and pangs of an immedicable lesion, that has been shortening his days, and hastening him "to the narrow house appointed for all the living," when he speaks out in its praise, who will doubt it! THE PETROLEUM IS A NATURAL REMEDY—it is put up as it flows from the bosom of the earth, without anything being added to or taken from it.

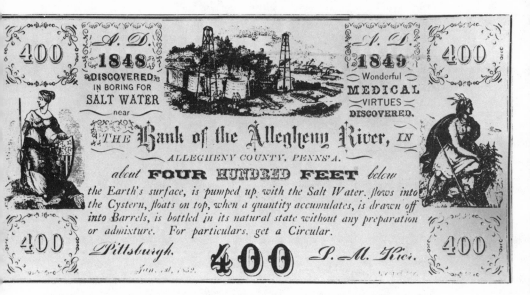

The enterprising Mr Kier's attempts to turn 'the devil's tar' to
account: (*opposite*) a circular, (*above*) a pseudo bank note – issued in
1852 – proclaiming the curative properties of Kier's Rock Oil.
(*below*) The original still used to rid the oil of its obnoxious smell.

(*opposite*) 'Colonel' Edwin L. Drake in top hat and 'Uncle Willie' at the world's first oil well; (*above*) Early drilling equipment; (*below*) the first oil train out of Bartlesville, Oklahoma.

Jeanette Dumont, first of the oil billionaire's five wives, and (*opposite*) her ex-husband together with their son George – apple of his father's eye as the only Getty of his generation to show any flair for the family business. George died three weeks after this photo was taken.

J. Paul Getty I and his granddaughter Claire, photographed at Sutton Place in 1975.

George Getty left an estate valued at $15,478,137. Apart from the $500,000 left to his son, he bequeathed $300,000 to his grandson, George F. Getty II, to be held in trust, $47,000 in gifts to various friends and relatives and $1000 to the Christian Science Publishing Society. The balance, more than 90% of the estate, went to his wife, making seventy-seven-year-old Sarah Getty the majority stockholder and occupant of the position Paul thought would be his. (The size of the estate was noted by several newspapers and, to Paul's anger and disgust, his mother soon began receiving dozens of marriage proposals through the post from total strangers.) Getty did not even name his son as executor, electing instead the Security-First National Bank of Los Angeles and his business manager, H. Paul Grimm, who were also to act as advisers to the ailing Sarah.

Devastated by the loss of the husband to whom she had been happily married for more than fifty years (they had celebrated their Golden Wedding with a big party only six months earlier), Sarah Getty was in no condition to take over control of George F. Getty Inc. She had no first-hand experience of the oil business – indeed, no experience of any business. She was elderly, in poor health, suffering greatly from rheumatism and almost deaf. She really wanted nothing more out of life than peace and quiet, but she was not the kind of woman to fail her husband. If he had wanted her to run the business, then that was what she would do.

It would, of course, have been much easier to hand everything over to Paul, particularly as such a move would probably have met with the approval of her late husband. But Paul's suggestion that she might care to consider this option fell on deaf ears; she showed not the slightest inclination to surrender the power she had so surprisingly inherited.

Although she would never admit it, Sarah did not entirely trust her only son. Deeply conservative herself, she thought Paul was all too willing to take risks and rely on luck. Her great fear was that he would one day overreach himself and lose everything, throwing them into the poorhouse. She had been at George Getty's side all through the years he had spent doggedly building the business. 'It's best not to carry too much sail,' he liked to say. 'One never knows when a sudden storm might strike.' He hated to borrow money and was inordinately proud of the fact that even when they were considered wealthy by any standards, the family's annual expenditure never exceeded thirty thousand dollars. Sarah inherited his fiscal conservatism and was determined not to allow her headstrong son to gamble with the family business. She wanted to preserve the family fortune, for the benefit of future Gettys.

While Paul had no wish to jeopardise what his father had created, he also had no wish to miss what he considered to be a unique opportunity to expand the business. 'My mother and the executors of my father's will were deeply worried about the economic situation and advised drastic retrenchment and curtailed operations. My own views were in direct opposition. Convinced of eventual economic recovery and firmly believing in the business dictum, buy when prices are low, I urged a programme of expansion. Stocks in publicly-owned companies with huge assets were selling at prices that made them barely believable bargains. There were shares selling for as little as a twentieth of their net underlying asset value. I argued that anyone who purchased them was, in effect, buying twenty dollars worth of stock for every dollar spent.'

Sarah had no hesitation in rejecting Paul's advice and siding with the directors, who were all long-standing friends of her husband. Thus was the stage set for a prolonged struggle between mother and son. Underlying the contest was Paul's obsessive compulsion to challenge his father's ghost and demonstrate his own worth by making even more money.

On 3 July 1930 Paul was elected president, treasurer and general manager of George F. Getty Inc., although ultimate authority resided with his mother as majority stockholder. The previous year had been a good one for the company under Paul's management, with rich strikes in deep sand at Santa Fe Springs and Long Beach occasionally boosting daily production above thirty thousand barrels and bringing in a profit of $1.6 million. But Paul's confidence in the future was not shared by his fellow directors, who were uneasy about his casual dismissal of the deepening Depression.

In the weeks following the Wall Street crash, stocks lost forty per cent of their value and the downward trend had continued intermittently. More than five thousand banks had closed, thousands of factories shut down and millions were thrown out of work – the Ford Motor Company cut its workforce from 128,000 to 37,000 and by the end of 1930 almost half the 280,000 textile mill workers in New England were unemployed. The newspapers were full of stories about incipient riots and the pictures showed ragged people with hollow eyes standing in breadlines in New York and children scavenging for food in trash cans. It was little wonder that the directors of George F. Getty Inc. were nervous about Paul's insistence that the time to buy stocks was when everyone else was selling.

'The first major problem the company faced after the death of George Getty was a threat to a valuable lease it had acquired in the fabulously rich Kettleman Hills field, a perfect dome some seventy-five miles north of Los Angeles. The big operators in Kettleman Hills were planning to carve up the field with a 'unit' scheme to regulate production and avoid a glut on the local oil market – the more units a company held, the more oil it would be allowed to produce and consequently the larger its profits. Such a scheme was potentially disastrous for small operators like George F. Getty Inc. and at a board meeting in early September Paul proposed buying shares in Pacific Western and Mexican Seaboard – both big leaseholders in Kettleman Hills – in order to increase their unit holding and so safeguard their interest.

Buying stock in other oil companies was an entirely new departure for George F. Getty Inc. and the directors, most notably Sarah Getty, were less than enthusiastic. Sarah thought it better to sacrifice the lease rather than borrow a cent from the bank; Paul argued that they would be throwing away their stake in one of California's richest oilfields. After a great deal of wrangling, Paul at last prevailed and the directors agreed – with conspicuous reluctance – to borrow $2,500,000 from Security-First National Bank of Los Angeles to finance the necessary stock purchases. The company bought 129,719 shares in Pacific Western for $2,102,481 and 75,000 shares in Mexican Seaboard for $1,176,285. Only Paul was happy.

The gloomy forebodings of Paul's fellow directors seemed to be confirmed when oil stock prices fell rapidly and the company's paper loss on its Pacific Western and Mexican Seaboard holdings climbed week by week until it approached one million dollars. Paul's chirpy reaction was to suggest further borrowing from the bank to buy *more* stock. It was a wonderful opportunity, he said, to take over both companies at rock-bottom prices. This time the board firmly rejected the idea. Mrs Getty staunchly supported the board against her son, quoting her late husband's maxim 'The last thing you should ever do is borrow. The first thing you must always do is repay your debts.'

Paul's authority with his fellow directors was not helped by the shambles of his private life. While his wife and baby son remained firmly resident in Germany, it was common knowledge in Los Angeles that Paul had become 'involved' with a young actress by the name of Ann Rork. Ann's father, Sam Rork, was a well-known Hollywood producer and the manager of Clara Bow; it was through his friendship with the 'It girl' that Paul first met Rork and his precocious daughter, then fourteen and still at school. She was just seventeen and working as a bit-part actress in early 'talkies' when Paul began escorting her about town. The Rorks were not a low-profile family and Ann was regularly photographed at nightclubs and parties squired by Paul.

On 28 November 1930 Paul sailed for Europe on the SS *Homeric* to try and sort out his personal life. He intended to see Fini and the baby, confess to his affair with Ann and ask for a divorce. While he was on his way across the Atlantic, oil stocks plunged to new lows and Sarah Getty held worried consultations with the executors of her late husband's will. All concurred that the kind of expansion envisaged by her son was reckless and ill-advised when the world was in the throes of a depression.

On Christmas Day 1930 Paul received a curt telegram in Berlin: 'YOUR MOTHER CALLED US AS EXECUTORS TO RESIDENCE AND DEMANDED THAT WE PREVENT FURTHER BUYING OF STOCKS WITH FUNDS OF ANY COMPANY AND INSTRUCTS US ADVISE YOU ON PROGRAM OF BUSINESS STOP PLEASE INSTRUCT DIRECTORS TO CANCEL ALL BUYING ORDERS AND RESOLUTIONS STOP ALSO PLEASE CABLE OUTLINE OF PLANS FOR COMING YEAR CONFIRM BY LETTER.' Paul meekly cabled a reply three days later, agreeing to cancel all buying orders and to devote the company's income to paying off the bank.

It was not, by any means, what he wanted to do but he was thousands of miles from the boardroom of George F. Getty Inc. and he had problems enough in Europe. To his astonishment he discovered that Fini, who had previously seemed amenable to a divorce, changed her mind the moment she heard about Paul's affair with Ann Rork. Meanwhile Dr Otto Helmle was still intent that his daughter should divorce Paul at the earliest opportunity, but not until he had negotiated a handsome settlement from this oil millionaire who had so deliberately trifled with his daughter's affections. He was demanding outrageous sums from Paul, not only for Fini, but for the baby too. 'I was forced to admit,' Paul noted ruefully, 'that in Doctor Helmle I had encountered a businessman who was most certainly my equal.'

In Los Angeles, Sarah continued to fret. She became convinced that the company was on the brink of collapse and took to summoning directors to meetings at South Kingsley Drive to grill them about the state of the oil business. The minutes of the 7 March board meeting recorded that 'Mrs George F. Getty had sent for Mr Rush Blodget, had indicated great concern over newspaper reports as to the oil business and had asked if the company was in a position safely to get through the slump. He assured her that the company would get through safely. He stated that Mrs Getty urged that the company buy no stocks and not deal in the stock market at all except to sell any securities necessary to carry on.' Emil Kluth, another director, reported a similar meeting, as did yet another, the appropriately named Mr Grimm. In April the board heard that the bank was demanding additional collateral to finance the company's borrowing. 'It was the consensus of opinion,' the minutes noted, 'that as Mexican Seaboard was selling at twenty dollars and over, it would be wise to sell sufficient to make one or two payments on its [George F. Getty Inc.'s] note to the bank and that sales should be made unless good reason was advanced by President J. Paul Getty to the contrary.' The President, still in Europe, was hardly in a position to advance such good reasons.

George F. Getty Inc. reported a profit of only $693,000 for 1930. The paper loss on its shareholdings in Pacific Western and Mexican Seaboard now stood in excess of a million dollars and nearly nine hundred thousand dollars had been lost on drilling dry holes. A great deal of money had also been spent setting up an Exploration Department to exploit a new technique of prospecting using torsion balances, but it found nothing but 'dusters' (dry holes). Most of the directors found it convenient to place the blame for the company's poor performance at the door of its wilful and absentee president. 'In the eyes of the directors and executors,' Paul confessed, 'my stewardship seemed to have been something less than an overwhelming success.'

Paul returned from Europe in August and 'married' Ann Rork in New York. As he had not yet managed to get a divorce from Fini, it was a rather simpler ceremony than normal. In a rented apartment on West 59th Street he told Ann he loved her and wanted to marry her. 'Do you want to marry me?' he asked. She said 'Yes.' 'We are married then,' Paul averred. 'We don't need any third person to say things over us.'

When Paul got back to California in early September, he found the climate in the boardroom extremely chilly. Things were no better at home, where Sarah had discovered his relationship with Ann Rork. What, she demanded querulously, was going on? Paul broke the news as gently as he could. His marriage to Fini was over, he said; divorce proceedings had been instituted in Mexico and he had agreed a settlement with her father, Doctor Helmle. As soon as he was free, he wanted to marry Ann Rork. (He did not bother to tell his mother about their unusual 'marriage' in New York, or that he had installed Ann in an apartment in Los Angeles.) Sarah wept bitterly at this; she had liked Fini and had hoped with all her heart that this time round, her son would finally settle down. Paul asked if he could bring Ann home so that his mother could meet her. Sarah shook her head. She had no desire, she said coldly, to see her or speak to her.

On 14 September, seven days after returning to California, Paul presided over a directors' meeting at which Rush Blodget resigned as vice-president, saying he could no longer support Paul. Blodget was one of George Getty's most trusted friends and advisers and his resignation did nothing to elevate Paul's standing with his mother. Not long afterwards, the company secretary similarly resigned. At the annual general meeting on 7 December the executors put the estate's twenty thousand shares firmly behind Sarah, confirming her ultimate control of the company. Although he was re-elected as president and general manager, Paul was still frustrated by his lack of real power. 'I was definitely deprived,' he said, 'of control of the company in which I had invested a million dollars of my own money. I believed my policy had been sound, had protected the company and had enhanced the value of its assets. The controlling stock interests, however, thought otherwise.'

Paul resisted the temptation to point out to his grudging fellow directors that much of the company's success in the previous six or seven years could be directly attributed to the five million dollars earned by the leases he had acquired as an independent operator and assigned to George F. Getty Inc. on a participating-partnership basis. It was not the time, he thought, to provoke further acrimony. Instead he suggested clearing the company's debts by selling the Kettleman Hills lease. It would, he said, produce a very substantial profit which would more than offset the paper losses of the Pacific Western and Mexican Seaboard holdings, about which the board was so concerned. (He declined, diplomatically, to point out further that the company only kept its stake in Kettleman Hills because he had forced through the purchase of Pacific Western and Mexican Seaboard stock.) The board, always inclined towards caution, was much more attracted by the idea of liquidating assets than acquiring them, and enthusiastically endorsed the proposal. The lease was bought by the Shell Oil Company in January for $4,500,000, returning George F. Getty Inc. to solvency.

While negotiations for the sale were taking place, one of Paul's friends offered him a further 160,000 shares in Western Pacific, enough to put George F. Getty Inc. in overall control of the company, which was one of the ten biggest oil producers in California. After some haggling, Paul got the offer price down to only seven dollars a share. At a special directors' meeting he pleaded with the board to take advantage of this 'once-in-a-lifetime' opportunity. As soon as the economy recovered – he was still convinced it would – the price of Western Pacific stock would soar and George F. Getty Inc. would be superbly placed for expansion and development. The risk was minimal in any case, he said, since Pacific Western's realisable assets were worth more than the market value of its stock.

The board heard him out, but took its cue from Sarah Getty. They were oilmen, not stock speculators, they said. The purchase of Western Pacific stock had only been approved for the sole purpose of protecting the Kettleman Hills lease. As soon as the price of the stock improved, the board wanted to dispose of it. They had no interest in taking over other companies. They were also worried about the company's liability regarding inheritance taxes to be levied on George Getty's estate, since valuation of the estate was being disputed by the government revenue service. Sarah nodded her approval throughout the discussion.

Paul was infuriated by their stubborn complacency and their willingness to pass up such an opportunity. Through February and March 1932 he had innumerable discussions with his mother and the other directors in the hope of changing their minds, but he won little support. In the end they half-heartedly agreed to allow him to buy the shares as an agent of the company, providing he used his own resources. They hinted that George F. Getty Inc. might be willing at a later date to reimburse him, once the question of the inheritance tax had been resolved. It was a rotten deal since he had to shoulder all the risk himself, but it was the best he could get. Using $1,200,000 of his money, he bought the shares on offer and on 1 May 1932 the field operations of the Pacific Western Oil Company and George F. Getty Inc. were consolidated.

A few days later Paul left for what was now becoming an annual trip to Europe, but this time he did not travel alone. When he boarded a transatlantic liner in New York he was accompanied by a young and pretty girl – Ann Rork, travelling as 'Mrs Getty'. Close observers might have noticed a certain healthy glow about her and a faintly matronlike plumpness. They stayed first in Paris and then moved on to Italy. In August the good news arrived that Paul's divorce from Fini had been finalised. On 7 September while they were on their way by ship from Genoa to Naples, Ann gave birth to a son, a month prematurely. They wanted to call the baby Jean Paul Getty II, but there was a muddle with the Italian authorities and the birth certificate named him Eugene Paul Getty.

In November Paul left Ann and the baby in Paris and briefly returned to California to check on the progress of a house he was having built for them on the beach at 270 Ocean Front, Santa Monica. (He knew there was no question of them staying with his mother at South Kingsley Drive.) Then he took a train to Washington to try and settle the dispute over the government's valuation of his father's estate. After negotiating with revenue agents he managed to reduce the original assessment of $20,000,000 by about half, which left George F. Getty Inc. with a tax liability of $1,300,000. He was pleased with the result, even though he felt it was somewhat unjust for his father to be heavily taxed after his death for his abstemious lifestyle. Getty never owned valuable objects of art, country estates or yachts and lived unpretentiously for a man of his means. 'Tax legislation today', his son noted, 'makes it doubtful if such moderation in expenditure is advisable.'

Back in California Paul sent a telegram to Ann telling her to meet him in Mexico, where they were married at Cuernavaca on 2 December; Paul was forty, Ann exactly half his age. Sarah Getty was not invited to the ceremony and had no desire to attend; she no longer wished to know anything about Paul's private life and even the birth of another grandchild did not soften her attitude, particularly as he had the misfortune to arrive before the wedding.

If Paul had learned anything from his previous attempts at marriage, he did not show it. They had barely moved into the beach house at Santa Monica before business immediately intruded in their relationship. The problem now was that Paul was involved in something really big, something which *had* to take precedence over wives and children.

Disregarding vehement opposition from his mother and his fellow directors, Paul had conceived a plan to build George F. Getty Inc. into an integrated oil company engaged not just in exploration and production, but transportation, refining and retailing; everything from the oil well to the gas pump. He knew if he missed his chance now, while stock prices were low and the Getty companies had cash and credit, it might never come again.

On 27 February 1933 Rush Blodget resigned from the board in protest at Paul's activities. He explained his reasons in a long letter to Sarah:

Dear Mrs Getty,
When I resigned in August, 1931, as Vice-President . . . you sent for me and requested me to remain with the companies as director and general counsel . . .

I have been happy to serve you, both for your own sake and in memory of my former employer, Mr George F. Getty. My service to you has on a very large number of occasions involved opposition by me to the wishes of your son, Mr J. Paul Getty, President and General Manager. This opposition happily has been free from acrimonious dispute, but has involved a heavy drain upon my vitality, as I have most of the time been opposed to his policies and to his decisions . . .

The difference of opinion between Mr Getty's views and mine is wide; and the difference between your views (as I understand them) and your son's, is wide. Apparently there can be no middle ground. I appreciate your desire to leave full management to your son, who is young, energetic and ambitious and I sympathise deeply with your apprehensions as to the future as the companies so cautiously managed by Mr George F. Getty, now are engaging in activities vastly different.

I cannot see any solution with contentment to you, except to immediately realise from your holdings a substantial sum adequate to keep you in comfort in the station in life to which you are accustomed. My own idea is that if you were to exchange your present position, with its apprehensions and worries, for a million dollars in good interest-bearing securities, you will have done what Mr George F. Getty would approve. I can assure you that I have every reason to believe, from evidence that has come to my knowledge, that you should insist upon a consummation of this plan, and not allow yourself to be deterred.

In the meantime, I can be of no help to you on the board of

directors and I feel that in justice to all concerned, I should resign.
  If, however, at any time I can be of service to you, I trust you will
not hesitate to command me.

Very sincerely yours,
Rush M. Blodget

Sarah was upset by Blodget's resignation but she was not ready to give
way to Paul, as he recommended, just yet. She viewed her responsibilities as a kind of sacred trust passed on by her beloved late husband
and while there was breath in her body she was not going to allow her
son to ride roughshod over her – or her husband's – wishes. Paul
claimed that their arguments about business never affected their relationship:

> My mother and I were always very close. A great bond of love and
> affection existed between us, and in so far as our personal relation-
> ship was concerned my father's death served to draw us even closer
> together. When it came to business, however, our opinions some-
> times differed greatly. We did not allow these differences to affect
> our personal relationship in the slightest degree. On the other
> hand we did not let the fact that we were mother and son prevent
> us from having and expressing our respective, independent – and,
> on occasion, vigorously opposed – views regarding business mat-
> ters. Needless to say this relationship, to the casual observer an
> ambivalent one, gave rise to many paradoxical and often delight-
> fully amusing incidents. Mama – as I called her from the time I was
> a child – and I often chuckled over the astonishment registered by
> some who saw and heard us arguing vehemently over business
> affairs one moment and then switching abruptly to an affectionate
> mother-son conversation the next.

This was a faintly rose-tinted view, designed for public consumption.
Paul saw his mother at least twice a week, usually for lunch or dinner.
Most weeks he also took her out for a drive in his car, often to the beach
at Santa Monica where she liked to feed the sea lions. It would have
been a heart-warming sight, the old lady leaning heavily on the arm of
her loving son as they walked across the sand, had they not invariably
been arguing about business. They disagreed, fundamentally, on what
George Getty would have been doing had he still been alive.
  Sarah believed her husband would never have wanted to borrow
large sums of money, particularly during a recession. She also thought
that he would probably not have speculated in the stock of other oil
companies, even if the economy had been booming. She was convinced
that if she let her son have his way, he would endanger the future of the
company. Paul argued that what he was doing was precisely what his

95

father would have wanted. 'Father never missed a chance to expand his business enterprises,' he said, 'and there will never again be opportunities such as there are today.' It was Paul's conviction that doing nothing presented a far greater risk to the company: stagnation and eventual liquidation would follow. His policy offered growth and an opportunity to build a thriving and powerful business. 'I was certain,' he explained, 'that if my father had lived to see the remarkable stock bargains that became available in 1932 he would have done just as I was doing.'

So the argument went on, with neither side giving an inch. Paul continued to buy stock, almost on a daily basis, and pressed his fellow directors to make good their vague promise to pick up some of the shares. By March 1933 he had spent more than two million dollars. At one point his resources had become so strained that he was forced to dump a block of fifty-eight thousand shares in Mexican Seaboard at an average price of around $10.25 a share in order to obtain additional funds. He had not wanted to do it, as he expected the shares to rise sharply in a few months. When they did, Paul calculated bitterly that he had lost a potential profit of more than half a million dollars – a profit he could have reaped had it not been for the reluctance of the board at George F. Getty Inc. to support him.

On 31 March he decided he had had enough of his lily-livered fellow directors and he tendered his resignation from the board, which was accepted. He retained his interest as a one-third stockholder, but wanted to be free to pursue his own long-term objectives. In May 1933 the stock market suddenly surged upward and George F. Getty Inc. belatedly offered to take over some of his shares. 'You're arriving at the party rather late,' Paul pointed out curtly. 'All the door prizes have been given out and most of the buffet supper has been eaten.'

At the beginning of August, with the stock market still buoyant, the board cautiously decided that it could risk purchasing stock on its own behalf and an account was opened with the stockbrokers E.F. Hutton and Company. Paul was invited to act as agent, with authority to purchase for George F. Getty Inc. He agreed, but objected vociferously to a spending limit proposed by the board of only three hundred thousand dollars. The limit had been imposed at the insistence of Sarah Getty and furious arguments took place between mother and son during the next few weeks. ('A great deal of friction,' a privately-printed history of the company noted discreetly, 'developed between George F. Getty Incorporated's two stockholders.') Paul succeeded in getting the limit increased to $400,000, then demanded it should be raised to $1,000,000. Sarah adamantly refused. They compromised at the end of the month on $650,000.

All this while, Paul's fourth marriage was falling apart. Ann was pregnant again, angry, resentful and bored. She thought she had married a businessman and found she had married a business. Ann knew nothing about the oil business and cared less. Left alone for long periods in their twelve-room clapboard house at Santa Monica, she filled the place with friends from show business and they sat about for hours on the deck overlooking the beach, drinking, talking, laughing and playing with baby Eugene. Ann told her friends about her marital problems – how she felt neglected, how Paul seemed to care more about the business than her and the baby. Her friends sympathised and stirred further trouble, teasing her about having a rich husband. 'Why has he only given you a Mercedes, darling?' they said. 'You should have a Rolls with a husband like that.' Or 'You've only got mink? He should dress you in sable!'

Paul made no secret of the fact that he considered Ann's 'claque' of show-business friends to be worthless – an ironic turning of the tables from the days when Paul's friends had been labelled Hollywood 'riff-raff' by his mother. If they were still around when he got home, he was coldly polite but took the first opportunity to disappear into his study with his business papers. He and Ann argued frequently. 'I wanted him to dote on me,' she said. 'I wanted romance and glamour; he wanted to build a business. Perhaps it was not his fault.' One evening Paul tried to explain why it was necessary for him to spend so much time on business and she threw a pin cushion at him and snapped: 'I'd rather be a pauper who spent his last penny like a prince.'

On 20 December 1933 Ann gave birth to another boy, Gordon Peter Getty. It was an event to which Paul gave little attention, for he was on the brink of finally persuading his mother, after weeks of negotiation, to release her grip on George F. Getty Inc.

Sarah Getty was tired of fighting with her son. She was eighty-one and her rheumatism was steadily worsening – she had to have an elevator installed at South Kingsley Drive so she could get upstairs to bed. All through 1933 she had been involved in constant arguments with Paul and she despaired of ever convincing him that it was she who was carrying out his dead father's wishes, not he.

A couple of days before Christmas, Paul visited his mother at South Kingsley Drive. He wanted to give her the good news that she had a fourth grandson, but more importantly he wanted to air his many grievances about the business. He had a lot to say and he reeled off his complaints point by point, accurately quoting dates and figures from memory.

First, he said, he had been hurt financially by loans which George F. Getty Inc. had made to the George F. Getty Oil Company, an ailing subsidiary formed to prospect for oil in New Mexico. A total of

$1,684,000 had been loaned to the George F. Getty Oil Company for the purchase of 25,000 shares in Pacific Western and another $700,000 had been advanced for the acquisition of leases and drilling of test wells. Paul had objected to both loans at the time but had been overruled. His principal objection was that he owned one third of George F. Getty Inc., but had no interest in the George F. Getty Oil Company, which was entirely owned by his mother. Therefore he was indirectly financing one third of the loan without the possibility of any benefit. Any appreciation in the value of the stock bought by George F. Getty Oil would go solely to his mother. He also had grave doubts that its assets matched the amount of money it had borrowed – he considered it was an unsound loan to have made.

'I stressed the point,' Paul explained, 'that George F. Getty Inc. had no right to advance money to a corporation owned entirely by her in order to enable it to speculate in oil property and stock. If her company made a fortune, it could then repay its borrowings; if it lost there was no stockholders' liability and George F. Getty Inc. could whistle for its money. It was a clear case of "Heads I win, tails you lose".'

At this point Sarah slyly offered to 'regularise' the position by transferring a third interest in the George F. Getty Oil Company to Paul. He was not interested. The loans were already 'under water', he said, and in any case the stock had no value.

Paul's next gripe was that he had been left 'holding the bag' by George F. Getty Inc.'s reluctance to pick up the stock he had been buying on its behalf. 'I recited again to mother the financial losses and hardships suffered as a result of my personal participation in the Getty companies' stock-buying campaign. I had aided them to the limit of my ability and to my own personal detriment during 1931, 1932 and 1933. The entire burden of the campaign had been assumed by me and I had received no profit for my services.'

He cited as an example of the losses he had sustained the fact that he had had to stop buying Mexican Seaboard stock as a personal investment and then was obliged to dispose of a substantial block of shares in order to support George F. Getty's stock purchases. 'Had I been able to hold the Mexican Seaboard stock a few months longer, I would have made a profit of over half a million dollars and had I continued buying – which I would have done had I not employed my money and credit helping George F. Getty Inc. – I would have had a personal profit in the spring of 1933 of at least one million dollars.'

If he had been dealing with an outsider, he added, it would have been a good business decision to refuse further help when it became clear the stock he was purchasing as an agent on behalf of the company was not going to be promptly picked up. He blamed his mother, accusing her of ordering the board not to reimburse him. As a result, he said, he had a personal debt with his stockbroker of $640,000 and was now being pressed for payment. In addition he owed George F. Getty Inc. $216,000 for stock which the company had refused to accept but for which, 'after many entreaties, it had consented to loan me the money.'

His final complaint was that settlement of his father's estate had been arranged in such a fashion that his mother benefited at his expense. In February 1933 George F. Getty Inc. paid Sarah Getty $1,609,160 for 643,664 Minnehoma shares, in order to provide the estate with funds which would enable the executors to pay its debts and distribute the assets to her. Paul complained that the price paid for the shares – $2.50 each – was based on a valuation made in 1930 and took no account of the collapse in share prices since that date. Not only that, but the price had been arbitrarily raised by fifty cents. Sarah had first accepted an offer of two dollars a share and then the board raised it to two dollars fifty. 'As a one-third stockholder,' Paul pointed out, 'this cost me $107,000.' Apart from the price, he also objected to the whole deal since it was of no advantage to the company but of substantial advantage to his mother. 'There was also,' he pointed out, 'no advantage to me.'

Sarah heard her son out, listening carefully to his lengthy litany of complaints and injustices. At the end of it, to Paul's intense surprise and pleasure, she told him that she thought it was about time she retired. She no longer wanted the burden of responsibility, she said, and would be content if she had nothing more to supervise than the running of her own home. It was Christmas, the season of goodwill, and even though she could not resolve her differences with her son she was ready to recompense him for the losses he had suffered.

Mother and son got down to business, and Ann and the new baby were completely forgotten while Paul was engrossed in making a deal which would at last give him control of the company. 'We were both anxious to avoid continued friction,' said Paul. 'Mother suggested that if I would allow George F. Getty Inc. to purchase her stock at its full value, she would agree to make a substantial contribution to me as a Christmas gift which would enable me to pay my pressing debts.'

The agreement they worked out was that George F. Getty Inc. would purchase eighteen thousand shares from her for $4,500,000. More than a million dollars would be paid in cash and the remainder in interest-bearing notes payable at agreed dates in following years. This would amply provide for all Sarah Getty's needs for the rest of her life and at the same time make Paul the sole stockholder in George F. Getty Inc. In addition there was Sarah's 'Christmas gift' to her son which included her remaining two thousand shares in George F. Getty Inc., stock in other Getty subsidiaries and various notes worth in total $1,018,156. It was, Paul admitted, 'very generous'.

Sarah insisted that precise details of how she was to be paid for her stock were drawn up in a formal letter to her son which bore little indication of Christmas bonhomie. 'This offer', it concluded, 'shall remain open to and until 12 o'clock noon, December 30, 1933, and if not accepted by you in writing on or before that date and hour shall be considered as withdrawn by the undersigned and shall be wholly terminated and be at an end. Very truly yours, Sarah C. Getty.'

Paul and his mother signed all the necessary papers on 29 December in the offices of George F. Getty Inc. at 1060 Subway Terminal Building, Los Angeles. On 2 January 1934 Sarah thankfully resigned from the board and on 1 February the board accepted her resignation. 'I'm sure,' she said slowly as Paul was driving her home, 'that father approves.'

The fourth Mrs Getty was privy to none of these negotiations, but did not much care. Abandoned at the beach house in Santa Monica while Paul devoted himself to business, Ann began to despair of ever making their marriage work. She hated playing second fiddle to Getty Inc., hated everything to do with the oil industry. She often compared herself with the long-suffering heroine in J.M. Barrie's play, *The Twelve Pound Look*, about the neglected wife of an overworked businessman who decides to pull out all the stops to save her marriage. One evening when Paul came home late, as usual, she insisted he sit down and watch while she played the climactic scene. She entertained a vague hope that it would impress upon him what was happening to them. He was singularly unimpressed; when Ann had finished, he got up and walked out of the room without a word. A few days later Ann told him she was suffocating in her 'gilded cage' and wanted a divorce. Paul raised no objection, packed his bags and moved back to South Kingsley Drive, back to mother.

It was not at all inconvenient for Paul to be back living with his mother, since he was still finding it difficult to impose his will on the company, even though he was the principal stockholder. He discovered to his dismay that Sarah had merely exchanged one kind of authority for another – as principal creditor. George F. Getty Inc. owed her more than three million dollars, a debt which conferred considerable weight on her wishes and her primary wish was to halt the purchase of more oil stock.

'I was forced to mark time,' her frustrated son noted, 'although I told her I didn't believe a creditor should dictate the company's policy. Mother warned me against combining two very speculative businesses, drilling for oil and buying oil stocks with borrowed money. I had done both on a large scale in a period of general business insecurity, she complained, and had thus exposed our capital to a double risk.'

Sarah's great fear was that if the stock market collapsed again, the notes she held would be worthless and she insisted that as dominant creditor she had every right to criticise her son's business policy if she thought it affected the security of her loan. Paul sympathised to some extent, but had no intention of abandoning his strategy and he began looking for ways to neutralise his mother's power.

It did not take him long to decide that the only way to do it was to persuade her to simply give him the notes. Knowing Mama as he did, he was not hopeful.

'When I broached the subject of a gift, I found her rather unreceptive to the suggestion,' he noted gloomily. But through the long evenings they spent together at South Kingsley Drive and whenever they went out for a drive to feed the sea lions at the shore, he never missed an opportunity to press his case. He constantly reminded his mother that she herself had admitted often enough that his father had made a mistake by not leaving him the business. The notes were entirely superfluous to her needs, he argued. She had an income of around seventy-five thousand dollars a year without the notes, and had never spent more than twenty-five thousand. He warned her that as the notes became due, she would have to face the additional worry of investing the money.

'I wish,' Sarah muttered wearily at one point, 'that I was out of the whole affair.' Towards the end of 1934, she was wilting under the continual pressure from her son. 'However,' she warned him, 'if I decide to give anything now it will be in trust for you and your children so that you will be protected against speculation.' Paul would have preferred a no-strings gift, but he was not averse to the idea of a trust since it would effectively excise his mother's authority in the business.

Sarah and her son reached an agreement on Christmas Day 1934, an unusual day on which to discuss business in any other household but the Gettys'. She was willing to relinquish notes worth two and a half million dollars, providing they were committed to 'an irrevocable spend-thrift trust' and providing he contributed one million dollars of his stock in George F. Getty Inc. He was to be the first beneficiary. After his death, the trust income would be shared between three of his four children – the old lady agreed to Paul's suggestion that Ronnie should be excluded as he would inherit his maternal grandfather's substantial fortune. (Paul also wanted Ronnie cut out to punish the Helmle family – he was still smarting over the divorce settlement extracted by Fini's father.) The exclusion would only last for one generation; when the last of Paul's children died, the trust would be equally divided among all Sarah's great grandchildren.

The Sarah C. Getty Trust was established on 31 December 1934. It would be, in the years to come, a source of bitter enmity, inexorably setting one Getty against another. But for the time being, it set J. Paul Getty free from the shackles imposed by his mother. He was at last ready for battle with an oil giant.

7. 'My first thought was this is THE girl'

Paul was invited to spend New Year's Eve 1934 at San Simeon, the candy castle between Los Angeles and San Francisco on which newspaper publisher William Randolph Hearst had squandered much of his fortune. Hearst had begun building San Simeon in 1919 and although it was still not finished in 1935, it nevertheless took Paul's breath away when he first caught a glimpse of it from the road. Set in the foothills of the Santa Lucia Mountains overlooking the Pacific, it shimmered like a fairy-tale confection, a rococo folly topped with twin towers, sparkling white in the winter sunshine. It was common gossip at that time that Hearst's obsession with San Simeon and his determination to cram it with art treasures from all over the world had seriously weakened the financial position of his publishing empire. Paul had recently read that there was a storeroom covering two acres under the main part of the building, full of European antiques which had not even been unpacked from their crates. He was appalled, but morbidly fascinated, by such extravagance and was very much looking forward to his visit.

He had met Hearst several times at parties at the home of the glamorous film star Marion Davies, who lived next door to Paul's beach house at Santa Monica. It was one of Hollywood's worst-kept secrets that Miss Davies was Hearst's mistress and that he had lavished over three million dollars on her Santa Monica mansion, which had more than a hundred rooms and was furnished with antiques. Paul used to complain wryly that it made his own place look like a cottage.

About twenty house guests had been invited to San Simeon for the New Year holiday and they gathered for dinner on New Year's Eve in the conspicuous grandeur of the great refectory, hung with Gothic tapestries and silken Sienese banners. High above their heads was a carved ceiling removed from an Italian monastery, the walls were panelled with choir stalls from a cathedral in Spain and huge logs blazed in a sixteenth-century French fireplace. It was not a particularly jolly party, partly because of the intimidating surroundings and partly because the host, then seventy-one years old, frowned on 'excessive' drinking and only allowed his guests one apéritif which was served at the table. Paul was seated next to Marion Davies, who was on the right of Hearst. Miss Davies, who liked to drink, downed her cocktail and

103

seeing that Paul had not yet touched his, leaned across to him and whispered: 'If you don't want your drink, Paul, may I have it?' Unfortunately, Hearst overheard her request and boomed 'No!' loudly enough to be heard around the table. Conversation, which had been more polite than animated, faltered and died. Marion Davies glared at the old man sitting at the head of the table, turned to Paul again and stammered 'P-please give me your drink, Paul.'

Getty had no idea what to do. It would be churlish and ungentlemanly not to hand over his drink to the lady, but at the same time it would undoubtedly offend his host. He reached uncertainly for his glass, conscious of all eyes on him and accidentally knocked it over, spilling the contents over the table. Two flunkeys leapt forward to mop it up and, the crisis past, conversation resumed haltingly. Later that evening while a film was being shown in the theatre adjoining the refectory, Hearst took Paul to one side and gruffly congratulated him on his diplomacy, brushing aside, with a wink, Paul's protests that it had been an accident.

Next day Paul took the opportunity to explore the estate and marvel at its treasures. He was admiring the fifteenth-century stained glass in the main part of the house, the Casa Grande, when a butler came up and told him he was wanted on the telephone, long-distance from New York. Paul picked up the receiver and said: 'This is Paul Getty.'

'Glad I managed to track you down,' said a familiar voice at the other end. 'Happy New Year.' It was Jay Hopkins, a Wall Street attorney who often acted for the Getty business. 'Jersey Standard have transferred their Tide Water shares to a holding company called Mission Corporation and they are going to distribute Mission Corporation shares to their own stockholders on a pro-rata basis.'

Getty's impassive countenance rarely displayed his emotions, but the news caused him to flinch visibly. If this happened, a vital block of shares he wanted would be widely dispersed.

'I am authorised,' Hopkins continued, 'by John D. Rockefeller Junior and certain other Standard stockholders to offer you their rights to receive stock in Mission Corporation at $10.125 a share. I think there are about two hundred thousand shares involved.'

This time Getty smiled, almost imperceptibly. 'I'll buy,' he said without hesitation. 'But Jay, suppose Jersey Standard's management hears that Rockefeller intends to sell. They'll try to talk him out of it.'

'Not a chance. He's aboard a train bound for Arizona. They can't reach him, and I have his authorisation to sell.'

When Getty put down the telephone at San Simeon he had closed a deal to buy 'rights' worth around $1.8 million. He was a happy man, convinced at last that control of Tide Water Associated Oil Company was within his grasp. He drove back to Los Angeles later that day to

104

orchestrate the next move in his long-term dream to transform the Getty oil business from a small independent operator on the West Coast into a major integrated oil company.

Paul Getty's campaign to take over the Tide Water Associated Oil Company had begun early in 1932. It was to be a long and dirty fight, much longer and much dirtier than he had ever envisaged when he set out, and it would involve alarming risks. 'It was unquestionably a gamble,' he said later, 'and by my standards an enormous one. I was then a relatively small wildcatting operator setting my sights on one of the nation's major oil companies. My stock purchases were financed by every dollar I possessed and every cent of credit I could obtain. Had I lost the campaign – and I was defeated in several preliminary skirmishes and came within a heart-stopping hair's breadth of total failure on several occasions – I would have been left penniless and very deeply in debt.'

What prompted Paul to undertake such a hazardous venture was his continuing conviction that with oil stock prices still depressed in the aftermath of the Wall Street crash, he should look for a company with good refining and marketing facilities to merge with the Getty interests, which were primarily concerned with exploration and production. The only question was, which company should he go for?

Most of the crude oil produced by George F. Getty Inc. and its associated companies came from wells in California and so it seemed sensible to Paul that he should choose one of the seven major oil companies operating in California. The list was headed by two giants – Standard Oil and Shell Oil – both of them totally invulnerable, because of their sheer size, to a takeover bid by an independent. Next in line came Union Oil, which was amply supplied with its own crude, as was General Petroleum. Three possibilities were left. Richfield Oil had a contract to purchase Getty's crude production, but had recently gone into receivership and Texas Oil also had its own adequate supplies of crude. There remained only the Tide Water Associated Oil Company.

Tide Water was an old established firm, founded in 1878 as the Tide Water Pipe Company to build and operate a 104-mile pipeline – the longest in the world – to transport oil from Titusville, where 'Colonel' Drake had drilled the first oil well, to Williamsport in Pennsylvania. Newspapers described it as the 'feat of the age' when oil first began to flow into the storage tanks at Williamsport. In the years that followed Tide Water expanded rapidly until by 1932 it was among the fifteen biggest oil companies in the United States. Large enough to attract Paul Getty's attention, it also met his two most important criteria – its stock was selling at a low price and it was sorely in need of extra crude production. An investigation of the company revealed no hidden snags: Tide Water looked like a plum ripe for the picking.

Paul made his first purchase of Tide Water stock on 15 March 1932, picking up 1200 shares for $2.50 each. Next day he bought another 2500 at the same price and a further 600 at $2.625. The day after that he got another 2500. The weekend interrupted his buying spree, but on Monday 21 March he acquired 2500 shares, on Tuesday 1700 and on Wednesday 3900. By the end of the month, he owned 15,100 shares of Tide Water stock; by the end of April he had 41,100.

On 1 May 1932 Paul Getty turned up at the annual stockholders' meeting of Tide Water Associated in New York, determined to obtain a voice in the company's management as a first step towards his eventual goal of merging Tide Water with the Getty companies. He confidently expected a friendly reception, since there was no conflict of interest: Getty oil needed marketing and refining facilities and Tide Water needed crude production. In Paul's view the benefits of amalgamation would be mutual.

To support his claim for a seat on the board, he had his 41,000 shares, plus the promise of a proxy for 126,000 shares owned by Petroleum Securities which he had negotiated through personal contacts in the oil business. To his surprise Petroleum Securities revoked its proxy just before the meeting, without a word to Paul. Deprived of this backing, his bid for election to the board failed. Afterwards he discovered that Petroleum Securities owned a gas plant in the Kettleman Hills which was buying gas from Tide Water, but he did not think there was anything suspicious in this connection until later when the fighting really started and he became aware that Tide Water management was prepared to go to almost any lengths to thwart his plans. As far as the board was concerned, young Getty was an upstart and an outsider. One of the directors spoke for them all when he said: 'Paul Getty should stay where he belongs – on a drilling rig!'

Undaunted by this first setback, Paul continued buying Tide Water stock on an almost daily basis. He told his broker in New York – an old school friend, Gordon Crary – that at current levels he would take 'an unlimited amount'. Crary, who worked for E. F. Hutton and Company, often got colleagues to buy Tide Water shares on the floor of the New York Stock Exchange to camouflage Getty's involvement and intentions. Week after week and month after month Paul patiently increased his stake in the company, sometimes paying as much as $5.125 a share, sometimes as little as $2.125.

Even though he had failed to get a seat on the board, as a minority stockholder he considered he had the right to make his views known and he bombarded management with criticism, ideas and suggestions for improving efficiency and reducing overheads. He believed that much of Tide Water's refining plant was approaching obsolescence and strongly advised the company to use its cash resources to embark on a comprehensive modernisation programme. He vigorously objected to the payment of big dividends on preferred stock at the expense of common stockholders. Checking through company records, he discovered that in some years a dividend of more than four million dollars was paid to preferred stockholders while common stockholders received nothing. His view was that Tide Water should buy up as much of its preferred stock as possible in order to pay bigger dividends on the common stock.

Tide Water management deeply resented Getty's interference in its affairs and rebuffed all his proposals. By the end of 1932 Paul had more than a million dollars of his own money invested in Tide Water and another half a million in the Petroleum Corporation of America which owned a substantial segment of Tide Water stock. With around 156,000 Tide Water shares in his pocket, he had made substantial progress in his campaign but he felt greatly handicapped by the continuing opposition from the other Getty directors, all of whom were opposed to the gamble. Despite their misgivings, his confidence never wavered. 'Had I received the promised support from mother and the other directors in 1932,' he said, 'I would have bought three times as much Tide Water stock as I did. The failure to fully exploit the bargain days of 1932 ruined the Getty companies' chance to acquire one third or more of Tide Water Associated's common stock, although this was not fully realised at the time.'

At the end of April 1933 Paul again boarded a train to New York in order to attend the annual meeting of Tide Water stockholders, which was to be held on Thursday 4 May. This time he did not need any proxies in order to be able to claim a seat on the board: Getty interests owned no less than 258,004 shares – more than enough, Paul declared, to justify claiming a voice in the management. This time, he could not be ignored and the Tide Water Associated Oil Company acquired a dynamic new director – forty-year-old J. Paul Getty. 'It was a comparatively minor victory in the campaign,' he was to say later, 'but it had the effect of establishing a Getty beachhead on a shore which, if not exactly hostile, was a step or two removed from being warmly hospitable.'

Paul had no experience of any kind in the boardroom of a major oil company, but he was not in the least inhibited by being the new boy. He immediately proposed that the company should use its surplus cash, about five million dollars, to buy back its preferred stock and eliminate the need to pay the compulsory six per cent annual dividend it carried. This, he argued, would make more cash available for distribution in dividends to the seventeen thousand common stockholders. The proposal was rejected as foolhardy by the other directors, all of whom believed that it was safer to hold a large cash balance than buy equities in the uncertain business climate still prevailing after the collapse of the stock market in 1929.

During the next few months, Paul learned a great deal about his fellow directors and was far from impressed. The board was made up of five Tide Water executives and seven outsiders, few of whom, it seemed to Paul, showed much interest in the business. In October 1933 the directors were invited on a tour of inspection of Tide Water plants in Texas and Oklahoma. Only one outside director accepted the invitation – the newest member of the board, J. Paul Getty. Subsequently he discovered, to his disgust, that none of the outside directors had ever bothered to visit the company's huge refinery at Bayonne in New Jersey, even though it was only a twenty-minute drive from New York and represented a major investment. And, in answer to Paul's question, the company comptroller told him he had only once been consulted by any of the outside directors.

It was not in Paul's nature to remain silent about such matters and his scathing comments at board meetings did not make him the most popular member, not that he was interested in making friends. What concerned him more was the almost routine dismissal of his ideas by men who were too idle to inform themselves about the nature of the business they were supposed to be managing. 'I had a large part of my fortune invested in the company's stock,' he groused, 'and was experienced and successful in the oil business. But I found that none of the outside directors ever consulted or paid any particular attention to my views, although I was an oilman and they were not.'

Throughout the year his stock-buying campaign quietly continued, boosted by belated support from the directors of George F. Getty Inc. whose fears had been stilled by a sudden surge in the stock market. With George F. Getty Inc. and Pacific Western both picking up Tide Water shares, the 'Getty interests' slowly strengthened their grip on Tide Water. In September veteran oilman Harry Sinclair offered to trade his three hundred thousand Tide Water shares for the Getty group's complete holding of two hundred thousand shares in Petroleum Corporation common stock. Paul could have realised a profit of around one and a half million dollars by selling the Getty stake in Petroleum Corporation, but he jumped at Sinclair's offer to trade and so virtually doubled his holding in Tide Water.

At a Tide Water board meeting held in December, which Paul was not able to attend, it was decided that it would, after all, be a good idea to buy back its preferred stock. When Paul had first suggested it that spring, the price was thirty-five dollars a share; by December it was sixty-five. Further embarrassment awaited the unfortunate Tide Water board when it discovered that the only preferred stockholder willing to sell was George F. Getty Inc. Paul authorised the sale of 18,400 shares of Tide Water preferred stock and cleaned up a profit of $428,316 for the family business. This money was immediately ploughed back into buying Tide Water common stock and by the close of 1933 the Getty interests could muster 743,154 shares in Tide Water Associated, about 7.5% of the outstanding stock.

In May 1934 Harold P. Grimm, a Getty executive, was voted on to the board of Tide Water, giving the Getty interests two of the twelve seats. By then Tide Water common stock was selling for $11.25 a share, which pleased Paul enormously since he had paid an average of only $3.59 for his first three hundred thousand shares. Paul was also pleased that William F. Humphrey, a man he liked and greatly respected, was appointed to replace the retiring president of the company. Humphrey, known as 'Big Bill' because of his imposing stature, was a corporation lawyer with an excellent reputation as a businessman; he had been involved with Tide Water for nearly twenty years and was well known as the founder of the Olympic Club in San Francisco.

That early summer of 1934, a little more than two years into his campaign, Paul could look back with quiet satisfaction at what had been achieved and look forward to further progress with confidence. His contentment was extremely short-lived, for he was shortly to receive a nasty surprise. In June 1934 Paul Getty discovered to his consternation that the Tide Water Associated Oil Company was not independent, as he had been led to believe, but was actually controlled by the mammoth Standard Oil Company of New Jersey!

Paul would never have considered taking on Tide Water had he known that it would mean a battle with one of the giant corporations dominating the American petroleum industry. As far as he had been able to ascertain from public records, Jersey Standard had divested itself of working control of Tide Water in 1930 when it sold 1,078,123 shares – then about twenty-three per cent of the company's stock – to Mission Securities, a holding company formed by a syndicate of Tide Water executives. Jersey Standard had subsequently picked up fifty thousand Tide Water shares on the open market, but that had appeared to be the extent of its interest.

What Paul did not know was that Mission Securities had bought the shares from Jersey Standard on a time-payment basis and had consistently defaulted. In June 1934 Jersey Standard declared the purchase forfeit and transferred the 1,078,123 shares back into its own name, thus regaining working control of the company. The effect on the

'Getty interests' was calamitous – instead of being influential stock-holders in an independent company they became, overnight, no more than a pawn in a game now dominated by Jersey Standard.

Once he had recovered from the shock, Paul weighed up the options open to him. There was not, in truth, a great range of choice – he could either admit defeat and back out, or continue the campaign regardless of the enemy's formidable reinforcements. He had always thought of the venture as a 'battle' and viewed his dilemma as similar to that of a general surveying his forces after a particularly bloody setback. 'I could on the one hand admit that I was outnumbered and outgunned,' he noted, 'or, on the other, I could stand and fight. I had been forced to make similar choices many times on payday nights in the Oklahoma oilfields. I had learned then that the bigger the bully, the better the brawl was likely to be; that no matter how tough the opponent who backed you into a corner, there was always a good chance of out-slugging, outboxing or outlasting him in the in-fighting. I decided to fight.'

But first, he attempted to parley. In October 1934 Paul sought a meeting with Jersey Standard's top management to 'talk matters over', in the hope of convincing them that they should not hold such a large stake in a competing company like Tide Water. No one would agree to see him.

He tried another tack. On 19 December lawyers acting for the Getty interests dispatched a terse letter to Jersey Standard.

> My clients, Getty Inc., a Delaware corporation, and George F. Getty Inc., a California corporation, are large stockholders in Tide Water Associated Oil Company. They are advised that Standard Oil Company is the holder of record of over 1,100,000 of its voting shares. Because of their interest in the company, they have a vital concern in the effect of retention and voting by Standard Oil Company of so large a block of the company's voting shares. They consider it is not to the wellbeing of Tide Water Associated Oil Company, or the public, that a competing business such as that of the Standard Oil Company be permitted to exercise control of Tide Water Associated Oil Company through such voting power. They further regard it to be the duty of the Standard Oil Company under the law promptly and in good faith to divest itself of such ownership or definitely commit itself to refrain from voting, either directly or indirectly, the stock so owned ...
>
> My clients have no desire, for the sake of Tide Water Associated Oil Company and their interests therein, to engage in controversy with Standard Oil Company either in the courts or elsewhere but the matter is of sufficient importance to the independent stock-holders in that company to justify recourse to the courts should

Standard Oil Company decline to relinquish the voting rights afforded by its stock ownership, or to distribute these shares to its own stockholders, or to make a bona fide sale, or other effective disposition thereof. It is hoped that Standard Oil Company will give this matter its careful consideration.

Jersey Standard chose not to reply to this letter, but took swift action to head off any possibility of a legal challenge from Getty. On 31 December 1934 Jersey Standard transferred its 1,128,123 Tide Water shares, and 557,557 shares in the Skelly Oil Company, to the Mission Corporation – a new holding company organised in Reno, Nevada. Jersey Standard's intention was to distribute shares in Mission Corporation as a dividend to its own stockholders.

The setting up of the Mission Corporation was a manoeuvre expressly designed to fend off any attempt by Getty to win control of Tide Water, now vested in the block of shares held by the Mission Corporation. Lest there by any doubt where Jersey Standard stood in the dispute between the 'Getty interests' and the incumbent Tide Water management, 'Big Bill' Humphrey, president of Tide Water, was appointed president of the Mission Corporation and two senior Tide Water executives occupied two of the remaining four seats on the board. Notably absent was anyone representing or supporting J. Paul Getty.

'This was,' said Paul, 'in effect a declaration of open hostilities between Tide Water and Jersey Standard on the one side and the Getty group on the other.'

Jersey Standard's strategy backfired from the start. Mission Corporation, originally set up to stop Paul Getty acquiring Tide Water, actually providing the means for him to achieve his objective. At existing market prices it would have cost him another eleven or twelve million dollars to buy control of Tide Water, well beyond the borrowing power of the Getty interests, which were severely stretched by three years of aggressive stock acquisition. But the Mission Corporation, a much smaller company, was another proposition altogether. And whoever controlled Mission in effect controlled Tide Water.

Unluckily for Jersey Standard John D. Rockefeller Junior, the sixty-year-old son of the founder of Standard Oil, was reviewing his investment portfolio when the Mission deal was announced. As he had no particular wish to receive Mission stock as a dividend on his Jersey Standard shares, he instructed his attorney to sell the rights to his allocation. It was Jersey Standard's further misfortune that Rockefeller's attorney also acted for Paul Getty, recognised he would be a

111

potential buyer and took the trouble to track him down to San Simeon.

Paul bought $1,802,135 worth of Mission Corporation stock from Rockefeller. A few days later, Rockefeller arrived back in New York to find that the chairman and president of Jersey Standard were anxious to see him. They explained that there was likely to be a proxy fight over Tide Water and they asked him not to sell his Mission Corporation share rights under any circumstances.

'It's too late,' Rockefeller replied. 'They've already been sold.'

'Sold? To whom, Mr Rockefeller?'

'Someone out in California.'

'His name isn't Getty, by any chance?'

'Yes. As a matter of fact I believe it is.'

The Rockefeller deal was not Paul's only stroke of luck. By another miracle of timing, on the same day that Jersey Standard set up the Mission Corporation, the Sarah C. Getty Trust was signed in Los Angeles: his mother relinquished power just in time to enable Paul to marshal all the Getty finances behind his campaign. Without the support of the old lady none of the other Getty directors could stand up to her dynamic son, so that Paul was free to buy stock whenever and wherever he wanted – so long as his credit held out.

His next move was to mop up some of the smaller Standard stock-holders by the simple method of spreading the word, via Jay Hopkins, that 'Mr Rockefeller deemed it wise' to sell. The result was predictable. If Mr Rockefeller thought it wise to sell, dozens of small investors also thought it was wise to sell.

Word that Getty was purchasing Mission stock soon leaked out. It did not take a great financial brain to work out what Paul was up to, causing alarm bells to ring in the New York offices of the Tide Water Associated Oil Company. Humphrey and the other directors, bolstered by the support and encouragement of Standard Oil, were determined not to relinquish control to young Getty, and new measures were drawn up in secret to frustrate his obvious intentions.

At a directors' meeting in March 1935 Paul was surprised to find a resolution on the agenda proposing that four of the company's directors should be elected for three-year terms instead of annually as usual – the alleged aim being to provide continuity of management. Paul argued strongly against the proposal, pointing out that it was contrary to accepted practice throughout the oil industry and inimical to the best interests of the stockholders. In private, his primary concern was being philanthropist. His first concern was for himself as pros-pective owner saddled, when he eventually won control, with a board of directors entrenched for three years.

After much heated discussion the board reluctantly agreed to submit the issue to the stockholders, inviting their votes by proxy. The exercise would teach Paul a great deal about the way big corporations waged a proxy fight. He naively imagined both sides of the argument would be fairly explained to the stockholders, so that they would be able to make up their own minds. Instead, he discovered the tawdry reality of boardroom politics.

The management's first tactic was to move fast – so fast, in fact, that Paul barely knew what was going on. While he was casually beginning to solicit support from some of the bigger stockholders, his fellow directors were finalising plans to run rings round him. On 3 April 1935 all Tide Water stockholders received a letter from the management asking them to sign and return a proxy form enclosed in the same envelope agreeing to the directors being elected for three-year terms. To Paul's astonishment, no mention was made in the letter of his opposing arguments. During the following weeks secretaries and clerks employed by Tide Water telephoned individual stockholders, urging them to sign the proxy and mail it back to the Tide Water headquarters.

Against such resources Paul was powerless, yet when the proxies were finally counted, the board had still not received the majority required to approve their motion. Paul was jubilant, until Bill Humphrey announced that as president of the Mission Corporation he would be casting Mission's 1,128,123 votes in favour of the proposal, thus achieving a majority. The 'Getty interests' were beaten, and Paul knew it. Four directors, Humphrey included, were elected for three-year terms. Paul was among those re-elected for one year; he was told he would have an opportunity of standing for three years in 1936 (by which time the Tide Water board would have other plans for him).

Throughout 1935 Paul continued to buy stock, concentrating on Mission Corporation and ingeniously juggling his finances to raise further credit. He had an astonishing ability to carry facts and figures in his head, which was just as well because his responsibilities were now formidable. To all intents and purposes he was running three important oil companies – George F. Getty Inc., Getty Oil Inc. and Pacific Western – along with nine or ten smaller companies in Oklahoma, California and New Mexico. He was sole trustee of the Sarah C. Getty Trust and he was deeply committed, financially and emotionally, to the Tide Water gamble. He was also, in 1935, entangled in a messy and acrimonious divorce.

Ann Rork had filed for a divorce from Paul in 1934, alleging 'extreme cruelty'. The hearing opened in Los Angeles in May 1935 and quickly attracted the attention of the newspapers. 'Teenage starlet tells of bizarre marriage to oil millionaire' – it had all the ingredients of a good, long-running story. Miss Rork certainly pulled no punches. Mr Getty, she said, became 'interested' in her when she was fifteen and they went through a 'form of marriage' in a rented apartment in New York before he was divorced from his third wife.

In court, Ann painted an extraordinary picture of life with Getty. She complained of being 'forced' to live in a 'dismal apartment' in Paris; her husband refused to take her out because she was pregnant and her 'only companion' was a little Scotch terrier called Sophie. When she was allowed to accompany him on a trip round Europe he made her hike, pregnant, to the inner crater of Mount Vesuvius and when she dared to complain, he snapped at her 'My God, you'd think you were the first woman ever to have a baby.'

Back in Los Angeles, she said, she was 'forced' to pay two hundred dollars out of her six-hundred-dollar monthly allowance for the rent of another 'dismal' apartment. He would not let her employ a nurse after the birth of their first child and refused to allow her a new wardrobe, calling her a 'gold-digger'. When she went out anyway and spent $750 on dresses, he cut off her charge account. One Christmas, Ann alleged, his only present to her was a carnation he pulled from his buttonhole. He was frequently absent from home, she said, philandering with other women. There were also hints of other marriages not revealed and bigamy charges – the headline writers had a field day.

At the start of the hearing, Ann's lawyers were demanding a division of community property which they estimated was worth in excess of twenty million dollars, but in September a settlement was agreed. Ann accepted $2500 a month for herself and $1000 for each of her sons. It was 'just too beautiful' she told reporters. In the light of Ann's settlement, Paul voluntarily increased the monthly payments he was making to Jeanette and Fini.

Paul was philosophical about his fourth divorce, blaming the lawyers rather than Ann for the public muckraking. 'United States divorce proceedings do not pay much attention to the truth,' he said. 'The man is supposed to take the blame. He either has too much money or too little. He either comes home to dinner or he doesn't. Either way, he is guilty of cruelty.'

During the divorce proceedings, Paul was living with his mother in the family home at South Kingsley Drive, Los Angeles, an arrangement he found convenient and comfortable. Ann had moved out of the beach house at Santa Monica, but Paul had no desire to live there alone, much preferring the company of his adored 'Mama'. He visited the beach house occasionally with girlfriends, but otherwise left it unoccupied.

Despite his wealth, he had shown very little interest in acquiring property or setting himself up in quarters reflecting his millionaire status. He liked being at home with his mother and when he travelled he was perfectly happy staying in modest hotels. But during 1935 the affairs of Tide Water were requiring him to spend more and more of his time on the East Coast and he decided to find a place of his own in New York. He opted for uncharacteristic hedonism and extravagance – a sumptuous penthouse apartment at 1 Sutton Place on the east side of Manhattan, furnished with the finest eighteenth-century French and English antiques and offered for rent by a Mrs Frederick Guest, a well-known socialite and antique collector. Paul was unaccustomed to such luxury, but not ashamed to enjoy it. 'The living-room is so big,' he told his mother on the telephone, 'that when I lent the place to a friend for a dance, he put a twelve-piece orchestra at one end of the room and you could not hear it at the other.' Old Mrs Getty managed a rare smile at her son's joke. Later, Paul would date his interest in eighteenth-century furniture from his time spent in the congenial surroundings of Mrs Guest's penthouse.

Not long after taking up residence at Sutton Place in November, he invited Betsy Beaton – an actress appearing in a play on Broadway – to drop by for tea. Betsy was an old friend from Los Angeles and she turned up one afternoon at the penthouse with a girlfriend in tow – a singer by the name of Louise Dudley Lynch. 'When I saw Louise,' Paul recorded, notwithstanding his previous abortive attempts to find THE girl, 'my first thought was this is THE girl.'

Louise was tall, auburn-haired, twenty-two years old and one of the first of the 'Society Chanteuses' – self-possessed young ladies from the social register who could be found singing in smart Manhattan supper clubs in the thirties. Brought up in Connecticut, educated at a convent in Paris and 'introduced into society' in 1932, she was the niece of Bernard Baruch, the multi-millionaire financier. Well-connected, beautiful and talented, she was irresistible to a notorious ladies' man, recently divorced. Paul took to spending his evenings at the Stork Club where Louise was singing nightly under the name of 'Teddy' Lynch. He would send flowers and champagne to her dressing-room and then sit alone at a corner table, never taking his eyes off her, while she ran through her popular repertoire, from 'Begin the Beguine' to 'Just One of Those Things'.

Naturally he tried not to allow his infatuation with Teddy to intrude on his business affairs, particularly the Tide Water campaign. By the close of 1935 the Getty interests had acquired 474,154 of the Mission Corporation's 1,399,000 shares and increased their Tide Water holding to a total of 836,254 shares. Acrimony between Paul and the other Tide Water directors had also sharply increased, as the controlling group led by 'Big Bill' Humphrey became more and more worried that the Mission Corporation was slipping, inexorably, from its grasp.

Newspapers had already latched on to the developing boardroom drama and Tide Water directors, with an eye to wooing the stockholders, did their best to blacken Paul's name, assiduously presenting him as a 'threat' to the stability of the company, an outsider disrupting the management and attempting to usurp the 'loyal' board to satisfy his own rampant ambitions. Paul, inexperienced in public relations and manipulation of the media, found himself powerless to counter stories portraying him as a ruthless opportunist.

Humphrey expected Getty to make an attempt to oust the board at the first meeting of Mission Corporation stockholders, due to be held in Reno on the second Monday in January 1936. In the preceding weeks Tide Water mobilised considerable resources to lobby proxy support and was slightly taken aback, when the proxies came to be counted, to discover that the incumbent management had carried the day by a substantial margin.

Paul realised, too late, that he had made a big mistake by not canvassing for proxies on his own behalf. Faintly distracted by Teddy, he had not sufficiently appreciated that proxy support to bolster his own shares could have tipped the balance in his favour and given him control of Mission. He had also been discouraged by the fact that many of the stockholders from whom he had bought Mission shares had refused to revoke their proxies and insisted on reserving the right to vote their stock in favour of Humphrey. (Paul considered it to be both unfair and unprecedented, but he wanted the stock.)

Unknown to Paul, Humphrey and his cohorts had made secret contingency plans to retain control of Tide Water for some years to come, even if Getty got control of Mission in 1937. Before the meeting, and with no official notification, they altered the bye-laws of the corporation, changing the date of the annual meeting from the second Monday in January to the second Thursday in May – a week after Tide Water's annual meeting of stockholders, which was held on the first Thursday in May. Thus Humphrey was assured of Mission support at Tide Water's next annual meeting and with three-year directorships firmly established, the board could stay in place for some years.

Paul did not uncover this subtle alteration in Mission's bye-laws until April, by which time he was engrossed in a head-on battle with the Tide Water board. In mid-April, three weeks before the annual meeting of Tide Water stockholders, the Getty interests mailed a letter, putting forward proposals to dilute the power exercised by the controlling group of directors and asking for proxy support.

A week later, stockholders received another letter headed 'Important Letter from ten of the twelve Directors of Your Company. Do Not Lay Aside. Please Act on It at Once.' It began in uncompromising terms:

You received an undated letter early this week, signed by J. Paul Getty and H. Paul Grimm, soliciting your proxies for the annual meeting to be held on 7 May 1936. This letter had the name of your Company at the top and was signed by Messrs Getty and Grimm as directors. It is possible that it may have been considered an official communication of your Company. It was not. If through error or misunderstanding you have signed the form of proxy sent to you by Messrs Getty and Grimm, and after reading this letter you desire to be represented by the Proxy Committee appointed by the Board of Directors, please date, sign and mail the enclosed proxy, which will automatically revoke any former proxy ...

The letter went on to dismiss all Paul's proposals as unnecessary, strongly hinting that his purpose was to 'advance his own interests' and take over the company: 'It is vitally important that stockholders understand the significance of Mr Getty's proposals and take prompt and decisive action, in order that these continuing threats to the efficiency and stability of the operations of your Company may be completely removed.'

Four days later Paul dispatched another letter to the stockholders, enclosing yet another proxy, appealing to them to stand up for their rights. 'This is your Company,' he began. 'The directors and officers are your servants. You have the right to dictate to them, not they to you ...'

He was, as he knew all along, probably wasting his time. Tide Water had put enormous resources into the proxy campaign, dividing the United States into districts and appointing a 'captain' for each district to supervise the canvassing. All the captains were secretly issued with detailed written instructions and orders to destroy the incriminating paperwork after they had digested the information. Such was their efficiency, Paul heard, that it was not unusual for a district captain to make a personal visit to the home of a stockholder with only one share in order to obtain another proxy. 'If the management of Tide Water was as efficient conducting the oil business as they were in conducting a proxy campaign,' Paul grunted, 'they would soon leave their competitors far behind.'

On 7 May the annual stockholders meeting of the Tide Water Associated Oil Company in New York had to be adjourned for several hours while the proxies were counted at the company's downtown office at 17 Battery Place. The result, predictably, was an overwhelming vote of confidence for the Humphrey management – 4,100,000 votes, compared to only 952,000 for the Getty interests. Paul's rout was compounded by being thrown off the Tide Water board. Due for re-election for a three-year term, he was defeated by a five-to-one majority. Before the meeting broke up, he was unable to resist acidly pointing out to those present that the controlling group on the board, which had sought so successfully to perpetuate its power, owned only 8.5% of the stock. Next day the *New York Times* reported the meeting under the headline 'TIDE WATER FIGHT IS LOST BY GETTY'.

But Paul had no intention of losing the Tide Water fight and was soon supervising a complicated inter-dealing transaction between the Getty companies in order to be able to purchase more stock in both Mission and Tide Water. He was particularly bitter that Humphrey had been able to cast Mission votes against him at the Tide Water stockholders meeting, regardless of the fact that he (Getty) owned about 44.5% of the Mission stock, and he was determined not to let it happen again.

For his part, Humphrey recognised that the ejection of Getty from the Tide Water board did not make him any less dangerous an adversary. As it now appeared that nothing could stop him from eventually winning control of Mission, the Tide Water management embarked on a financial restructuring of the company aimed at greatly increasing the number of shares, thus diluting the voting power both of the Mission block and Getty's Tide Water holdings. By 1 January 1937 more than 1,100,000 voting shares had been added to the capital of Tide Water Associated, reducing Mission's stake in the company from about 20% to only 16.5%. This was further reduced to 13% by exercising a Jersey Standard-inspired option to buy 250,000 Tide Water shares from Mission.

Despite this manoeuvring, Mission remained Tide Water's biggest stockholder and, as such, the single most important element in the battle for control of the company. With their backs firmly to the wall, Tide Water directors played their last card. On Thursday 15 March it was announced that a special meeting of Mission directors would be held at 9.30 a.m. on Monday 19 March in Reno, Nevada, to write up the assets of the company prior to distributing its Tide Water holding to Mission stockholders. Such a distribution would sever the link between the two companies, destroying Getty's hopes of using Mission as a stepping stone to Tide Water.

Paul, in New York, did not learn about the meeting until Thursday evening. He could scarcely believe that his opponents would dare to try such a trick: their motives were so patently obvious and so blatantly born out of self-interest. There was only one conceivable reason to break up Mission's block of Tide Water shares – the now imminent danger that control of Mission would pass out of the hands of Tide Water directors. Paul picked up the telephone in his Sutton Place penthouse and dialled Dave Hecht, a bright young attorney who had been appointed New York counsel for the Getty interests less than a year earlier. Paul rapidly briefed him on this latest development and ordered him to use whatever legal options were available to delay the 'surprise' meeting in Reno and prevent the Mission board proceeding with their outrageous plans until the stockholders could be consulted. Time was not on their side: the meeting was due to be held in only three days, which included the weekend.

Hecht worked all through the night studying company papers and legal documents. Early Friday morning he was joined by Harold Rowland, a senior Getty executive, and together they spent the day collating all the facts and figures they would need, constantly conferring with Paul at Sutton Place and with other Getty executives on the West Coast. By late afternoon they had prepared a case for a restraining order to be served on the Mission directors and at dusk, with the weather closing in, they were driven out to the airport to catch the last aeroplane leaving New York City for Reno. It was Hecht's first flight and an extremely unpleasant baptism – squalls and blizzards forced the plane to make several unscheduled stops along the way.

Paul anxiously followed their progress via telegrams dispatched by Hecht from each halt. 'GROUNDED CHICAGO. HOPE TO TAKE OFF AGAIN IN A FEW HOURS.' 'WEATHER FORCED US TO LAND IN ST LOUIS.' He began to fret that they would not even arrive in time for the meeting, let alone in time to apply for a court order.

Sleepless, unshaven and exhausted, Hecht and Rowland finally arrived in Reno on Saturday evening, exactly twenty-four hours after leaving New York. A local law firm, Hawkins, Mayotte & Hawkins, had been hired to help prepare the necessary papers and was standing by. While Hecht and Rowland took it in turns to catnap, the entire team worked straight through the night and into Sunday.

On Sunday afternoon Hecht began to try and find a judge willing to hear an application for a restraining order out of court, since the Mission meeting was due to start next morning before the courts were in session. But Mission directors had foreseen that Getty would try to stall their plans by legal action and had contacted every judge they could find in the area, requesting that no restraining order be issued without prior notification to Mission's counsel. With the help of local attorneys, Hecht eventually tracked down a state judge with a reputation for impartiality. When Hecht arrived at the judge's house, a maid said he was out at a party. Hecht said he would wait. Shortly before midnight, the judge returned home to find an extremely tired and dishevelled New York attorney camped on his doorstep. After listening to what he had to say, the judge agreed to meet Hecht in his chambers at eight-thirty the following morning.

Hecht returned to his hotel, put through a long-distance call to New York to apprise Getty of the day's events and crawled thankfully into bed after instructing the front desk to send *two* bellboys up to his room to wake him at six-thirty.

At nine twenty-three on the morning of Monday 19 March, seven minutes before the directors of the Mission Corporation were due to meet, the judge signed a restraining order forbidding the meeting to take place until a court hearing later in the week.

Having won valuable breathing space, Hecht immediately set about preparing a detailed submission to prove that the Mission directors were proposing a course of action which was not in the best interests of the shareholders and was harmful to the future prosperity of the company. Expert witnesses – economists and local university professors – were briefed to give evidence on behalf of the Getty interests, subpoenas were served requiring Mission to produce company records in court and Harold Rowland shuttled backwards and forwards between Reno, Los Angeles and New York, gathering evidence. Meanwhile, attorneys acting for the Mission Corporation were similarly occupied putting together a case to justify the board's action.

Hecht did not finish work until after midnight on the eve of the trial and he decided to drop by at a local bar for a drink before turning in. To his surprise, he found the New York attorney representing Mission already standing at the bar. They knew each other vaguely and although in court the following day they would be implacable opponents, they had a friendly drink together and a guarded chat about the case. The Mission attorney seemed somewhat worried by Hecht's confidence and his assertion that the Mission directors would 'never get away with it'. Getty, Hecht said, was prepared to subpoena all the directors to keep them in Reno until after the annual stockholders' meeting. The only way for Mission to 'save face', he added, was to put the issue before the stockholders and let them decide.

Next morning, before the case opened in court, the Mission attorneys offered a compromise settlement. Mission directors were prepared to put the matter to the stockholders, provided both sides would abide by a 'gentlemen's agreement' to avoid an acrimonious proxy fight. It was agreed that each side would be allowed to state its views in a simple, 'dignified' letter accompanying a proxy form. Both letters would be enclosed in the same envelope and mailed to all Mission stockholders with the relevant proxy for them to sign and return.

Hecht packed his bags and returned to New York, satisfied that the Getty interests had been protected – Paul Getty had made it clear from the start that he was content to let the stockholders decide the issue. The letters were written and dispatched, as per the 'gentlemen's agreement' and Paul settled back to wait for the outcome. It soon transpired that not all the parties to the 'gentlemen's agreement' were gentlemen.

A week before the last day on which proxies could be filed Edward

L. Shea, who had recently taken over from Bill Humphrey as president of the Mission Corporation, secretly dispatched another letter to Mission shareholders attacking the motives of the Getty group and complaining about the 'many misleading statements and inferences' in the letter from the group that the board had 'permitted' to be enclosed with its own recent proxy form.

The first Paul knew of this was when an associate, purple with rage, burst into his study and thrust a piece of paper into his hand. 'Read this!' he said. Paul read the letter with mounting anger. 'It is like a story,' he muttered, 'from the days of Drew and Gould.' (Daniel Drew and Jay Gould were notorious nineteenth-century 'robber barons'.) Hecht was hurriedly summoned and a meeting was arranged for the following day to include all the parties to the 'gentlemen's agreement'. It was held in an atmosphere pregnant with rancour and unconcealed bitterness. Charge and counter-charge were flung across the table and at the end the Getty group announced that it considered the 'gentlemen's agreement' was terminated and the 'lid was off'.

That night Paul, Hecht and a handful of Getty executives drafted another letter answering Shea's charges. It began:

You have recently received a letter from Mr Shea supplementing his original report to you and accusing us of misleading statements and inferences. We ask you to take particular note that Mr Shea does not support this serious charge with proof of any specific instance where we have made a misleading statement or inference. We stand by every statement in our first letter without reservation. Rather, it is his argument which would tend to confusion and misunderstanding ...

The letter went on to discuss motives 'since the subject has been raised by Mr Shea'. Why were the directors suddenly intent on distributing the Tide Water shares held by Mission? The crux of the matter was simple and simply stated:

While in control of Mission Corporation, Mr Shea and his associates have voted the Mission holdings of Tide Water Associated in favour of continuing themselves in office in that company. He and his associates now face loss of control of Mission Corporation and consequently of the opportunity to vote the block of Tide Water Associated stock in their favour.

All available Getty personnel – secretaries, clerks, typists and executives – were asked to work through the night to duplicate the letter and address envelopes so as to get the letter out to stockholders before the deadline for filing proxies expired. They made it with no more than a couple of days to spare.

The annual meeting of Mission Corporation stockholders was held in Reno on 13 May 1937. When the proxies had been counted, Mr Shea glumly announced that 310,314 votes had been cast in favour of the board's proposal to distribute the Tide Water shares and 802,478 votes opposed the proposal.

Getty had won an overwhelming victory and, with it, control of Mission Corporation. At the end of the day, Getty nominees sat in six of the seven seats on the Mission board. They included Jay Hopkins, Dave Hecht and Harold Rowland.

From that moment, it was only a matter of time before Getty achieved his ambition of taking over Tide Water, laying the foundations for the creation of a veritable business empire. As the *New York Times* reported from Reno: 'The two-year fight of J. Paul Getty for a dominant position in the Tide Water Associated Oil Company appeared successful today . . .'

Later in life, Paul would describe the Tide Water campaign as 'the major triumph' of his business career.

At first glance, it might seem as though the campaign involved nothing more than going into the market and buying the company's stock. It was nowhere near as simple or easy as that.

There were millions of Tide Water common shares outstanding. Only a relatively small percentage of these were ever on the market at any given time. Great blocks were held by individuals and interests desiring to maintain control over the company. Many other shares were owned by people who just did not want to sell for any number of reasons. Others who might have sold hoped the contest for control would run up the price of the stock, and they determined to hold on to their shares and see what happened.

Consequently our campaign had to be conducted on several fronts simultaneously. First, we had to buy as much stock as we could when it became available on the market – subject, of course, to the availability of funds for that purpose. Then, it was necessary to obtain voting proxies from stockholders who did not wish to sell their shares. Naturally, these stockholders had to be shown that it was to their advantage to give the Getty interests their proxies. They had to be convinced that control by the Getty group of independent stockholders would benefit the company, increase the value of their stocks and mean larger dividends for them in the future.

There were countless ramifications and complications at every step of the way. New problems and obstacles seemed to present themselves constantly as the campaign progressed. My associates and I worked tirelessly, and round the clock, during many critical stages in the contest. All-day meetings followed by all-night conferences again followed by all-day meetings were not unusual. I shall always be grateful to my associates who, bone-weary and hollow-eyed as they frequently were, none the less always somehow managed to find the strength and energy to do just a little bit more, a little bit extra.

In so far as I am personally concerned, I think the principal qualities which made it possible for me to achieve my goal were determination, persistence – and mulish stubbornness.

8. *'Teddy phoned. Miss her so much'*

On 16 August 1936, at the height of the Tide Water takeover shenanigans, the *New York Times* carried the following brief item of social news:

> Mrs L. Ware Lynch, of Lyncroft, Belle Haven, Greenwich, Connecticut, announces the engagement of her daughter, Louise Dudley Lynch, to Mr J. Paul Getty. Miss Lynch attended the Greenwich Academy and Marymont Convent in Paris. She was introduced into society in 1932 at Greenwich and has been singing professionally under the name of Teddy Lynch.

With four disastrous marriages behind him and the dust barely settled from the last rancorous divorce, it might have been thought that Paul Getty, at the age of forty-three, would be leery of undertaking so soon another stab at matrimonial bliss. But he was as unconventional and adventurous in his private life as he was in business and having fallen for the beautiful Teddy, he did not hesitate for a moment to propose marriage. Teddy was a headstrong, temperamental young woman. She did not concern herself in the least with Paul's lamentable record as a husband or his reputation as a philanderer and hastened to accept. Thus was contracted the longest of Paul Getty's five marriages and perhaps the most unusual.

As a 'society chanteuse' Teddy was a popular attraction on the supper-club circuit, but her real ambition was to be an opera singer – she had adopted the stage name of Theodora after a friend told her that Louise was not distinguished enough for opera. Night after night, while she was warbling 'Pennies from Heaven' and 'It's De-lovely' for the benefit of the smart set at the Waldorf-Astoria or the Stork Club, she would be longing for the glory and drama of grand opera. But while she had a voice with a remarkable range, from contralto to coloratura soprano, and claimed to have received encouragement from the great diva Amelita Galli-Curci, Teddy's was not an outstanding talent. She had herself photographed dolled-up as an opera star, wearing an extravagant low-cut ball gown and peering haughtily at the camera from behind a spread fan, but it was the closest she would ever come to operatic stardom.

Paul thought Teddy was a wonderful singer and offered to finance her operatic lessons. This lovelorn gesture was cloaked as a business arrangement – she had to agree to pay him ten per cent of her future earnings – but he did not honestly expect to get any money back. In the first flush of rapture, he was happy to pander to Teddy's every whim: when she expressed a desire to learn by watching the great stars perform, he booked two seats for every Friday night of the season at the 'Met' – the Metropolitan Opera House in New York. Afterwards they could be found tête-à-tête at the ritzy Diamond Horseshoe, where Loge No. 4 was reserved every Friday night in the name of Getty.

That he was able to conduct a passionate affair in tandem with his enormously complex business activities was testimony to his remarkable talents and his individual, not to say eccentric, business style. Paul had a horror of bureaucracy and ran his burgeoning empire virtually single-handed and almost entirely by telephone. Whether he was at the penthouse in New York or staying with his mother at South Kingsley Drive or travelling in Europe, his daily routine hardly varied. He would rise late, glance through the newspapers, read his mail and then get on the telephone, sometimes talking for hours at a stretch to the key executives on whom he relied to carry out his instructions. He believed in delegating and believed implicitly in what his father used to say – 'If you can trust a man, a written contract is a waste of paper. If you can't trust him, a written contract is still a waste of paper.'

Although he maintained a small personal office in Santa Monica, he could rarely be found there. (Yet every day of his life, no matter where he was in the world or what he was doing, he dressed in a sober business suit, as if for a day at the office.) He had no time for offices, for conferences, business lunches or paperwork: he could make decisions in an instant on matters that a board of directors might deliberate over for weeks. Neither did he need a retinue of personal assistants or high-powered secretaries or filing clerks – he kept his files in his head. If he had to reply to a letter, he scrawled a note in the margin, put it in an envelope and posted it himself.

He held strong views about office efficiency: 'One of the serious wrongs in American business is the penchant for wallowing in welters of paperwork and administrative detail. Some companies have literally hundreds of people keeping records on each other and passing inter-office memoranda back and forth. Very often, there appear to be more memo writers and readers than productive workers. The cost of this over-administration is staggering, not only in salaries paid to paper shufflers, but in the general slowdown it has on all operations.'

During 1937 and 1938, after his Mission victory, Paul directed a complicated consolidation of the Getty interests. 'It had long seemed,' he said, 'that there were too many Getty companies, some of them

125

formed by my father, others by me.' The object was to simplify the structure and create in embryo the integrated oil company which was constantly in the forefront of his mind. Eight companies were dissolved and the remaining holdings were amalgamated under the umbrella of George F. Getty Inc., which then had assets valued in excess of thirty-five million dollars. Paul alone controlled George F. Getty Inc., which in turn controlled the Pacific Western Oil Corporation, which in turn controlled the Mission Corporation, which in turn controlled the Skelly Oil Company. (Skelly was an unexpected bonus that came with Mission – Paul did not learn that Mission held fifty-seven per cent of Skelly stock until the latter stages of the proxy fight). The Tide Water Associated Oil Company was not yet fully under the Getty umbrella, but it was only a matter of time before it, too, would be swallowed up.

During this reorganisation Paul decided, with some regret, to wind up the Minnehoma Oil Company which his father had founded more than thirty years earlier in Oklahoma. Minnehoma had been inactive for some time and had no real future, nevertheless Paul was sorry to see it go. 'It had been the pioneer Getty company,' he wrote in a nostalgic postscript, 'on which the Getty oil business and the Getty fortune were founded. It had been as a Minnehoma Oil Company employee that I served my apprenticeship in the Oklahoma oilfields. The very name "Minnehoma" was sufficient to evoke countless associations and memories of my childhood and youth – and above all, memories of my father. Liquidating Minnehoma caused a sharp tug at my heartstrings.'

In the midst of this corporate revamping Paul decided to buy the Hotel Pierre in New York, for no other reason than the simple, alluring fact that it was a bargain. The Pierre – on the corner of 5th Avenue and 61st Street, overlooking Central Park – was not only the most modern hotel in New York, it was *the* hotel in New York in the thirties. As a guide to the city pointed out, the Pierre 'caters to only those of refined tastes who can afford the best in the way of hotel luxury'. Spencer Tracy, Gary Cooper and Constance Bennett always checked into the Pierre when they were in New York and Auguste Escoffier, probably the most famous French chef ever, worked for a time in the Pierre's kitchen.

Built in 1929 on the site of a mansion once owned by Elbridge Gerry, a signatory to the Declaration of Independence, the forty-storey Hotel Pierre cost more than fifteen million dollars and was a majestic neo-Georgian building with Italian marble floors and four hundred rooms furnished with English antiques. It should have been an enormous success, but events conspired against it. Planned in the free-spending, carefree twenties, it opened its doors in October 1930 when the country was on the threshold of the Great Depression. While the Pierre proved instantly popular with hordes of fashionable overnight guests, the expected number of permanent residents – essential to the hotel's profit – simply did not materialise and after only a few years in business the owners were obliged to file for bankruptcy.

In 1938 the Pierre was put up for sale for the astonishingly low figure of $2,500,000, less than a fifth of its assessed value. Paul, who cheerfully admitted he knew nothing about the hotel business, nevertheless decided it was a good moment to diversify and added the Pierre to the Getty interests, having knocked the price down to a trifling $2,350,000. 'So great was the bargain,' he said, 'I never understood why it was not snapped up long before I even heard that it was for sale.' A story was soon circulating in New York that he had gone to the Pierre for lunch and that a waiter was rude to him when he complained about his steak. He had promptly bought the hotel, it was rumoured, in order to fire the waiter! No one who had ever met Paul Getty believed such a fanciful yarn: one look at his lugubrious countenance, his wary hooded eyes and thin, down-turned mouth, was enough to know that he was not a man who acted on impulse – so far as business was concerned, at least.

In the spring of 1938 Teddy sailed for England, with Paul's blessing, to further her operatic ambitions. She was to take singing lessons in London with one of the most respected teachers in the world, Madame Blanche Marchesi, and vowed she would never return until she had attained a perfect high C. Paul kissed her goodbye on the pier in New York and promised to meet her in London when he made his customary trip to Europe later in the year.

Paul had been in the habit of making an annual visit to Europe for many years now, travelling first class across the Atlantic in one of the big liners and spending several months touring the Continent in a rented car, usually an American model if he could find one. Constantly on the move, he was in daily contact with New York and Los Angeles by telephone or telegram, mail was forwarded from hotel to hotel and money was telegraphed to American Express offices for collection as he needed it. In this way he wandered Europe, visiting museums and galleries and generally seeing the sights, usually alone but completely content. He made many friends along the way, particularly ladies, and kept a bulging address book which would normally produce an agreeable female companion in any of the major European cities.

In June 1938 Paul joined Teddy in London, where they enjoyed several happy weeks together. Paul decided that he, too, would take singing lessons with Madame Marchesi to keep Teddy company and in the evenings they did the rounds of the theatres and nightspots. More orthodox engaged couples might have chosen to spend as much time together as possible, but Paul did not want to stay in one place for the duration of the trip and Teddy did not want to break from her singing lessons. As each was as strong-willed as the other, they parted again in

July, quite amicably. Paul set off for Paris, keeping a meticulous record, as always, of his journey and providing some insight into his complex character as well as tracing his erratic path across Europe.

Saturday 27 August 1938: 'Left Paris 7.30 p.m. Dined at the Grand-Veneur on the Paris side of Fontainebleau – forty francs, table d'hôte. No rooms in Fontainebleau. Drove on to Sens, arriving at about 11.00 p.m. Room at the very good Ecu d'Or – thirty-five francs. Bal de Fleurs at the nearby Hôtel de Ville – noisy till all hours.'

Sunday, 28 August: 'Saw Sens Cathedral. Climbed to the top and enjoyed the beautiful view. The country here is lovely – winding river, green meadows and scattered woods. Good lunch at the Ecu for thirty-five francs. Filled gasoline tank with fifty-five litres. Put air in tires, 1.7 all round. Left Sens at 3.40 p.m. Drove leisurely the few miles to the charming little town of Villeneuve-sur-Yonne. A gay and colorful water carnival drew most of the inhabitants from their usual activities. My 1937 Lincoln Zephyr runs like a charm. On past Auxerre and its magnificent Cathedral to Avallon. Went to the Hôtel de la Poste, secured rooms for forty-five francs. Fête till all hours; very noisy!'

Monday 29 August: 'The Hôtel de la Poste is very good as well as ancient. Napoleon stopped here in 1815. Left Avallon after an excellent lunch and drove to Vezolay, a side trip of ten miles. The location of the town with its historic Abbey is superb – on a hill, dominating everything. The church, restored by Viollet-le-Duc in 1840-60, is pre-Gothic, very pleasing and grand. Returned to Avallon through picturesque country during a thunderstorm. Drove from Avallon to Dijon. Spent fifteen minutes in the famous Hôtel de la Cloche. Sorry I was too early to stop for dinner and the night, for I remember the wonderful cuisine from 1932. Like Dijon very much. Left Dijon for Auxonne and Dole. Pleasant country with a suggestion of the nearby Alps. Arrived at the Grand Hôtel about 7.00 p.m. Had a very good dinner and afterwards a walk through the picturesque eighteenth-century streets of Dôle. Drove 116 miles in all.'

Tuesday 30 August: 'Left Dôle for Pontarlier. Weather rainy, and in the mountains a perfect cloudburst. Put in fifty-five litres of gasoline. Car used fifty-five litres in four hundred kilometers, an average of about seventeen miles a gallon. Arrived at Pontarlier for lunch about 12.30 p.m. Indifferent lunch. Then to the Swiss frontier in a perfect deluge. No examination of luggage. Everybody very courteous. Coming downhill the weather improved. Reached Lausanne about 4.00 p.m. Went directly to the Lausanne Palace – my first visit here since 1932. Lausanne is beautiful but the weather is miserable. Am worried about the possibility of war. Had my watch cleaned for 4.50 francs. Read until 2.30 a.m.'

Wednesday 31 August: 'Up at 10.00 to find it is still raining. Sorted correspondence until lunch time. Paid hotel bill – sixteen francs for room and eighty-odd francs for telephone and dinner last night. Left Lausanne at 4.00 p.m. for Geneva in miserable, dull, threatening weather. Sixty kilometers of grand scenery along one of the most beautiful lakes. Stopped at Hôtel des Bergues – twenty-five francs for bedroom and sitting-room with bath. Bought sixty francs worth of Baedeker guides. Resolved: To eat fruit every day but not with other food. Also to sit straighter.'

Thursday 1 September: 'Went to the Casino last night. It was free night. Very decent appearing crowd of townsfolk. A few danseuses, including a negress. Good music! Thursday morning I took a sunbath and after lunch received mail from the Lotti in Paris. First mail since Paris. Got my car from the garage. It now has automatic signals – sixty-two francs. Arrived at the Majestic Hotel at Chamonix about 8.45 p.m., after driving fifty-two miles. This is my first visit since 1931. Everything is just the same. After dinner I took a walk in the village. Bought an Alpinisme magazine and a few views. Then had a beer at "Out A" – twelve francs. Good music! Only a few people there, but there was plenty of life outside in the streets. Many people wore hiking or mountain-climbing clothes. The girls looked cute.'

Friday 2 September: 'Awakened late. A heavenly day. Sun shining in a cloudless sky. I took a sunbath in my room and admired the view until lunch time. The view from Chamonix valley is almost unrivalled. The great glaciers and the unique needles, Dru, Grands-Charmoz, Grepon, Blaitiere and Midi, are but two to four miles away. The needles are fantastic and unbelievably steep. I have never seen their equal. Everything is terrifyingly grand! Mont Blanc itself is all that a monarch should be. Spent the afternoon walking around and admiring nature in her grandest mood. Evening cold. Had dinner at the hotel. Drank too much Asti Spumante and to crown it, ate a lot of chocolate. Read Alpinisme late – then couldn't sleep because of indigestion. Finally to sleep about 4.00.'

Paul's diary entries consistently reflected two prominent traits in his personality: a passionate concern for value for money (always noting the price of hotel rooms and meals) and a neurotic obsession with his health (scrupulously documenting frequent bouts of indigestion, their cause and effect). Paul was a hopeless hypochondriac. Perhaps because he had never been really ill, he thoroughly enjoyed imagined poor health, escalating minor ailments into life-and-death crises. If he had a headache, he immediately assumed it was a brain tumour; every gripe in his stomach was always appendicitis. He allowed no twinge to go untreated, always sought second opinions, patronised every kind of quack and healer, and lugged a box of dubious patent medicines around with him wherever he went.

Convinced that diet was one of the secrets of good health, he periodically abandoned a normal diet in favour of a cranky regimen of his own design – he would fast for twenty-four hours, then eat nothing but bran and fruit interspersed with liberal doses of vitamin pills for the next twenty-four hours. Like so many of his countrymen, the workings of his bowels was a matter of absorbing interest to him. When he was only eleven years old, he wrote in his diary: 'Awful pain in the bowels. Bed. No solid food.' It marked the beginning of a lifelong fascination with his intestines and their wellbeing.

The parsimony which was such a constant feature of his diary was based upon the simplest creed: he could not understand why, just because he was rich, he should be expected to pay more for everyday services than someone who was poor. He hated to pay over the odds for anything, whether it was a meal or an oil well, abhorred ostentation and never threw his money around. If he was required to tip a waiter or a porter, he never offered more than the accepted percentage and was truly mystified when people accused him, later in life, of being a skinflint.

When Paul was not logging prices or details of his indigestion as he journeyed around the European fleshpots, he made copious lists of what he had seen and admired in museums, along with an occasional note of having bought something for his art collection. Strange juxtapositions resulted: one day he would mention that lunch had cost him five francs, the next he would note that a picture had cost him twenty thousand dollars. It rather appeared as if he was undecided which was the more significant event.

Paul had been interested in art ever since he was a young man. He read voraciously on the subject and enjoyed visiting museums and galleries, but even though he was a millionaire at the age of twenty-three, he didn't seriously consider becoming a collector himself until much later as he thought twenties' prices were ludicrously inflated. 'In the late twenties it appeared to me the days of collecting were just about over,' he said. 'Men who had made their millions before I'd started in business – or even before I was born – swept up just about everything worthwhile that found its way on to the market. The old aristocratic British and European families who still possessed treasure troves of fine art were, for the most part, still very well situated financially. And even if they were not and decided to sell an item or two, they had been conditioned to the idea of entertaining only the most staggering offers for their possessions.'

But then came the Wall Street crash. The events of 1929 shook the art world quite as much as the financial world and the bottom dropped out of the art market. Prompted by the same rationale that persuaded him the time was right to buy shares, Paul began buying pictures and antiques. 'Choice items suddenly became available,' he said, 'as many of the strong hands that formerly held some of the finest examples of art on the face of the earth were forced to relax their grip. Prices dropped to levels that would have been inconceivable a few years earlier.'

He made his first serious purchases in 1931 at an auction of the Goldschmidt-Rothschild Collection in Berlin, paying less than $1500 for a number of old English prints, a small oil painting by Gajon and an antique rug. Two years later in New York he attended the auction of the Thomas Fortune Ryan Collection at the Anderson Gallery and bought twelve paintings by the Spanish impressionist Joaquin Sorolla y Bastida. Experts expected the pictures would fetch in excess of forty thousand dollars – Getty got them for slightly under ten thousand.

Moving into the penthouse at Sutton Place in New York aroused his enthusiasm for eighteenth-century furniture and tapestries, then Georgian silver, followed by Greek and Roman antiquities. He was eclectic in his taste, buying whatever took his fancy with no particular plan for a cohesive collection. Although he had a natural 'eye' for the genuine article and became more knowledgeable with each purchase, he was always suspicious of being 'taken for a ride' and never bought a work of art without first having it authenticated by an expert, usually employing a stenographer to record the expert's assessment – he found he learned a lot by studying the notes later. But despite his growing reputation as a collector, he remained unsure of himself in this esoteric world. When Sir Alec Martin of Christie's told him a painting he had recently bought for a thousand guineas was not worthy of a place in his collection, he immediately gave it away – to the man who had advised him to buy it. On another occasion, during a sale at Christie's, he nodded agreement to a remark made by a friend sitting next to him and discovered he had bought a frightful landscape for one hundred guineas.

By 1938 Paul had acquired a reputation as a 'serious' collector, one of the diminishing band of millionaires to survive the thirties with sufficient funds to buy important works of art although, if his diary is any guide, it was the cause of no great excitement. On 7 September in Bern he wrote: 'Telephoned Lowengard in Paris and bought Duveen's carpet for fourteen thousand pounds after offering thirteen thousand and being refused. Drove along shore of Lake Lucerne ...'

'Duveen's carpet', so casually and briefly mentioned in his journal, was an exquisite sixteenth-century Ardabil Persian carpet woven on the Royal looms in Tabriz for the mosque of Safi-ad-Din and said

131

by the Persians to be too beautiful 'for Christian eyes to gaze upon'.

One of the finest Oriental carpets in the world, Paul had wanted it from the moment he first saw it at the Persian Art Exhibition in Paris. 'With its magnificent pattern, colours and sheen,' he said, 'it was one of the most beautiful things I had ever seen in my life.' Lord Joseph Duveen, an art dealer who owned the carpet and had loaned it to the exhibition, at first refused to sell, bluntly declaring that 'no one has enough money' to persuade him to part with it. But the ominous turn of events in Europe that summer of 1938 and the fear of war prompted Duveen to change his mind and he let it go. Later King Farouk of Egypt, seeking a suitable wedding present to give his sister on her marriage to the Shah of Iran, offered Paul two hundred and fifty thousand dollars for the Ardabil. He turned it down.

His visit to Europe in 1938 turned out to be a veritable buying spree. Apart from the Ardabil carpet, he bought a collection of French eighteenth-century furniture and a fine Louis XIII Savonnerie carpet at Christie's and then picked up a Gainsborough portrait of Thomas Christie, founder of the firm, for £7500. At a sale at Sotheby's a week later he bought a number of minor paintings for less than £250 – one of them, the 'Madonna of Loreto', listed in the catalogue as 'after Raphael', would later prove to be a genuine Raphael. Paul paid forty pounds for it.

Further purchases were laconically noted in his diary, along with the inevitable price of every hotel room, as he drove from Switzerland into Germany, then south through Holland and Belgium to Paris, then to Vienna and back to Berlin. He covered thousands of miles without ever appearing to be tired and without ever explaining in his diary why he was moving from one place to another. His stamina was certainly remarkable: one particular day he was staying overnight in Antwerp and set off for Brussels in the morning. On the way, he noticed a sign to a seventeenth-century castle and made a detour to take a look at it. He arrived in Brussels in time for lunch at the Palace Hotel, after which he hired a guide to show him round the city. At four o'clock he was back on the road, heading for Paris. He stopped for an hour for dinner and checked into the Hôtel Lotti in Paris at ten-thirty that evening, taking a room without a bath for seventy-five francs. Still disinclined to call it a day, he spruced himself up and went out on the town, first to the Bal Tabarin, 'the best show in Europe' and then to the Melody Bar, 'always fun!' Arriving back at the hotel at three o'clock in the morning, he read until four.

He happened to be in Berlin, staying at the Adlon Hotel, for the two weeks in September while the world held its breath as British prime minister Neville Chamberlain parlayed for peace with Hitler at Berchtesgaden. Paul was completely unconcerned by the 'war scare' and disregarded the friends telephoning him every day warning him to leave Germany.

> Friday 23 September: 'Up at ten-thirty. Lunch at Adlon. Model said "Get out of Berlin." Saw *Melodie der Nacht* – excellent show – ten marks for best seats. The audience was nervous and bought newspapers between acts. Announcer called "Achtung!" Everybody jumped, but he only announced a pause. It looks as if war may come!'
> Saturday 24 September: 'Lunch at Adlon. Draht called, said "Get out of Germany – war is coming!" Beautiful summer weather continues. It is real swimming weather ...'
> Sunday 25 September: 'Up at ten. Draht called, said "Urgent, get out!" His wife and child are leaving tomorrow. Saw the National Galerie, upper floor. There are some very good works by Menzel, Thoma, Marée and Bocklin. The entrance charge is ten pfennigs. Everybody seems apprehensive about war. The Führer is making a speech tomorrow night. Dinner at Eden roof. Gay!'

Paul had no desire to leave since Berlin, with its exuberant nightlife, was one of his favourite cities and he was never short of female companionship:

> 'Met Hansi and Phyllis. To the Femina for a cup of chocolate and cake – 1.80DM. There was an amusing crowd, good music and show. To the Staatsoper at eight for *Margarete* – splendid uncut performance. After the opera, dinner at the Atelier, then a quick visit to the Roxy Bar, which was crowded, then to Ciro's. It was very crowded and gay as usual.'
> 'Had chocolate at Kroll's with Dora. Met Hildegard at the Opera at eight. We saw *Otello*. It was a very good production.'
> 'Saw *Frau Warren's Gewerbe* at Grosses Schauspielhaus. Hansi came at end of the second act. Took Hansi home.'
> 'Saw *Der Opern Ball* at the Theater am Nollendorf Platz. It was a good show; and Dr Goebbels has beautified the theatre. Gretchen enjoyed it.'
> 'Lunch at the Adlon with Gretchen. Met Gretchen again for dinner.'
> 'Met Gertrude for a dance.'
> 'Met Charlotte. She looks well. Saw her new apartment. Later I went to the Scala with Hildegard.'
> 'Teddy phoned. Miss her so much!'
> 'Left Berlin at 6.15 p.m. after saying goodbye to Elisabeth.'

On 30 September Paul was joined by Teddy, who had flown from London to meet him in Amsterdam. They travelled together to Paris, where they visited the Louvre and Versailles and toured the leading art

dealers. Paul bought a magnificent eighteenth-century secretaire for
£1500, then noted in his diary that he had had new rubber heels put
on his shoes for 110 francs. Teddy left after ten days and a few days
later Paul could be found dining with a lady called Lonny. 'We had
dinner at the Tout Paris, then went to the Ambassadeurs. Saw
Georges Carpentier, also Lonny's friend, Lou La Riviere, with a peppy
blonde. He pulled her off the floor when the Lambeth Walk was
played.'

By mid-October Paul was back in Suite 355 at the Adlon Hotel in
Berlin. 'Saw Dr Salomonski', he wrote. 'Since 1 October the poor man
has been unable to continue his practice except for Jews.' From Berlin
he took a brief train excursion to Vienna where he met a lady called
Josephine and saw the Rothschild palace 'blazing with light and full of
police'. Back in Berlin, his friend Charlotte told him that a new law
involving the Jews might mean the Rothschilds would have to sell their
furniture. She promised to keep him posted.

In November Paul decided it was time to return to the United States.
He had a brief reunion with Teddy in London before his departure and
tried, but failed, to persuade her to leave with him.

Saturday 5 November: 'Up at nine. Met Teddy at Mme Marchesi's
at 12.15 p.m. Mme the same as ever. Wonderful character, but she
has plenty of self-appreciation. Teddy sang well. Proud of her.
Lunch at Teddy's. Wonderful food! Everything very neat. She
keeps a New England household. Took the 5.09 boat train. Teddy
with me. Arrived Southampton 7.10 p.m. Teddy left me. Desolate
moment! Tender left at 7.35 p.m. Arrived at the *Normandie* 9.30
p.m. *Normandie* left 10.30 p.m. Ran ten minutes and went
aground. Aground till 2.15 a.m., then succeeded in backing off.
Slight fog.'
Sunday 6 November: 'Cabin 364. Slept well. Exhausted. Awoke
10.00 a.m., 9 a.m. ship's time. Heavy swell, wind, 4 to 5. Good
lunch. Dull, gloomy weather. Read, walked and saw movie –
Three Sisters with Bette Davis, Errol Flynn – good. After dinner, I
tried unsuccessfully to telephone New York.'
Monday 7 November: 'Up at 11.45 a.m. ship's time. Weather
fairly good. Telephoned twice to Teddy. 733 miles in twenty-five
hours. Saw marvellous eclipse of the moon about 9.30 p.m. lasting
about an hour. Walter Footer and Leslie Howard watched it with
me. Beautiful clear night. Ate too many raisins. Upset stomach.
Poor night!'
Tuesday 8 November: 'Up at 9.00. Had tea, toast and steak for
breakfast. Dreary windy day. 741 miles. Light lunch. I certainly
miss Teddy and my own dear mother. Read and saw movies whole
afternoon. Dinner at eight. Read. Foghorn is blowing. We are off
the banks.'

Wednesday 9 November: 'Run at noon, 736 miles. Sea moderate. Wind twenty miles. Not much sun. Walked an hour in afternoon. Saw movies *Mad Miss Manton* with Barbara Stanwyck and Henry Fonda, also *Normandie*'s *Cruise to Rio*. After dinner there was a three-out-of-five table-tennis match between the ship's professional and the world's champion. Latter won, 21-12, 21-10, 21-10. Am reading Irving's *Mountaineering* and a Hashknife story, then Pendexter's *Bird of Freedom*.'

Thursday 10 November: 'Up at 9.30. Beautiful, calm, sunny weather. Picked up pilot at 9.45 in sight of dear old USA. Docked at noon.'

In many ways Getty was an infuriating diarist, since it was his habit to keep a scrupulous record of trivia of all kinds, while glancing over significant events. On Tuesday 15 November, five days after his return to America, his diary entry consisted of just ten words: 'In New York. Got results of Mensing auction in Amsterdam.'

The 'result of the Mensing auction' was that Paul acquired a Rembrandt, the portrait of Marten Looten. Painted in 1632 when Rembrandt was a young man, the picture was previously owned by Anton W. Mensing, a wealthy Dutch collector whose worthy lifetime ambition had been to restore the best-known Dutch masterpieces to their native land. While he was in Europe, Paul heard that the Mensing Collection was being broken up and authorised a Dutch dealer to bid up to a hundred thousand dollars on his behalf for the Marten Looten. Mensing had paid more than two hundred thousand dollars to bring the picture back to Holland in 1928; with the war scare depressing prices in 1938, Paul got it for sixty-five thousand.

There was a public outcry in Holland when it was learned that the Marten Looten, one of only forty fully authenticated Rembrandt paintings in the world, had been sold to 'an anonymous American'. Paul was blithely indifferent to Dutch sensibilities – he had bought the picture, it was his to do what he liked with. He hung it in the sitting-room of his New York penthouse.

Paul spent Christmas 1938 in Los Angeles with his mother, then eighty-six years old, and for the first five months of 1939 he remained in Los Angeles dealing with the day-to-day problems of the business – the purchase of new oil leases, a well that turned up water, continuing friction with the directors of Tide Water, legal difficulties about taking possession of the Hotel Pierre ... every day, almost every hour, it was something different.

In the evenings he laboured over the writing of *The History of the Oil Business of George F. and J. Paul Getty from 1903 to 1939*, a book he intended to have privately printed as a testimonial to his father's career. It was a painstakingly detailed opus, listing every lease they had acquired during their first thirty-six years in the oil business.

If he dined out in the evenings, he usually dined alone, either at Lindy's or the Biltmore Coffee Shop. He wrote to Teddy in London regularly and was largely faithful to her, except for the occasional lapse. Barbara Denny, a twenty-two-year-old poetry student, briefly took his fancy and he enjoyed a few nights out with her at the Trocadero (Errol Flynn's favourite nightspot). Another evening he took a girl called Virginia to the Grove nightclub to see Veloz and Yolanda, but it can hardly have been a riotous frolic as he only bought Virginia one cocktail (thirty-five cents) and he had an ice cream (also thirty-five cents). The bill, he noted with satisfaction, was $2.70, including cover charge. He liked going to the movies ('Walked down to Western to see a movie. Had already seen *Gunga Din* so walked back.') and went to the Louis-Roper fight at Wrigley Field in April, but otherwise led an uncharacteristically low-key social life.

At the end of May he took a few days off to visit the World's Fair in San Francisco, taking the cheapest suite available at the St Francis Hotel for twelve dollars a night. He hired a 1939 Chevrolet from Hertz, renewed acquaintanceship with an old girlfriend, Ellen, and diligently visited all the exhibits at the Fair, dining every night on Crab Louis at DiMaggio's on Fisherman's Wharf.

On the evening of Monday 29 May he said goodbye to Ellen and boarded the Overland train for the fifty-seven-hour journey to Chicago. Crossing Nevada next day, he fell into conversation with a lady from Mexico City, a Miss Concepcion Eddy, and arranged to meet her in New York. After a seven-hour stop in Chicago, Paul and Miss Eddy boarded the 'Twentieth Century' for the overnight leg to New York, arriving at nine o'clock on the morning of 2 June.

Paul stayed in New York for three weeks, devoting much of his time to problems at the Pierre where he was enormously impressed by Hildegard, the cabaret singer in the Pierre's roof restaurant, but less so by the hotel's exorbitant operating costs. He demanded stringent economies to cut back its losses, then running at about $150,000 a year. When he was not at the Pierre, he spent many happy hours fending off approaches from high-class New York art dealers hopeful of lucrative sales. The Duveen gallery wanted to sell him a fine collection of eighteenth-century French furniture for $1,500,000 – Paul offered $400,000.

One afternoon he laconically responded to the dollar prices being quoted by a despairing dealer with his own sterling estimate of what each picture would fetch at auction. The dealer asked $95,000 for a Vigée-Lebrun portrait of Madame du Barry. Getty looked at it impassively and pointed out that it would go for only £6000 at Christie's in London. Next was a Van Dyke for $150,000 – Getty said '£12,000.'

Finally the dealer produced a Rubens, a full-length portrait of a beautiful woman, for $250,000. '£20,000,' said Getty and walked out.

On Saturday 10 June, he joined the crowds lining 96th Street to watch the King and Queen of England drive by during their state visit to America. He also found time to visit the New York World's Fair, where he was pleased to see that his Rembrandt and his Gainsborough – which he had loaned for exhibition – were well-placed and compared favourably with the other pictures on view. He liked the Petroleum exhibit with its working model of a drilling rig, but was most impressed by the 'World of Tomorrow' exhibit in the Perisphere, which he thought was breathtaking.

Most nights, Paul dined alone at Schraft's (indulging his sweet tooth one evening with *three* maple nut sundaes). But he was never, of course, short of female company. Ellen turned up from San Francisco 'looking very pretty' and Miss Eddy from Mexico City accepted an invitation to lunch at his Sutton Place penthouse. Then there was Gloria ('met Gloria at the Ambassador'), Nancy ('took Nancy to dinner and a show'), Geri ('met Geri at 9.30 p.m. Went to see *Mr Chips*'), May ('met May at the Langdon and took her to "21" for dinner') and Joy ('Joy came over and drove us out to the Fair').

None of these ladies posed any serious threat to his intended marriage to Teddy, which they now tentatively planned should take place in the romantic city of Rome. On Friday 23 June Paul sailed once again for Europe, ignoring dire warnings that war was imminent. That year Pan-American Airways began regular scheduled flights on the *Dixie Clipper* across the Atlantic, but Paul was frightened of flying and did not for a moment consider it as a serious alternative to his usual sea passage. Instead he booked a first-class cabin on the *Saturnia*, bound for Lisbon. Four days out into North Atlantic, excited passengers lined the starboard rail after dinner in the belief that a light in the sky was the *Clipper* flying overhead. Paul was unmoved and gratified when the captain announced that it was not Pan Am, but Jupiter.

Arriving in Lisbon on 2 July, Paul took a train for Paris via Salamanca and Biarritz. He checked into his regular room, number 324, at the Hôtel Lotti and spent two days visiting museums and the Louvre before leaving on the night train for Geneva where he had arranged to see his ex-wife, Fini, and his nine-year-old son, Ronnie, who was at school in a small town about twenty kilometres outside Geneva.

Although he always liked to pretend that he was an adoring father, Paul's four sons did not figure prominently in his life. George, who was then sixteen and at school just outside Los Angeles, had seen so little of his father and was so in awe of him that he addressed him as 'Mr Getty'. Little Paul, aged eight, and his brother Gordon, aged six, were boarders at the California Military Academy and could count the number of times they had seen their father in the previous five years on the fingers of one hand. Similarly, Ronnie, at school in Switzerland, was not accustomed to a visit more than once a year.

Paul met Fini at the American Express office in Geneva and they drove together in a rented car to Ronnie's school where the teachers gave the boy a good report, praising his intelligence and character, marred only by a tendency to be 'babyish' at times. In honour of his father's annual visit, Ronnie was given special permission to take a short holiday with his parents and the three of them drove across the border into France to the off-season skiing resort of Chamonix, in the Alps. Paul was on perfectly good terms with Fini; although he was still bitter at the terms of the divorce settlement, it was her father he resented, not Fini herself. They loafed happily in Chamonix for three days, enjoying the scenery, sunbathing and watching the climbers on Mont Blanc. Paul took Ronnie swimming and was pleased to see the boy could swim 'quite well'. On 14 July they moved on to Aix-les-Bains, where Paul was due to catch the night express to Genoa to meet Teddy. He found a room for Fini and the boy at the Europe Hotel, took them to the casino in the evening to watch a firework display, then kissed them goodbye and hurried to the station.

Teddy was waiting on the platform at Genoa station when the express pulled in at nine-thirty the next morning. It was the first time they had seen each other since the previous November. She threw herself into Paul's arms, then joined him on the train for Rome where she was to continue her operatic training under yet another teacher, Madame Cahier. Arriving in Rome at three-thirty in the afternoon, they booked into separate hotels – a mile apart – for the sake of propriety. Teddy was in the Hotel de Russie, Paul in the Excelsior.

For the next seven weeks, Paul immersed himself in the Eternal City and its glorious monuments to the creative imagination of the past. He was enthralled by the palaces and galleries and spent hours every day working his way through each museum, room by room, intent on missing nothing. Occasionally he would agree to drive out with Teddy to the beach at Ostia for a swim, but he could hardly bear to be parted from the city's vast store of antiquities. One afternoon when he was poking around the Pantheon, he was caught in a sudden heavy thunderstorm and he stood watching the rain fall through the gap in the dome on to the marble floor 140 feet below, mesmerised by the beauty of the scene.

Soon determined to add some Graeco-Roman trophies to his art collection, he found a fine head of Agrippa which he had authenticated by the assistant to the director of the Vatican Museum before buying at $2500 for shipment to New York. The same dealer came up with the bust of a Roman lady – probably Augustus's daughter – which Getty acquired for $7000, delivered to Los Angeles. He also decided he would have a bust made of himself by a local sculptor, Pier Vangelli, lamely explaining to Teddy that it would make a 'nice present' for one of his sons. Meanwhile, on the telephone to London, he bought a Beauvais Boucher tapestry at Sotheby's for £2700 and the famous 'Coronation carpet' at Christie's for six thousand guineas. He was particularly pleased with this last coup – it was a sixteenth-century Persian carpet that had been laid before the throne in Westminster Abbey at the coronation of King Edward VII in 1902.

During their first few weeks in Rome, Teddy often accompanied Paul on his museum tours and he, in turn, usually attended her singing lesson with Madame Cahier each evening. But there were soon disagreements between them. Paul wanted Teddy to return to the United States with him after their marriage, whereas Teddy was determined to stay in Rome to continue her studies, war or no war. There was also the tricky question of a property settlement agreement, drawn up by Paul's attorneys, which he insisted she sign before the ceremony. He believed it to be a sensible precaution – if their marriage failed, he had no desire to find himself facing another murderous divorce settlement like that negotiated by Fini's father.

One day at lunch, Teddy refused to eat anything when Paul criticised her extravagance for spending ninety-five lire postage on a single envelope. Four days later, when they were discussing 'the way to live' over dinner, Teddy broke down and ran out of the restaurant in tears. She was happiest, undoubtedly, on the evenings they spent together at the opera. At a performance of *Rigoletto* at the Baths of Carracalla, they sat only fifty feet from Mussolini, Il Duce. Paul was much impressed by his bearing and the spontaneous ovation he received from the crowd. 'He is the greatest son of Italy since Augustus' he wrote in his diary that night.

Towards the end of August, Paul started to worry for the first time about the prospect of being trapped in Europe by a war that now seemed inevitable. The newspapers were full of alarming reports that a German invasion of Poland was imminent, and Paul knew what that would mean. He decided on the spur of the moment that they should leave for Switzerland without delay. They travelled separately, Teddy by car with a friend and Paul by electric streamliner train via Milan, where he could not resist taking the time to visit the La Scala, the Poldi-Pezzoli Museum and the Brera Gallery. On the streets, the only hint of the coming storm that he could observe was the way people grabbed the latest editions of the newspapers as soon as they appeared on the stands.

Neither Paul nor Teddy had any problems crossing the border from Italy into Switzerland and they met, as arranged, at the Bear Hotel in

Grindelwald on the evening of 28 August. For the next seven days they did little but listen to the radio. On the morning of Friday 1 September they heard a broadcast of Hitler's speech in the Reichstag announcing the annexation of Danzig. The ten o'clock news from Stuttgart that evening carried details of the German advance into Poland. Two days later, Swiss Radio News announced at midday that England and France had declared war on Germany.

Paul had many friends in all three countries and his immediate reaction was to hope that the United States would be able to remain neutral and stay out of it. Indeed reassuring evidence that it was business as usual in America arrived in the form of a cable from Los Angeles, telephoned through to Paul by the porter at the Bellevue Hotel in Bern, to announce that a new well had been brought in and was good for 4500 barrels.

Neither of them had any particular wish to stay in Switzerland and on 4 September, the day after war had been declared, Paul telephoned the US Consul in Bern to ask if it was safe to return to Italy, which was maintaining an uneasy neutrality. Assured that they would be all right, they left next day for Rome by train. Paul returned to scouring the museums as if nothing had happened, but he made a point of listening to the radio news every evening, although the war seemed far distant from the tranquil purlieus of the Vatican and the Villa Borghese and the Sistine Chapel.

Curious about the effect of the war on Germany, Paul decided at the end of September to visit Berlin to look up his friends there. As his train rattled through the night across Germany, he sat in the dark, looking out at a mysterious shadowy landscape without a light showing anywhere. Arriving in Berlin he found the streets similarly dark, virtually deserted and the skyline silhouetted by searchlights probing the night sky. His taxi drove on hooded side lights to the Adlon Hotel, which looked curiously cold and forbidding in the gloom. Once inside, he was relieved to find the lights blazing and an orchestra playing 'gay music'.

He stayed nearly two weeks, lunching and dining with various lady friends, going to the opera in the evenings and enjoying Berlin's nightlife, which continued unabated despite a ban on dancing. There were fewer taxis on the streets and rationing made life rather more austere, but otherwise he found the city barely inconvenienced by the war. One day when he was strolling along Wilhelmstrasse, he saw von Ribbentrop drive by and noted in his diary that the crowd gave a 'hearty cheer'. A couple of days later, he wrote: 'Saw a column of troops just returning from Poland. The column was several miles long. Everything was motorised – no marching soldiers! The equipment was superb and the men fine-looking, honest fellows. The Berlin populace, especially the girls, gave them a warm welcome.' On the following day he saw Hitler, Goering, Hess, von Ribbentrop and Goebbels on their way to the Reichstag; he listened to Hitler's speech and thought it 'worthy of consideration'.

On 7 October, his last day, he had lunch with Charlotte, said goodbye to Gretchen at his hotel in the afternoon, met Hilda for dinner and left with her for the station at 9 p.m. He arrived back in Rome on the morning of Monday 9 October, took a taxi to his hotel and telephoned Teddy to arrange to meet her for lunch.

The next four weeks passed uneventfully, except perhaps for seeing Il Duce haranguing a wildly enthusiastic crowd in the Piazza di Venezia. Sunday 12 November found Paul and Teddy driving through Pincio in an open carriage, discussing their forthcoming marriage. Neither gave an inch. Paul was adamant he had to return soon to the United States. Teddy was adamant that she intended to stay in Rome in pursuit of that elusive high C. She had found a new teacher and where was a better place in the world to study opera? Next day they visited the American Consulate to make the wedding arrangements and in the afternoon they both signed the property settlement papers.

At noon on 14 November 1939 Paul and Teddy were married in the romantic setting of a palatial room in the Campidoglio. The event merited no more than a single line in his diary. They celebrated with lunch at the Ambassador with a friend. Paul spent the afternoon packing, had dinner alone with Teddy, then caught the eight-thirty train for Naples. Teddy went to the station to see him off. 'Much disappointed', he wrote in his diary, 'that T. decided not to go.'

The new Mrs Getty spent her bridal night alone in her room at the Ambassador Hotel in Rome. Her husband spent the night alone in a room at the Excelsior Hotel in Naples. Next day at noon, he departed for the United States on board the Italian liner *Conte di Savoia*. 'Stood on the deck for an hour,' he wrote, 'watching the matchless beauty of the bay of Naples gradually fade in the distance.'

9. 'My dearest darling left to join Papa'

The *Conte di Savoia* docked at the pier in New York at nine o'clock on the morning of Thursday 23 November 1939 – Thanksgiving Day. A posse of reporters and photographers, in pursuit of stories about the war in Europe, rushed on board as soon as the gangways were lowered and it did not take them long to discover that an oilman by the name of J. Paul Getty was on board who had recently been in Berlin. Paul, not displeased to be the sudden centre of attraction, dealt with their questions with his usual courtesy and patience before disembarking and taking a taxi to Sutton Place, where he was welcomed home by the housekeeper, Elsa.

Like the dutiful son he was, Paul immediately telephoned his mother in Los Angeles to tell her he was safely home. Then, after riffling through the mail and a pile of messages and pausing for a moment to admire anew the Ardabil carpet now on the floor of his sitting-room, he telephoned the doorman and asked for his Cadillac to be brought round to the front. He had been invited to spend Thanksgiving with Teddy's family in Greenwich, Connecticut, and by midday he was at the wheel of the Cadillac heading north out of Manhattan.

Mrs Lynch greeted her new son-in-law enthusiastically; she liked Paul and was apparently untroubled either by his four previous marriages or the fact that he was more than twenty years older than her daughter. The whole Lynch family, with the exception of Teddy, had gathered for Thanksgiving and Paul enjoyed meeting them. If there was any whispering behind his back about him being old enough to be Teddy's father, he did not notice it. In his diary that evening, Paul remarked on the 'fine dinner' and added 'everyone missed Teddy'.

Paul stayed in New York for two weeks, largely occupied by problems at the Pierre. Its reputation was beginning to suffer at the hands of the George F. Getty Inc. executives to whom Paul had entrusted the running of the hotel. It was Paul's view, as an oilman, that if you were a good executive in the oil industry you would be a good executive in any business and he had had no qualms about replacing many of the Pierre's highly trained and professional managers with his own colleagues. He had even put a retired prizefighter, an old friend, in charge of the kitchen. The food at the Pierre and the general standard of service deteriorated rapidly and Paul realised he had blundered. He solved the problem by hiring Frank Paget, an experienced Swiss hotelier, as general manager and giving him a free hand to make the Pierre the 'best hotel in New York', cautioning him at the same time to 'avoid waste'.

On the evening of Tuesday 5 December he left New York by train for Tulsa, Oklahoma, where he planned to look over Skelly Oil, the company he had unwittingly acquired in the package that went along with control of the Mission Corporation. Paul knew Bill Skelly from the old days when they were both wildcatters and used to hang around the lobby of the Tulsa Hotel in 1914, hoping for a whisper of a promising new lease.

William Grove Skelly was fourteen years older than Paul, a bullish, domineering autocrat with a powerful physique and huge ego. He started in the oil business as a roustabout and scraped together four hundred dollars to begin drilling on his own account. By the mid twenties Skelly Oil was one of the fastest-growing companies in the mid-continent and Skelly himself was known as 'Mr Tulsa', having built the first air-conditioned office block in the city and financed the construction of a huge sports stadium named after him. In 1928 he bought the Spartan Aircraft Factory and the flying school attached, and enthused by the potential of air travel, he helped incorporate Safeway Airlines which ran the first scheduled flights between Oklahoma City and St Louis, Missouri.

Like so many other self-made businessmen with an inclination to speculate, Skelly was hit hard by the Wall Street crash and the subsequent depression. He sold his interest in Safeway Airlines to help pay his debts but by 1934 he could no longer meet his commitments and was obliged to hand over control of Skelly Oil to Standard Oil of New Jersey. He remained as president of the company, although helpless to prevent its becoming embroiled in Getty's fight for control of Tide Water. When Jersey Standard transferred its Tide Water holding, and its 57% holding in Skelly Oil, to the Mission Corporation, Bill Skelly could do nothing but sit back and watch while young Getty slowly swallowed up his business. When it was announced in May 1937 that Getty had won control of the Mission Corporation and, with it, Skelly Oil, Bill Skelly flew into a towering rage. He burst into Tide Water's office in Tulsa brandishing a gun and threatening to shoot whoever was responsible for 'cheating' him out of his business. Thereafter, Skelly nurtured a deep animosity towards Getty. It was thus not surprising that when Paul arrived in Tulsa on 7 December to inspect Skelly Oil, he learned that Bill Skelly had been 'unavoidably detained' on business in Kansas City. Undeterred by his absence, Paul spent the morning going over the leases and figures. He noted with satisfaction that the company estimated it had reserves of between two hundred and two hundred and fifteen million barrels.

During lunch at the Mayo Hotel Paul ran into Josh Cosden, another of the wildcatters with whom he had shared a boarding house near the Tulsa Hotel back in 1914. Cosden, a multi-millionaire by the time he was thirty, had fallen on hard times. When Paul said he had just arrived from New York, Cosden smiled ruefully and said he didn't even have enough money left to raise the fare. Fearful of being asked for a loan, Paul departed hurriedly, explaining his time was short.

In the afternoon he drove out to the Spartan Aircraft Factory and found it to be a run-down little plant, employing no more than sixty assembly workers. It transpired that the factory was plagued by production problems, its aircraft range was outdated and its order book was thin. By contrast the Spartan School of Aeronautics next door was a flourishing enterprise, with fifty-one training aircraft and more than 150 US Army Air Corps cadets enrolled on flying courses. Paul was told that the students were logging around 180 flying hours every day and that Spartan had become one of the biggest flying schools in the country.

He was greatly impressed by 'Captain' Max Balfour, the swash-buckling veteran in charge. Balfour had learned to fly in France during World War One and served with great distinction as a combat pilot in the 213th Pursuit Squadron. After the war he survived two horrific accidents – on one occasion the wings of his aircraft fell off in midair and on another he crashed in flames, sustaining serious burns. Invalided out of the Air Corps, he became personal pilot for an international playboy in Europe before joining Spartan in 1938. Balfour told Paul he had won a government contract to train air cadets through the good offices of a general in Washington with whom he had served in France in 1918. It was the kind of initiative that Paul admired.

Late that night, Paul drove to Wichita and boarded the Chief for Los Angeles. The following day as the Chief huffed across the high plains of Kansas towards the Rocky Mountains, he could be found deep in conversation with one Ruth Donaldson of Minneapolis, a young lady he had met on the train. Although he was approaching fifty, Paul found a pretty face quite as irresistible as he had when he was a young man. Whether he was sitting in a hotel lobby in Europe, or strolling the deck of an ocean liner, or crossing the American continent by railroad, he never failed to notice an attractive young woman and he was usually able to contrive an introduction. Ingenious and diligent in the pursuit of the opposite sex, in hotels he often bribed hall porters for the names and addresses of ladies who took his fancy. He would then devote a considerable amount of time to checking through his network of friends and enter into complicated arrangements for a dinner party, inviting friends of friends in order to ensure that a certain young lady would be present.

Although he was no Rudolph Valentino, he was intelligent, widely-travelled, amusing, rich and loved female company. In the presence of attractive women he abandoned his usual sour and taciturn demeanour and positively sparkled, with considerable effect. He was also a perfect gentleman, never pressing his suit beyond the bounds of decency. While his motivation was always sex, his advances were discreet and rarely caused offence.

Certainly Ruth Donaldson was happy to have such a charming fellow passenger during the long journey on the Santa Fe railroad from Wichita to Los Angeles. Paul was very disappointed to learn that she was intending to get off at Lamy in New Mexico, but discovered she was planning to continue on to Los Angeles later and asked her if she would like to accompany him one evening to the Beachcombers Club. She accepted. Paul did not permit himself to consider whether dating young girls was appropriate behaviour in a man so recently married and on the verge of middle age.

At the imposing new Union Station in Los Angeles, opened earlier that year, Paul was met by the family chauffeur in his father's old Duesenberg and driven directly to South Kingsley Drive for a reunion with his mother. 'She looks very well', he wrote in his diary. 'Dinner at home and then drove out to see Ronnie and Fini.' After all the fuss at the time they were married over Fini's wanting to live in Germany close to her family, the rise of the Nazis and the prospect of war soon changed her mind and she had moved to California with her son a few months previously. Paul was happy with her decision (and not displeased that it undoubtedly caused Dr Helmle considerable grief).

Over the next few weeks, Paul rediscovered his sons and also saw quite a bit of his ex-wives. He had dinner with Ann Rork at the Brown Derby and took Fini to the movies to see *Elizabeth and Essex*. On the Saturday before Christmas he met Ann, with young Paul and Gordon, in the toy department at Robinson's store downtown and bought presents for the boys and on Christmas Day all four of his sons visited South Kingsley Drive – the first time they had been in the same room together. It was a subdued little gathering. George was a plump fifteen-year-old, soon to graduate from the Webb School of California in Claremont. He barely knew his younger half-brother, Ronnie, who was sulky and self-conscious, perhaps because his native tongue was German and his English was poor. The little ones, whom Paul called 'Pabby' and 'Gordo', were only seven and six years old respectively and had nothing in common with the older two.

Happy to play the unaccustomed role of fond father, Paul was nonchalantly unaware of any awkwardness between them. 'We had a lovely tree in mother's sitting-room and heaps of presents,' he recorded in his diary. 'Mother enjoyed it like a youngster.'

Paul spent most of 1940 in Los Angeles, living at home with his remarkable mother who celebrated her eighty-eighth birthday in January. He devoted himself diligently to business, wrote often to Teddy in Rome and led an active social life – as always, with plenty of female companionship. (He took several different girlfriends to the Beverly Wilshire Hotel when Ray Noble's band, which he thought was marvellous, was appearing there.)

His tussle with Tide Water was in the news again in the spring. On 3 May 1940 the *New York Times* reported that a truce had been negotiated. Under the headline 'GETTYS END FIGHT FOR TIDE WATER OIL' the story began, 'The long fight of the George F. Getty interests to get control of the management of the Tide Water Associated Oil Company apparently has ended ...' It went on to disclose that Tide Water had reached an agreement with Pacific Western and George F. Getty Inc. for joint operations in California.

The report was both inaccurate and premature. While such an agreement did exist, Paul never considered it marked the end of his ambitions. Although he had scaled down the action ever since winning control of the Mission Corporation, he was still buying Tide Water stock and still wanted to take over the company. If there was any change in his attitude, it was that he was now in less of a hurry. After nearly eight years of knee-and-gouge in-fighting, he held more than twenty-five per cent of Tide Water's voting stock and it seemed to him inevitable that he would eventually win overall control. He could wait.

Meanwhile Paul followed the progress of the war in Europe, through the newspapers and the radio, with increasing anxiety for Teddy's safety. On 10 June, when Italy declared war on Britain and France, Paul cabled Teddy: 'COME HOME.' She replied, cheekily: 'VICE VERSA.' Teddy was having a fine time in Italy, despite the war. As well as continuing with her singing lessons, she had landed a commission to write a weekly column from Rome for the New York *Herald Tribune* and she was thoroughly enjoying her glamorous new status as a newspaperwoman.

In November Paul voted for the re-election of F.D.R., whose policies he strongly supported, and then took off for a holiday in Mexico with his cousin, Howard 'Hal' Seymour. Four years older than Paul, Cousin Hal was as different as it was possible to be. He was a carefree bachelor, totally disinterested in money or material possessions and devoid of all ambition. In a colourful and chequered career he had navigated iron-ore ships on the Great Lakes, played trumpet in a band, prospected for gold in Alaska and led an expedition on mules to search for a lost gold mine in the Yucatan. He hated responsibility and loved life with exuberant passion. Hal and Paul had been close friends since childhood, united by a common bond of trust and respect born out of their differences: each admired the other intensely.

They set off at the end of November in a new Edsel Ford Mercury which Paul had bought for the trip and arrived at the Hotel Reforma in Mexico City on 2 December 1940. On the road south Paul got a piece of cinder in his eye which he was naturally convinced would cause permanent damage and when they checked into the hotel, doctors were instantly summoned to 'save his sight'. After the fragment had been removed, Paul was advised to 'rest' for a week. Hal tolerated this ludicrous incident with his usual good nature and when the doctors had at last convinced Paul that he was completely recovered, they resumed their journey, intending to spend some time on the coast at Acapulco.

The highway leading south from Mexico City had only been paved a few months previously and they discovered Acapulco to be a charming little Mexican town, completely unspoiled and huddled on a narrow strip of land between the harbour and the steep mountains encircling the bay. The scenery, surroundings and climate were all perfect and they agreed that it would be pointless to travel further. They rented a simple apartment facing the beach and whiled away the days swimming, sunbathing and beachcombing.

Paul had originally intended to be away for only three weeks, but Christmas came and went without either of them showing any inclination to return. They kept promising themselves 'just one more week' and the days drifted lazily by, their even tenor unaffected by the outside world.

Towards the end of January, Paul met a young Englishman in a bar and got into casual conversation with him in the faint hope of making an impression on his extremely pretty girlfriend. The Englishman kept talking about how he had discovered 'the most beautiful beach in the world', and the evening ended with them all agreeing to an expedition the following day to look at it. Paul instantly regretted the decision next morning when the Englishman turned up in an ancient truck and said they would want to drive fifteen miles along a rough track through dense tropical forest to get to the beach. The journey was even worse than he had expected. Clinging to the battered sides of the truck, they were soon covered in dust. Once into the forest, the truck bounced and jolted viciously and they were tormented by swarms of mosquitoes. But when at last they trundled out of the trees and on to the shore, Paul had to admit the Englishman was right – it *was* the most beautiful beach in the world. He had never seen anything like it, even in the Mediterranean. Known as Revolcadero Beach, it was a sweeping crescent of white sand, fringed by tropical forest interlaced with sweet-water lagoons and sheltered by an inland mountain range.

Over the next few weeks Paul went back to Revolcadero Beach

several times and, never slow to seize an opportunity, was soon discussing with Hal the possibility of buying land in the area and building a resort hotel there. The problems were formidable: a proper road would have to be built through virgin forest and the cost of clearing the land alone would be staggering. On top of that, it would mean dealing with the notorious red tape of Mexican bureaucracy and finding a way round a law forbidding foreigners to own land on the coast. But Paul was never deterred by problems: he telephoned Dave Hecht in New York and told him to get down to Acapulco immediately.

By the end of February 1941 Hecht had set up a partnership deal with a wealthy Mexican construction engineer to avoid the prohibition on foreigners owning land and Paul had bought a nine-hundred-acre site on Revolcadero Beach. In the middle of March Paul and Hecht returned to the United States, leaving the amiable Hal behind to 'tie up the details'.

Back home in Los Angeles, Paul went to work with a will, spending his spare time putting the finishing touches to another book on which he had been working intermittently ever since finishing the history of the Getty oil business. *Europe in the Eighteenth Century* was a scholarly work born out of research he had originally undertaken to educate himself as an art collector. Like the family history, he had it privately printed – perhaps to avoid the indignity of a publisher's rejection slip.

It was a slim volume of only 113 pages but impressive for all that, considering its author was neither a writer nor a historian. In the introduction, dated July 1941, Paul made no claims to literary posterity. 'We of the twentieth century', he wrote, 'have been profoundly influenced by the manners, customs, philosophies, politics and arts of the eighteenth century. I hope that this little handbook may serve to acquaint the reader with the life and accomplishments of that splendid period in the world's history.'

A much less splendid period in the world's history was being enacted in Europe while Paul was finishing his manuscript. Hitler, apparently invincible, ordered the invasion of Russia in June and the jackboot strode across the Steppes, crushing Kiev, Odessa and Kharkov under its heel. In August, Churchill and Roosevelt met off the coast of Newfoundland and signed the Atlantic Charter: Paul approved, wholeheartedly. His views on the war had changed radically during 1940. Like many Americans he had at first clung to the hope that America would be able to 'stay out of it', but listening to Ed Murrow's moving reports from London during the Blitz had made isolationism seem untenable. By the beginning of 1941 he had come to realise that freedom itself was at stake and he no longer believed that it was morally possible for the United States to turn its back on the struggle against Hitler, particularly after Japan joined the Axis.

When Roosevelt broadcast an uncompromising address in September, aggressively declaring his determination to protect US shipping on the high seas, Paul dispatched a congratulatory telegram to the White House: 'YOUR SPEECH TONIGHT IS A GREAT DOCUMENT IN AMERICAN HISTORY. IF AXIS RAIDERS AND SUBMARINES WERE PERMITTED TO CONTINUE THEIR PRESENT ACTIVITIES, WAR WOULD SEEM INEVITABLE. IF THEIR AGGRESSION CONTINUES YOU WILL HAVE A UNITED NATION SHOULD YOU ASK FOR A DECLARATION OF WAR. MAY GOD BLESS AND STRENGTHEN YOU IN YOUR GREAT RESPONSIBILITY.'

In November tension between the United States and Japan increased and on 26 November the US Secretary of State dispatched a blunt note to the Japanese, demanding their withdrawal from China and Indochina. Three days later, the first item on the ten o'clock news was that President Roosevelt had returned hurriedly to Washington. 'If this means war with the Axis,' Paul wrote in his diary that night, 'I am for it. The time has come for the United States to be united in support of the President's foreign policy. He said from the beginning that appeasement would not work with the Axis, and we must ruefully admit that he was right.'

On Sunday afternoon 7 December Paul and his mother planned to listen to a concert on the Columbia Broadcasting System. A few minutes after three o'clock, as the New York Philharmonic was tuning up for Shostakovich's Symphony No. 1, an announcer broke in: 'We interrupt this programme to bring you a special news bulletin. The Japanese have attacked Pearl Harbor.'

Once the initial shock and outrage had subsided, Paul reacted like millions of others: he tried to enlist. James Forrestal, the Undersecretary of the Navy in Washington, was an old friend and on Sunday evening Paul dispatched a telegram offering his services: 'DASTARDLY JAPANESE ATTACK CALLS CIVILIANS TO GIVE EVERYTHING TO DEFEAT THE ATTACKERS. I AM FORTY-NINE BUT IN GOOD HEALTH, HAVE OWNED THREE YACHTS AND AM EXPERIENCED IN THEIR CARE AND MAINTENANCE. IF NAVY CAN USE ME IN ANY CAPACITY, PLEASE ADVISE. REGARDS. PAUL GETTY.'

The millionaire received a polite reply the following day: 'YOUR MESSAGE APPRECIATED. REFERRED TO BUREAU OF NAVIGATION. FORRESTAL.' As a former yacht owner, Paul did not appear to think it at all unrealistic that he should be considered potential officer material for the US Navy. He would, of course, expect to be assigned to sea duty and hoped to be offered a command without too much delay. He fondly pictured himself on the bridge of his own ship, a destroyer perhaps, forging across the Pacific to beat the hell out of the Japs. Captain

J. Paul Getty, US Navy; yessir, it had a certain intrepid air about it.

Unfortunately, his qualifications were not impressive. The declaration of war against Japan had provoked a rush to the recruiting offices and there was no shortage of rather younger men clamouring to serve in the navy. And as for his 'experience' ... it was true that he had owned three motor yachts in the early thirties, but that hardly made him a sailor. Millionaires were expected to own yachts and on each occasion that Paul had bought one, it was in the expectation of enjoying leisurely ocean cruises; in fact, he never seemed to find the time for such pleasures and his yachts rarely left harbour. He sold the last one in 1936.

Whether or not Paul seriously thought he would be considered for active service in the US Navy (he was still a week short of his forty-ninth birthday when he sent the telegram to Forrestal; if he was that keen, he might have been better advised to say that he was forty-eight), he nevertheless pressed his suit with some persistence, writing to Forrestal again on 11 December and presenting himself at a naval recruiting station in Los Angeles two days later as a volunteer.

When he got home after his medical examination, he found there was a message from Washington waiting for him. Instead of news about his application to join the navy, he learned that Teddy had been arrested in Rome.

Teddy had been warned to leave Italy in October, but had encountered interminable difficulties in obtaining an exit visa. She had finally got all the papers together, but on the day before the raid on Pearl Harbor all American exit visas were cancelled. Teddy was not unduly concerned – the war seemed a long way from the sunny terrace of her apartment and she continued with her daily singing lessons. On 11 December she stood in the Piazza di Venezia and 'listened incredulously to the roly-poly marionette on the balcony declare war against my own country'. When she got back to her apartment, she found two policemen waiting to take her to the police headquarters.

'I was put into a small room, unfurnished except for a table and a picture of Mussolini. The uproar was amazing, as people ran up and down outside my room and shouted to each other and into the telephone. I sat on the table for four hours and was then taken before the chief, who told me I was to be sent to a nunnery for the night.'

The 'nunnery' turned out to be a vile women's prison under the Tiber, where Teddy was put into a corridor with fifteen other women – all the cells were full – and given a bundle of straw to sleep on.

I spent the night huddled on my straw, vainly trying to keep warm

150

and cursing myself for not having brought an extra sweater. But the police chief had told me I would be released in a day, so I remained fairly cheerful. We were roused at five for mass. I was stiff with cold, exhausted and hungry, and the sights and smells of the ragged dirty bodies clambering to their feet was too much. We washed without soap at a cold-water spigot. The toilet was a foul hole in the floor with a smell that made me dizzy.

For breakfast we were herded into a line and served black bread and bitter black coffee. I spent the morning locked in a cell with four other women. The morning was broken by a fifteen-minute promenade in a small court. Then came a lunch of vegetable soup, followed by a deadly long afternoon of wondering when I would be released. No word came. We were led away for more prayers at five-thirty, at which all the sinners around me sobbed and moaned. I lay awake all that night, unable to sleep because of the cold and the snoring of the other women. On the morning of the fifth day I was told that a group of American correspondents had been interned in a hotel and I was to join them.

There was nothing Paul could do in Los Angeles to help Teddy and, in any case, he had his hands full at home. On the morning of Saturday 20 December he had arranged a rare excursion with his eldest son, George, to look at the Athens oilfield in Los Angeles where he had made so many big strikes when he was a young man. George was then seventeen, about to go to Princeton and had told his father that he intended to study law. Paul approved, but had no intention of allowing his son to be a lawyer – he wanted George to follow him into the family business and the trip to the Athens field was intended to arouse the young man's interest in the oil industry.

When they got back to South Kingsley Drive at midday, Paul was met by the family doctor who told him that his mother had had a stroke. He rushed upstairs to her room and found the old lady sitting up in her favourite chair, testily insisting there was nothing the matter with her. Outside her room, the doctor, grim-faced, warned Paul that while she had only sustained a slight cerebral haemorrhage affecting her right side, there was a strong likelihood she would have another, more severe, stroke within the next few days which might prove fatal.

Paul was grief-stricken at the prospect of losing his 'dearest darling'; it was the first time he could ever remember his mother being ill. He went back into her room to sit with her and when she demanded to be taken out for her usual afternoon drive, he did not have the heart to refuse – regardless of the fact that the doctor had said she should not be allowed to leave the house. He stayed at her side through the weekend. On Monday morning he was due to go into the office to sign some cheques, but the doctor cautioned him not to go. The words sent a chill through Paul.

For the next three days the old lady clung to life while her son alternated between despair and hope. He did his best to amuse her and make her comfortable, but on Christmas Day she weakened noticeably and he began to lose heart. 'Christmas Day was a sad one because of Mama', he wrote in his diary. 'She is very ill and has, I am afraid, little chance to recover. I was hopeful until this afternoon, but then became alarmed. Mama took three cups of hot water from me. She recognised me and kissed me. Afterward I went out of the room and cried.'

On the next day her condition worsened. Paul sat by her bedside all day, holding her hand. In the early evening she squeezed his hand faintly and asked him, in a whisper, to leave her alone for a while. Paul thought she probably wanted to sleep for a while. He tiptoed out of her room and went into the garden for some fresh air. Standing on the lawn under her bedroom window a few minutes later, he suddenly looked up in time to see one of the servants drawing the curtains. Tears welled up in his eyes and coursed down his cheeks.

For a hard-headed businessman approaching fifty, Paul confessed in his diary to an extraordinary anguish at the loss of his mother. She was only a few weeks short of her eighty-ninth birthday, but Paul grieved as if she had been cut off in her prime and he was a lonely orphan, utterly lost without her.

December 26: 'I can't think of anything but Mama. In the evening, quietly and modestly, my dearest darling left to join Papa.'

December 27: 'What can I say? I only know I am desolate. Telephone calls, telegrams and messages. What loving friends my mother had! What a task it is to be worthy of two wonderful parents! I have tried to be worthy, but I must try harder.'

December 28: 'How I miss her! No one ever had a better mother.'

December 29: 'Mama, Mama.'

December 30: 'Mama is gone; everyone is so kind to me.'

December 31: 'A sad New Year's Eve with Hal at home. Resolved to do my best to be worthy of Mama and to help my country crush its enemies to the last ounce of my strength.'

This return of patriotic fervour was prompted by a call from the Navy Recruiting Office: he had failed his first eyesight test and was required to undergo another examination. On 3 January 1942 he was passed as fit for service in the US Navy but warned that it was extremely unlikely, in view of his age, that he would be recommended for sea duty. Undeterred, Paul enrolled at the University of Southern California for a course in navigation and seamanship. 'If I go in the navy,' he explained, 'I don't want to be a duffer.'

A few days later he was offered a job by the Office of Petroleum Coordinator – a government agency set up to oversee oil supplies for the war effort. The suggestion was gently put to him that he would be of more use to his country working in the oil industry than he would in the navy. He indignantly rejected the idea. 'I pointed out that my companies were well-organised and efficiently run by the men who formed their executive and managerial staffs. They were entirely capable of running the companies at peak efficiency without me. I wanted to serve in the navy – and I wanted sea duty.'

Weeks passed with no call from the navy and news from the front worsening by the day: Allied forces were being routed by the Japanese in the Pacific. Paul, his patience wearing thin, took a train to Washington in mid-February, intending to buttonhole someone in the Navy Department to find out what had happened to his application. He was passed from one office to another and given the same dispiriting message everywhere he went – he was too old. If he joined the navy, he was told, he could not expect anything more glamorous than an administrative job on shore, probably at a supply base. 'It appeared,' he noted sadly, 'that sea duty was out of the question. I was too old to serve as a junior officer aboard a warship and did not have sufficient experience to qualify for higher rank in the combat branches of the US Navy.'

On the evening of 17 February Paul ran into an acquaintance, Jack Swerbul, in the lobby of the Mayflower Hotel in Washington. Swerbul was the boss of Grumman Aircraft and had a particular reason for being pleased to see Getty, since he knew that Getty interests controlled the Spartan Aircraft Company. Over a drink, Swerbul told Paul a few home truths about Spartan. Grumman employed the firm as a subcontractor, he explained, to supply components for combat aircraft. The quality of its product was extremely poor and it was months behind schedule. 'Spartan stinks!' he said. 'We've had to reject practically every goddamned thing it has produced.'

To underline what he was saying, Swerbul produced from his briefcase a confidential report on the NP-1 Primary Trainer being built by Spartan at Tulsa. It alleged that the aircraft was nose-heavy, poorly welded and nine months late with deliveries.

Paul was shocked by what Swerbul had to say. He had very little idea of what was going on at Spartan and certainly had no inkling that its management was so disorganised and inefficient. Liability for running the company rested with Skelly Oil, several removes from the hub of the Getty operations where he sat, and he had had little reason to interfere in its affairs. Nevertheless, as head of the conglomerate, Paul felt a keen sense of personal responsibility for the company's poor reputation, particularly as it was involved in war production.

Three days later Paul had an appointment with Frank Knox, the

Navy Secretary. Knox confirmed that there was no chance of Paul's going to sea. 'You qualify for a commission as an administrative or supply officer,' he said. 'But sea duty is out of the question.' He paused for a moment, then said, 'I understand you hold a large interest in the Spartan Aircraft Company.' Paul admitted that he did, wondering what was going to come next.

'We need aircraft, aircraft components and trained fliers desperately,' Knox continued. 'To obtain them, we must have experienced businessmen running our factories and flying schools, men who can rapidly expand manufacturing and training facilities and raise production to unprecedented levels. The most useful thing you can do for the navy and for your country is to forget about putting on a uniform, drop all your other business activities and take over direct personal management of Spartan.'

That night, Paul boarded a train for Tulsa. Before he climbed into the bunk of his sleeping compartment, he wrote in his diary: 'I have an important job – getting the Spartan factory into mass production for the navy and the army.'

No one at the Spartan Aircraft factory in Tulsa knew quite what to make of the tall, slightly stooped man with a long face, big nose and doleful expression who turned up in February 1942 and announced that he intended to take over the running of the factory. He arrived in a taxi wearing a dark grey double-breasted suit with a white handkerchief in his top pocket and spent the morning slowly walking round the factory, staring glumly at the plant and the twitching assembly-line workers with lizard eyes darting this way and that, revealing nothing, missing nothing. He appeared never to smile, even when he was shaking hands with someone while being introduced and they observed that when he spoke, which was rare, he had a curious habit of swallowing his words, chewing on the syllables with his cheeks working as if masticating a particularly indigestible lump of gristle.

At lunch time he joined the queue of blue-overalled workers in the staff cafeteria, sat at a table with three visibly nervous Spartan executives and solemnly munched a salad with no obvious sign of enjoyment. In the afternoon, he summoned all the managers into an office for a meeting behind closed doors which went on for hours. Getty told them he had been personally asked to take charge of the company by the Navy Secretary in Washington. Spartan had a vital contribution to make to the war effort but it was falling down on the job – it had a lousy reputation for quality and reliability. Getty intended to change all that. Henceforth all managers would be directly responsible to him for meeting delivery dates and quality control. There would be no backsliding; anyone discovered to be lazy or incompetent would be 'invited to resign'. Getty was going to make Spartan the best aircraft factory in the United States.

On the production lines the workers exchanged whispered gossip and what few titbits of information any of them had been able to glean about J. Paul Getty. Beyond the fact that he was an oilman with no experience of aircraft manufacture, they knew virtually nothing. It was said that he was a ruthless businessman (certainly, he looked the part) and that he was fabulously rich. No one could understand why he should want to take over a one-eyed dump like Spartan if he was so rich and so successful. By the time the day shift clocked off, there was a rumour circulating that Getty might be mad.

Next morning, a memo was pinned up on notice boards all over the factory announcing that Mr J. Paul Getty had been 'elected' as the new president of the Spartan Aircraft Company and the Spartan Aeronautical School in place of Mr W. Skelly. That afternoon, a framed photograph of Mr Getty was hung *above* the photograph of Mr Skelly already adorning the cafeteria. It was impossible not to observe that Mr Getty's picture was also considerably larger than that of his predecessor.

Later he addressed the shop-floor workers, in his usual ponderous tones:

A battle is being fought every day in every one of the United nations and in every one of the Axis nations. It is the battle of production. In the greatest production battle of all time we are the men behind the men behind the guns. What we do in the school and factory is just as important, if not heroic, as though we were on the battlefield itself. Great factories and modern machine tools will not win this battle. All they can do is help us to win. The war is a personal matter for every one of us. I will do my best, and I know you will too.

Paul's blunt self-confidence disguised the considerable trepidation he felt about the whole undertaking. Ever since agreeing to do the job, he had been worrying about it, worrying if he would be able to make a success of it. In the end he convinced himself that although he knew nothing about the manufacture of aircraft (he did not even like to fly in them!), a business was a business, no matter whether it was making aeroplanes or drilling wildcat wells. 'I realised,' he said, 'that I had to apply the same principles, rules and yardsticks as I had always used throughout my business career.'

For the first couple of weeks, Paul spent most of his time learning about the business. He asked endless questions, spent hours talking to workers on the factory floor and pored over paperwork late into the night in his suite at the Mayo Hotel in downtown Tulsa. All his life he had possessed a remarkable facility for soaking up information, even of the most technical nature, and it was not long before he was able to talk about tooling up and machine tolerances and complicated welding processes, using the jargon of the industry and earning considerable respect, if not affection.

When he was ready to start making changes, things happened fast. He brought in a plant designer to reorganise the work flow and eliminate bottlenecks, introduced daily progress charts and split the plant into competing production teams requiring the unhappy supervisor of any lagging team to sit behind a cardboard cutout eight ball until he increased output. Anyone who dared to suggest that his production targets were not technically feasible was treated to a growled aphorism: 'I don't have to be a cow to know how much milk a cow can give.'

Paul was as unsparing of himself as he was of his executives. He put in very long hours, always working late at night and often missing meals. He talked for hours on the telephone chastising suppliers and chasing scarce raw materials. When he noticed that some of his managers were in the habit of arriving up to thirty minutes after the day shift had clocked on, he did not bother to issue warnings about the need for diligent timekeeping or setting an example – he simply convened a daily production conference at seven-fifteen each morning, forty-five minutes before the day shift started work. All management personnel were obliged to attend.

Production began rising steadily and quality control procedures drastically reduced the rate of rejects. On 21 March Spartan delivered seven NP-1 trainers to the US Navy – its highest-ever daily output – all of which were tested and accepted without a fault. 'Felt proud of the planes,' he scrawled in his diary, 'as they were flown away at noon by seven splendid boys.'

Morale increased tangibly as production improved. When he arrived in February, he loudly wondered if anyone on the Spartan payroll knew that there was a war on. By April, he had every employee donating a day's labour to make a gift of an extra plane to the US Navy. The idea was adopted enthusiastically and the entire work force gathered for the formal presentation of an NP-1 trainer, named the *Spirit of Spartan*, to the Navy Secretary.

Realising that he was likely to be in Tulsa for some time, Paul bought a large apartment in the Sophian Plaza – the most fashionable and expensive residence in town. Seriously alarmed by the prospect of air raids against the United States, he ordered the construction of an elaborate air-raid shelter in the grounds of the Spartan factory. It had eighteen-inch thick walls reinforced with steel rods and cost a hundred thousand dollars. Paul, who had a highly developed regard for his own safety, considered it money well-spent.

In May negotiations by neutral intermediaries secured Teddy's release from the hotel in Siena where she had spent five months interned with a group of American correspondents. 'On the whole, it could not have been pleasanter,' she said. 'Our hotel was extremely comfortable. We had the run of the city, took walks and bicycle trips almost every day, played tennis or sat lazily on the hotel terrace in the sun. I had a grand piano in my room and was able to practise every day. We had cocktails together before dinner and spent almost every evening in long debates liberally laced with alcohol, or even longer bridge games.'

She was, nevertheless, understandably pleased to be going home and arrived back in the United States on 1 June 1942 on a Swedish Red Cross ship, the *Drottningholm*. On the way across the North Atlantic, she entertained her fellow ex-internees with a new lyric to 'Home on the Range':

> Oh, please take me home on the old *Drottningholm*,
> Where the unemployed diplomats play,
> Where seldom is heard an intelligent word,
> And the bar remains open all day.

Paul was delighted to find Teddy was quite unscarred by her experience, which she described to him as being 'straight out of Warner Brothers'. She accompanied him back to Tulsa, although she was less than thrilled when she realised that Paul expected her to make her home there for the duration of the war. For a few weeks she played the dutiful wife. She attended a dance at the Spartan factory in aid of Naval Relief and sang for the workers. She cooked pot roasts for her husband when he got home from the factory, and played pool with him after dinner. Cousin Hal, to whom Paul had given a job at Spartan as a manager, was a frequent dinner guest despite baldly announcing to Teddy one evening that he did not think her voice was 'big enough' for the opera. After a month sampling the limited social delights of Tulsa, Teddy could stand the boredom not a moment longer and fled to New York, telling Paul she wanted to resume her career as a singer.

Paul was unhappy that she left so soon, but he was engrossed in a particular challenge at Spartan which was occupying much of his time. In April, Spartan was given a subcontract to manufacture wings for the navy's Grumman fighter. Washington's technical experts estimated that it would take Spartan fifteen months to tool up, train its labour force and get into full production. Paul instinctively distrusted 'so-called experts' and after a conference with key personnel at Spartan, he loftily informed Washington that Spartan would have the Grumman wings in full production within six months. Officials in Washington were extremely sceptical, which served only to make Paul even more determined to fulfil his promise.

Fifty of Spartan's best line workers were sent to California for on-the-job training at Grumman's plant, while the factory in Tulsa began tooling up frantically. Encouraged by Paul, everyone in the factory responded to the idea of teaching the 'experts' in Washington a lesson. Ten jigs were ready by the time the first group of workers returned from California. To keep up the pace, Paul had big wooden clocks hung above every jig showing how many hours it took to produce a single wing: production time dropped rapidly. A few days before the six-month deadline, Paul informed Washington that the Spartan Aircraft Company was in full production.

At a critical moment in this 'beat-the-experts' operation, Paul had to go to Chicago on Spartan business and on the return journey to Tulsa he missed his train connection in St Louis. He was so anxious to get back to the factory that he steeled himself to continue by air. He had only ever 'been up' once before – on a joy ride in 1917 in a Jenny – and quite enjoyed it, but had subsequently developed a phobia about flying so overpowering that he always travelled by train around the continent, no matter how long the journey. This time, however, he decided to risk the scheduled flight from St Louis, perhaps recognising that it was slightly ludicrous for the boss of an aircraft factory to be frightened of flying.

It was a nightmare. Just a few minutes out of St Louis, the aircraft ran into a series of thunderstorms. Paul gripped the arms of his seat with white knuckles as the plane bucked and yawed across the sky and lightning crackled around the fuselage. He prayed for the pilot to land so that he could get out, but they battled on through one storm after another. When they eventually landed in Tulsa, he had to be helped from the plane, ashen-faced, by a stewardess. He would never fly again.

Adolphine 'Fini' Helmle, the woman Getty pursued halfway across Europe to marry. It lasted less than five years. Married in 1928, they were divorced by 1932.

(*above*) J. Paul Getty II (on the left) in his capacity as head of Getty
Oil Italiana in 1959: every inch the young executive. (*opposite*) Eight
years later, in his hippie avatar, taking part in a demonstration
against the Vietnam War in Rome together with the exotic Talitha Pol
– Dutch actress and his second wife. Gail, Paul II's first wife, is
pictured below with three of their four children: (from left to right)
Arlene, Ariadne and Mark Getty.

(*opposite*) The ill-fated J. Paul Getty III in his palmier days as the Golden Hippie, veteran of several boarding schools and running wild in Rome. (*above*) With Martine Zacher, his wife-to-be, practising for the career in photography they had planned together before disaster struck.

Gail with attorney Jacavoni, announcing to the press her willingness to pay a ransom for the safe release of her son J. Paul Getty III.

The newly released Paul, fresh from the hands of his kidnappers, minus an ear and marked for life by his traumatic experience.

A solitary figure: the man who resolutely refused to pay his grandson's ransom, cultivating the special rapport he believed he had with animals and so demonstrably lacked with his own family.

10.   'A simple Irish girl of deep spirituality'

With production of the Grumman wings in full swing, Paul did not feel the need to spend such long hours at the Spartan factory. Teddy was still away in New York and Paul, being Paul, began to seek out amiable young ladies with whom to spend his evenings. One of them was a voluptuous redhead by the name of Joan Barry.

Miss Barry was an actress, twenty-three years old and trouble. Paul had had a brief, hectic affair with her in Los Angeles after he returned from Mexico in March 1941. Two months later she met Charlie Chaplin at a dinner party, having been introduced as 'Paul Getty's girlfriend'. Joan told Chaplin she had quarrelled with Getty and made it clear she was 'available'. Chaplin was fifty-three, had recently broken up with his third wife, Paulette Goddard, and was more than usually vulnerable to the charms of a sensual young woman making a play for his affections. Within a few weeks, they were lovers. Paul was not much concerned: he and Charlie were old friends and of an age when they could pass a paramour from one to the other without falling out about it.

Chaplin became convinced that Barry had star potential. He put her under contract to his studio at $250 a week, enrolled her in an acting school and offered her a part, as a 'simple Irish girl of deep spirituality', in his next film. It was all too much for Joan Barry to handle. She began to drink and behave erratically, showing up at Chaplin's house at all hours of the night. One evening, hopelessly drunk, she crashed her Cadillac into a tree in his driveway. Chaplin, worried that there would be a scandal if she was picked up by the police, ended their affair.

But it was not, by any means, the end of his troubles with the troublesome Miss Barry. She took to telephoning him in the middle of the night. When he would not answer her calls, she turned up at his house in Beverly Hills and banged on the door. When he refused to open it, she started smashing the windows. In the summer of 1942, she decided she did not want to be an actress after all and offered to tear up her contract if Chaplin would give her five thousand dollars and pay her fare to New York. He paid up willingly, happy to be rid of her.

Joan Barry did not go to New York, but to Tulsa where a lonely oilman gave her a warm welcome. She stayed at the Mayo Hotel and they saw each other 'frequently', but at the beginning of December Paul was obliged to get rid of her as he had arranged to spend the weeks leading up to Christmas with Teddy at the beach house in Santa Monica. He paid her bill at the Mayo Hotel, gave her a cheque for $249 to settle an outstanding account at the Beverly Hills Hotel and another cheque for $93.80 made out to the Santa Fe Railroad for her fare to New York, then he bade her farewell. Like his friend, Charlie Chaplin, he perhaps imagined it was the last he would see or hear of Miss Joan Barry: how wrong they both were.

Christmas at the beach house was idyllic. Teddy joined Paul there in time to bake him a cake for his fiftieth birthday on 15 December and for several weeks they enjoyed a normal life as husband and wife, living together under their own roof. They slept late, took long walks along the beach and talked a lot. Teddy cooked dinner every evening and afterwards she would sing for Paul or they would sit together on a sofa listening to opera on the phonograph. On Christmas Day Teddy gave Paul two Scottie puppies, four weeks old, which he named Hilda and Jocko.

After a 'quiet celebration' on New Year's Eve, Teddy returned to New York where she had a singing engagement and Paul caught the train for Tulsa to resume his duties as the boss of the Spartan Aircraft Company. At the end of January, George arrived in Tulsa to see his father before enlisting in the US Army. 'He has lived up to all my expectations,' Getty wrote in his diary, 'but it is hard for me to realise he is twenty years old. [He wasn't – he was eighteen.] George is eager to get into the fight against the Axis. He is already in the Enlisted Reserve Corps and will be called up after 8 February. He will probably have thirteen weeks of basic training and then thirteen weeks in officers' school. I love him and pray that he comes through safely.'

The Spartan Aircraft Company went from strength to strength under Getty's tireless direction. He kept a meticulous monthly record of production figures and the man-hours required to manufacture individual parts, making it a matter of personal pride that the figures improved each month. The work force doubled, then tripled. By June 1943 Spartan had so many contracts that a further three hundred thousand square feet was added to the factory's floor space. When that proved to be inadequate, Getty ordered the construction of a mezzanine floor to accommodate further plant.

He became obsessively proud of the factory and its men. When a delegation of bureaucrats from Washington came on a visit and dared to question whether the ailerons being manufactured for B-24 bombers were of a sufficiently high standard, Getty riposted in his deep, somnolent tones: 'Spartan parts are like diamonds round a sow's neck.' Once he knew he could trust his own men, Paul supported them through thick and thin. When Spartan welding engineers complained that US Navy inspectors were rejecting components that were completely up to standard, Getty told the navy inspectors that every disputed component would be sent to the National Bureau of Standards in Washington for independent inspection. The rate of rejection dropped significantly.

While he was intensely loyal to his work force, he never let them forget that he demanded in return the highest standards of diligence and honesty. Anyone who 'wasted the taxpayer's money' by reading newspapers at work or dawdling over lunch found his wages docked at the end of the week. An executive who was discovered running personal letters through the company's postage meter was immediately 'invited to resign'. Paul told him that although he had only cheated the company of a few dollars, his behaviour constituted 'petty larceny' which not only meant a loss to the company but a loss to the taxpayer, too, since they were engaged on government contracts.

Even easy-going cousin Hal found himself pilloried for misuse of company property by collecting some scraps of wood around the factory to build a kennel for a stray dog he had befriended. When Paul found out about it, he insisted that Hal draw up a full inventory of everything he had used, down to the last nail. He was then presented with a bill, plus a twenty per cent surcharge for overheads. Paul wanted to make an example of Hal precisely *because* he was his cousin. 'I made sure everyone knew about this incident,' Paul said, 'so they got the message that there was only one set of basic rules and regulations and it applied with equal vigour to everyone.'

Although he devoted most of his attention to the factory, Getty kept a benevolent eye on the flying school which was thriving under the leadership of the redoubtable Captain Balfour. More than 1500 pilots were in training at the Spartan Aeronautical School, many of them Royal Air Force volunteers sent to the United States when flying schools in Britain could no longer produce sufficient pilots to replace the horrific losses sustained during the Battle of Britain and the bombing raids over Germany. Paul always attended the graduation ceremonies at Spartan, insisted on laboriously signing all the diplomas himself and kept in touch with the exploits of Spartan-trained pilots, many of whom were in action even before Pearl Harbor, flying as volunteers with the Eagle Squadron. Wing Commander Lance Wade, the ace who probably shot down more than a hundred enemy aircraft but who never claimed a kill, was a Spartan graduate.

In June Paul picked up a newspaper in Tulsa and found, somewhat to his consternation, that Joan Barry was in the headlines. Barry had turned up in gossip columnist Hedda Hopper's office and sobbed out a pitiful story that had all the lurid ingredients of a first-class scandal. She was pregnant by Charlie Chaplin, she said, and when he found out he had her thrown out of his house and arrested for vagrancy. As the story developed over the next few days, Chaplin was vilified as a licentious, black-hearted scoundrel while Miss Barry was portrayed as a sweet, innocent waif corrupted and left destitute by the millionaire film star.

What had actually happened was that Barry had returned to Beverly Hills intent on pestering Chaplin. One night she broke into his house through a window and threatened him with a gun. After an hour and a half he managed to persuade her to hand over the gun and gave her some money. When she broke in again a week later, he called the police. She was given a ninety-day suspended sentence, disappeared for a couple of weeks then broke into Chaplin's house for a third time. She was again arrested and spent thirty days in jail on a vagrancy charge. After her release she continued to harass Chaplin – standing fully clothed under the sprinklers of his lawn one afternoon, then driving a car at breakneck speed round the circular drive as if it was a racetrack. In October 1943 Barry gave birth to a daughter and announced she would be pressing a paternity suit against the father of her child, Charlie Chaplin.

Even before the Barry story broke, Chaplin had been having trouble with the press. He was widely criticised for supporting the call for a second front in the war against Germany and accused of being a 'commie' sympathiser. His 'failure' to become a US citizen was cited as further evidence of latent anti-American inclinations. Thus when Joan Barry stepped into the limelight, the newspapers were delighted to show Chaplin in the blackest possible light.

Federal authorities were also taking an interest in his alleged 'un-American' activities and seized upon the Barry case as an opportunity to 'get Chaplin'. In February 1944 Chaplin was indicted before a federal grand jury and accused of 'feloniously transporting Joan Barry from Los Angeles to New York for immoral purposes' in violation of the Mann Act, an obscure piece of legislation passed by Congress in 1919 to combat organised prostitution.

In Tulsa Paul was distressed to read of all the misfortunes falling upon his friend, but fervently hoped he would not be dragged into the case. During the first weeks in February he took a day off from Spartan to make a nostalgic pilgrimage to Bartlesville, where his father had started in the oil business more than forty years earlier. The visit was recorded in his diary in the usual maudlin and emotional tone generated by any reference to his beloved parents: 'The Rightway Hotel is gone, also my favourite candy store run by a kindly Greek. When I went to the bridge [over the Caney River] for some reason tears came suddenly to my eye. It has been forty years since I walked across that bridge with Jip. I am a man of fifty-one, older than my father was then. My darling parents were not waiting for me to come home to them at the hotel.'

When he got back to Tulsa, he found a federal agent waiting for him at the Spartan factory with a subpoena requiring him to give evidence in the case against Chaplin. His appearance on the witness stand, a week later, was more comical than sensational. Without a flicker of expression on his long face, he agreed that he knew Miss Barry, had seen her frequently in 1941 and in November 1942 in Tulsa, Oklahoma. When it came to the embarrassing details of the money he had given her, he hastened to point out that they were loans offered in order to help her with her career. Getty said he had insisted on holding security for the loans – Miss Barry's coat. There was a ripple of laughter round the courtroom at this, which Getty seemed not to hear. When he was asked to stand down, he wondered why he had been called to testify at all since the questions were so trivial.

Chaplin's defence rested primarily on his counsel's contention that it was ridiculous for him to transport Barry almost four thousand miles to have intercourse with her in New York when the girl would have 'given him her body at any time or place'. The jury agreed and acquitted Chaplin, but his ordeal was not yet over since the paternity suit still had to be settled. Blood tests had proved conclusively that Chaplin could not be the father of Barry's child, but a judge in Los Angeles refused to dismiss the case, ruling that the 'ends of justice' would be best served by a 'full and fair trial of the issues'.

The paternity suit opened in April and dominated the headlines for several days, editors everywhere rightly guessing that the public would be grateful for a titillating break from the grim news of the war. Apart from the evidence provided by the blood tests, Chaplin's counsel also called on a Tulsa lawyer who testified that Barry had told him she was having an affair with 'an Oklahoma oilman' at the time her child was conceived. Getty was called once more to give evidence and swore he had not had 'intimate relations' with Miss Barry.

To the astonishment of virtually everyone, the jury ignored the medical evidence and ruled against Chaplin by an eleven-to-one majority. It was clear that the issue was no longer whether he was the recalcitrant father of an illegitimate child, but whether he was a commie fellow traveller and an anti-American: the jury had few doubts. Understandably, Chaplin was bitter and he was furious with Getty whom he clearly believed was the most likely candidate to be the father of Barry's child. Chaplin would not speak to Getty outside the court and continued to snub his former friend for many years.

Apart from his reluctant court appearances in connection with the Barry scandal, Paul spent all of 1944 in Tulsa. By the spring of 1945 the Spartan Aircraft Company was employing a workforce of 5500 and was recognised as one of the most efficient component manufacturers in the

United States. Getty noted proudly that during the years he had been in charge, the factory had manufactured 90 NP-1 trainers, the rudders, ailerons and elevators for 5800 B-24 bombers, hundreds of wings for Grumman Wildcat fighters, thousands of control surfaces for Douglas dive bombers, 2500 engine mounts for P-47 fighters and much else besides. 'I like to think,' he wrote in his diary, 'that I have made a worthwhile contribution to America's war effort and without any thought or possibility of financial profit.'

That summer of 1945, as events moved inexorably towards the cataclysmic end of World War Two at Hiroshima and Nagasaki, no one could have blamed J. Paul Getty for concluding that he had 'done his bit'. True, he never got to be captain of a destroyer in the Pacific, but he had built Spartan Aircraft into an efficient and reliable supplier of vital components for fighters and bombers in the front line. And factories like Spartan had helped win the war quite as much as the pilots who flew the planes.

Everyone who knew Paul expected him to return immediately to the Getty oil business at the end of the war; he was, after all, first and foremost an oilman. Instead he confounded his friends by throwing himself with great enthusiasm into an entirely new, and distinctly humdrum enterprise – the manufacture and sale of trailers or 'mobile homes', as he preferred them to be called.

Why a brilliantly successful oil millionaire with a labyrinthine network of companies would want to go into the trailer business was not immediately obvious, but a single entry in his diary that summer explained all: 'Damned if I'll just blow the whistle and have the Spartan factory turned into an ice-skating rink.'

Getty had been worrying about Spartan's uncertain future for some time. For all his reputation as a hard-headed and heartless businessman, he had conceived a curiously emotional attachment to the little factory and felt a sense of personal responsibility for the work force, most of whom owed their jobs to the expansion that he had instigated and directed. The Getty oil business was getting along perfectly well without him and after three years in Tulsa he simply did not have it in his heart to let Spartan wither away as the war contracts dried up.

'I had taken over the company in 1942,' he explained, 'and nursed it through its many and varied wartime growing pains. I could not bring myself to abandon it in what, in a manner of speaking, was its time of need. My personal interest in Spartan was far too keen, and my pride in its achievements too great, to allow me to do that.'

On 25 June, when Spartan produced its last B-32 aileron, Getty was already discussing options for the future with executives at the factory.

His first hope was that Spartan would be able to find a niche in the commercial aircraft market; before the war the company had produced a moderately successful all-metal monoplane, the *Spartan Executive*, with a top speed of 190 miles an hour. They debated ways in which the *Spartan Executive* could be updated and drew up tentative plans for a new eight-passenger aircraft, the *Spartan Skyway Traveller*, suitable for use by the growing number of feeder airlines.

A publicity brochure printed around that time was full of confidence. 'Spartan Aircraft Company has far-reaching plans for the future', it announced. 'Busy working for victory today, but planning for the great commercial "air age" tomorrow, it will start production of single and twin-engined all-metal personal transports as soon as the needs of the war programme are satisfied.'

After V-J Day, Getty suddenly changed his mind about Spartan's 'far-reaching' plans. 'I could not help but feel,' he confessed, 'that many serious drawbacks and pitfalls were concealed beneath their promise.' Foremost among the drawbacks he could foresee were the tens of thousands of aircraft produced for the war effort which could easily be modified for passenger-carrying and would soon flood on to the market as war surplus. Even if there was a demand for new commercial aircraft, it would mean Spartan trying to compete with well-established and enormously successful manufacturers like Boeing, Douglas, Cessna and Northrop.

Much as Getty hated to admit defeat, he was also a realist and he came to the conclusion the odds were stacked against Spartan so heavily that the company should look for a future in a field outside of aviation. They talked about making refrigerators, small domestic appliances, home heaters and even automobiles, but discarded them all for one reason or another. It was Captain Balfour who came up with what appeared to be the most likely idea – mobile homes and trailers. Very little housing had been built during the war and thousands of service-men would soon be returning to their families and looking for a place to live. Not only that, but America had become a highly mobile society: families were accustomed to travelling great distances to look for work.

Getty did not for a moment consider allowing anyone else to supervise the conversion of the Spartan Aircraft Company into Spartan Mobile Homes. 'By rights,' he said, 'I suppose I should have gone back to work expanding my oil business. But I had come to regard Spartan as my personal responsibility.'

For the next two years the oil millionaire was proudly in charge of the manufacture and sale of a range of superior trailers to suit every pocket, from the basic 'Spartanette' to the luxurious 'Royal Mansion'.

*　　*　　*

Teddy, ignored in Los Angeles, could just about understand why Paul had felt the need to be in Tulsa during the war. But she found it extremely difficult to understand why he wanted to be in Tulsa *after* the war manufacturing *trailers*. Teddy did not know much about trailers and the folk who lived in them and, frankly, did not consider she had missed very much.

Since their wedding in 1939 they had spent no more than a few weeks together, as both of them were equally determined to pursue their own careers. Teddy had not achieved her ambition to be a star of the opera, but she had had some success as a singer having been invited on a concert tour of the southwest and, on one occasion, performing at the Hollywood Bowl. She got her most regular work dubbing songs for the movies, although she had actually appeared in a small part in *The Lost Weekend* with Ray Milland. Ironically, she played an opera star.

In the hope of getting more work in films, she had moved into the beach house at Santa Monica and equipped herself with the accoutrements of a star – a manager, an agent, a publicist and a personal masseur. She also bought herself a Lincoln Continental on the strength of a promised recording contract. When Paul first saw it, during a rare visit to Los Angeles, his reaction was typical. He eyed its magnificent dimensions and grunted: 'I can't afford a car like that.'

There was a moment, in the spring of 1945, when it seemed that their marriage might have a chance. Paul decided it was time they had a permanent home of their own and he bought a ranch house on seventy-five acres of land fronting on to the Pacific Coast Highway at Malibu. The property was part of an old Spanish land-grant hacienda and was formerly owned by a Los Angeles judge, who had built the existing house in the twenties. Paul paid $184,000 for the house and $600,000 for the land and was comforted by the knowledge that he had got a bargain. He told Teddy that when wartime building restrictions were lifted, he would renovate and extend the house, adding a museum wing for his art collection and a small concert theatre for her.

Meanwhile they spent some time together in the beach house, a short way down the coast at Santa Monica. Paul had no desire to move back to South Kingsley Drive, with its attendant memories of his 'dearest darling'; in any case he liked the beach house and found it wonderfully soothing to sit at nights listening to the soft lisp of the surf. Teddy had all the rooms redecorated and planted a lawn in the front garden and for a while they pretended they had a marriage. But each of them found it increasingly hard to conceal from the other a single, daunting truth – that Teddy was much more interested in her career than she was in Paul and Paul was infinitely more interested in his business than he was in Teddy. He was soon back at the factory in Tulsa and Teddy bitterly joked to her friends that she had been jilted for a trailer.

In February 1946 a further complication was added to their deteriorating relationship. Teddy discovered she was pregnant, as a result of Paul's brief trip home the previous Christmas. When she telephoned Paul in Tulsa to break the news, he seemed pleased but rather more excited by events in the factory. He told her proudly he expected production to reach more than seventy units a week in March and that already Spartan mobile homes were being described as the 'Cadillacs of the trailer industry'. Teddy said she was happy for him.

From the moment he decided Spartan would go into the trailer business, Getty was determined to demolish the idea that mobile homes were only fit for 'low-class bums'. Thus the quality of Spartan trailers, even the bottom-of-the-range 'Spartanette', was exemplary. All of them had large picture windows, proper insulation and heating and fully-fitted interiors finished to a high standard. 'In the past,' he said, 'trailers were rather sleazy affairs, little more than shacks on wheels. Ours were real homes, designed and built for comfortable, pleasant living and were radical departures from most of those built previously.'

On 14 June Getty received a telephone call from a hospital in Los Angeles to say that Teddy had gone into labour unexpectedly and had given birth to a boy at nine o'clock that morning. The baby was two months premature and weighed only four pounds fourteen ounces. Teddy was all right, but the doctors were worried about the baby. 'I can't express my disappointment at not having been with her,' Getty wrote in his diary next day, 'but she wasn't expecting the baby until August. Exciting to talk to her. Sent masses of roses.'

So involved was Getty at Spartan – it was a 'most crucial period' he explained, a trifle unconvincingly – that he felt unable to take a train to Los Angeles to see his new son, who was to be called Timothy Ware Getty, until the beginning of July. Between times he resolved to fast for a few days. One of the many quack doctors he often consulted told him that fasting 'cleansed the system' and was not only beneficial to his bowels but also tested his willpower and was thus good for his brain. From after dinner on 20 June he ate nothing for a week and drank only water. 'My first meal after seven days and nine hours', he wrote in his diary, 'was a small broiled rare steak.'

Timothy was still in hospital when Getty finally arrived in Los Angeles. The doctors warned him that the baby had a very frail constitution. Getty's concern was reflected in his diary over the next few days.

8 July: 'To hospital to see my son. Timothy now weighs six pounds but is anaemic; his red-cell count is only sixty-five. Poor little man, he has had a hard time.'

10 July: 'Timothy came home today. He has two nurses.'

13 July: 'With Teddy and Timothy to hospital, where he had a blood transfusion. His red count was down to forty-seven. Much anxiety and fear until the danger passed after his transfusion.'

Something happened to Paul Getty while he was watching his sickly newborn son fight for life. He marvelled that such a tiny scrap of humanity, the fruit of his loins, should exhibit such a determination to survive against the odds. When the immediate crisis passed and Timothy returned home to the beach house once more, Paul could not have been more proud that his son had pulled through; he felt as if it was a personal triumph. Thereafter, Getty made no secret of the fact that Timothy was his most adored and favourite son.

George, Ronnie, Paul and Gordon did not suffer overmuch from their father's favouritism since they saw so little of him and, in any case, they were growing up. George was still in the army (having spent two years in the Pacific as an infantry officer, he had been assigned to a war-crimes prosecution team in the Philippines after V-J Day); Ronnie was soon to enrol at the University of Southern California; and young Paul and his brother Gordon were both at St Ignatius High School in San Francisco, where their mother now lived.

Paul's devotion to Timothy did not, of course, prevent his returning to the trailer factory in Tulsa where there was still much to be done. With around seven hundred mobile homes rolling off the production lines every month, Paul began to concern himself with the sales side of the operation. He soon learned that Spartan lost many customers because they were unable to raise loans or arrange insurance. 'Some of the nation's banks and insurance companies apparently thought of trailer owners as irresponsible nomads,' he noted tartly. 'When lending institutions did deign to finance house-trailer purchases, they called for terms which made it difficult for the average worker, serviceman or retired person – the people who accounted for the bulk of trailer sales – to buy them.'

As a wealthy oilman Paul had considerable clout with financial institutions and he took the problem to the Bank of America, where he received a much more sympathetic ear than the average trailer manufacturer could expect. With the cooperation of the Bank, Getty set up the Minnehoma Financial Company and the Minnehoma Insurance Company (the names commemorated his father's first oil company) to assist the purchasers of Spartan trailers. Whereas previously customers had been obliged to find forty per cent of the purchase price as a down payment and pay ten per cent interest on their loans, Minnehoma slashed interest rates to five per cent and reduced the minimum down payment to only twenty-five per cent. The line on the sales graph in Paul's office in the Spartan factory rose dramatically.

Spartan Mobile Homes lost two million dollars in 1946, due primarily to the high capital cost of retooling, but by 1947 the company was solidly in the black and Getty was able to spend more time in Los Angeles where he interested himself once more in what was happening in the Getty oil business. Back with at least one hand on the helm, he judged that the moment had come to reactivate his long-running Tide Water campaign. Although he had been preoccupied with matters at Spartan for some years, he never for a moment lost sight of the goal he had set himself in 1932 – to merge Tide Water with the Getty interests to create a major integrated oil company.

In 1946 he had approved the merger of George F. Getty Inc. into Pacific Western to form the Pacific Western Oil Corporation. By 1947, Pacific Western and the Mission Corporation together owned thirty per cent of Tide Water. During that year, Getty proved that he had lost none of his old skills and directed a dazzling and complex corporate juggling act to increase the Getty interests' leverage over Tide Water stock. It involved setting up another holding company – Mission Development – to swallow up Tide Water stock as Mission Corporation acquired it, and constant transferring of dividends and stock between different companies. At the end of a year of ingenious manipulation Getty had increased his Tide Water holding to thirty-five per cent. He was well-satisfied.

While Getty was thus occupied, his son George returned from the Far East, having been discharged from the army. To Getty's well-disguised delight, George announced that he did not intend to return to Princeton to graduate. 'I know I want to go into the oil business,' he told his father, 'so why waste time?' By the summer of 1947 he was working as an 'independent' oil producer (with very considerable help from his father) under the aegis of Pacific Western to gain experience in the business.

Early in 1948 Getty, Teddy and Timmy moved at last into the ranch house. Building and renovation work had taken two years but the old hacienda, with its white stucco walls, elaborate wrought-iron work and red-tiled roof, had been transformed into a luxurious modern house entirely suitable for a millionaire art collector and his family.

The property was approached through iron gates set in a stone wall fronting on to the Pacific Coast Highway. A steep, winding drive bordered by old trees led up, past two life-size lions carved in white marble, to a walled courtyard with a tall Italian marble fountain splashing softly in the centre. The view from the courtyard was spectacular – a huge expanse of velvet lawn gently sloping down to clumps of lemon and olive groves, intersected by a crystal stream fed from a spring trickling out of a nearby canyon wall. Beyond the garden was the shimmering ocean, startlingly blue and flecked most days with little white sails. The house itself was long and low, recognisably Spanish in style, with all the rooms overlooking the sea and opening on to the terrace. Behind it was a stand of huge eucalyptus trees and the dark green flanks of the Santa Monica mountains.

Paul, who had never before been able to gather together his art collection under one roof, turned the house into a showcase for his treasures. There was a long picture gallery, in which the Rembrandt and the Gainsborough took pride of place among a large collection of paintings of the seventeenth-century Dutch School. One room was furnished entirely with exquisite pieces from the Louis XVI period, another was devoted to Louis XV and hung with eighteenth-century French tapestries. In the 'classical room' the floor was a first-century Italian mosaic which he had bought when he was in Rome in 1939; the dining-room was Queen Anne and the library was panelled with fifteenth-century English oak. Among the books on the shelves in the library was every G.A. Henty novel Paul had ever read and his father's Ohio law books.

In the grounds of the ranch house was a miniature zoo which included a lioness called Teresa, two brown bears, a pair of bison and a white wolf. Getty liked animals and liked to think he had a special rapport with them. He took a great interest in the zoo and visited it every day when he was at the ranch house to make sure the animals were well-fed and cared for.

Although Teddy had three giant sequoia trees planted at the top of the drive to mark the three of them taking up residence, in truth she much preferred the beach house. She thought of the beach house as her *home*, whereas it was hard to think of the ranch as anything but a museum for her husband's art collection. It certainly was not the kind of place to bring up a small child – little Timmy was learning to walk and loved to clear table tops by delightedly sweeping everything on to the floor. As the ranch was crammed with valuable antiques, the little boy had the capacity for causing thousands of dollars worth of damage if left alone for more than a moment.

Paul did not share Teddy's reservations. He was enormously proud of the ranch and felt it gave him the opportunity to enjoy his possessions at last. He never tired of showing visitors round, particularly other collectors. As far as he was concerned, the ranch had only one fault – the automatic opening device he had had fitted to the iron gates on the Pacific Coast Highway sometimes failed to work, with embarrassing consequences. An 'electric eye' in his Cadillac was supposed to open the gates as he approached and close them behind him after he had driven through. At first it worked perfectly and Paul found it amusing to drive full speed at the gates, particularly if he had someone with him in the car. But one day the gates did not open as they should have done and he was forced to brake furiously at the last minute to avoid crashing into them. On another occasion the gates closed too soon and, to his annoyance, squashed the rear of his car.

Because Teddy and Paul felt so very differently about the ranch, Teddy stayed at the beach house with Timmy whenever she could and Paul was often alone at the ranch. It did nothing for their marriage. A Dutch art dealer whom Getty invited to stay saw nothing of Teddy or the baby the whole time he was there. When he nervously inquired about them, Getty grunted that they were 'out of town' and changed the subject.

Getty might have been happy to spend the rest of his days at the ranch, either with or without Teddy, but towards the end of 1948 something happened which changed the whole course of his life.

One morning in November he received a cable from Kuwait which contained just four words – 'STRUCTURES INDICATE OIL – WALTON.'

PART THREE

THE RICHEST TYCOON
1949-64

11. 'In the name of God, the Merciful and Compassionate ...'

The existence of oil in the Middle East had been known for centuries. Noah was said to have used pitch to caulk the Ark, Herodotus spoke of a bitumen substance in the walls of Babylon and Genesis described an oily slime used as a mortar to build the Tower of Babel. Oil seepages along the Jabal Zait ridge in Egypt prompted the Romans to name it Mons Petroleus and a gas escape on the banks of the Euphrates which burst into flames five hundred years before the birth of Christ was thereafter venerated as the Eternal Fires of Nebuchadrezzar.

Although the ancient civilisations of the Middle East made use of oil wherever it appeared (if for nothing else, it was always prized for its medicinal properties), it was not until the dawn of the twentieth century that serious attempts were made to extract it from the ground in commercial quantities. In 1901 the first European prospectors in the Middle East were granted a concession by the Shah of Persia to drill for oil. Working in wild and mountainous country where the temperature in the summer reached 110 degrees Fahrenheit before seven o'clock in the morning, plagued by locusts and outbreaks of smallpox, and constantly sniped at by hostile local tribesmen, they toiled for six dispiriting years without a strike. On the brink of abandoning the operation and with their funds virtually exhausted, they resolved in March 1908 to sink one last hole on the site of an ancient fire temple at Masjid-i-Sulaiman. At four o'clock on the morning of 26 May, the drill struck oil at a depth of 1180 feet and the prodigious Middle Eastern oil industry came into being. By 1914 a pipeline stretched across the desert from the Masjid-i-Sulaiman oilfield to a refinery on the coast and Persia was producing an impressive 273,000 tons of oil a year.

After World War One major oil companies in Europe and America competed in an undignified scramble for drilling rights in the Middle East, somewhat to the mystification of ruling sheikhs and local potentates who found it difficult to comprehend why the infidels got so excited about the thick black liquid in the ground. Competition hotted up considerably after a sensational strike at Baba Gurgur in Iraq, only a mile and a half from the Eternal Fires of Nebuchadrezzar. On 15 October 1927 a drilling crew at Baba Gurgur broke into one of the

175

biggest oilfields in the world, with terrifying consequences. Two members of the crew were killed instantly as the well blew out, demolishing the rig and sending a jet of oil into the air so high that it could be seen twelve miles distant. For more than a week the well 'flowed wild' – out of control – spewing some 12,500 tons of crude over the surrounding country every day. It was the first real indication of the bonanza to come.

Three years later in neighbouring Saudi Arabia Abdul Aziz Ibn Saud, absolute monarch of that vast and forbidding desert kingdom, reluctantly agreed to allow foreigners into his country to seek oil, in the hope of filling the kingdom's severely depleted coffers. Ibn Saud was a descendant of the family which had ruled much of Arabia before being driven into penniless exile in Kuwait in the latter half of the nineteenth century. In 1901 Ibn Saud, then twenty-one, led a raiding party of forty loyal tribesmen on camels back into Arabia in a bold attempt to regain control of his family's lands. They slipped into the capital, Riyadh, by night and stormed the castle at dawn, killing the governor.

This daring exploit rallied supporters to Ibn Saud's cause and for the next twenty years he rampaged across central Arabia, determinedly reconquering Saudi territory. Tall, charismatic, powerfully built and fearless, he was a born warrior and inspired the fanatical devotion of his Bedouin followers. As a devout Muslim he fostered religious fanaticism as a means of defeating his enemies, founding an extremist Muslim brotherhood known as the Ikhwan and encouraging it to plunder and massacre his opponents with ruthless zeal. Members of the Ikhwan believed the Koran to be literally the word of God and were happy to shed their blood for Ibn Saud, for to die on the battlefield was a passport to paradise. By the end of the twenties Ibn Saud and his puritanical army had killed, captured or put to flight all their enemies and Ibn Saud was the undisputed ruler of four fifths of the Arabian peninsula, stretching from the Persian Gulf to the Red Sea.

With no one left to fight, the great desert warrior unified his dominions into the Kingdom of Saudi Arabia and instituted an autocratic regime of medieval ferocity. Drinking or smoking was punished by the lash, thieves had their hands chopped off at the wrist. Sexual intercourse, even with wives or concubines, was unlawful during the hours of daylight. Men found guilty of committing adultery during Ramadan were beheaded, women were stoned to death. It was forbidden to laugh in the street or to sing, or to listen to music, or to exhibit 'arrogance' on pain of a public whipping.

The king found none of these restrictions onerous, for he had pleasures in plenty, notably what was tactfully described by a courtier as a 'marked tendency to uxoriousness'. By the time he was fifty Ibn Saud proudly claimed he had married 135 virgins and enjoyed concubines without number. While he never exceeded the four wives allowed to him by Koranic law, he often tired of them rapidly after the wedding night; some he divorced without even bothering to remove their veils. Each of his four wives had a house of her own with a full complement of servants, while the king occupied a palace where a changing rota of four concubines and four favoured slave girls shared his embraces. To add to these immoderate domestic expenses, Ibn Saud fathered forty-four sons and they in turn produced an alarmingly large number of grandsons, all of whom expected to be kept in princely style.

Excess also marked another of the king's pursuits – hunting. Unfortunately, the arrival of the car and the machine gun in Saudi Arabia rather changed the nature of this particular sport. Whereas once he would have ridden out into the desert on horseback with a hawk and a rifle, he was now driven by chauffeur and blazed away at anything that moved with a machine gun mounted on the back of the car. Ibn Saud killed for the sheer joy of it – he once slaughtered a complete herd of rare gazelle in less than fifteen minutes. The king and his hunting companions quickly managed to reduce much of Saudi Arabia's wildlife to extinction levels. Ostriches, which were common before 1930, were completely wiped out and the few surviving ibex and gazelle sought refuge high in the mountains where even the king's resourceful Italian chauffeur was unable to follow.

Only one little problem curbed the king's pleasures or caused him concern – he was always short of money. Saudi Arabia's sole source of income was from the pilgrims who flocked every year to Mecca, but the world recession and continuing unrest in the Arabian peninsula had greatly reduced the scale of the pilgrimage and the revenue it produced. With so many wives and sons to support, not to mention the concubines and slaves, Ibn Saud's profligate lifestyle ensured that the kingdom teetered constantly on the brink of bankruptcy.

One of the king's closest advisers was an eccentric Englishman by the name of Harry St John Philby. An Arabist scholar and explorer, Philby had previously worked for the British colonial service in Baghdad but resigned in protest at British treatment of the Arabs and shocked his countrymen by 'going native': he embraced the Muslim faith and set up home in Mecca. In the process, he became close to Ibn Saud and it was commonly said that he was the only man at court who dared to argue with the king or offer advice unasked.

One afternoon in 1930 while out for a drive in the desert with Philby, the king confessed to his worry about the country's economy. Philby, who recognised the oil potential of the area, bluntly told the king that he was 'asleep on the site of buried treasure' and quoted a favourite passage from the Koran: 'God changeth not that which is in people unless they change that which is in themselves.'

Challenged to make my meaning clear [Philby explained later], I said I had no doubt whatever that his enormous country contained rich mineral resources, though they were of little use to him or anybody else in the bowels of the earth. Their existence could only be proved by expert prospection, while their ultimate exploitation for the benefit of the country necessarily involved the cooperation of foreign technicians and capital. Yet the government seemed to have set its face against the development of its potential wealth by foreign agencies.

Ibn Saud pondered Philby's words and clearly decided they made sense. A few weeks later an American geologist, Karl Twitchell, was invited into Saudi Arabia to prospect in the desert for oil. Twitchell's reports were highly favourable and he was asked to return to the United States to communicate to American oil companies the king's willingness to discuss concessions. There was only one problem – the king wanted to be paid in gold. This condition caused consternation and some delay among oil companies unfamiliar with the foibles of Middle Eastern rulers. Standard Oil of California, which had recently drilled successful wells in Bahrain, eventually managed to scratch together thirty-five thousand pounds worth of gold bars and won the concession. In September 1933 geologists from Standard Oil waded ashore on the coast of Saudi Arabia at Damman, hired camels and soon located a promising structure only five miles inland at Jabal Dhahran.

Six years later, King Ibn Saud was invited to attend the formal opening ceremony of the Dhahran oilfield. He arrived with an entourage of two thousand slaves, servants, wives and concubines after a journey of a thousand miles across the desert and camped outside the prefabricated oil town which had grown up around the oilfield. On the following day, he turned a valve on a pipeline and the oil began to flow. During two days of celebrations, the king and his party were entertained on the deck of an American oil tanker moored offshore and he reciprocated with a huge banquet laid out on the sand by the flickering light of the oilfield flares. Standard Oil executives presented the king with a Cadillac to mark the occasion and he handed out carved golden daggers in return.

Ibn Saud would never have to worry about money again. Within a few years, his personal income jumped from $200,000 a year to $2,500,000 *a week*.

J. Paul Getty followed developments in the Middle East with consuming interest and more than a twinge of frustration. In 1932 he had been offered the chance of a concession in Iraq, but had turned it down. It was a mistake he would never repeat and never forgot. Even when he was an old man, whenever he was asked by journalists if he had ever made any mistakes in his career he would always recall, with a rare wolfish smile, what he liked to describe as his 'classic boner'.

It was the fabulous strike at Baba Gurgur in 1927 that had originally stirred his interest in Iraq. All the geological surveys of the area and test-drilling by European prospectors indicated the presence of vast petroleum deposits under the sand of the Mesopotamian desert. 'I thought then it would be an excellent idea to get in on the ground floor,' he said, 'and I appointed a representative in Baghdad to negotiate an exploration and drilling concession with Iraqi officials.'

Early in 1932 he received a message from Baghdad that a potentially lucrative concession would shortly be available. 'The initial cost would have been minimal,' Getty confessed, 'a matter of some tens of thousands of dollars.' But at that moment, Paul suffered an uncharacteristic crisis of confidence. Several factors were involved. One of them was a sudden break in US crude prices following the opening up of huge oilfields in east Texas. American crude was selling for ten cents a barrel and less and the industry was thrown into a temporary panic. More importantly, the tempting prospect of acquiring Tide Water had appeared on the distant horizon and he was already deeply involved in tussles with his mother and the other Getty directors over the question of buying stock.

> I should have jumped at the chance and grabbed the concession – but I didn't. Much of my capital was tied up in Pacific Western stock and in other ventures. I hesitated to risk large capital outlays on operations in the Middle East; I was afraid I would be spreading my resources too thinly. After debating the question with myself for several weeks, I decided against the Middle Eastern venture and instructed my agent in Baghdad to break off negotiations. My decision was a classic boner, one that I would rue and regret in the years that followed. I allowed a fantastically valuable concession to slip out of my hands even though it was being offered at a comparatively negligible price.

By the end of World War Two, Paul considered it to be imperative for the Getty companies to obtain a foothold in the Middle East. 'It was evident,' he said, 'that the Middle East was the key to the world's oil supply in the future and unless we had a stake in the Middle East we would be hard-pressed to meet the heavy competition that would soon develop for overseas markets.'

Other oil companies felt the same and after V-J Day there was a rush for concessions virtually anywhere in the Middle East. Getty bided his time and was glad of it – several of his rivals bought exploration and drilling rights in North Africa for large sums, only to discover that the whole territory was thickly sown with land mines left behind after the war. Clearing the mines cost millions of dollars and when at last it was thought safe for test-drilling to begin, no oil was found.

Getty's chance came in October 1948, soon after he had moved into the ranch house at Malibu, when he learned that offers would shortly be sought for a half-share of the drilling rights in a place called the Neutral Zone. He did not at that time know precisely where the Neutral Zone was, but one look at the map stirred his interest.

The Neutral Zone covered 2100 square miles of desert bordering the Persian Gulf between Kuwait and Saudi Arabia. An arid, trackless wasteland virtually uninhabited except for a few hardy nomad tribes, the zone was established in 1922 by an agreement between the Sheikh of Kuwait and Ibn Saud that there should be a neutral buffer zone between their frontiers where tribes from both countries would retain grazing and watering rights, but no forts would be built. Sir Percy Cox, the British high commissioner in Baghdad who had helped negotiate the agreement, expected that in time firm frontiers would be fixed and the zone would eventually disappear, but it never happened.

Neither the politics of the Neutral Zone nor its desolate topography mattered much to Getty: what interested him was that there were producing wells both to the north and to the south. It was hard to believe there was no oil under that broad tract of burning sand.

Complications involving joint ownership – both Kuwait and Saudi Arabia had the right to grant oil concessions within the zone – had prevented test-drilling previously. Ibn Saud included the Neutral Zone in the concession he granted in 1933 to Standard Oil of California, but Standard Oil could not prospect in the area without a similar concession from Kuwait, which it had been unable to obtain. Sheikh Ahmad-al-Subah of Kuwait was in no hurry to grant drilling rights in the Neutral Zone, correctly guessing that the longer he delayed the higher the price would be.

In 1946 Sheikh Ahmad judged the time had come to see what he could get for his fifty per cent share of the Neutral Zone's mineral resources. He announced he was ready to auction drilling rights to the highest bidder, but warned interested parties that 'derisory' offers of the kind that had been accepted for concessions before the war would not be entertained. Gulf, Burmah, Shell and a number of other British and American oil companies immediately declared their intention to bid, but they were all pre-empted by an astonishing offer from an outside syndicate.

Veteran oilman Ralph K. Davies – a former director of Standard Oil of California – put together a syndicate of ten independent oil companies, called the American Independent Oil Company (Aminoil), and made a spectacular pitch for the Kuwait concession in the hope of forcing the 'majors' out of the market. The terms, when they were revealed, brought gasps of disbelief from oilmen everywhere. Aminoil offered an immediate down payment of $7,250,000, plus guaranteed annual payments of at least $625,000 and a royalty of thirty-three cents per barrel of oil produced – the highest, by far, in the Middle East. Even so, the canny Sheikh Ahmad did not immediately accept, producing instead a list of further conditions he would require written into any agreement. He wanted, among other things, a promise that Aminoil would build a refinery and a new hospital and provide educational facilities for Kuwaiti employees. Aminoil acquiesced to all his demands.

The major oil companies were horrified by the deal and accused Aminoil of 'ruining' the market. Just a few years earlier, the concession for the whole of Kuwait had cost only $170,000 and Standard Oil had acquired 440,000 square miles of Saudi Arabia – as big as Texas, Louisiana, Oklahoma and New Mexico put together – for less than $200,000. Ralph Davies made no apologies for Aminoil's apparent generosity. He held the view that the 'majors' had unscrupulously exploited many of the rulers in the Middle East, some of whom were completely unaware of the true value of their countries' resources. In the developing years of the Middle Eastern oil industry, the Arabs had been the last to benefit and the 'majors' often paid more in tax to their own governments than they did to the countries which owned the oil. Davies believed it was high time oil companies started to pay a fair price for the Middle East's mineral wealth.

Two months after the Sheikh of Kuwait signed the Aminoil agreement King Ibn Saud, ever with an eye to boosting his income, declared that he was ready to consider offers for Saudi Arabia's interest in the Neutral Zone. (Standard Oil, now renamed the Arabian-American Oil Company, had been persuaded to relinquish its drilling rights in the zone in return for an offshore concession along the coast of the Persian Gulf.) Among the oil companies immediately posting an intention to bid was Pacific Western, owned by J. Paul Getty.

Although Getty detested paying a cent more than the going rate for anything, whether it was a shoeshine or an oil company, he largely shared Ralph Davies's views about the terms offered by the 'majors' for oil concessions in the Middle East. 'When I go into the Middle East,' he said, 'I don't want to feel I have to run down an alley every time I see an Arab approaching.'

Nevertheless the Aminoil deal gave him pause for thought, for he knew enough about the Arabs to realise that Ibn Saud would be strongly disinclined to accept less than the Sheikh of Kuwait for Saudi

Arabia's share of the Neutral Zone and would be very likely to demand a great deal more.

In the library of the ranch house at Malibu Getty sat for hours at a mahogany desk, munching maple-sugar candy and slowly reading through geological reports and surveys. He had asked his personal assistant, a young moon-faced accountant by the name of Norris Bramlett, to provide him with every scrap of known information about the Neutral Zone and its surroundings and he methodically plodded through an enormous pile of research, filing detailed information in his head and rarely taking a note. Although he was in his mid-fifties – his hair was thinning and grey at the temples – he was still able to command astonishing powers of concentration over long periods without ever appearing to tire: the lights in the library customarily burned until two or three o'clock in the morning. When he was satisfied that he had read everything there was to read, he was sufficiently encouraged to call in some expert advice.

One morning in early November 1948 a small light aircraft took off from a sand airstrip in Kuwait and headed south towards the Neutral Zone. On board, sitting next to the pilot, was Doctor Paul Walton, considered by Getty to be one of the world's finest petroleum geologists. For the next two hours the plane flew low over the barren dunes of the Neutral Zone while Walton stared intently through the window, squinting in the glare and jotting notes on a pad resting on his knee. Occasionally they encountered Bedouin tribes and the men on the ground shook their fists at the noisy machine frightening their camels. When the fuel ran low, the pilot nudged Walton and jabbed a finger in the direction of Kuwait. The geologist nodded and sat back to enjoy the return flight, convinced he had seen enough. At the cable office in Kuwait, Walton scrawled 'STRUCTURES INDICATE OIL – WALTON' on a crumpled cable form and addressed it to J. Paul Getty at 19875 Pacific Coast Highway, Los Angeles.

The instant Getty read Walton's cable, he telephoned Dave Hecht in New York and said he wanted to open negotiations immediately with King Ibn Saud to bid for the oil concession in the Neutral Zone. On 8 December 1948 Hecht's partner, Barnabas Hadfield, left for Saudi Arabia with instructions to outbid the opposition and secure the concession for Pacific Western.

In Riyadh, Hadfield found there was already aggressive competition for the concession. Aminoil were in the bidding, hoping to tie up the Neutral Zone entirely for themselves, as was the huge Royal Dutch-Shell combine. But every time Hadfield cabled Los Angeles for authority to increase Pacific Western's offer, Getty gave his unhesitating approval. 'I confidently increased my offers,' Getty said simply, 'until the others gave up and dropped out.'

The agreement finally hammered out between Pacific Western and Saudi Arabia for oil and gas rights in the Neutral Zone filled forty-six pages and was even more startling than the Aminoil deal with Kuwait. The contract document, signed by Hadfield and King Ibn Saud on 20 February 1949, opened with the words: 'In the Name of God, the Merciful and Compassionate. This agreement entered into in Riyadh on the twenty-second day of the month of Rabie 11, the year 1368, corresponding to the twentieth day of February 1949 ...'

It was not the flowery preamble that raised eyebrows throughout the oil industry but the onerous, some said outrageous, terms that followed. Pacific Western agreed to make an immediate down payment to Ibn Saud of $9,500,000 followed by annual payments of $1,000,000 *regardless of whether or not oil was found* in the Neutral Zone. These annual payments would be an advance on an agreed royalty of fifty-five cents per barrel, should oil be discovered. Pacific Western further consented to:

*Pay twenty-five per cent of its net profits in tax to the government of Saudi Arabia

*Build a 12,000 barrel refinery and 150,000 barrel storage facilities

*Deliver 100,000 gallons of gasoline and 50,000 gallons of kerosene to the government every year following the opening of the refinery

*Allow Saudi government representatives to attend Pacific Western board meetings

*Provide pension, retirement, insurance and other fringe benefits for all Saudi Arabian personnel employed by the company, along with free medical care

*Provide educational facilities for the children of Saudi employees, including further education for promising pupils and scholarships to the United States

*Build a mosque, housing, office accommodation, post office, telephone facilities and water supply systems for the benefit of all employees.

'The terms made me realise,' Getty noted drily, 'that I had come a very long way since the days when I bought my first lease for five hundred dollars.'

If the Aminoil deal horrified the major oil companies, the Getty deal provoked widespread anger, condemnation and dismay. As Howard

Page, of Standard Oil of New Jersey, said: 'This could change everything in the Middle East.'

Getty was denounced for 'upping the ante' to such an extent that future profits were likely to be severely circumscribed, even if there were profits to be made at all. None of the oil companies in the Middle East had any doubt that every caliph, sultan and sheikh would soon be demanding more money and terms similar to those negotiated by Ibn Saud.

As he was risking no one's money but his own, Getty remained serenely unperturbed by the reaction of other oilmen or by frequent predictions that the Neutral Zone adventure must inevitably lead to his ruin. 'There were many individuals in the industry,' he cheerfully agreed, 'who, for the umpteenth time in my career, freely predicted I would bankrupt my companies and myself.'

In fact, he very nearly did. As soon as the covenant with Ibn Saud was signed in Riyadh, Getty met Aminoil representatives in Los Angeles to discuss conducting joint operations in the Neutral Zone. As production would have to be equally shared, it seemed eminently sensible for the two concessionaires to work together and Getty was anxious to come to an arrangement with Aminoil without delay.

Ralph Davies agreed on the need to cooperate, but made it clear he wanted Aminoil to take the lead. Aminoil was the senior company, he claimed, inasmuch as it had obtained its concession first, but more importantly, the syndicate included a number of oil companies bigger than Pacific Western and could call on greater technical and organisational resources than those available to Getty. Davies proposed that Aminoil should conduct all the initial exploration and test-drilling, thus avoiding wasteful duplication of effort. He suggested that Pacific Western should send only a small skeleton team to the Neutral Zone; Pacific Western's role would be 'consultative' and, of course, financial, since Pacific Western would be expected to contribute its full share of the development costs.

While it was true that Pacific Western did not have the same resources available to Aminoil, Getty was deeply averse to the idea of effectively handing over control of the Neutral Zone venture to outsiders. Nevertheless, much against his better judgement, he grudgingly accepted Davies's proposition. 'I am not much of a believer in allowing others to take my responsibilities or do my work for me,' he said. 'However, I allowed myself to be talked into the arrangement.' It cost him dear.

To protect his interests, Getty dispatched his eldest son, George, to the Neutral Zone in March 1949. George Franklin Getty II was by then twenty-four, tall, dark-haired and heavily built, a likeable enough young man with a winning smile that gave an impression of more confidence than he in reality possessed. Following his father's advice, he had been working as an 'independent' oil producer for Pacific Western for nearly two years and had opened the South Crane field in Texas. Getty fondly believed that George displayed a natural aptitude for the business, despite an unimpressive academic record at school and university.

As the newly-appointed manager of the Saudi Arabian Division of the Pacific Western Oil Corporation, George was enormously pleased and flattered to be entrusted by his father with such an important enterprise, even though Pacific Western would be taking a back seat in the Neutral Zone operations. Wasting no time, he established a headquarters office in Jeddah, the administrative capital on the Red Sea coast, and spent his first few months in Saudi Arabia studying the operations of other oil companies in the Middle East.

He found the Gettys were far from popular: as predicted, the Getty deal had considerably 'upped the ante' everywhere. King Ibn Saud, for example, craftily inquired of the Arabian-American Oil Company why it was that if one man could pay $10,500,000 for the opportunity to prospect in a part of Saudi Arabia where oil was yet to be found, Aramco had only paid $28,000,000 in 1948 for all the oil flowing out of Dhahran? Ibn Saud said he wanted more money and not only money. He also wanted schools and roads and hospitals; he even wanted a ludicrously uneconomic railroad to be built from Riyadh to Dhahran at a cost of $160,000,000. Fearful of losing their concession, Aramco acceded to the king's demands even though it sometimes seemed there would be no end to them.

George discovered to his discomfort that because his name was Getty, he shouldered the blame for encouraging the king's avarice and he was not sorry when the time came for him to set off for the Neutral Zone with two Getty geologists, Dr Paul Walton and Emil Kluth, the veteran petroleum geologist who had been with the Getty companies since the days of the Minnehoma Oil Company in Oklahoma. They arrived in November 1949 and found that Aminoil had set up a floating base camp on an old tank-landing craft anchored offshore.

Nothing, not even the rigours of service in the Pacific during World War Two, prepared George for the Neutral Zone: it was, he soon determined, one of the most inhospitable places on the face of the earth. In November, at the beginning of the 'winter', the oilmen sweltered during the day and froze at night when the temperature plummeted. Along the coast, humidity was frequently one hundred per cent so that the slightest exertion drenched the body in perspiration. Even when it rained, there was no relief: sudden cloudbursts, often of hail, could turn the desert green, as if by magic, overnight – but it was a transformation that invariably attracted swarms of locusts, darkening the sky with their loathsome voracity. Between the fitful downpours the wind whipped up fierce dust storms, the dreaded *tauz*, which could last for days and clogged the eyes, mouth, nose, hair and ears with sand.

George soon learned to wear thick leather boots on shore to provide protection from the giant scorpions and vipers that infested the sand dunes. He also quickly found himself immune to the allure of the warm blue waters of the Persian Gulf: the sea which lapped so invitingly along the coast of the Neutral Zone was teeming with sharks and shoals of pink jellyfish capable of inflicting painful stings.

As if the stress caused by the climate and environment was not enough, there was also the problem of culture shock: the sense of stepping back through time to a Biblical society of incomprehensible barbarity, superstition and ignorance. In the makeshift camp for locally-recruited labour, set up on shore close to the anchorage, it seemed that every child was covered by suppurating sores crawling with flies. Hot branding irons applied to the skin was the accepted remedy for stomach cramps and the urine of female camels was used to 'sterilise' open wounds.

When the oilmen reported an Arab youth to the local emir for stealing their supplies they were appalled to discover, when they next saw him, that he had a bloody stump where his right hand used to be. Later, George read with mounting horror another oilman's account of a public execution in Al Hufuf:

> They had shaved off his hair and his beard and they brought him on to this platform with his hands tied behind his back. The poor guy looked surprisingly calm and resigned. There were two executioners, big Negro slaves with chests like barrels, each with a huge curved sword in his hand. They made the man kneel down and one of the Negroes went and stood in front of him and suddenly started to dance! He waved his sword above his head and spun around in his sandals and the crowd cheered him. As for the poor guy on his knees, he was watching, fascinated. While his attention was distracted, the real executioner was getting ready behind his back. Suddenly he moved his own sword, quick as a flash. I saw the end of it prick the back of the man's neck. His head jerked back and then so fast that all you could see was a blur of silver, the sword came down and the head was off and rolling on to the platform and blood was gushing out of the neck.

The man had been found guilty of committing adultery during Ramadan.

In December Aminoil set up a small drilling camp at Wafra, in the centre of the Neutral Zone, and prepared to sink their first test hole. It was to cause even more problems for poor George, because both Pacific

Western geologists warned him that Aminoil was drilling in the wrong place. The Aminoil team was using unreliable seismic research: they should be drilling far to the west where surveys had indicated clear evidence of Eocene limestone formations. As manager of Pacific Western's Saudi Arabian Division, George sought to raise the doubts of his geologists with Jim MacPherson, Aminoil's veteran director of field operations, but he was airily dismissed. MacPherson, who had first come to the Middle East with Standard Oil, was not inclined to have some kid wet behind the ears and fresh out of college tell him where he should be drilling for oil.

'The area is practically floating in oil,' George wrote despairingly to his father, 'but the people running things are spudding their wells wide of the mark. I've argued myself hoarse. It does no good.'

When the first well at Wafra was abandoned as a dry hole at five thousand feet, Getty sent urgent messages to the Neutral Zone asking for the next hole to be drilled at a site suggested by his own geologists. Aminoil ignored his entreaties and started a second hole at Wafra at the height of the summer, in fierce noon temperatures as high as 165 degrees Fahrenheit. That, too, was a duster. Getty again dispatched a flurry of cables to the zone, insisting that the advice of his geologists be followed. Again he was ignored. In order to try and convince Aminoil of its folly he hired the Anglo-Iranian Oil Company's top geophysicist to make an independent survey of the zone, but the Aminoil team would heed no one and nothing but their own seismic research, even though seismology was still poorly developed as a prospecting tool.

Getty was furious that Aminoil continued to disregard his advice and alarmed by the escalating costs of the Neutral Zone operations. Each dry hole added another $250,000 to the bill and all the time other expenses were rising sharply. As there was no water in the area, tanker lorries from Kuwait drove in convoys across the desert to supply the drilling camp with fresh water. Prefabricated huts were shipped from the United States, with air conditioners and generators to run them. The heat took a fearsome toll of the drilling crews and the Aminoil doctor had his hands full just keeping enough roughnecks at work to man the rig.

In deference to the sensibilities of their prickly hosts, no alcohol was allowed on any of the shore-based camps although many oilmen were prepared to risk smuggling it in and there was a lively illicit trade in bootleg liquor. Considering the conditions in which they worked, it was hardly surprising that men exhibited an inclination to get drunk after coming off a rig but the oil companies knew that their continued presence in Saudi Arabia demanded they adopt a severe and unforgiving attitude towards illegal drinking. King Ibn Saud and his emirs made little secret of the fact that the American infidels were only there on sufferance and would be instantly kicked out if they were not prepared to abide by the strict Koranic laws that prevailed in the kingdom. Sixty lashes was the minimum punishment for the crime of consuming alcohol, applicable both to Muslims and infidels.

One evening in August 1950 George Getty was found drunk at the drilling camp at Wafra. He was hustled out of the country next day, on the pretext of urgent business in the United States, in the hope of avoiding a scandal. By the time news of the incident reached the ears of the Saudi authorities, George was safely back in California and to Aminoil's relief the matter was overlooked and soon forgotten. George had to face a sticky interview with his father at the ranch house and was then dispatched ignominiously to Pacific Western's office in Texas. He was not, in truth, all that sorry that he had been obliged to depart the Neutral Zone so precipitously. After a brief and ill-fated romance with the pretty daughter of Ben Lyon and Bebe Daniels, in 1951 he met and married Gloria Gordon – a nice girl from Denver, Colorado. His father did not attend the wedding.

Aminoil continued drilling in the Neutral Zone, well by well, throughout 1950, 1951 and 1952 without finding a drop of oil. After three dusters at Wafra they tried their luck at Fuwaris, close to the western border of the zone, and drilled a hole to 9400 feet before giving up. A fifth well, at Al-Hasani in the south, was abandoned at 4730 feet.

By the end of 1952, Getty had invested $18,000,000 in the Neutral Zone without receiving a cent back in return. 'The men on the spot,' he said, 'continued to have high hopes. But that was about all.'

Rumours began circulating in the oil industry that Getty had overreached himself at last. No one, it was said, could continue pouring money away at such a rate and stay out of the bankruptcy court.

12.   'Where is the oil, where is the money?'

If Paul Getty was worried that the Neutral Zone adventure would break him, he certainly did not show it. While Aminoil drilled one dry hole after another in the Arabian desert, Getty unconcernedly carried on with his life in the United States much as he had always done. There was plenty to occupy him – his oil companies in California, the trailer factory at Tulsa, the Pierre Hotel in New York and the continuing prospect of taking over Tide Water Associated, a corporate war of attrition he had been waging for nearly twenty years. He also had a wife and son, of course, although Teddy and Timmy were by now firmly relegated to second place in his attention, after business – the lowly status eventually occupied, with varying degrees of regret, by all his wives and all his sons.

In the late spring of 1949, while preparations were being made to start drilling in the Neutral Zone, Getty decided to take a trip to Europe – alone. Teddy was not invited to accompany him, but then she had no desire to go. She knew that Paul would trek around the capitals of Europe from hotel to hotel, talking business all day or touring museums, galleries and auction rooms. The prospect of dragging round after him with little Timmy, then nearly three, in tow, was unalluring.

Getty contrived to justify the trip on both commercial and altruistic grounds. He wanted, he said, to organise a European marketing operation to handle the huge quantities of oil he confidently expected would be produced in the Neutral Zone and in this way 'do his bit' to assist in the rehabilitation of industrial Europe. 'I was determined,' he said, 'to do whatever I could to help in rebuilding the shattered economies of the war-ravaged European countries'.

Fine ideals, indeed, although not entirely the whole story. Getty was quite as interested in profits as he was in rebuilding Europe and he believed that the market for crude in the eastern hemisphere was likely to expand enormously in the postwar years. But he was mainly going for the simple reason that it had been his inflexible habit – ever since 1927 – to spend some months each year in Europe, 'war-ravaged' or not. As an art collector and a man with a keen interest in history, he was comfortable there, feeling it to be his spiritual home, and he had made many friends, touchingly cherished, in the 'top drawer' of European society.

Getty arrived at the Ritz Hotel London in May 1949 and was shocked to see for himself the damage done by the Luftwaffe. 'I'll never forget my first sight of the City and the East End,' he said. 'They'd been blitzed almost to oblivion. Everyone still looked careworn and sort of shabby. Most of the department stores had been bombed and there was very little merchandise available, let alone on display.'

He spent two weeks in London, much of it at the elegant Mayfair home of Margaret Sweeny, a beautiful heiress and socialite, recently divorced. The 'very best people' could usually be found gathered at the parties at Mrs Sweeny's house in Upper Grosvenor Street. Indeed, she was a hostess of such celebrity on both sides of the Atlantic that she actually made an appearance in Cole Porter's lyrics for 'You're the top' sandwiched, somewhat unfortunately, between Mussolini and Camembert cheese:

> 'You're the nimble tread of the feet of Fred Astaire,
> You're Mussolini,
> You're Mrs Sweeny,
> You're Camembert.'

Getty did not much like large social gatherings, being shy and uneasy in the company of strangers – he often worried about being a poor conversationalist – but he found European 'society' irresistible. Mrs Sweeny's soirées provided him with the entrée to a glittering world far removed from the oil business and he counted her among the closest of his friends in London.

The ravishing Mrs Sweeny, then thirty-two, was deeply fond of the American oilman and sometimes contemplated the possibility – Teddy notwithstanding – of becoming the sixth Mrs Getty, although in the end it came to nothing. 'There was a time in the late forties when we might have married,' she confessed, 'if it had not been for the intervention of a certain mutual woman "friend" who deliberately convinced Paul that I was interested in an American colonel. This was quite untrue.' (She could not have been too upset, for within eighteen months she would marry the Duke of Argyll, a relationship that ended in one of the most sensational divorce suits of the century. But as Margaret, Duchess of Argyll, she remained a close friend of Getty for the rest of his life.)

After London, Getty went on to Paris to stay with his friends Sir Charles and Lady Elsie Mendl, 'leading figures,' he noted with satisfaction, 'of Continental society'. The Mendls entertained a great deal at their villa in Versailles and Getty was delighted to discover Greta Garbo was among the house guests when he arrived. No one could ever have accused him of being a gossip – he abhorred 'small talk' – but in later years he liked to recount an acid little exchange he witnessed between Miss Garbo and her hostess:

> One morning, Greta and I were sprawled in deck chairs beside the Mendls' swimming pool. I was unshaven and haggard, quite disreputable in my appearance, I'm afraid, but Greta and I chattered away. Then Elsie appeared at the poolside. 'Paul!' she snapped. 'I'm ashamed of you! How can you sit there with Greta looking the way you do?' I flushed with embarrassment. Greta merely arched an eyebrow. 'Elsie, what a horrible colour you're wearing this morning,' she murmured. It was probably one of the very few times in her life that Elsie Mendl had ever been outpointed. She didn't even glance at me, but beat a hasty retreat.

While in Paris, Getty made a sentimental visit to the *petit meuble* at 12 rue St Didier, which had been his 'twice-divorced bachelor's pad' in 1927. 'Countless memories tumble through my mind,' he wrote in his diary. 'Those were wonderful days. How much Paris – and the entire world – have changed since then!'

In August he checked into the Amstel Hotel in Amsterdam, intent on fulfilling a promise he had made to himself ten years earlier. The last time he was in Europe, in 1939, he had resolved to return the following year and devote some time to researching the history of his Rembrandt, the portrait of Marten Looten, about which little was known except that it was the artist's second commissioned portrait. The war had put paid to the idea, but he had not forgotten it.

For the next four weeks, Getty was absorbed by his self-imposed research project, poring over documents and records at the Municipal Archives in Amsterdam every day and typing up his notes each evening in his hotel room on a 'Baby Hermes' typewriter. He interviewed leading art historians, traced the origins of the Looten family, visited Rembrandt's birthplace at Leiden and painstakingly investigated the mystery of what was written on the letter Looten was holding in the painting. He concluded it was nothing more than a prop, with four lines of meaningless scrawl, to improve the composition.

'With long hours of research and study behind me,' Getty explained, 'I felt that if Marten Looten ever did step out of the canvas and begin to talk, I would be able to greet him and converse with him as though he were an old acquaintance.'

Before leaving Amsterdam he asked for an interview with Professor van Dillen, the country's foremost authority on Rembrandt, posing as an American journalist researching an article on the great artist. Van Dillen had been one of the most outspoken critics when it was revealed in 1938 that the Marten Looten had been sold to an 'unnamed American' and Getty wanted to try and make his peace.

The professor invited Getty to tea in his apartment at the top of an old narrow house overlooking a canal on the Ruysdaelkade. After the two men had been talking for some time, with Getty constantly introducing the subject of the Marten Looten, the professor suddenly said: 'May I inquire whether you have any specific reason for wanting all these details of the Marten Looten?'

Getty hesitated, stood up, crossed the room to the window and turned to face the professor. 'Because, sir,' he said dramatically, 'I am the "unnamed American" who purchased it in 1938.'

The professor, taken aback, apparently said nothing. Getty later furnished several accounts of the address he then delivered, all of them displaying an unlikely rhetorical aplomb.

'"I can understand how you felt about it sir," I continued. "However, the Marten Looten is not lost to the Netherlands for it, like every Rembrandt, will forever be Dutch. The portrait is in America, that is true. However, it is acting as a cultural ambassador of your country and its heritage." I went on to describe where and how the painting had been exhibited, how it had been viewed by millions and would be viewed by millions more, for I was soon to donate it to the Los Angeles County Museum. The professor's face gradually softened and finally broke into a huge and sincere smile. I had won not only my goal, but a friend.'

On his way back to Los Angeles Getty stopped for a few days in New York, staying at the Pierre Hotel, having given up his rented penthouse apartment at Sutton Place as an 'unnecessary extravagance'. The millions of dollars he was pouring into the Middle East did not curb his activities as a collector, for the day after his arrival in Manhattan he could be found browsing through the galleries of Rosenberg and Stiebel, antique and fine art dealers, looking – he said later – for something to rank with his Rembrandt, or his Ardabil carpet. The gallery had recently acquired some French furniture from the Rothschilds, but none of it was of sufficient quality to attract Getty and he was about to leave when one of the partners whispered in his ear that there was something in the private office that might interest him. He was ushered, almost furtively, into a room with a huge safe and the door was locked behind him before the safe was opened. A small piece of furniture wrapped in a white cloth was brought out and set in front of him.

Getty's cold, mask-like countenance did not register a hint of the surprise or excitement he felt when the wraps were removed. Standing before him was a fine Louis XV green lacquer table with a top of Sèvres porcelain, identical to one he had seen and admired many times in the Louvre. Up to that moment, the existence of a companion piece had been completely unknown. Getty examined it carefully. It seemed genuine enough and was signed 'B.v.R.B.' – the initials of an eighteenth-century craftsman recognised as the greatest cabinet-maker in the world, whose full name at that time was still unknown.

In answer to Getty's questions about the provenance of the piece, the dealer refused to reveal the previous owner but hinted strongly that it had come from a member of the British royal family. The table, he said, was presumed to have been originally the property of Madame du Barry and was a gift from King Louis XV. Getty judged the piece to be worth at least forty-five thousand dollars and he coughed unconvincingly to hide his momentary exultation when the dealer said he was asking fifteen thousand dollars. He immediately said he would buy it, providing it was authenticated by his friend Mitchell Samuels. In response to a telephone call, Samuels soon arrived at the gallery and confirmed Getty's opinion. 'It is probably the most important piece of French furniture in the United States,' he hissed in Getty's ear. 'Had I seen this wonderful little table one minute before you, I and not you would be its present owner.'

There was nothing in the world Getty liked more than finding a bargain for his art collection and he returned to Los Angeles to pick up the threads of his life with Teddy and Timmy in an unusually happy frame of mind. The lacquer table was installed among his other treasures at the ranch, but Getty stayed at the beach house so he could be with Teddy – she still refused to make her home at the ranch. 'Strange, charming elf that she is,' Getty wrote in his diary, 'she can be impossible, too.'

For several months they managed to lead something approaching a 'normal' home life, or as normal a relationship as could ever exist between a frustrated thirty-six-year-old opera singer and an obsessive tycoon aged fifty-seven. Getty relaxed sufficiently to book a $178 course of twenty-five lessons at Arthur Murray's School of Dancing. 'My dancing is good but needs improvement,' he explained in his diary, 'and I don't know the samba or jitterbug. I also don't lead well and do some unorthodox steps. I have a good sense of rhythm and timing, so says the teacher.'

He stepped out with Teddy to some of their favourite spots – the Coconut Grove at the Los Angeles Biltmore, the Brown Derby and the Mocambo, a regular haunt of the stars on the Strip. If they went out for dinner, it was usually to the Beachcombers – famed for its Hawaiian delicacies – where they rounded off their meal with the speciality of the house, 'coffee grog'.

Getty also tried to spend some time with Timmy. At the age of three and a half, Timmy had grown into a loveable little boy. Although he was frail and often sick, he remained constantly cheerful and more concerned about others than himself. Even when he was lying ill in bed, deathly pale and with dark shadows under his eyes, he could always manage a smile for his father. And he never forgot to include his mother and father in his prayers, which he said every night kneeling by his bed.

In February 1950 Teddy accompanied Getty on a trip to the Texas oilfields and ended up with a business of her own. They were on the road from Amarillo, heading for New Mexico, when their Cadillac broke down near a town called Hereford. While the car was being repaired, Paul and Teddy waited in a restaurant and got into conversation with a few of the locals who boasted about the quality of the town's water, which was so pure that people around and about never lost their teeth. 'Only dentists go broke here,' the owner of the restaurant confirmed. 'Dig three feet and you find water.' Teddy tried a glass and confirmed it had the fresh, clear taste of a natural spring.

Before their Cadillac was back on the road, she had come up with the idea of bottling the water commercially. Paul agreed to put up the money – for a percentage of the profits, naturally – but otherwise did not want to get involved. 'Oil and water don't mix,' he said with a thin smile. Teddy bought 120 acres near Hereford from the Santa Fe Railroad and launched the 'smallest bottled-water business in the United States'. Marketed as 'Theodora's Tap', it got a mention in *Time* magazine but was not an enormous success despite its alleged popularity with Hollywood movie stars.

After their return from Texas Getty suffered, to judge by his diary, from a prolonged bout of hypochondria. No less than three doctors were summoned to the beach house on 27 March. 'After a sharp pain in the muscle over my left kidney, I walked the floor in great pain for half an hour. Doctors L. A. Scola and Adams came within forty-five minutes. I'd never had such an attack before. Dr Gorfain pronounced prostate all right. No stones or kidney lesion. Bladder had a filtering delay. He said ten per cent had recurrence. Periodic check-up.'

Doctor Gorfain was back again in three weeks, prescribing a diet involving more fluid. 'Dr Gorfain thought a stone had existed due to lack of sufficient fluid ... The last few months I have been drinking no fluid before noon.'

A week later, the services of Dr Aremon, the chiropodist, were required. 'He treated my left toenail. Must paint every other day with iodine and grind down every four or six weeks.'

A fifth doctor came into the picture in May. 10 May: 'Drove through pouring rain to Dr Ward for a checkup. Blood pressure 126/86, heart good, prostate normal.'

In July, a sixth and seventh doctor were called in. 24 July: 'Disabling pain in lower back. Could hardly walk upstairs. Dr Oscar Hug recommended four weeks hot mud baths.' 25 July: 'To hospital. Dr

Prago said everything normal except fifth lumbar vertebra, which sclerosed. I think yesterday's disablement due to my strenuous efforts on Thursday, Friday and Saturday to bend over and touch the floor without bending my knees. I used to be able to do this, with some difficulty, but hadn't tried it for ten or fifteen years.'

Six days later, an eighth doctor appeared: 'Dr Trautman injected a varicose vein in my left leg.'

By this time, Getty was back in Europe. Given his record as a husband and father, it was perhaps not surprising that he soon tired of the joys of family life and felt the need to escape once more.

He meandered round Europe for several months, had a portrait of himself painted in Paris, won a thousand francs at the casino in Trouville, met 'an attractive twenty-two-year-old' by the name of Pamela Connink who amused him by declaring 'US girls are *interessées*, English girls are un-moral and French girls are unselfish and romantic.' In Vienna he was astounded by the vivacity of one Elsie Wittouck who, although fifty-five, was 'considered the beauty of the town'. He toured Switzerland with a friend called Irmgard. 1 August 1950: 'Drank a litre of milk in two hours. Took the Harderbahn up the mountains with Irmgard. Two Swiss alpinists advised us not to proceed on foot to the summit and she returned with them. I proceeded alone. Very steep, stony descent. Huge trees blocked the path in places, blown over in the last two or three days by thunderstorms. A distant thunderstorm was approaching, and after an hour's strenuous effort I was glad to reach the valley. To the casino in the evening, but very stiff.'

Before leaving for home Getty had dinner in London at White's with his 'close friend', the Duke of Argyll, who was by then deeply involved in a romance with Mrs Sweeny. The duke was permanently short of money, largely due to the upkeep of his crumbling ancestral home, Inverary Castle, and casually mentioned to Getty over coffee that he intended to sell an eighteenth-century desk he had inherited. Getty was not keen to make the trek up to Scotland and asked a dealer of his acquaintance next day if the duke had inherited any furniture of importance. He was assured not and forgot about it.

Later Getty learned that his dealer 'friend' had immediately driven up to Inverary Castle and discovered the piece of furniture that the Duke wanted to sell was an extremely rare double desk, signed by B.v.R.B. and possibly made for the twin daughters of Louis XV. Getty was outraged by this dirty trick and although he eventually acquired the desk from a dealer in New York, he was vexed by the price he had to pay for it and he bitterly regretted missing the opportunity of buying it before the duke had been 'alerted to its value'. He had absolutely no qualms about admitting that he would have bought the desk from his 'close friend', the duke, at a price far below its real value and liked to recount this cautionary tale as a warning to collectors to act swiftly. It could also have been taken as a warning about the nature of J. Paul Getty's 'friendship'.

In May 1951 the Getty interests at last won 'clear-cut numerical control' of Tide Water Associated Oil, a quiet triumph of persistence and patience on Getty's part. Considering the bitterness of the struggle for control of the company in the thirties, Getty's eventual victory was a distinctly low-key affair, passing virtually unnoticed by the newspapers. 'One must know how to wait,' was his only recorded comment when asked how he had achieved such a coup.

The fact was that the battle for Tide Water had been fought and won in the thirties. For years it had been accepted that it was only a question of time before Getty had enough shares in his pocket to take control. His 'clear-cut' control was vested in an extraordinary corporate maze: he only held 14% of Tide Water stock directly, but owned 42% of Mission Development Corporation (which owned 47% of Tide Water) and 47% of the Mission Corporation (which owned 10% of Mission Development and 3.5% of Tide Water).

Getty had prepared detailed plans for the rapid expansion of his now integrated and self-contained oil company, but he was effectively hamstrung by his investment in the Middle East. Until oil was found in the Neutral Zone, the future of the Getty oil business was uncertain. As he explained: 'Truth to tell, I had absolutely no assurance they would ever find any oil at all. Under such circumstances, whatever plans I made had to be very flexible and highly tentative.'

Thus it was that as the summer of 1951 rolled round, he could see no reason why he should not make his usual trip to Europe. He sailed from New York in June, intending to start his visit in London to see the Festival of Britain. He had no idea, as he leaned on the rail of a liner, watching the skyline of Manhattan disappear over the horizon, that he would never step foot in the United States again.

For the rest of his life, Getty kept promising himself he would return home to the United States. As early as 1952, he wrote in his diary on Christmas Day: 'This is my last Christmas away from home. I am resolved to return to the United States before the next holiday season comes around.'

Fourteen years later he was beginning to fret that he might actually die without returning home and on 11 May 1966 he dispatched identical letters to six close friends.

I would appreciate it very much if you would do me a favour. As you know, I am a Californian. I plan to return to my home in Santa Monica when my work is finished and I retire. If anything happens to me such as a stroke and I am unable to speak or write, please see that I am sent back to my home in California with a minimum of delay as I do not wish to end my days in a foreign country.

With all best wishes,

J. Paul Getty.

But Getty never did go back to California, although he made plans for the trip times without number. He often booked a first-class cabin on a liner leaving Southampton, but never made the sailing. On one famous occasion, his luggage was actually packed and loaded into his Cadillac and a chauffeur was standing by to drive him to the ship. But at the last minute he telephoned for a weather report and decided the crossing might be too rough.

Not even the prospect of seeing the fabulous museum he was having built in the grounds of the ranch house in the early seventies could persuade him to make the journey back across the Atlantic and he died still in self-imposed exile.

That Getty did not plan to stay in Europe for the rest of his life is quite clear. His trip to Europe in the summer of 1951 was to be like every other trip and began like every other trip. In London he stayed at the Ritz as usual and assumed, as usual, the twin roles of a culture-hungry American tourist and millionaire art collector. He plodded doggedly through all the pavilions at the Festival of Britain, attended the Opening Day of the Royal Academy, visited museums and stately homes and poked around the fine art and antique dealers in Bond Street. At Spink's he was told that the Lansdowne family might be willing to part with a marble statue of Herakles, dating either from the first century BC or the first century AD, for ten thousand pounds. Getty offered six thousand pounds. 'I very much doubt,' the Spink's representative sniffed, 'whether your offer will be accepted.' It was.

From London he went to Paris, where he bought some eighteenth-century carved oak panelling, painted in grey and gold, for the ranch house. The cost, including shipping it to Malibu and installation, was a little more than a hundred thousand dollars. There was no incongruity, in his view, about filling the ranch house with such an eclectic collection of treasures. In a rare moment of picturesque soliloquy he once said:

To me my works of art are all vividly alive. They're the embodiment of whoever created them – a mirror of their creator's

197

hopes, dreams and, yes, frustrations too. They've led eventful lives
– pampered by aristocracy and pillaged by revolution, courted
with ardour and cold-bloodedly abandoned. They've been
honoured by drawing-rooms and humbled by attics. So many
worlds in their lifespan, yet all were transitory! What stories they
could tell, what sights they must have seen! Their worlds have long
since disintegrated, yet they live on – and for the most part as
beautiful as ever.

After several weeks in Paris, Getty drove to Munich and spent some
time, Baedeker guide in hand, visiting the castles built by King Ludwig
II of Bavaria. From Munich he went to Bayreuth for the Wagner
Festival and to Salzburg for the Music Festival. October found him in
Rome, having a bronze bust made of himself; in November he was in
Athens, clambering over the great fallen stones around the Acropolis.

November was the month when, under normal circumstances, he
would have started making plans to return to the United States. This
time, however, he put off the decision and returned to Paris, to his
modest two-room suite at the Ritz Hotel. He wrote to Teddy saying that
he thought he ought to be 'on the spot', ready to exploit the European
market when the Neutral Zone began producing. Thereafter, there was
always a multitude of reasons why he needed to be in Europe.

Getty lived a strange, lonely nomadic existence in anonymous hotel
suites for the whole of the fifties. He shuttled regularly between London
and Paris and drove thousands of miles around Europe in his Cadillac,
visiting other cities as business demanded or whim suggested.
Everywhere he went, he carried his files and his patent medicines in a
huge steamer trunk, a couple of battered suitcases and a varying
collection of cardboard boxes tied with string.

He was perfectly content: hotels provided him with almost everything he needed – a bed, a telephone, food, a forwarding address,
laundry and room service. The only other service he required on a
regular basis was sex, and that he was perfectly capable of providing on
his own account. Despite his advancing years, Getty's sexual appetite
was undiminished – he boasted of having five different women in a
single day when he was sixty – and he had many girlfriends all over
Europe, some of them already collecting regular monthly cheques at
their nearest American Express office, courtesy of the libidinous old
millionaire, for services rendered. 'I have an appointment,' he once said
to the writer Bela von Block, 'with a young lady who is an absolute
master in the art of oral intercourse. She has a friend. Would you care to
come along?'

Getty did not apparently consider his lifestyle to be in any way
bizarre or eccentric and while there were clearly times when he suffered
pangs of homesickness, it was his home *country* he was missing, not his

home. He regularly shipped antiques and pictures back to the ranch house at Malibu with instructions where they should be put, but had no particular desire to see for himself how they looked, although he did ask for photographs to be sent to him showing the French panelling installed in the tapestry room and the Louis XVI room.

The only reminder of family life that he carried with him was a folding picture frame in brown leather, containing four photographs, which he liked to prop up on his bedside table. The first picture was of a grey-haired gentleman in a check suit who could be no one but Getty's father, such was the likeness. In the next frame was his mother, wearing a high-necked dress with her hair swept up severely and pinned with a comb on the top of her head. Next to her was a little girl with a bow in her hair – Getty's sister, Gertrude Lois, who died before he was born. The last picture was of Getty aged eight, a chubby little boy in a high collar and lace-trimmed smock. None of the four faces staring out of the sepia tints was smiling.

Getty's extended trips to Europe before the war had proved to his satisfaction that he was perfectly capable of running his business from a hotel room and, assisted by legions of loyal *concierges* who ensured his mail was forwarded, he settled into a daily routine which suited his somewhat individual business style. Rising late each morning, rarely before ten o'clock, it was his habit to read the leading national newspaper of whatever country he was in, as much to exercise his linguistic ability as to find out what was happening in the world. Urgent papers and cables were delivered to his room each morning by courier in a brown overnight bag. By the time he finished going through the contents of the bag, his mail had invariably arrived – in a bundle. He worked his way through it, envelope by envelope, putting to one side letters that would require him to make a telephone call during the day. If a letter needed a written reply, he simply scrawled a note in the margin and readdressed the envelope. Those few, usually very few, letters he wanted to keep were 'filed' in the steamer trunk and the remainder were unceremoniously thrown away. It did not normally take him long to deal with his mail.

His telephone was usually ringing by eleven o'clock and he might easily spend six or seven hours of each working day on the telephone, often with visitors waiting in the hotel lobby to see him. 'Twelve-hour workdays were anything but uncommon,' he said, 'and many stretched to fourteen or more. Steady streams of telexes, cables, written reports and letters of all kinds poured in from, it seemed, every conceivable corner of the globe. Then there were the telephone calls – local, international and transoceanic – and executives of Getty companies and engineers, accountants, attorneys and other businessmen who had to be seen personally.'

Because of the different time zones, he was not able to make business calls to the West Coast of the United States until about five o'clock in the afternoon and so the early evening was always a particularly busy time. If he was not going out in the evening, he liked to sit quietly in his room reading through business papers and reports, sipping a rum and Coca-Cola, until one or two o'clock in the morning.

Food meant little to Getty and his eating habits were erratic. If he was not fasting, he liked to prepare his own midday meal of fruit and bran, mixing together all the ingredients with milk and throwing in whatever quack health foods were popular. He chewed each mouthful thirty-three times, faithful to his mother's advice. In the evenings, he often warmed up a bowl of gruel on a hotplate in his room to help digest his vitamin pills and the sulphur he swallowed in the belief it would stop his hair going grey.

Author Ralph Hewins was astonished when he visited Getty in Paris in 1958 and discovered just how many pills and potions he lugged around with him.

> We were rummaging through cartons, which passed for a filing system, in his vestibule, looking for a document. And we unearthed a sample of his potions: medicines, eyewash, dates, cranberries, soup, cereals, chocolate candy, barley sugar, maple syrup and other 'nourishing' or 'energising' substances. These were all jumbled up with bottles of sweet rum to go with his Coca-Cola and Scotch for his whisky and ginger ale, photographs, maps, books, art magazines and a pair of sneakers.

The working day always ended with a touching little ritual. Before preparing for bed, Getty liked to tot up the day's balance sheet with 'Income' in one column and 'Expenditure' in the other. Under the 'income' heading he listed the latest figures from his bewildering network of companies, usually in thousands, if not millions. Under 'expenditure' he would scrawl: 'Newspaper – 10 centimes; bus fare – 5 centimes; lunch at Les Ambassadeurs – someone else paid; haircut 25 centimes, tip 2 centimes.' In this way comforted and convinced of his solvency, Getty could go happily to sleep.

Very occasionally, Getty confessed to moments of self-doubt in his diary, as on 12 April 1952 in Rome: 'I don't know why I continue to be active in business. Force of habit, I suppose. I'd be much better off to sell out and go into tax-exempt bonds.' Several months later he was on the Côte d'Azur: 'André Dubonnet is a good friend and companion. Lunched at his villa. It is a dream – modern, luxurious, directly over the water. I must try and complete my business over here so that I can return and once more enjoy my own house.'

It was nothing but idle jotting. In reality Getty was determined to remain in Europe, as he was to prove when his resolve was put to a chilling test. He tried to ensure he telephoned little Timmy every week, making a pathetic attempt to fulfil his responsibilities as a father across a crackling transatlantic telephone line. But that summer of 1952, his adored Timmy was taken seriously ill: a tumour had been discovered on the optic nerve. Teddy, frantic with worry, telephoned to say she had taken the boy to New York, where the finest neurosurgeon in America was to operate.

Getty telephoned every day, wept frequently and copiously, prayed for the boy's recovery – and stayed in Europe, pleading that pressure of business made it 'impossible' for him to leave. He could, perhaps, have taken a couple of days off and booked a seat on a scheduled flight across the Atlantic – but not even the plight of his favourite son could bring him to overcome his fear of flying.

The boy recovered from the operation, although with his eyesight severely impaired. When at last he was able to talk to his father, Timmy said he had been praying for him. Getty broke down, unable to speak for several minutes.

Pressure of business did not, however, prevent Getty from allotting a great deal of time and energy to protracted negotiations to buy three of the infamous 'Elgin Marbles', pieces of the Acropolis removed from Greece by Lord Elgin at the beginning of the nineteenth century. Most of the collection was in the British Museum, but Getty had been tipped off that the Elgin family might be prepared to part with a few pieces still in their possession and immediately threw his hat in the ring as a potential purchaser. He eventually bought, for an undisclosed sum, two carved stone slabs, dating from the fourth century BC, and a small marble statue of a female figure, dating from the early fifth century BC. 'Needless to say,' he pointed out, 'lengthy and delicate negotiations had to be made, export permits obtained and many other details attended to before the three precious pieces were mine. As a collector, it was one of my great triumphs.'

Encouraged by this success he casually asked Professor Bernard Ashmole, keeper of Greek and Roman antiquities at the British Museum, how much it would cost to acquire the Parthenon frieze. 'More money than you've got, Mr Getty,' was the professor's withering reply.

In November 1952 Getty renewed his acquaintanceship with another, rather more famous, exile – the Duke of Windsor. They had first met in 1912 when they were both students at Oxford and Getty was inordinately proud to be on first-name terms with a former King of England, name-dropping shamelessly in his diary.

1 November 1952: 'Dinner at Dorothy Spreckel's lovely
apartment at 12 rue Murillo. Dorothy – tall, blonde, slender –
looked most attractive, but all eyes were on the Duke and Duchess
of Windsor. They are devoted to each other. People will still be
talking and reading about this fascinating couple and their ideal
marriage a century from now, when most other celebrated figures
of today will be long forgotten.'

6 November 1952: 'Dinner at the Duke and Duchess of
Windsor's. David looks extremely fit and is the same as ever.
Wallis is the perfect hostess – but then she is a perfectionist in all
things.'

15 December 1952: 'I am sixty today and apparently in good
health. I feel sad at leaving the fifties.'

In March 1953 Getty received the cable for which he had been waiting
for more than three years: oil had at last been found in the Neutral
Zone. The sixth hole to be drilled in the zone known as 'Wafra No. 4'
had struck oil in the 'first Burgan sand' at a depth of 3800 feet and was
producing at the rate of 2500 barrels a day. By that date, Getty
calculated that his total investment in the Neutral Zone poker game was
approaching thirty million dollars.

Although he never admitted it publicly, he was on the point of giving
up the concession and admitting that he had lost the greatest gamble of
his career. 'If that sixth well had been a dry hole,' said his close aide
Norris Bramlett, 'Mr Getty was going to pull out and write off the
investment. It was a do-or-die hole. It was very frustrating for him,
because if they had drilled where he wanted them to in the first place,
they would have found oil in 1950.'

The quality of the crude produced by Wafra No. 4 was disappointing
– it was heavy oil with a high sulphur content which required special
refining – but Getty had hopes that it would lead to the development of
a big field in the area. Further encouragement was provided in
June when another well was completed in the extreme southwest
of the zone and turned out to be a producer, although a small
one.

Mightily relieved at the prospect of recouping some of his money,
Getty remained convinced that the full potential of the zone had yet to
be realised and that his partner, the Aminoil syndicate, was failing to
exploit the concession fully. Since Aminoil had persistently ignored all
his communications, Getty decided that the only way he could push his
suit was to visit the Neutral Zone himself. In preparation he bought a
Linguaphone 'Teach Yourself Arabic' course and as Christmas 1953
approached, he could be found sitting in his room in the Ritz at Paris,
listening to Linguaphone records and mouthing phrases in Arabic.

When Paul Getty came to deal with the Arabs, it was going to be in their own language.

On 18 February 1954 Getty left Paris on the Orient Express, bound for Istanbul, where he was due to pick up his Cadillac. Even though he was sixty-one years old, he was not in any way discomfited by the prospect of a gruelling two-thousand mile drive across Turkey, Syria, Iraq and Kuwait to Mina Saud in the Neutral Zone where the Aminoil/Pacific Western base camp was established. He took it in 'easy stages', he explained, as he wanted to enjoy the scenery and stop to see places of historical interest. On the final leg to Kuwait he drove alongside the trans-Arabia pipeline, which provided a convenient guide across the desert.

Arriving in Mina Saud on 2 March, there was no time for him to rest for protocol demanded that he should immediately make a courtesy call on Saudi Arabian government officials at Riyadh – 350 miles away across the desert. Driving into Riyadh in his dust-smeared Cadillac, Getty was gratified to observe what oil wealth was achieving: a small oasis of mud-brick dwellings in the centre of the desert was being transformed into a modern city with paved highways, hotels, hospitals and schools.

On his second day in the city he was invited to an audience with Crown Prince Faisal, the king's half-brother.

> The reception I received exceeded all my expectations. An honour-guard escorted me into the courtyard of his palace. Thirty of his retainers were ranged there in symbolic greeting, each with a falcon on his arm. Prince Faisal's personal welcome was warm and most gracious. We talked for almost an hour. It was evident he possessed a keen brain and much wisdom, even then – and these qualities were to make him an outstanding ruler of his people in later years.

Next night Getty attended a banquet for sixty guests given by King Saud, who had succeeded to the throne on the death of his father, Ibn Saud, the previous year. Getty was seated second from the king, with the Turkish ambassador in between them, and bravely struggled to converse with the king in Arabic.

The king brusquely dismissed Getty's attempt at polite conversation and demanded: *'Wain zait, wain fluss?'* ('Where is the oil, where is the money?')

Getty replied at length, saying he had high expectations of oil being produced in the Neutral Zone in large quantities and that money would soon be pouring into the Saudi exchequer. He quoted projected figures and explained in detail how he thought the concession might be best exploited to their mutual advantage.

The king smiled at last and said: 'You know, of course, what your President Roosevelt said to my father?'

Getty nodded and quoted F.D.R.'s widely-reported comment: 'I am essentially a businessman and as a businessman I am interested in Saudi Arabia.'

The king looked at Getty and said: '*You* are a businessman.' Getty took it as a high compliment.

Back at Mina Saud, Getty galvanised the drilling operation. He toured all the wells, looked at everything, was scathing about the laxness of Aminoil's operations and administration and boosted the morale of his own men. He marked out the sites where more exploratory drilling should take place and warned the Aminoil men that unless his advice was heeded, he would start drilling on his own account. He impressed – and sometimes terrified – everyone who crossed his path.

'Even the jellyfish seemed to get out his way when he took a swim in the Gulf,' said one of the Aminoil roughnecks. 'He was the only man I ever knew who bathed every day and never got stung once. The jellyfish wouldn't have dared – Getty would have stung them right back!'

While Getty was still in the Neutral Zone, Pacific Western and Aminoil played host to King Saud and the Sheikh of Kuwait at a reception on board the old tank-landing craft still being used as Aminoil's headquarters. It was one of the few occasions the King of Saudi Arabia and the Sheikh of Kuwait had ever met and the idea was to give both rulers an up-to-date briefing on the progress of the exploration and the potential for future exploitation of the Neutral Zone's mineral resources. Carpets were laid out on the deck of the ship and maps spread over the carpets. Getty, with a pointer in his hand, began explaining – in Arabic – the geology of the region where drilling was presently taking place and where more oil might be found in the future. Before long, both the king and the sheikh could be found poring over the map on their hands and knees. 'See,' said King Saud to the sheikh when Getty had finished, 'he is able to tell us where the oil is in Arabic.'

13. 'I don't believe in giving my competitors a head start'

Production in the Neutral Zone increased from 7559 barrels in 1953 to 2,977,094 barrels in 1954. Now certain that one of the biggest gambles of his business career would pay off, Getty set in motion a massive programme of investment and expansion. Directing operations from the remote reaches of hotel rooms in Europe, he began building – unaided – a business empire of astonishing range and complexity spreading halfway round the world.

In Wilmington, Delaware, bulldozers were levelling a five-thousand-acre site bordering the Delaware River, in preparation for the construction of a two-hundred-million-dollar refinery for Tide Water. It would be the biggest and most modern refinery in the world, designed for handling the low-gravity, high-sulphur crude being produced in the Neutral Zone. Dredgers were cutting a deep ship channel, three miles long, to accommodate the tankers that would soon be forging up the river.

On the West Coast the Tide Water refinery at Avon, not far from San Francisco, was undergoing extensive modernisation – a sixty-million-dollar project which included the installation of a forty-two-thousand-barrel-a-day fluid coker, the biggest in the world.

In the sprawling shipyards of St Nazaire, at the mouth of the river Loire in France, the keel of a huge new tanker was being laid – the first of a fleet that would be delivered before the end of the decade to move Neutral Zone crude from the Persian Gulf to Wilmington, Delaware.

In the Neutral Zone itself teams of Arab labourers were laying pipelines across the desert to link the oilfields with the storage tanks being built at Mina Saud, on the shore of the Persian Gulf. A refinery was also under construction on the coast and a submarine pipeline was being laid to the deep-water anchorage offshore, where the tankers would take on their cargoes. Mina Saud, once a miserable little huddle of prefabricated bungalows, now accommodated hundreds of oilmen in air-conditioned trailers, shipped from the United States and supplied, of course, by the Spartan factory in Tulsa, Oklahoma.

In Mexico, a paved road was being laid through the virgin forest which screened Revolcadero Beach and the footings were being dug for Getty's second luxury hotel – the Pierre Marques, due to open in 1956.

In Los Angeles, Tulsa and New York, architects were drawing up plans for skyscraper office blocks to contain the thousands of people who now worked for J. Paul Getty.

Tidewater (which condensed its name and dropped 'Associated' around this time) sold its mid-continent marketing operation – where it was competing with Skelly Oil, also owned by Getty – but allocated about $120,000,000 to double its roster of two thousand Veedol service stations on both coasts. Getty had orchestrated the election of all the Tidewater directors in 1953 and pushed the company into international expansion. It bought a forty-nine per cent interest in a refinery owned by the Mitsubishi Corporation at Kawasaki, just outside Tokyo, and a stake in the consortium operating the oil industry in Iran; exploratory drilling was also taking place as far afield as Turkey, Pakistan, South America and Canada.

While all this was going on, Getty became 'involved' with the young wife of one of his English friends. As he often liked to say: 'A man's driving force is sex.'

Penelope Kitson was twenty-nine years old, the mother of three young children and the wife of a wealthy, well-connected Cornish landowner when she first met J. Paul Getty. Her husband, a close friend of the foreign secretary Sir Anthony Eden, invited Getty to stay one weekend when he was in Cornwall looking at some paintings.

Getty was instantly charmed by Robert Kitson's wife. She was very tall and slender, striking more than beautiful, intelligent, entertaining and the epitome of a well-bred Englishwoman. Penelope's marriage was not happy and before the end of the year she had separated from her husband and moved to London with her children, to an elegant, double-fronted mansion on Campden Hill in Kensington where she frequently entertained Getty when he was in London.

A slight complication intruded on their developing relationship in June 1955, when Teddy arrived in Paris with nine-year-old Timmy in a forlorn attempt to patch up their marriage. Getty, who had not set eyes on either wife or child for four years, seemed pleased to see them. They moved into his suite, number 801, at the George V hotel (where he now stayed in preference to the Ritz) and pretended they were a happy family on holiday together. Getty and his son were photographed by the Eiffel Tower – Timmy, freckle-faced in a white shirt and sports jacket, looking up admiringly at his father through the thick spectacles he had had to wear ever since his operation; Getty staring down at the boy with his lips stretched into the grimace which was, for him, an affectionate smile.

After two weeks in Paris they moved to the Ritz in London, where Getty took them to Spink's, the art dealers. Rudolph Forrer, Spink's

disinterested and did not even plan to send a wedding present until Penelope, frankly appalled at his lack of concern, insisted.

Young Paul, who was twenty-three, had no expectation of his father turning up for the wedding and, in truth, no real desire for him to do so. Getty senior was no more than an elderly stranger to whom he would write 'once in a while' and from whom he received an occasional letter in a spidery scrawl. Paul sent his father a cutting from the *San Francisco Chronicle* at the time of his engagement the previous summer: 'Judge and Mrs George B. Harris gave a cocktail party at the Red Room in the Bohemian Club to present friends to their daughter's fiancé, Mr E. Paul Getty. The bride-elect is a senior at Dominican College in San Rafael and a graduate of the Convent of the Sacred Heart.' If the old man was impressed by the credentials of his future daughter-in-law, he kept it to himself. The only other Getty at Paul's wedding was his younger brother, Gordon.

By the beginning of 1956, Mrs Kitson's presence in Getty's life had been thinly legitimised: impressed by what he considered to be her particular talent as an interior decorator, he hired her to select the colour schemes in the cabins of the oil tankers he was having built – a detail he had previously been happy to leave to the ships' designers. 'There is no earthly reason,' he explained somewhat self-consciously, 'why a tanker should be any less attractively decorated than one's home or office. I called therefore upon Mrs Penelope Kitson to advise on the decoration of the living quarters, messing and recreational rooms aboard the tankers.'

It was presumably in the interests of 'research' that Mrs Kitson also accompanied him on his second visit to the Neutral Zone in 1956. Instead of taking the train to Istanbul, as he had done previously, this time Getty decided to drive all the way from Paris. The uncomplaining Norris Bramlett was summoned from Los Angeles to act as major-domo and Getty also invited along an old friend from pre-war days, Melville Forrester, known to everyone as 'Jack'.

Forrester was a colourful New Yorker who began his career as a dancer with Maurice Chevalier in Paris, then turned to film production. He was recruited as an OSS agent in Europe during the war and afterwards became a millionaire businessman based in Paris. He was as outgoing and extrovert as Getty was shy and introvert, but the two of them somehow became firm friends. Forrester owned a few shares in Getty Oil and used to tease his friend by telephoning from different parts of the world demanding to know how many hours Getty had worked that day.

The four of them – Getty, Penelope, Bramlett and Forrester – set off from Paris at the beginning of April 1956 in Getty's Cadillac. Penelope took her turn at the wheel along with the men and they arrived at Mina

Saud at the end of the month after a four-thousand-mile journey across much of Western Europe, the Balkans and the Middle East.

Getty was greeted, uneasily and without much affection, by his son Ronnie, a tall young man with a slight paunch, prematurely receding hair and a small toothbrush moustache which added years to his appearance. After graduating from the University of Southern California in 1953, Ronnie had joined Tidewater as an executive in the marketing department and was now–at the age of twenty-six–doing his stint in the Neutral Zone just as his older half-brother, George, had done. Although they had not met for more than five years, father and son had little to say to each other: Ronnie was quite as much in awe of his father as George and was considerably less personable. Getty soon made it clear he preferred the company of his cronies and Ronnie was left to kick his heels.

While 'Pen' occupied herself organising the decoration of Getty's air-conditioned bungalow overlooking the Persian Gulf, Getty spent the first two weeks out in the field with Norris Bramlett. 'I dragooned Norris into acting as a sort of combination stenographer and Man Friday,' Getty said. 'Thrusting pad and pen into his hands, I took him with me everywhere, dictating memos, orders, suggestions and ideas to him.' Accompanied by Bill Scott, the superintendent of field operations, and Wally Smith, the drilling superintendent, they drove across the featureless desert from well to well. At every drilling site Getty stopped to talk to the crews, both American and Arab, asked endless questions and minutely inspected each rig. No detail was too small for his consideration: when he discovered it cost six cents to flush a lavatory with fresh water, he instantly wanted to know why sea water could not be used. There was no reason, except no one had thought of it. Thereafter, every lavatory in the Neutral Zone was flushed with the waters of the gulf.

Although he was sixty-three years old Getty appeared tireless and impervious to the blistering heat, even in the middle of the day. He never bothered with a hat and wore a lightweight grey suit, with a collar and tie, every day. He was not, however, unaware of how tough it was to work on a drilling rig in one of the hottest places in the world. 'I was greatly impressed,' he said, 'by the difficulties and hardships the crews encountered.' At a rig in the southwest corner of the zone, he asked the driller if there was anything special he needed.

'Hell, yeah,' the man replied. 'You could start off by sending over Sears, Roebuck and the Rockettes and work your way down from there.' He laughed and then added: 'Seriously, boss, we want what you want – more oil.'

Getty was quite moved. 'His reply proved,' he said later, 'that oilfield workers are the same, whether employed in Oklahoma or Arabia. They are as much infected by oil fever in 1956 as they were in 1906.'

Actually, none of the oilmen in the Neutral Zone in 1956 had any reason to complain that not enough crude was being pumped out of the desert. After the initial, nerve-racking years of disappointment, the zone was proving to be a phenomenally rich oilfield. Production in 1955 soared to 4,351,741 barrels and by the time of Getty's visit it was running at about 25,000 barrels a day. The first strikes in the Wafra field had been supplemented by the discovery of oil in Eocene limestone at the comparatively shallow depth of 1200 feet and a year later another, much deeper, layer of oil was found in a stratum called New Ratawi Limestone at around 7000 feet. Conservative estimates of the Neutral Zone's oil reserves exceeded thirteen billion barrels.

'Continued exploration and drilling,' said Getty, 'proved that the Neutral Zone was like an enormous layer cake, with numerous huge reservoirs of petroleum sandwiched between strata of rock and soil at various depths beneath the surface of the ground.'

On Friday 1 June Getty took the day off and spent the morning sitting in a canvas chair outside his bungalow, sunbathing and chatting with Pen, Forrester and Bramlett. All of them were in bathing suits. At around noon they noticed that a large steamer out in the gulf had altered course and was heading directly for Mina Saud. As no passenger ships ever called at the camp, they were mystified by the vessel's approach until Forrester suddenly leapt to his feet and said: 'Holy smoke! That's King Saud's yacht!'

As they watched, the ship anchored offshore, davits were swung out and a launch was lowered into the water. Realising they were going to get a visit, they rushed into the bungalow, hurriedly pulled on more suitable clothes, then lined up at the water's edge as the launch approached. The unmistakeable robed figure of King Saud could be seen standing in the centre of the boat, staring towards the shore through thick dark glasses. As the launch softly slid on to the sandy beach, the king stepped out on to a makeshift jetty and greeted them in Arabic. Getty, acutely aware that he had not shaved that morning, introduced him first to Mrs Kitson who curtseyed confidently, then to Forrester and Bramlett both of whom bowed stiffly. One of the king's equerries explained the king wished to visit the local emir but would be graciously pleased if they would join him for dinner on his yacht that evening.

Getty said they would be honoured, but when the time came for them to set out for the royal yacht in Aminoil's small motorboat, the light breeze that had been blowing all day had strengthened considerably and the sea was choppy. Eyeing the pitching and wallowing motorboat, Getty suddenly refused to go. There followed a farcical scene on the beach as the four of them – the three men in grey suits and starched white shirts and Penelope in a dark blue cocktail dress and diamond earrings – argued about whether or not it was safe to venture out and the diplomatic consequences of not showing up. Penelope settled the matter by hitching up her skirt and wading out to the motorboat. 'For heaven's sake, Paul,' she said, '*come on.*' Getty followed with the greatest of reluctance and sat miserably gripping the gunnels as the boat slewed laboriously out to where the king's yacht was moored. Once on board, he cheered up enormously and he was to look back on the evening with some pleasure:

> It was like something out of an *Arabian Nights'* tale. Even the gangway slung against the yacht's side was carpeted with thick, priceless oriental rugs. There were considerably more than a hundred guests in the dining-saloon. Dinner, course after course, was served on the finest porcelain, each plate decorated with the Saudi emblem, a sword and palm tree. A good-sized army of retainers was posted around the dining-saloon, ready to wait on the king and his guests. The feast, marked by all the colour and grandeur befitting the court of an oriental potentate, lasted nearly three hours.

The Royal Yacht sailed away the following day and Getty returned to work, preparing the ground for a rapid increase in production. He ordered more plant and pipeline, arranged improved housing and facilities for the oilfield workers and took steps to ensure construction of the refinery at Mina Saud went ahead without delay.

At the beginning of August, after four months in the zone, Getty and his friends loaded their bags into the Cadillac for the long drive back to Paris. Mrs Kitson, whose presence had provoked much nudging and winking among the drilling crews, took many souvenirs home with her – among them a photograph of herself wearing an Arab headdress and shorts, perched uncertainly on the hump of a camel and surrounded by barefoot Bedouin tribesmen striking martial poses.

Getty's hopes of expanding production in the Middle East and marketing the oil in Europe suffered an unexpected setback not long after he returned to Paris. In October 1956 a combined force of French and British paratroops invaded Egypt in a disastrous attempt to regain control of the Suez Canal, which had been nationalised by Egypt's newly-elected president, Colonel Gamal Abdel Nasser. The Egyptians promptly scuttled a number of ships to block the canal, cutting the artery through which Europe received most of its oil.

Oil tankers made up two thirds of the traffic through the Suez Canal, all of which suddenly had to be rerouted round the Cape of Good Hope, adding thousands of miles to the journey. The effect of the Suez crisis on the oil industry was devastating – the cost of transporting a barrel of oil from the Middle East tripled and the carrying capacity of the tanker fleets operating out of the Middle East was reduced by two thirds now that the round trip took so much longer. With the Suez Canal closed, the industry had to face up to the fact that there were not enough tankers in the world to shift all the crude being produced in the area.

Getty was better placed than many since he already had his own tanker fleet and was thus less vulnerable to the skyrocketing charter rates. The first of his 46,500-ton tankers, the SS *Veedol*, was delivered in December 1955. At that time construction of nine other tankers was well-advanced at cut-price shipyards in both France and Japan, and sixteen more were on order. When the Suez crisis flared up there were seven tankers at sea flying the Tidewater flag, but even so Getty was obliged to cut back temporarily on production in the Neutral Zone and order the construction of additional storage tanks to cope with the excess – particularly as two new wells in the Wafra field had been brought in at more than four thousand barrels a day, pushing output above fifty thousand barrels daily.

Bigger ships – the *George F. Getty* and the *Minnehoma Getty*, each of 53,000 tons – began sliding down the ways at St Nazaire in France early in 1957 and eased the problem. Getty, with typical foresight, was already talking about building the first supertanker of 130,000 tons. 'My competitors have been burdened with small tankers,' he told *Time* magazine in March 1957. 'I am determined to obsolete their fleets by building a new super-fleet at a lower cost. Whoever has the cheapest transportation has the advantage – and I don't believe in giving my competitors a head start.'

Getty was very proud of Tidewater's tanker fleet and followed each phase of the shipbuilding programme with intense interest and his usual attention to detail, even down to the number of coats of paint applied to the bulkheads. He was particularly pleased with the decoration of the cabins. 'Mrs Kitson adroitly managed to add a subtle woman's touch,' he recorded, 'without in any way impairing the essentially masculine quality that any ocean-going vessel with an all-male complement must possess. Officers and crew have been unanimous in their praise for the warmer, pleasanter atmosphere that prevails aboard the ships.'

To show his gratitude he invited Penelope to launch two of the tankers in France, ceremonies she performed with her usual assurance while the assembled dignitaries no doubt wondered who she was and speculated about the precise nature of her relationship with the owner. In the shipbuilding business, it was not usual for the lady who had chosen the colours of the ship's accommodation to be awarded the honour of cracking a bottle of champagne over the bows at the launching ceremony.

Getty spent three days on board the *George F. Getty* after her maiden voyage to check the specification, but was otherwise incurious about what he owned around the world. The four-million-dollar Pierre Marques Hotel opened at Revolcadero Beach in Mexico in 1956 and was an instant success, being chosen as the venue for the first official meeting between President Eisenhower and President Adolfo Lopez Mateos of Mexico. Its owner glanced briefly at photographs taken after the opening, but only concerned himself thereafter with the hotel's balance sheets.

At the ranch house in Malibu five rooms had been turned into a museum in 1953 at the suggestion of Norris Bramlett, who advised Getty that by opening his house to the public he could claim a charitable tax deduction. The J. Paul Getty Museum opened to the public on Wednesday and Saturday afternoons. It rarely attracted more than a few people, despite the treasures to be found therein which included Rubens's 'The Death of Dido', the Gainsborough portrait of Thomas Christie, a Titian and a Tintoretto, the entire collection of Louis XV and Louis XVI furniture and the Boucher tapestries (the Rembrandt and the Ardabil carpet were on permanent loan to Los Angeles County Museum). Early in 1957 a gallery was built on to the house to accommodate the growing number of Graeco-Roman antiquities Getty was shipping from Europe. He never saw his own museum and showed no particular desire to see it.

In May 1957 Tidewater's new refinery at Wilmington, Delaware, opened with a fanfare and the notable absence of the majority share-holder. Hailed as 'the refinery of the future' by the authoritative *Oil and Gas Journal*, the plant boasted one of the world's biggest single-fluid catalytic crackers, processing 102,000 barrels a day. The principal refining units extended in a straight line for nearly a mile along the shore of the Delaware river and the whole plant was as 'automated' – a new word to many people – as it was possible for a refinery to be.

Getty, exercising his flair for mental arithmetic, liked to quote the construction statistics. Levelling the site involved moving more than three million cubic yards of earth; fifteen million cubic yards of sand were dredged from the ship channel, which was three miles long and four hundred feet wide; ten thousand freightcar loads and seventy-five thousand truckloads of supplies and equipment were delivered to the site; and at one time there were nine thousand workers on the con-struction payroll ...

'I believe my new generation of refineries will force other oil companies to scrap theirs,' Getty said, 'as no patchwork outfit can compete with a plant modern in every respect.' The opening of the

Wilmington refinery certainly impressed the stock market, as did Getty's policy of ploughing profits back into expansion. A single share in Getty Oil – originally incorporated back in 1916 when father and son first formalised their partnership, and merged with Pacific Western in 1956 – cost $3 in 1932 and was worth $152 in 1957. Skelly Oil stock, which was selling at $26 when Getty took over in 1937, had climbed to $231, and Tidewater stock had quadrupled in value during the six years Getty had been in control.

But only two months after the Wilmington refinery came on stream, Getty was in trouble again. By encouraging the build-up of production in the Neutral Zone and investing two hundred million dollars in a new refinery in the United States to process the output, he had gambled that foreign oil would be freely marketed in the United States for the foreseeable future. He lost. In July 1957 President Eisenhower announced the imposition of 'voluntary' quotas to restrict the import of foreign crude oil. The effect on Getty's grand design was potentially disastrous. He was by then the biggest individual oil producer in the Middle East with fifty-six producing wells – but without refining capacity, all the crude gushing out from under the white sand of the Neutral Zone was virtually worthless. 'There were those who were predicting,' he said, 'that the Getty interests would soon drown in their oceans of excess crude oil.'

The predictions, as usual, were wrong. Getty at first openly flouted the quota system. The Wilmington refinery's import quota was set at 34,200 barrels a day, less than half the input it required to operate efficiently; Getty blithely ignored the restrictions and maintained crude imports at an average of 64,000 barrels a day, almost double his quota, arousing much bitterness and resentment among his competitors and those oil companies abiding by the quota restrictions. It did not bother Getty in the slightest. He was happy that the rest of the industry toed the line, since it kept imports under the overall quota and made the US government powerless to act against Tidewater – it could hardly make quotas mandatory for a single company.

Nevertheless, Getty knew that he was probably only buying time and that the government might soon be forced to crack down. In anticipation of that unwelcome day, he began conducting an urgent search – from his suite at the Ritz in London – for further refining facilities around the world. Instructions were cabled to the Neutral Zone to speed up the construction of the refinery at Mina Saud. Hours of talking on a long-distance telephone line to Japan resulted in a doubling of the capacity of the Tidewater-Mitsubishi refinery at Kawasaki, which promised to take up to ten thousand barrels a day from the Neutral Zone. He put out feelers to the West German government with a tentative proposal to build a new refinery there, but was rebuffed. Next he tried Denmark, this time dispatching his old friend Jack Forrester to act as emissary. Forrester made good progress and agreement was rapidly reached to build a forty-thousand-barrel-a-day refinery at Kalundborg, sixty miles west of Copenhagen.

Meanwhile Getty heard that an oil company in Italy, Golfo Industria Petrolifere, was in trouble. Golfo had recently built a new refinery and storage facilities for 1,300,000 barrels at Gaeta on the coast between Naples and Rome, but because of financial difficulties the refinery was virtually standing idle. 'I learned that a controlling interest could be purchased,' Getty said, 'at a price far below the replacement value of the plant and I immediately began preliminary negotiations.'

While Getty was thus occupied, a totally unexpected event occurred which was to completely change his life. In October 1957 *Fortune* magazine published the names of the richest men in America. At the top of the list, above the Hunts of Dallas, the Rockefellers, the Mellons and the Fords, was a name that many people had never heard of – J. Paul Getty.

14.   'A billion dollars isn't what it used to be'

Until October 1957 Getty had enjoyed relative obscurity. He had figured briefly in the newspapers during the battle for Tidewater in the thirties and the wartime scandal over Joan Barry. Each of his divorces had merited a further mention, but they were soon forgotten and so other than an occasional appearance in a trade journal or the financial press, he remained virtually unknown outside the oil industry. This was a situation which suited him admirably.

Fortune magazine changed all that. Not only was there widespread astonishment that a formerly anonymous businessman could suddenly be 'richer than Rockefeller', but *Fortune*'s assessment of Getty's wealth revealed him to be *much* richer. The magazine declared him to be a billionaire twice over, holding stocks worth $1,138,600,000 and controlling companies with net assets of $1,271,900,000. His personal fortune was estimated at between $700,000,000 and $1,000,000,000.

Getty knew nothing of the *Fortune* article until one afternoon he found the lobby of the Ritz Hotel suddenly full of journalists, all of them clamouring for an interview with the 'richest American'. The magazine had not yet appeared on the newsstands, but advance copies had been distributed to newspapers and wire services and it had taken no time at all to discover that the richest American lived in hotel suites in Europe and at that moment was at the Ritz in London.

All my life I had managed to avoid the limelight or, to be more accurate, the limelight avoided me. Although I had hardly lived the life of a recluse, and made no conscious efforts to elude the press, I had succeeded in achieving a very large, and quietly gratifying, degree of personal anonymity. I had always been able to attend premieres, parties or nightclubs without eliciting much attention from the press. Reporters and photographers covering functions at which I was present generally detoured around me to seek more interesting game elsewhere; for all I know, they took me for one of the waiters. My name did not appear in gossip columns and my photograph seldom, if ever, adorned the pages of any publications less prosaic than the *Oil and Gas Journal*.

This pleasant and peaceful state of affairs came to a halt when I was labelled, unbeknown to me, the 'richest American'. To my acute discomfort I became a curiosity, a sort of financial freak, overnight. In the opinion of many reporters I had also become 'hot copy'.

217

Getty was not quite as bashful as he made out. In fact, he rather enjoyed talking to the reporters and read every word that was written about him. By and large, he emerged unscathed from his first major encounter with the world's press. Even though he was repeatedly asked 'exactly' how much he was worth – one anxious newshound even wanted to know how long it would take him to count his money – he was unfailingly polite, patiently explaining that fluctuations in the stock market made it impossible for him to calculate his fortune with any degree of accuracy. He admitted that he might, if pushed, be able to raise a billion but hurriedly pointed out: 'Remember, a billion dollars isn't what it used to be.'

Most reporters declared themselves to be impressed by his quiet, thoughtful manner, his old-world courtesy and the depth and range of his knowledge, particularly about history. 'The cool air of detachment with which Mr Getty discusses himself and his career is very remarkable,' the London *Sunday Times* noted. 'It is made attractive by a manner which is compounded of modesty, shyness and a kind of courtesy which has a slightly old-fashioned, and very American, charm. There is charm, also, in the evidence Mr Getty gives in conversation of an intensely serious mind, which is widely educated and deeply cultivated.'

For less serious newspapers, Getty's lifestyle, his attitude towards money and such eccentricities as sticking twice the necessary number of stamps on important letters as a precautionary measure, provided the best copy. Acres of newsprint were devoted to descriptions of the richest American sitting in his lonely hotel suite manipulating his huge empire and rummaging for business papers in cardboard boxes tied up with string. It was perhaps to be expected that slight embellishments crept into the coverage: his modest hotel suite, for example, soon became a single room and his single room soon became the cheapest room. From being the richest American, he was soon 'the richest man in the world'.

Reporters chasing 'skinflint' stories about Getty found there was a rich vein to be tapped. It didn't take them long to excavate the dog-show incident – when he waited with his guests for half-price admission – and an ex-girlfriend was persuaded to volunteer the story of the time when Getty took her out to dinner late one night and asked her to wait outside the restaurant for the orchestra to finish playing so that he did not have to pay a cover charge for music. It was revealed that he liked to save pieces of string and was 'delighted' when he had enough to tie up a parcel. Dining with a lady friend at the Pavillon d'Armenonville in Paris, he was alleged to have hurried her past the maître d'hôtel with the warning: 'Don't talk to that man – the slightest word with him and he expects to be tipped.'

Not all the anecdotes were strictly accurate. It was said, for example, that he once took a party of sixteen friends – including Elsa Maxwell – to dinner at Maxim's in Paris and then refused to pay the bill of 140,000 francs. What actually happened was that he was among the guests at the dinner, but at the end of the evening the 'host' took the maître d'hôtel to one side and told him to 'send the bill to Mr Getty'. 'I refused to pay,' said Getty, 'because I am not in the habit of being taken for a ride.'

The image of Getty as Scrooge was curiously enhanced by every photograph ever taken of him. The moment a camera was pointed at him, he turned down the corners of his mouth and scowled, almost as if he was *trying* to look like an old miser. 'Mr Getty was not very photogenic,' said Norris Bramlett, 'but that was hardly his fault. He did smile, except when he was in front of a camera.' His lugubrious expression, the three deep converging furrows above his long nose, his beady eyes, thin mouth and pointed chin combined to endow him with a undeniably curmudgeonly aspect. 'He can send shivers down an oil shaft,' the *Herald Tribune* commented.

In a fanciful cover story under the headline 'The Do-It-Yourself Tycoon', *Time* magazine alleged that as a young man Getty once tried to sell his mother a well, on Signal Hill in California, that bottomed out on an adjoining lease. Warned by a friend against buying, the old lady is said to have replied: 'What you are trying to tell me is that Paul is a crook. But he's awfully smart, isn't he?' The same article also reported that he had had his face lifted in a London clinic and dyed his hair.

None of this was true, but Getty did not much care. He was secretly amused at being portrayed as something of a 'character' and rarely bothered to deny even the most outrageous fabrications, although he was upset by one news magazine which said he wore frayed sweaters out at the elbow. 'I haven't worn long-sleeved sweaters since I was eleven years old,' he groused to friends.

What Getty really found irksome was not the publicity itself but the astonishing aftermath, which was not long coming and a lot less welcome. A week after the publication of *Fortune* magazine, he was swamped by thousands of begging letters.

They came from all over the world, variously addressed – one simply said 'Castle Getty, Arabia' – but inexorably finding their way to the Ritz in London thanks to the irrefutable law which ensures international postal services handle useless mail with particular diligence and ingenuity.

Getty was both appalled and intrigued by the deluge. 'I never cease to be amazed,' he said, 'at the economic illiteracy of people. They seem to think I have millions lying around in my room and all they need to do is drop me a line and I'll send them a few bundles of it.'

Although he had no intention of obliging any of his correspondents, he found it hard to resist reading their letters, some of which displayed breathtaking audacity. A banker wrote to confess he had embezzled a hundred thousand dollars and pleaded with Getty to make good the loss before he was found out. An inventor hoping to perfect a 'death ray' asked for a million dollars, as did a woman economics teacher from a Midwestern high school who simply wanted to 'do good'. An African requested a modest fifty dollars to buy a wife, while an aspiring entrepreneur put in a bid for two hundred million to build a canal across Nicaragua to compete with the Panama Canal. A lady in Brussels asked for twenty thousand dollars to buy her son an aeroplane and a doctor in Honolulu solicited seventy-five thousand dollars for a wildlife safari, offering to donate his trophies to Getty in return. 'You can display them in your home,' he wrote, 'and tell your friends you bagged them yourself. Part of the consideration I offer in return for the seventy-five thousand is the promise that I will never reveal your secret.'

Many people candidly admitted that they did not really need the money, but thought they would write anyway as 'he had so much'. Getty was mystified that anybody could think he would be so naive as to respond to such letters:

Dear Mr Getty,
I am thirty-five, married and without children. I have a pretty good job, earning a little over nine thousand dollars a year. But it's hell to work at thirty-five – during the prime of one's life. It's a time when a man and his wife should be enjoying themselves.

Having had so many divorces, you probably appreciate that more than most people. That's why I'm so certain you'll lend a sympathetic ear to what I am going to ask. It's really not much by your standards – not even petty cash. I would like to take two years off work and travel lazily around the world with my wife. We've checked into this with a travel agency, and we can do it comfortably for seventy thousand dollars.

So if you'll send the money, you'll make two people very happy and very grateful to you ...

A fair proportion of the mailbag comprised marriage proposals, most of which Getty rather enjoyed:

Dear Paul Getty,
You should not be living alone and as a bachelor – not at your age and with your money. I am only twenty-three, blonde, healthy and strong. I could look after you. I am willing to marry you for a hundred thousand dollars, cash payable at the time of the wedding, plus a hundred thousand a year for as long as you live. We can discuss the terms of your will after you have sent me the first-class air fare to England. I enclose some candid photographs of myself in the nude so you can see what you'll be getting ...

Not all such young ladies wrote on their own account; many had mothers making representations on their behalf, like this hopeful from Pennsylvania:

Dear Mr Getty,
A magazine article I just read says you have been married and
divorced five times. You should give yourself another chance and
make it an even half-dozen. My daughter will be eighteen next
month. She has already won three beauty contests and is a
wonderful dancer. She would make you a good and very sexy wife,
I'd see to that. I think ten thousand dollars a month for her and
five thousand a month for me would be a fair arrangement ...

Getty calculated that on average each mailbag brought in requests for a
total of around a hundred thousand dollars. He only ever responded
once to a begging letter and immediately got his fingers burned. A nun
in Australia asked him for a donation to a children's charity and he sent
a cheque for ten dollars without, perhaps, considering the implications.
The nun was immediately offered a hundred dollars for the cheque as a
souvenir, a local reporter picked up the story and it was soon being
flashed around the globe as an irresistible titbit for newspapers
everywhere: the richest man in the world had just donated *ten dollars* to
charity.

Getty knew after this incident that he was never going to escape
ridicule or vilification, no matter what he did. In fact he made
substantial contributions every year to certain favoured charities –
among them, the World Wildlife Fund and the American Hospital in
Paris – but he made quite sure his gifts were kept secret for fear of being
inundated with further requests from institutions or organisations with
which he was less sympathetic. 'If I were convinced,' he said, 'that by
giving away my fortune I could make a real contribution towards
solving the problems of world poverty, I'd give away 99.5% immediately.
But a hard-eyed appraisal of the situation convinces me this is not the
case. The best form of charity I know is the art of meeting a payroll.'

He claimed, not entirely truthfully, he gave a 'million dollars or more'
to charity every year. *Time* counterclaimed that the 'only recorded
instance in which Paul Getty has ever loosened his purse strings' was
when he donated part of his art collection to the Los Angeles County
Museum. Even this gesture was tainted: it was widely rumoured,
incorrectly, that he received some tax advantage.

A man labelled a billionaire really can't win [Getty explained]. If
he spends freely, he's accused of being a wastrel and of trying to
make an impression by splashing his money around. If he lives
quietly and without ostentation, he's castigated for being a
tightwad. Even the simple, everyday matter of tipping can become
a major problem. If I tip well, someone is certain to accuse me of
showing off. If I don't overtip that same someone will be the first
to sneer that I am a penny-pincher. I shouldn't be expected to tip
more than the average man. It's rude and inconsiderate to overtip

– it only makes things difficult and embarrassing for people who are not as rich as I am.

In a comparatively rare moment of real insight, he added: 'Money is a wonderful commodity to have, but the more one possesses, the more involved and complicated become dealings and relationships with people.'

The legions of journalists who trooped up to Getty's suite at the Ritz to ask him how much he was worth made little attempt to explore the labyrinthine complexity of his business. In between interviews Getty was still desperately trying to locate more refineries to process the Neutral Zone production and he was also moving gingerly, step by step, towards a a final rationalisation of his oil interests.

Planning the merger of Tidewater, Skelly and Getty Oil required him to perform a tricky corporate balancing act to maintain control of the component companies while keeping Wall Street in the dark. If investors got wind of his next move they could push up the price of stock he needed to acquire and endanger the whole plan, since he ran the risk of losing control of one company if he had to pay out too much of its stock in exchange for another.

Getty was anxious to avoid reporters inquiring into his plans for the merger and he also politely sidestepped questions about a more personal matter then causing him extreme anguish – the health of his youngest son, Timmy.

After returning to the United States with his mother in the summer of 1955, Timmy enrolled at Daycroft Private School near Norwalk, Connecticut. He settled down well and proved to be exceptionally bright, with a natural talent for music – much to the delight of his mother – and a passionate enthusiasm for baseball. Getty resumed contact with the boy by way of weekly transatlantic telephone calls, a situation to which Timmy was perfectly accustomed. They always discussed, in heart-rending detail, what they would do together when they next saw each other. Timmy seemed perfectly well and happy until July 1957, when the tumour re-emerged behind his eyes. He was driven to New York for a second operation and when he had recovered sufficiently to write, he sent his father a reassuring little poem composed in his hospital bed:

> God protects me through the night,
> God will help me win each fight,
> I know that God is ever here,
> I know in God I cannot fear,
> God will show me day by day,
> If I follow in his way.

Getty was deeply moved when he read Timmy's poem in his hotel room on the other side of the Atlantic. He folded the paper carefully and put it in his wallet, taking it out frequently in the years to come to reread the words and weep anew.

Teddy moved into the Hotel Pierre to be near her son, spending every day at the hospital with him. He was very weak after the operation, but always cheerful. It soon became clear that the tumour had not been completely removed and that he would have to undergo yet another operation. He faced up to the news with extraordinary courage, appearing to be more concerned about the worry he was causing his mother than the ordeal of more surgery.

Timmy had to have a third operation before the year was out, as a result of which his eyesight further deteriorated. By the time surgeons pronounced themselves satisfied that the last traces of the tumour had finally been removed, Timmy was nearly blind. Getty followed events from his suite at the Ritz, agonising about not being with his son but never contemplating taking enough time off from his business affairs to return to the United States. Teddy telephoned him every day to keep him in touch, although she no longer wasted her breath asking him to come back.

While Getty unquestionably fretted over Timmy, he perhaps derived some small consolation from the fact that his other sons had all joined the business by the end of 1957. George was then thirty-three and the proud father of three young daughters: Anne, aged six, Claire, four and Caroline, two. He was a stocky, good-looking man with few of his father's facial characteristics and a cheerful disposition. After the contretemps in the Neutral Zone, when he offended against the Saudi liquor laws, he was obliged to spend a considerable period in the wilderness before regaining his father's confidence. After his penitential stint in the backwater of Pacific Western's mid-continent headquarters at Midland, Texas, he was sent to Tulsa, Oklahoma – to the Spartan Aircraft Company which had long since completed its switch to the manufacture of trailers.

As he had left Princeton to become an 'oilman' he was hardly thrilled to find himself working at a factory producing mobile homes, but he knuckled down and proved to be a creditable executive and a worthy successor to his grandfather's name. He was promoted to vice-president of Spartan and appointed president of the Minnehoma Financial Company and the Minnehoma Insurance Company – the subsidiaries set up by his father to boost trailer sales. Both companies flourished under his direction and in July 1955 he moved his family back to Los Angeles to take up a position as executive vice-president of Pacific

Western. Less than a year later he joined the Tidewater Oil Company in New York as a director and vice-president.

It was a remarkable rise, after a slow start, up through the ranks of the Getty empire, but he vigorously denied any charge of nepotism. 'Mr Getty is the smartest businessman I know,' he said. 'He would never promote anyone just because he was his son. With him, performance is the thing.'

By 1957 George was making frequent trips to Europe to discuss business matters with his father (he had been entrusted with handling the Tidewater-Skelly merger negotiations), although there was little familiarity between them. To George, his father was always 'Mr Getty', which was understandable in many ways since they hardly knew each other – George reckoned that he had spent no more than six weeks with his father since he was one year old. Getty, nevertheless, was quietly proud of George F. Getty II and already viewed his eldest son as his natural successor. 'The concept of primogeniture,' he said, 'is deeply engrained.'

Getty certainly considered George had proved himself to be an able businessman and in Getty's eyes nothing was more important in life than to be a good businessman. He was less sure about Ronnie, his second son. Ronald was twenty-eight and still a bachelor. Having done his time in the Neutral Zone, he had been appointed Tidewater's vice-president in charge of marketing – a post he had filled reasonably satisfactorily but without much obvious flair. Getty was obliged to keep his two oldest sons apart since Ronnie loathed his half-brother, George, quite as much as George detested him. While they were growing up they were virtual strangers, but once they were both on their father's payroll they had ample opportunity to discover just how much they disliked each other, an enmity they communicated to Getty by exchanging letters of hate – copies to their father.

As both were now vice-presidents of the same company, Getty tried to avoid friction by dispatching Ronnie to Hamburg to take over Veedol Petroleum International, Tidewater's European marketing subsidiary. Ronnie could speak fluent French and German and might have been considered an obvious choice for the job, but he signally failed to impress. He had not been at Veedol very long before he wrote plaintively to his father, asking if he could take some extra holiday as he was putting in so much 'overtime'. Getty was furious. 'I wrote back and told him,' said the old man, 'that executives did not get overtime and he was an executive.'

Ronnie's younger half-brothers, Paul and Gordon, had flown to London in the summer of 1957 to discuss their careers with their father. Neither of them had seen him for six years and their meeting at the Ritz was an awkward little occasion of marked formality. Getty suggested, as they had anticipated he would, that they should join the family business. Both timidly agreed with the wisdom of this advice and promptly returned to California to become management trainees with the Getty Oil Company, although neither of them were exactly cast in the conventional oilman mould.

Paul was twenty-five, but could easily have passed for a teenager. He was a serious young man, quiet, shy, painfully thin and, with his horn-rimmed spectacles, rather scholarly in appearance. He had majored in English at San Francisco University and retained an enduring interest in literature, particularly of the Wilde-Beardsley 'decadent' school. His young wife, Gail, a water-polo champion at university, was exceptionally pretty, although quite as unworldly as her husband. In November 1956 their first child was born, a boy baptised J. Paul Getty at St Dominic's Church in San Francisco.

Gordon was fifteen months younger than his brother and no better equipped to enter the oil business. Tall, curly-haired and rarely without a sunny smile on his face, his passion was music and his ardent ambition was to be an opera singer and composer. Gordon knew so little about his father's business that he was quite as astonished as the rest of America when J. Paul Getty was revealed as the richest American. 'At school,' said Gordon, 'I never thought of him as being wealthier than any of the other fathers. The other kids in the class all knew the Gettys had a rich Daddy, but there was always a Joe or a Frank around whose Daddy was *really* rich. The *Fortune* article came as a complete surprise.'

After Getty became suddenly famous for his wealth and notorious for his parsimony, Gordon noticed that his favourite cartoon character, Scrooge McDuck, began to exhibit characteristics curiously reminiscent of his father. 'Scrooge McDuck was Donald Duck's rich uncle,' he explained. 'He could make me roll on the floor with laughter. Father was always close with a buck and when he became well-known, I am sure the man who created Scrooge McDuck saw to it that the duck imitated my father.' Gordon thought that Scrooge McDuck as a caricature of his father was even funnier.

Paul and Gordon began their careers, as management trainees, pumping gas for four hundred dollars a month at a filling station just across the bay from their home in San Francisco. After three weeks they were sent to work as labourers at the Avon refinery, then they became warehousemen, then clerks, then salesmen, following the same intensive programme all trainees were put through.

In March 1958, when they had completed their basic training, they flew to Paris to spend some time with their father. 'It was to be partly holiday and partly work,' Gordon explained. 'We spent a few hours with him every day, taking letters, sitting in at conferences, dealing with the correspondence and generally learning the business.' Getty was staying in his usual suite at the George V but required Gordon and Paul, with his wife and baby son, to stay in a cheap hotel a couple of blocks distant.

It was Getty's first meeting with his daughter-in-law, Gail, and his grandson, Paul III, and he was charmed by them both. Gail was young and shapely, which was enough to make her immediately popular; what was completely unexpected was that the old man should suddenly become a doting grandfather. The baby, Getty noted, was a 'bright, red-headed little rascal, who possessed a remarkable ability for making his grandpa obey his commands'.

Getty took them all to visit the World's Fair in Brussels and amazed everyone by frequently dandling the baby on his lap. One afternoon in the hotel baby Paul was sitting on his grandfather's knee without a diaper and the inevitable happened: a dark stain spread across Getty's trouser leg. Paul and Gail stared at it with horror, wondering what to expect. Getty suddenly lifted the baby up and looked at his trousers. His jaw dropped momentarily and then he let out a great sonorous guffaw, as if it was the funniest thing that had ever happened to him.

In May, Gordon left for the Neutral Zone. The original plan had been for Paul to go, too, but Getty changed his mind and decided to send Paul to Italy to assist with the negotiations to take over Golfo. A desire to have his grandson around may have played some part in this decision. Paul and Gail were certainly happy to move to Italy and they rented a small apartment at 1 Piazza Duse in Milan, where the Golfo administrative headquarters was located. In June Paul shyly asked his father for permission to change his name from Eugene to Jean, so that he could become J. Paul Getty Junior. Getty was touched and naturally agreed.

Around this time, Getty heard the good news from New York that Timmy had recovered sufficiently to be moved into a rehabilitation hospital. After nearly a year in bed he was very weak and unable to walk unaided, but Teddy was confident the boy would soon get his strength back. Getty spoke to him on the telephone and asked him what he would like for his twelfth birthday. 'I want your love, Daddy,' Timmy's thin little voice piped over the transatlantic line, 'and I want to see you.'

Getty was in Rome in July discussing the Golfo takeover. At the end of the month, he checked into the Hotel Francia-Europa in Milan to spend some time with his grandson.

1 August 1958: 'To 1 Piazza Duse to see Paul and Gail's apartment and my loved ones. I saw little Paul asleep in his crib, lying on his stomach. Paul arrived from the office at eight. I am proud of my little family. Milan newspapers are featuring stories about the unbearable heat of the last few days, but although their apartment

is not air-conditioned, Paul and Gail were cheerful and uncomplaining.'

That same day, Hoen, the doctor in charge of Timmy's case, telephoned from New York and recommended cosmetic surgery to cover the scars of the previous operations and correct a sunken spot in the bones on the boy's forehead. Timmy had made a good recovery, he said. The pressure in his head was normal and he could walk around the room with help of a brace on his left leg, but the boy was worried by the scars and kept putting his hand up to his forehead. The doctor said he thought it would be a good idea to remove all trace of the operations before Timmy finally went home.

Getty asked if there was any risk and was told it was negligible; it was a simple cosmetic operation and the boy would only have to be in hospital for a couple more days. Teddy came on the line and said she agreed with the doctor, but Getty had a premonition about it and at first refused his permission. Only when little Timmy picked up the telephone and begged his father to approve the operation did Getty reluctantly give his consent. He still had misgivings about it when, two days later, he left for a series of business meetings in Lugano with representatives of a Swiss consortium holding a controlling interest in Golfo's refinery at Gaeta.

On Thursday 14 August Timmy had his operation in New York. Teddy telephoned Getty to say the boy had recovered well, was very bright and cheerful and looking forward to going home to see his black-and-white mongrel sheepdog, Tippy. Getty was much relieved.

At three o'clock in the morning on Sunday 17 August the telephone rang in Getty's suite at the Hotel Splendide, Lugano. It was Teddy. Timmy had had a relapse and was very ill. 'I am distraught,' Getty wrote in his diary. 'Said a prayer. Couldn't go back to sleep. Worked on reports and correspondence in an effort to occupy my mind.'

At four o'clock next morning, in the middle of a thunderstorm, Teddy telephoned again, nearly incoherent with grief. Timmy's heart had failed. He was dead.

Monday 18 August: 'Darling Timmy died two hours ago, my best and bravest son, a truly noble human being. Words are useless. I blame myself for permitting Dr Hoen to operate. I had refused to allow any further operation, but Dr Hoen assured me there was no danger in the operation. I still hesitated, but finally gave my consent. Had I not been assured the operation was a slight one, I would have gone to NY to be present as there was no urgency about the operation. Dear Teddy! How brave she is! Darling Timmy, the world is poorer for your loss and I am desolate.'

Tuesday 19 August: 'Can think only of Timmy.'

Wednesday 20 August: 'After dinner talked to Mr and Mrs Lund of London and their very pretty daughter, Robina. She is an excellent pianist ... Timmy, it is hard for me to be brave about losing you. My own darling boy.'

Thursday 21 August: 'It is cool today, a touch of autumn. Tore up old letters and business papers. I can't carry heavy luggage.'

Friday 22 August: 'Crude demand 1958, UK 724, Ger 410, Japan 360, Italy 340. Just reread a touching poem written by my Timmy ...'

Timmy was buried at Forest Lawn Memorial Park in Los Angeles, not far from his grandparents, Sarah and George Getty. His father was not present at the funeral service.

Getty buried himself in work, the only palliative, he believed, for grief. But he took some solace from the presence of baby Paul who was developing, in the Italian sunshine, freckles just like Timmy's.

Wednesday 27 August: 'Taxi with Paul to his apt. for lunch. Baby Paul came running into the parlor to greet us. He was most cheerful and cute. He can't talk yet. Gail had a nice lunch for us. Back to this hotel, worked with June [June Cassell, his secretary]. Paul and Farbach came to see me re meeting tomorrow. Madelle phoned, the Rubens is $130,000. Hilde arr. at 5.30, dinner with her. Took 500 mg. Terramycin at noon, 250 mg at 6 p.m., 250 at 12 a.m. GOC producing capacity in the NZ now seems bottlenecked by actual daily production of the Wafra wells accruing to GOC. Aminoil is taking 3/4 of the Burgan, the Ratawi is curtailed by Aminoil to 16000 BD, the Eocene does 26000 BD, GOC does 45000 BD, the terminal can handle 100000 BD, the 18" and 10" can handle 100000 BD or double present production. When the 16" is completed and a 2nd sea line completed the capacity will be 200000 BD or 4 times present GOC field production. The Burgan seems to have an MER of 45000 BD or 22500 BD to GOC. This requires GOC to get 178500 BD of Eocene and Ratawi. Present market demand for GOC NZ crude inc. fuel oil is 50000 BD to Del, 10000 BD to Avon. Next year, say 45000 BD to Del, 30000 BD to Avon, 8000 BD to MOC. Total potential would be 75000 BD to TW, 40000 to MOC, 35000 to Gaeta plus say 15000 BD of product sales from MS to the trade. TW has ample tanker capacity to handle everything foreseeable up to 1963, thus no new tanker orders before 1962. The tanker industry needs a suspension of new tanker orders for 3 years, 1958, 59, 60 and will probably get it. This 3 year close season plus cancellations and changes to ore carriers and dry cargo ships will probably eliminate the surplus by 1964 when owners will again be ordering tankers. Rates, however, may improve gradually from now on. Rates next year may be 10% to 20% higher than this year, or say PG US USMC – 55%.'

Timmy made a last, chilling, appearance in Getty's diary on Wednesday 3 September: 'Funeral bill for Darling Timmy. A sad day. Sent cable to Zone that Aminoil can have 50% of Eocene by giving us 50% of Burgan and paying 10c per bbl handling ...'

By the end of 1958 Getty had completed the takeover of Golfo, relocated the offices in Rome, closer to the Gaeta refinery, and changed the name of the company to Getty Oil Italiana. He knew that Paul and Gail would be happy to live in Rome and he convinced himself that Paul was capable of assuming major responsibilities.

'I am going to leave you here on your own,' he told Paul. 'Think you can handle things?'

'I'll try my best,' Paul replied.

Getty was satisfied and returned to London, leaving his twenty-six-year-old son to be general manager of Getty Oil Italiana after almost two years in the oil business. When they arrived in Rome, Paul and Gail found that the famous film director Federico Fellini was making a movie in the Via Veneto called *La Dolce Vita*.

For a young, unsophisticated American couple innocent of the ways of the world and on their first visit to Europe, what better place was there to set up home? What worse place?

Thousands of miles away in the Neutral Zone, Paul's brother Gordon was not having a happy time: he had managed to get himself arrested.

Gordon was surprised to discover on his arrival that the Neutral Zone was no longer the wild, romantic desert wilderness he had expected. 'It was more like suburbia USA,' he said, 'except there was no television.' The port at Mina Saud was now a settlement of air-conditioned concrete cubes with a swimming pool, a sports field and a golf course with miraculous green lawns growing in the sand. At Wafra oilfield, thirty miles inland, conditions were a little more primitive, but the sprawl of Spartan trailers made the place look much more American than Arabian. Gordon was quite disappointed.

The first task with which his father entrusted him was a matter requiring great tact and a deep understanding of Arabs and Arabia. Gordon had neither. Getty believed that the local emir, the governor appointed by King Saud to look after Saudi interests in the Neutral Zone, owed money to the Getty Oil Company. It was a trifling matter, no more than a couple of small, unpaid bills, but Getty hated to see debts outstanding and instructed Gordon to press for payment.

Gordon, obviously anxious to please his father, anticipated no difficulties. He made an appointment to see the emir and politely proffered the bills. The emir was friendly but explained through an interpreter that there was a mistake, he owed Getty Oil nothing: the items for which he was being billed were clearly a goodwill gift and he had accepted them as such. Gordon, blushed, apologised and departed.

He forwarded this intelligence to his father in London and received a curt cable in reply telling him that Getty still expected the bills to be paid. Back went Gordon to the emir, this time receiving a distinctly less amiable reception and the same story. The emir was perhaps unable to understand why the young American was not getting his message – the money Getty Oil was demanding was his rightful *baksheesh,* the toll he expected in return for his cooperation. It was the way business was conducted throughout Saudi Arabia and he was affronted by the persistent demands from this young Getty that he should give up his *baksheesh.*

When older hands with more experience in the Middle East explained to Gordon what was going on, he was all for letting the matter drop; but his father would not hear of it, insisting as a matter of principle that Gordon should continue to press for payment of the bills. It was not long before Gordon was extremely unpopular with the emir.

That summer, an Arab driver working for the Getty Oil Company crashed his truck into a pipeline and caused considerable damage. He promptly fled and was never seen again. Accidents of this kind were not unusual and under normal circumstances would not have aroused the interest of the Saudi authorities. But the goodwill the emir formerly possessed towards the Getty Oil Company no longer existed and he insisted that the driver's immediate superior be punished for the accident. This was perfectly lawful under Saudi Arabia's harsh judicial system.

Gordon was shocked, although some of the other oilmen told him it could have been worse – if a driver knocked down and killed a pedestrian in Saudi Arabia, relatives of the dead person not only had the right to demand the driver's life in return but they could appoint the executioner and decide on the method of his dispatch.

Appalled by the brutality of Saudi law, Gordon now found himself posed with a moral dilemma. He could hardly countenance the punishment of one of his men for an offence he had not committed. On the other hand, advising him to leave would almost certainly result in another arrest – Gordon's. (He was beginning to have an uncomfortable suspicion that this might perhaps be the emir's object.) In the end, when the man the emir wanted to arrest – a young Englishman who had been working in the Neutral Zone for several years – asked Gordon if he should stay and face the music, or drive up to Kuwait and take the first flight home, Gordon replied that he was not a policeman: he could neither order him to stay nor prevent him from leaving. The Englishman left that night.

Next day, the hapless Gordon was arrested and charged with

(*above*) Louise Dudley 'Teddy' Lynch, fifth and last of J. Paul Getty I's wives, and (*below*) the English *pied-à-terre* – Sutton Place – which supplanted her. Teddy cited her husband's refusal to return from Europe as evidence that their marriage was no longer extant.

The Sutton Place house-warming party 30 June 1960
(*opposite*) Between 2500 and 3000 people attended, less than half of them invited. (*above*) The milk bar erected for the occasion, which came complete with real-live cow. (*below*) The pool where photographer David Steen came to grief.

The Getty Girls

(*opposite*) Rosabella Burch, the alluring Nicaraguan widow whom Getty set up in a little house not far from Sutton Place; (*above*) Mary Tessier, high society art expert and interior designer; (*right*) the well-connected Penelope Kitson, his chosen companion for many years and (*below*) Robina Lund, his friend and longtime legal adviser in Britain.

The high life

(*opposite*) With his billions for an entrée, J. Paul Getty I rubs shoulders with the great and the famous: (second from the left) Victor Lownes, then managing director of Playboy Enterprises in London, Stirling Moss and Beatle Ringo Starr. (*above*) A tête-à-tête with a title, the Duchess of Bedford, and (*below*) old sparring partners: Jack Dempsey was a friend from Getty's Hollywood days.

For all his forays into society, J. Paul Getty I liked to keep the world at arm's length – on the other end of a telephone line for preference.

assisting a prisoner to escape. Because he was a Getty and thus a person of some note in Saudi Arabia, he was not thrown into jail but held in the governor's house at Damman, the capital of the eastern province of Saudi Arabia.

The trial, a week later, was conducted entirely in Arabic as a result of which Gordon did not understand a word of what was going on. But at the end of it, he gleaned that he had been found guilty and sentenced to a week's house arrest. 'It was not too bad,' he said, 'it gave me time to catch up on my reading.'

Getty was more than a little vexed when news of Gordon's arrest was relayed to London. He immediately blamed his son for the whole embarrassing incident and sent instructions that Gordon was to leave the Neutral Zone as soon as he was released.

Gordon flew back to London for a frosty reunion with his father in August 1959. 'Father was *reasonably* understanding,' he said, 'but I think he felt there must have been some darned way I could have handled it more adroitly.' If he had any doubt about this analysis, it was removed when he found himself summarily dispatched to Tulsa, Oklahoma, with instructions to learn the trailer business. A few months later, the boss of Spartan wrote to Getty threatening to resign. 'I just cannot work with Gordon,' he explained.

Not long afterwards, Gordon decided he was perhaps not cut out to be a businessman and resolved to leave the company to study full-time the Conservatoire of Music in San Francisco. Although he reluctantly accepted that he did not have a good enough voice to be an opera singer, he still had hopes of making a career in music as a composer.

'Father did not oppose my decision at all,' Gordon said. 'I think he might even have been pleased.'

By the summer of 1959, Getty had been living in hotel rooms for the best part of a decade. At the age of sixty-six, he had no thoughts of retirement, although for some time he had been warming to the idea of settling down and establishing a base somewhere in Europe. He envisaged something like a large country house close to a European capital, a place that would provide him with a comfortable and permanent home and at the same time be big enough to act as a corporate headquarters.

France was his first choice. He was a confirmed Francophile, adored Paris and Parisian women, and had recently been invested as a Chevalier of the Legion of Honour in recognition of the employment he had created by having many of his tankers built in French shipyards. A château not too far from Paris would, he thought, suit his purpose admirably. But political unrest in 1958 and the election of Charles de

Gaulle as president persuaded him that France was not such a good idea. He could not imagine that foreign businessmen would be particularly welcome under the imperious de Gaulle, and began looking elsewhere.

In June 1959, while he was staying at the Ritz in London, he was invited to a dinner party with the Duke and Duchess of Sutherland at Sutton Place, their country estate near Guildford in Surrey, some thirty miles from London. Sutton Place was a fine old manor house with seventy-two rooms and was considered to be the finest example of Tudor architecture extant. 'Geordie' Sutherland had bought the estate in 1917 for £120,000 but was finding the maintenance to be an increasing burden on the family finances. Over dinner, he confessed to Getty that he would like to sell the place and find somewhere smaller.

A couple of days passed before it dawned on Getty that Sutton Place was precisely the kind of property for which he was looking. It was certainly big enough, was close enough to London and would make a perfect setting for much of his art collection. The strange coincidence of the name – Getty's first home in New York was the penthouse at Sutton Place – made it, somehow, an even more attractive proposition. Getty asked Dudley Delevigne, a leading London estate agent and a close friend of Mrs Kitson, to make discreet inquiries of the duke as to the price he would expect for Sutton Place. The duke, it transpired, was extremely short of cash and exceedingly anxious to sell: Delevigne reported back and said that Getty could probably acquire the whole property, the house and its sixty-acre park, for less than sixty-five thousand pounds. The price was low, the agent explained, because most buyers would be deterred by the huge maintenance costs of a house of that size.

Getty never dithered much, particularly if he thought he might miss a bargain. He instructed Delevigne to open negotiations with the Duke of Sutherland to purchase Sutton Place at the earliest opportunity and he retained a young woman solicitor, newly qualified, to supervise the transaction and set up a company to run the estate. She was Robina Lund, the 'very pretty daughter' of Mr and Mrs Lund whom he had met the previous year at the Hotel Splendide in Lugano. Before the end of the year, the finest Tudor house in Britain passed into the maw of the Getty corporate labyrinth. Work on extensive renovations and improvements started immediately under the direction of Mrs Penelope Kitson, who faced little competition for the commission.

On 29 June 1960 Getty wrote in his diary: 'Left my suite, 611-612, at the Ritz for the last time. From now on, my address will be Sutton Place – but for how long? I am hoping to get all the loose business ends tidied up within the next year at most. I long to dive into the surf at Malibu Beach again.'

15. 'Good, old-fashioned, vulgar fun'

Sutton Place was built between the years 1521 and 1530 for Sir Richard Weston, a favourite at the court of King Henry VIII, and was the most important of the great Tudor houses started after Cardinal Wolsey began building Hampton Court in 1514.

Sir Richard, who had served as the king's emissary in France and accompanied him to the Field of the Cloth of Gold in 1520, was seemingly much influenced by the Italian style of architecture then popular on the continent – an influence reflected in the particular grace and elegance of Sutton Place and the extensive use of moulded terracotta tiles to embellish the brickwork. Probably the first manor house in England constructed without fortifications, its large mullioned windows of painted glass gave the interior an airiness and sparkle unusual for the period.

Henry VIII, then trying to disentangle himself from the first of his six wives, was a frequent visitor to Sutton Place with his young mistress, Anne Boleyn; they liked to play tennis with Sir Richard's son, Francis. Games might have continued off the court after Henry's marriage to Anne for in 1536, when she was committed to the Tower of London accused of adultery with a number of men, one of them was named as young Francis Weston. He was found guilty of being one of the queen's lovers and was beheaded, at the age of twenty-five, on Tower Hill. Anne Boleyn followed him to the block a few days later. Her ghost, so it was said, returned to haunt the echoing rooms at Sutton Place where she was alleged to have trysted with her lover.

In 1542 the estate was passed on to Sir Richard's grandson, Henry, who married a cousin of Anne Boleyn's daughter, Queen Elizabeth I. After the Reformation the Westons remained staunchly Roman Catholic and virtually disappeared from public life, although Henry's son, the second Sir Richard Weston, was a noted agriculturalist: he introduced the theory of crop rotation and conducted extensive farming experiments on the land surrounding Sutton Place.

The estate remained in the hands of the Weston family until the end of the nineteenth century when it was leased by the newspaper magnate Alfred Harmsworth, the first Viscount Northcliffe, who had a nine-hole golf course laid out in the grounds. In 1918 Northcliffe suffered a breakdown brought on by megalomania and Sutton Place was acquired by the fifth Duke of Sutherland, a descendant of an ancient Scottish landowning family which could trace its title back to the thirteenth century. The duke held on to the estate for nearly forty years, until the expenses became crippling.

When Getty bought Sutton Place in 1959, it was still substantially the same house Sir Richard Weston had built more than four hundred years earlier, except for the conversion of a number of rooms into bathrooms and the installation of an ancient central-heating system and a coal-fired range in the kitchen. Most of the fine armorial painted-glass windows were still in place, as were the stone fireplaces carved with the pomegranate emblem of Henry VIII's first wife who was still in favour at the time the house was being built. All the oak panelling was original, although it had been covered by countless layers of varnish over the centuries, and there was a considerable amount of furniture dating from a 1542 inventory. Sir Richard would have noticed few alterations to the two-storey Great Hall with its minstrels' gallery at each end, or the Long Gallery on the upper floor which Tudor occupants used for brisk constitutionals on rainy days.

Few improvements had been made during the Duke of Sutherland's tenure and the Sutton Place Property Company, which had been set up by Getty to run the estate, embarked on an extensive programme of renovation and modernisation. All the outdated bathroom fittings were ripped out and replaced, the kitchen was completely gutted and re-equipped with the latest American appliances, many of the ceilings were lowered, a new oil-fired central-heating system was installed, all the oak panelling was stripped to reveal the original wood and the entire house was redecorated from top to bottom, all seventy-two rooms.

Getty decided not to pillage his art collection in California in order to furnish Sutton Place. He purchased from the Duke of Sutherland some of the furniture, paintings and tapestries that were already in the house, then embarked on a veritable orgy of buying. He bought Gains-borough's 'Portrait of Anne' for $104,000 and another Rembrandt, 'Saint Bartholomew', for $532,000, then guiltily wrote in his diary: 'I think I should stop buying pictures. I have enough invested in them.' His resolve did not last long: during the next few months he acquired a Canaletto, two Renoirs, a Corot, two Degas, a Bonnard and Rubens's 'Diana and Her Nymphs Departing for the Hunt'.

He bought two complete collections of gold and silver plate, much of it by Paul Lamerie, more than a dozen old Flemish wall tapestries and Oriental rugs, innumerable pieces of sixteenth- and seventeenth-century oak furniture and two huge Tudor tables – for the dining-room at Sutton Place – from the William Randolph Hearst collection at St Donat's Castle in Wales.

Penelope Kitson was buying, too: hundreds of square yards of carpet and curtains, velvet wall covering for the library, two grand pianos for the Long Gallery, hundreds of towels and dishcloths, 128 pairs of sheets and 250 pillowcases . . . There was, said Getty, a 'dry-goods-storeful' of lesser items to purchase.

The Sutton Place Property Company took on all the staff formerly employed by the estate, except for a few family retainers who moved on with the duke and duchess. There were about thirty-five employees in all, including an estate manager, gamekeeper, five gardeners, two woodsmen, two maintenance men, eight security men, a chauffeur, a cook and assistant cook, head housemaid and two assistants, two secretaries, an odd-jobman, a footman and a butler. The two key personnel were Francis Bullimore, a magisterial butler who might have stepped straight out of the pages of P.G. Wodehouse and Albert Thurgood, the estate manager. 'We weren't too worried about Mr Getty taking over,' said Thurgood. 'The staff knew that the house had become too much for the duke and they were worried that if the estate was broken up they would all be out of work. They knew that Mr Getty had a reputation for being mean, but they were happy that they had all kept their jobs.'

While renovation work was under way at Sutton Place, Getty remained in his suite at the Ritz although he visited the estate frequently to check progress, usually travelling from London by train because it was quicker and cheaper than by road – the second-class train fare from Waterloo to Woking, the nearest station, was only seven shillings and sixpence. Richings, the chauffeur, met the train and drove Getty to the property. He liked to walk around the house to see what everyone was doing and he was genuinely excited when a priest's hole was discovered behind the panelling in the Long Gallery and the original bread oven, complete with bacon hooks, was found behind the fireplace in the drawing-room. Not long afterwards, he could be found poring over reference books in the library to try and find out what kinds of food would have been cooked in a Tudor oven.

News that the 'richest man in the world' (as Getty was now almost invariably known) intended to make his home in England, in a Tudor manor house, naturally attracted a great deal of attention in the media and inevitably his friends began asking him, more in jest than hope, when the 'house-warming' party was going to be. Getty had not given a party for years but the more he thought about it, the more he liked the idea, particularly as it would be tax-deductible. Sutton Place Property Company administered the property as a 'liaison centre' for the Getty interests; a house-warming would be tantamount to an official opening of a corporate facility.

At the beginning of April 1960 the sixty-seven-year-old billionaire decided that there *would* be a house-warming, and not just a modest gathering of a few friends but a once-in-a-lifetime party to remember, with guests invited from all over the world. It would, Getty thought, be excellent public relations – he could invite senior management personnel from all the Getty companies, top executives from other industries, leading politicians and influential society figures. Work on the house was scheduled to finish between 30 April and 15 May. Allowing a safety margin for delays, he took out his diary and circled Thursday 30 June.

The guest list, when it was finally drawn up, contained no less than 1200 names. Formal printed invitations were sent out in May, but not many days passed before Getty began to regret the whole idea. There seemed to be thousands of people who thought they should have been invited and Sutton Place was inundated with telephone calls and letters requesting invitations, many from 'friends' of whom he had no recollection. Still more difficult to deal with were the people who *had* been invited and who telephoned to ask if they could bring friends; some even wanted a stack of blank invitations.

Getty suspected, probably correctly, that few of them would have had the temerity to make such a request of any other host. Sometimes he wondered if it was simply because he was an American that people felt they could treat him differently, but he concluded that it was probably because of his unwanted status as 'the richest man in the world'. The shoals of begging letters which continued to arrive had greatly exacerbated his jaundiced view of humanity and the undignified wrangling for invitations to his party confirmed his prejudice. He was neither surprised nor particularly angry when newspapers reported that there was a healthy black market in invitations, with 'singles' selling at up to a hundred pounds and 'doubles' for as much as two hundred and fifty.

Of more immediate concern was the question whether or not the building work would be completed in time.

I began to have unnerving visions of guests arriving for the party and banging their heads on ladders and scaffolding and tripping over buckets of paint. For her part, Mrs Kitson was verging on panic. Despite her best efforts to hold contractors to their promises, certain phases of the work had fallen behind schedule and many of the items she ordered had not been delivered on time. As the day of the party approached, large sections of wall were still unpainted, and much of the great house was a jumble of heaped lumber, stacked pipe and workmen's tools.

Getty was not able to move into the house until 29 June by which time, with the renovations far from finished, most of the staff were run off their feet covering up the remaining scaffolding, tucking step-ladders, tools and tarpaulins out of sight, closing up the undecorated rear bedrooms and filling gaps in the furnishings with huge flower arrangements.

Getty's old friend Jack Forrester, who had been invited to stay over, arrived early from Paris wearing a smart vicuna coat which Getty greatly admired.

'Why don't you try it on, Paul?' said Forrester.

Getty slipped it on over his suit, stroked the material and said: 'It's beautiful. How much?'

'About fifteen hundred dollars,' Forrester replied cheerfully.

Getty's face registered utter horror. 'I could never afford anything like that,' he muttered, struggling out of the coat as if it had suddenly become contaminated.

On the morning of the big day, Getty noted in his diary: 'Everyone is working like mad to get ready for the party.' It was hardly an exaggeration. Caterers were bringing in food and drink in vans and the house and grounds were swarming with workmen. A dance floor was being laid alongside the swimming pool in the walled garden, floodlights and torches were being set up, pegs were being hammered into the lawns for marquees and, some distance from the house, scaffolding was being erected for the firework display. The three orchestras who were to play for the guests arrived in the afternoon, as did the 'Oriental' clairvoyant who would be telling fortunes in her incense-perfumed tent. A cow which was to be tethered in the 'milk bar' chewed at a bale of straw and stared at all the activity with lustrous, uncomprehending eyes.

The most honoured guests, numbering around a hundred, had been invited for dinner at eight-thirty; the remainder were due to start arriving after ten o'clock. At eight o'clock Getty discovered he did not have a dress shirt to wear with his white tie and tails, but the imperturbable Bullimore proved perfectly capable of coping with this crisis. He offered the master one of his own crisply-laundered dress shirts. It hung on Getty like a bell tent, but Bullimore calmly pinned tucks in the back to take up the material normally spread over his own ample girth. Thus accoutred, Getty arrived downstairs to greet his guests a few minutes before eight-thirty.

The dinner – caviar, consommé, roast veal and fraises de bois, all served on gold and silver plate – was a great success. Fifty people were seated around the long table in the dining-hall and about the same number were accommodated at round tables set up in the drawing-room. Getty sat at the head of the table in the dining-hall with the wife of the Venezuelan ambassador on his right and Mary, Duchess of Roxburgh, on his left, gamely struggling to make polite conversation while chewing each mouthful thirty-three times. One of the platoon of perspiring waiters slipped with a tray of ice cream and tipped it over himself, to the enormous enjoyment of the diners, but otherwise there were no hitches. Outside, it was a rather different story.

By the time coffee was being served, the other merrymakers were beginning to assemble amid scenes of increasing confusion. For security reasons guests had been asked to enter Sutton Place through the gates fronting on to the main London-Guildford road, the A3, and it was not long before a huge traffic jam developed. With a three-mile queue of limousines backed up along the A3, harassed local policemen hired to provide security began waving cars through the gates without bothering to check the invitations.

The gate-crashers could hardly believe their luck. None of London's loutish party-going set wanted to miss such a shindig and none were deterred by the lack of an invitation, particularly as the host was only some rich American. Cars crammed with six or seven hopeful revellers gained access on the strength of a single invitation; many others got in by simply flashing old invitation cards to other parties. It was particularly frustrating for those couples who had taken the trouble to hide in car luggage compartments to be told on their release, once safely inside the grounds, that they need not have bothered. Elsewhere around the estate, young gentlemen in dinner jackets and young ladies in ball gowns were crawling through hedges or climbing over walls and sauntering across the lawns as if back from a little stroll in the grounds. Around and about the party, various gate-crashers could be heard congratulating each other on having sneaked in: 'Good show, Jack's here', 'Oh well done, Fiona, you're in', 'George has made it, good old George, that makes all of us.'

In the Great Hall Getty stood in his pinned dress shirt at the head of a receiving line, politely shaking hands with the guests as they arrived. He had taken up this position at ten-thirty and was still there at midnight, by which time the house and grounds were crammed with more than two thousand people and there were still cars streaming through the gates.

Some of Getty's closest friends were expecting fireworks long before the firework display, since he had naturally invited a selection of his mistresses, many of whom had never set eyes on each other before. That there was no love lost between them was evident early on when Mrs Kitson made her entrance down the grand stairway in a gown which she had had made for the occasion by a Paris couturier. Halfway down the stairs she noticed a woman in the crowd wearing precisely the same dress. Another of Getty's friends, Ethel Le Vane, who hated Penelope, could not resist clapping her hands with a thrilled *'Très bon!'*

Mrs Kitson, however, demonstrated what it meant to be a well-bred Englishwoman. Without pausing for a moment, without a word, she simply turned and retraced her steps. Ten minutes later, she reappeared in yet another beautiful dress, a stunning peacock creation. By then a delicious rumour was circulating that the incident was not just a coincidence but had been deliberately arranged to humiliate Penelope. It was said that Mary Tessier, a Russian friend of Getty's who lived in France, had found out where Penelope was having her dress made and arranged for a copy to be made. She had then lent it to a woman with a notoriously dubious reputation and obtained an invitation for her on the strict condition that she was standing about when Penelope made her appearance.

No one ever admitted responsibility for engineering the prank, but it was noted that while Penelope and Mary Tessier were not exactly bosom friends before the party, they were bitter enemies afterwards. And Mrs Tessier not only lived in France, but also knew most of the leading designers.

Getty was unaware of this little drama. Having excused himself from the receiving line some time after midnight, he wandered about the party uncomfortably conscious that his house was full of total strangers, all of whom seemed to be assuaging their ferocious thirsts with his champagne. So unimposing was his presence that when he wanted to go up to the Long Gallery for a dance with Robina Lund, he was at first unable to persuade the guests sprawling over the staircase to make way for him. 'Later I managed it,' he said, 'and enjoyed dancing. Then I went outside to the swimming pool to enjoy the gay scene there.'

It is axiomatic at a party attended by scions of the British upper class that if a swimming pool is within reach, someone has to be thrown in, fully dressed. They chose a Fleet Street photographer, David Steen, one of ten photographers and thirty reporters allocated invitations to cover the event for the world's press. While Steen was taking pictures near the pool, a couple of young bloods gave him a hefty shove and there was a splash as he fell over backwards into the water with his cameras round his neck and his electronic flash pack over his shoulder. Everyone laughed except Steen, who was momentarily terrified that the powerful flash pack would short-circuit in the water and electrocute him. (Later when Steen threatened legal action against those responsible, he was warned off and badly beaten up by a band of thugs waiting for him outside a country club.)

In the early hours of the morning a lobster buffet was served for the carousing hordes, who now numbered between 2500 and 3000, less than half of them invited. They fell on the food like starvelings, fearful there was insufficient to go round, piling their plates, scooping great spoonfuls of Beluga caviar and hastily returning for the strawberries and cream.

Getty was too much of a gentleman to indicate his displeasure at the behaviour of some of his 'guests', not that there was much he could have done about it, short of trying to have those who were especially objectionable thrown out. It would have been difficult, perhaps impossible, to end the party early: there were just too many people intent on enjoying themselves at his considerable expense. He resigned himself to the realisation that it was a party that was going to have to run its course, ending either when fatigue or boredom set in, or when the last champagne bottle was uncorked, whichever was the sooner.

Determined to see it through to the end, at six o'clock in the morning as the dawn light filtered through the painted-glass windows he could be found in the Long Gallery dancing with 'Pen' to the music of a tired fourteen-piece orchestra and a crooner hoarse from singing all night. Getty went to bed soon afterwards, although it was ten o'clock before the last of the revellers departed, no doubt having filled their cigarette cases.

The extra staff who had been hired to clean up after the party could barely believe their eyes when they arrived at midday. A pair of electrically-operated gates hung useless on their hinges having been forced open by departing guests. The trimmed lawns surrounding the house had been churned into mud and were strewn with bottles and glasses, burnt-out fireworks, cigarette ends, broken plates and cutlery. A statue of a nymph in the forecourt carried a firework in one hand and an empty champagne bottle in the other; a matching statue nearby sported a red hat cocked over one eye.

Inside the house, the scene was even worse. To show their appreciation guests had smeared ice cream over antique tapestries, ripped the new velvet wall coverings, left cigarettes burning on eighteenth-century French furniture or ground them into the Persian carpets, spilled drinks everywhere and helped themselves to a great number of souvenirs, including one of a pair of Paul Lamerie sugar sifters valued at fourteen thousand pounds. 'It was heartbreaking,' said Robina Lund, 'to see the amount of damage done.'

Getty would never again host such a party. If there was any consolation for him, it was that the occasion drew mostly favourable notices from the press. 'Easily the most fabulous evening since the war,' said William Hickey, the gossip columnist in the *Daily Express*, describing the party as 'good, old-fashioned, vulgar fun'. *Time* reported that Getty, the 'prototype of a penny-pinching billionaire, went pound-foolish with a vengeance' and *Queen* magazine's story, under the headline 'The Battle of Gettysburg, 1960,' spoke of an 'amazing number of uninvited long-haired people'. One enterprising reporter estimated that the party probably cost something in the region of thirty thousand dollars, but uncharitably calculated that during the ten hours it lasted, profits from the Getty empire probably swelled the host's personal fortune by about sixty-seven thousand dollars.

Few newspapers failed to be impressed by the guests' Homeric consumption of food and drink. They swilled 34 bottles of vodka, 39 bottles of gin, 54 bottles of brandy, 174 bottles of whisky and more than 1000 bottles of champagne and gorged nearly 100 pounds of Beluga caviar, hundreds of lobsters and several hundredweight of strawberries. 'Yesterday and today the newspapers are full of stories and photos of the party,' Getty wrote in his diary. 'The press has been very complimentary in its articles and comments.'

Before the departure of those guests who had been invited to stay at Sutton Place, there was more skulduggery attributed to one or another of Getty's inamoratas. He had arranged for the lady who was to enjoy his favours to be installed in a suite next to the master bedroom, but on the day after the party someone switched the room allocations. When Getty retired for the night, he slipped through the interconnecting door into the adjoining suite and found himself trying to explain his presence to an irate, middle-aged and extremely respectable family friend.

It was but a taste of events to come.

The passions stirred in Tudor times when Anne Boleyn secretly met her lover at Sutton Place, were as nothing compared to the jealousy, greed and intrigue that would mark Getty's occupancy. For nearly a decade he had conducted his numerous amours from the anonymity of hotel rooms, constantly moving from place to place around Europe. It was unusual for any of his lady friends to meet; often, they knew little of each other's existence and the harmony of the courtly billionaire's exuberant philandering was rarely interrupted. Everything changed when he moved into Sutton Place.

Getty could see no reason at all why he should make any adjustments in his private life just because he no longer chose to live in hotels. Indeed, he very much looked forward to being able to squire his coterie of mistresses in the sumptuous surroundings of Sutton Place and he issued invitations without entertaining a moment's concern for the effect the arrival of another lady would have on those already present. In consequence Sutton Place was turned into an arena for open warfare between the ladies in the court of J. Paul Getty, many of whom fondly imagined themselves in the role of mistress of the house. Within its mellow red-brick walls they schemed and fought, listened at keyholes, poisoned the old man's mind against each other and jockeyed for his favours.

It was not at all unusual for three or four women to be staying in the house at one time, all of them competing for his affection and attention. The staff became quite accustomed, in their phlegmatic English way, to this arrangement and took to referring to Mr Getty's changing roster of female companions as 'the harem'.

'The place became a cathouse,' said Bela von Block who spent a great deal of time at Sutton Place while ghost-writing Getty's autobiography. 'You could sometimes hear the women screaming at each other. I've never heard bitchiness like it. If Mr Getty was in a room with the door closed, you could be sure someone was listening on the other side. On two occasions he opened a door and a woman literally fell into the room. I remember taking a walk in the garden with him one afternoon while the ladies of the entourage tiptoed behind us – literally tiptoed – to try and hear what we were talking about.'

Getty seemed oblivious to the blazing passions within the 'harem', or chose to ignore them. Most of the time he affected not to notice the constant sniping, but if the ladies looked as if they were about to start scratching each other's eyes out at the dinner table, he would simply push his chair back, dab his lips with his napkin, murmur 'Excuse me, I have some business to attend to', and leave them to it.

Von Block was convinced that the old man actually took pleasure in the constant hostilities: 'I once asked him if he enjoyed having women fighting over him all the time. He said something about how he would prefer people to get on with one another, but he couldn't stop himself smiling. I think he loved it, absolutely loved it. Sometimes he would play one woman off against another just to get them going.'

To Getty's credit, he did not necessarily accord preferential treatment to the mistress – or mistresses – of the moment. Women who were friends and no more, women who occasionally shared his bed and women who formerly shared his bed – all met with the same urbanity. His affair with Mrs Kitson, for example, had come to an end but she remained a close friend, retaining all her privileges. Although she still had her house in London, Getty had given her the use of 'the Pavilion' – a small property on the estate – as a weekend cottage and she spent a great deal of time with him at Sutton Place. She was, in truth, thankful that she was no longer in contention with the other women and she viewed the warring entourage with the greatest possible disdain. 'The women were at each other's throats all the time,' she said, 'and hated me more than you could imagine. I got frightfully fed up with it.'

Those women harbouring faint hopes of becoming the sixth Mrs Getty were all destined to be disappointed, for a fortune-teller once told the billionaire that he would die if he married for a sixth time. He was deeply superstitious and it was quite enough to deter him. He also had few illusions as to why so many women wanted to get him to the altar. 'I think they all hope,' he used to say to friends, 'that I would not live more than thirty days afterwards.'

In interviews with journalists, Getty was usually willing to discuss his abysmal record as a husband and his attitude to women: 'I was rotten husband material because I was so immersed in my work, I didn't notice what was going on in my personal life. My wives did not feel important enough in my life. A marriage needs a great deal of personal attention and I never had it to spare. Fortunately, I have a small circle of women friends close to me who keep me company. I like best to relax with women and as I've grown older I've learned to appreciate women more.'

Actually, he did propose marriage to a couple of lady friends when he was in his seventies, but he was probably pretty sure that he would be rebuffed. He regularly proposed to his young legal adviser Robina Lund, for example, and was just as regularly turned down. He was not in the least offended: they remained the firmest of friends.

Robina established an unusual relationship with the old man, often affectionately berating him like a rather naughty schoolboy. Once when he asked her to turn the frayed cuffs of a shirt, she indignantly refused and marched him to a shirt-maker next day, pushing him through the door with a peremptory warning: 'I am not going to sit down to dinner with you any more while you're wearing shirts with frayed collars and cuffs, so in you go and buy some new ones.'

'I had not the slightest interest in being one of his harem,' Robina said. 'As far as I was concerned he was old enough to be my grandfather, and apart from our working relationship I looked on him as a sort of adopted elderly relative of whom I was very fond.'

Getty also proposed to Baroness Marianne von Alvensleben, an attractive young widow he had met in Germany in the early fifties. 'Sutton Place was like a second home to me,' said the baroness. 'Paul always said "Come to Sutton whenever you are tired and stay as long as you like." I was very happy there but I never stayed for very long because in the end the atmosphere would always become too much and I would go back to Germany.'

The baroness never considered Getty to be anything more than a good friend and when he formally proposed to her, she sought to deter him by pointing out that there were other men in her life.

'That's all right,' Getty gruffly replied, 'I will have my mistresses, too.'

The tension always present among the house guests at Sutton Place increased noticeably with the arrival of Mrs Rosabella Burch, a comely and vivacious Nicaraguan widow with limpid green eyes. Just twenty-nine years old and recently widowed, Mrs Burch had been invited by Claus Von Bulow, a Danish-born barrister then working as Getty's personal assistant, to a luncheon party held at Sutton Place on 15 December 1961 to celebrate Getty's sixty-ninth birthday. (Von Bulow would later figure in a sensational court case in the United States, accused of the attempted murder of his socialite wife, Sunny.)

Rosabella said later that she was immediately attracted to Getty, even though there was a forty-year age gap between them. 'Men of his age usually lose the attraction they hold for the opposite sex, but he has something that attracts women very much. It's not the money, although I'm sure that's part of it. He has a sort of physical presence which holds them.'

For his part, Getty was very taken by the young widow and virtually ignored everyone else at the lunch. As Rosabella was preparing to leave, he took her hand and said: 'Why do you have to go?' They kept in touch by letter and telegram and by the summer of 1962 Mrs Burch had succumbed to Getty's entreaties and moved into Sutton Place – to the undisguised fury of two ladies already resident, Mary Tessier and Lady Ursula d'Abo, each of whom claimed to be the one true love of Getty's life.

Mrs Kitson, who would be witness to much of the brawling between these three ladies in the years to come, had no time for any of them. 'One was a drunk,' she said, 'one was totally unbalanced and the other was a trollop.'

Madame Tessier, the former wife of an Italian hotelier, met Getty in Paris in 1958 and they became lovers a year later. Her grandfather was a cousin of the Tsar of Russia, a birthright to which her hot temper was usually attributed. She had been known, in moments of pique, to pick up the nearest object to hand and hurl it across the room: favoured missiles were Sutton Place's glass ashtrays. Even Getty, who was tolerant to a fault with his mistresses, lost his temper on occasion with Tessier – particularly if she had been drinking – and snapped: 'That's enough Mary. I think you should go to your room.'

More than anyone, Mary detested Penelope, even though Penelope's affair with Getty was long over. Mary hated Penelope's voice and constantly ridiculed her English upper-class accent, perhaps because she was frightened of Penelope's power over Getty. Certainly whenever Getty went to London to visit Penelope, Mary was always in despair.

Lady Ursula d'Abo, a sister of the Duke of Rutland, also hated Penelope. 'Her head rules her heart – if she has one,' she said. Lady Ursula, who was forty-four, was tall and slim with a fine bone structure and blue-black hair swept back off her face, revealing a prominent widow's peak. She had trained as a nurse during the war and thought of herself as pre-eminently qualified to be the mistress of Sutton Place. Unfortunately, of all the ladies of the 'harem' she found it hardest to cope with the daunting competition. She was tortured by Getty's faithlessness and his determination to bring other women into the house and she could often be found weeping and wailing, beating her breast and loudly proclaiming that it was she, and she alone, who *really* loved Paul.

Rosabella swept into this hotbed of envy, suspicion and resentment and quickly managed to antagonise everyone around her – with the exception of Getty, who liked to surreptitiously pat her enticing bottom with a bony hand as she passed his chair. The general consensus of opinion was that Rosabella was 'common', a judgement she unquestionably confirmed by affecting ludicrous airs and graces. If Getty did not make an appearance for a meal, Rosabella rushed to sit in his chair in order to play the role of bountiful hostess while Bullimore stood to one side gritting his teeth. When a Getty Oil executive visiting Sutton Place asked her name, she graciously suggested that he should address her as 'Lady Burch'.

Common she may have been, but locked in combat with her gently-bred adversaries, she could more than hold her own. Getty did not like cars to be parked in front of the house, and for a while the ladies amused themselves by driving each other's cars round to the front of the house and leaving them in prominent positions – a manoeuvre in which Rosabella excelled. When Lady Ursula appeared for lunch in a pair of tailored trousers, Rosabella flashed her green eyes over them and sweetly inquired: 'Been working on your car again, darling?' Baroness von Alvensleben was present one evening when they were all watching television. Rosabella was sitting at Getty's feet and Ursula on a couch behind Getty's chair. Ursula asked if someone would pass her a napkin, whereupon Rosabella picked one up from a nearby table and casually threw it over her shoulder without a word.

Such was Rosabella's colourful behaviour that although she was to remain prominent in the old man's affections for many years, in the eyes of Getty's friends she came to epitomise the kind of women who passed in and out of his life, via his bed, in astonishing numbers, even when he was well into his seventies. 'There were lots of Rosabellas at Sutton Place at various times,' Baroness von Alvensleben explained. 'While I was staying there I must have seen at least twenty come and go.'

No mention of Getty's voracious sexual appetite ever appeared in the newspapers, perhaps because there was still plenty of lineage available in variations on the popular 'penny-pinching billionaire' theme: early in 1961 it was revealed that the richest man in the world had had a pay-phone installed in his Tudor mansion, so that his guests did not need to feel they were imposing on his 'generosity' when they wanted to make a telephone call.

It was a wonderful story that went round the world and produced gasps of disbelief from everyone who read it. A posse of photographers turned up at Sutton Place, pushing and shoving to take pictures of the enamelled 'Public Telephone' sign the Post Office had screwed to the Tudor oak panelling. It became, unquestionably, the most famous pay-phone in the world and effectively scuppered any hopes Getty might still have cherished of returning one day to obscurity, for he had acquired an unforgettable rider to his title as the 'richest man in the world'. The public now had him committed to its collective memory, fixed forever, as 'the richest man in the world, you know, the one who's got a pay-phone in his house'.

Getty was baffled that he should be so widely satirised and reviled. In vain did he explain that he neither owned Sutton Place personally, nor took the decision to have the pay-phone installed. It was nothing to do with the old man. The directors of the Sutton Place Property Company discovered that workmen and casual callers at the house, particularly journalists, were phoning all over the world and talking for hours to long-lost relatives in Australia and the Far East and South America. One call alone notched up a bill of £101. It was the same aberrant reaction suffered by the 'guests' at the house-warming – an overwhelming desire to abuse Getty's hospitality for no other reason than that he was supposed to be the richest man in the world.

Locks were put on all the telephones accessible to anyone who might just happen by and if such visitors wanted to make a call, they were politely directed to the pay-phone. It was never intended, as so fondly imagined, that Getty's rich and titled friends would be obliged to stand pushing pennies into a coin box because their host was too mean to let them use his own telephone. Indeed once the renovation work had finished at Sutton Place and all the security arrangements were in operation, the pay-phone was removed.

The myth, however, endured. When Getty opened Sutton Place to the public (as he did, occasionally, to fulfil his responsibilities as the occupant of an historic stately home), he was depressed to be told that many of the visitors showed little or no interest in the fine paintings and antiques. Instead, the first question they asked the guide was: 'Where's the coin-box telephone?'

In fact, Getty did little to help shake off his venal image. In July 1961 he unwisely agreed to be interviewed on television for the first time by Richard Dimbleby, the rotund and respected presenter of BBC's 'Panorama'. Getty had been assured beforehand that at least half the interview would be devoted to his business affairs, but Dimbleby went straight for the old man's jugular – first emphasising how much he was worth and then trotting out the hoary old stories of his money-grubbing, among them how he had waited for half-price admission to the dog show. Getty, poker-faced, admitted the incidents were true, adding that on such occasions he saw no need to pay more than necessary.

'Is that because you are mean?' Dimbleby rapped.

'No,' Getty replied slowly. 'I have always watched things like that. I do not see any particular point in throwing away those pounds for no reason at all.'

'Are you the richest man in the world?'

'I make no claims for that.'

'Are you one of the richest men in the world?'

'I would not even know that. I am not familiar with all the men in the world.'

So it went on, with Dimbleby firing off his relentless questions about Getty's enormous wealth and contriving in the process to portray him as Scrooge personified. Admitting that he might be worth three thousand million pounds in 'barrels of oil in the ground', Getty went on to mumble: 'I have been short of money all my life.'

Afterwards the old man professed himself to be quite pleased with the interview as he had managed to mention 'Veedol' three times, even though he had been asked beforehand not to refer to trade names as advertising was not allowed on the BBC.

In reality, the programme was a public-relations disaster. What the great British public saw on their television screens was a joyless, scrawny, stooped old man with an unsmiling, hangdog countenance and dewlaps, who looked as if he had been made thoroughly miserable by his money. If Getty had set out to impersonate Scrooge, he could not have done better. Thus did the oil billionaire indelibly stamp his image on the public consciousness.

Only his closest friends knew there was another, sunnier, Paul Getty, never revealed to strangers. Robina Lund could recall dinner-party guests at Sutton Place convulsed with laughter at Getty's devastating lampoon of Hitler addressing a Nazi youth rally, or his parody of a thoroughly wet upper-class Englishman, complete with a limp handshake. 'He had a wicked sense of fun at others' expense,' Mrs Kitson confirmed, 'and loved slapstick humour.'

One day, Bullimore was alarmed to hear noises like Indian war whoops emanating from behind the closed door of the study. He opened the door to find his septuagenerian master and Miss Lund bouncing up and down on a new sofa which had just been delivered. 'It's all right, Bullimore,' Getty said between whoops, 'we're just testing the springs.' A few days later, two of the gardeners were somewhat surprised to observe the master walking around the lawn in front of the house and striking a curious pose each time he halted. He was, they learned later, showing some of his friends how a few statues might look on the lawn.

No outsider would have believed, or perhaps wanted to believe, that Getty was capable of such frivolity. It was comforting for ordinary folk to think that he was permanently miserable and that 'money can't buy happiness', and newspapers were reluctant to disabuse their readers of this notion. Getty was trapped in his own caricature – even engaged in an act of pure philanthropy. When he started giving parties for orphans at Sutton Place, photographers inevitably persuaded him to put on a party hat and thus ludicrously adorned he scowled, as usual, into the cameras. He looked like an unhappy old miser in a silly hat who had somehow found his way, by some ghastly mistake, into a children's party.

Perhaps it did not matter. Perhaps the rehabilitation of J. Paul Getty was in any case beyond the dubious scope of public relations. When Gordon came to visit his father at Sutton Place, he tactlessly let slip that he had been obliged to pay for his room. On another occasion when the lovely Empress Farah Dibah accepted an invitation to lunch, Getty ordered the gold plate to be fetched from the safe in honour of the occasion – then served shepherd's pie on it. Visitors to the great house in winter reported that the place was usually cold because Getty had calculated he could save fifty pence per room by using small electric fan heaters rather than the central heating: in the severe winter of 1962/3 the heating was turned down so low that the whole system froze solid and was out of action for weeks.

Everyone had their own favourite Sutton Place story. Bela von Block liked to tell how he had heard Getty lecturing Mrs Richmond, the housekeeper, on the need for economy after she had been reckless enough to serve six portions of apple stew when there were only four people for lunch.

Ethel Le Vane told how she suggested Getty should send some silk ties to the art critic Bernard Berenson, who had helped with the research for a book about art collecting on which they had collaborated. Getty agreed but when he noticed that Miss Le Vane was writing on the card accompanying the ties 'To Bernard, from Paul and Ethel', he asked her to pay half the cost. 'You're getting half the credit,' he explained. It seemed, to Getty, a perfectly reasonable and logical attitude.

Although the entire world knew, as Gordon put it, that his father was 'close with a buck', this had no discernible effect on the volume of begging letters arriving at Sutton Place – probably because his address was now also widely known. By staying in one place, Getty became prey to every sycophant, scrounger, crackpot, con man, freeloader and gold-digger and they sometimes wrote him up to a thousand letters every day.

He no longer had the time, or the inclination, to read them all himself but he did take the trouble to compose a long standard reply, which was printed in five languages, to try to explain why he was not able to accede to requests in begging letters. Under the circumstances, it was a model of restraint and humanitarianism.

I apologise for not having been able to give more time and personal attention to your letter. Like most people, I suppose, I always used to be thrilled at the thought of getting mail. It was considered a misfortune if the postman came and went without leaving any mail – but that was years ago.

I have had a great deal of publicity in the international press, radio and television; most of it in connection with the reputed size of my fortune. The public seem to jump to the conclusion that my fortune, or a big part of it, is in cash. They don't stop to think that my money is invested in business since I am an active businessman, and it is generally true that active businesses are short of cash for their business requirements and even the largest business organisations are frequent borrowers of money. These large business organisations don't borrow money just to prove that they can do so but because they are in urgent need of cash. I don't mean to imply that I am short of cash to the extent that I can't pay my personal bills or buy a new car when the old one wears out. I merely mean that I don't have large sums of ready cash not required for my business.

Like most people I contribute substantially, in accordance with my means, to various recognised charities and public welfare projects in which I am particularly interested and, in general, which I have supported or helped to support for many years. Like most active businessmen I get a large amount of business mail every day and I have to spend, on an average, several hours a day reading and answering this mail. If I didn't do this I would not be looking after my business on which so many people depend.

In addition to my regular business mail I have received in recent years a tremendous and almost overwhelming amount of mail from the general public. This mail from the general public is almost entirely due to the unwanted publicity I have had regarding the alleged size of my fortune. Like most people, I suppose I don't object to a reasonable amount of publicity if it is of the right sort, but I don't like publicity which seems confined almost entirely to how much money I am supposed to have. I personally think it is vulgar, boring and generally inaccurate. There may be lots of people who have more cash than I have.

Nevertheless, due to this publicity I am, and have been, faced with the problem of how to reply to thousands and tens of thousands of people from seventy-five or more countries who write to me at the rate of anything from fifty to a thousand letters a day. How can I personally read and reply helpfully to this flood of mail? Many of the letters are from five to fifteen pages long and written in a script that is barely legible. Nearly all of them want something – gifts, loans, contributions, financial help, advice, personal interviews, offers to sell, jobs, investments – or express a wish to be 'pen-pals'. If I could reply to each letter personally in an average of four minutes, which would be a very short time, I still could do only fifteen letters an hour. Since like most people, I have my own work to do I could not possibly answer more than a very small fraction of the letters written to me. I regret this; I like people; I like to be helpful when I can; I try to do the best I can.

A friend of mine who has also had a lot of publicity about his supposed fortune also receives thousands of letters, nearly all of them requesting financial assistance, advice, employment or offering something for sale. He has given up trying to answer his public mail and tells me it is all thrown into the fire. It is too big a burden to answer. Nevertheless, I feel people, if at all possible, should have the courtesy of a reply. I have engaged secretaries to read and answer my mail from the general public to the best of their ability. I regret that I am unable to aid individuals. I am sure that nearly always they are truthful and sincere in what they write. If there were only a few of them I could do something but since the requests come in by the hundreds and thousands, it is just impossible for me to investigate and, if the cases are found worthy, to assist. No private fortune in the world would last more than a very short time under such conditions and it would take a tremendous organisation to administer the money during the short time it lasted. Again I say I apologise because I was not helpful. I just wanted you to know what some of the reasons and problems are.

J. Paul Getty

Towards the end of 1964 Rosabella discovered she was pregnant, an event which provoked a great deal of below-stairs gossip at Sutton Place, despite Bullimore's disapproval of what he described as 'tittle-tattle'. It was not Mrs Burch's expanding waistline which excited interest so much as the fact that in December Mr Getty would be seventy-two years old. The conclusion, repeatedly voiced behind Mr Bullimore's back, was that there was very definitely 'life in the old dog yet'.

It had been an unhappy year for the ladies of the harem. Firstly, Getty had agreed to loan Sutton Place to Mrs Kitson for the coming-out party of her seventeen-year-old daughter, Jessica, and in consequence they had had to put up with Penelope sashaying about the place as if she owned it, then playing bountiful hostess at the ball. Secondly, a tall and beautiful American woman with whom Getty had had a passionate affair almost twenty years earlier arrived on a visit from California.

Mary Maginnes was twenty-four and working as a booking clerk for the Santa Fe Railroad in Santa Monica when she first met Getty in 1946. He had telephoned to book a ticket and given his name as Paul Getty; she had not heard his surname properly and thought he was someone she knew called Paul and gave him a 'cheeky answer'. The next thing she knew he was standing outside the booking office, having come over specially to see who this cheeky girl was.

Mary had only recently moved to California and was missing her friends back east. When Getty offered to take her out for a drive, she accepted without hesitation. He took her all along the coast, told her about the history, showed her where he was building his ranch and bought her dinner at his favourite fish restaurant on Santa Monica pier. It was not long before they were lovers – to the intense disapproval of Mary's mother who considered Getty, then fifty-four, to be far too old for her pretty daughter. When Getty left the United States for the last time in 1951, he asked Mary to go with him to Europe but she refused. Her mother was alone and ailing and she felt her duty was to stay and look after her. 'Besides,' she said, 'Paul was a man of different moods and I thought there would be other women to suit them. I didn't think he was the homely type.' Mary never married but Getty kept in touch with her, always sending her a card at Christmas and flowers on her birthday. He was delighted when she accepted his invitation to visit Sutton Place in 1964.

'Delight' was not the word to describe the reaction of the resident ladies, particularly as they sensed that Miss Maginnes was someone rather special to Getty, not 'just another Rosabella'. Getty, as usual, pretended to be completely unaware of the seething emotions all around and made no secret of the pleasure he took in Mary's company. 'She is a thoroughly nice person,' he noted in his diary.

Soon after Miss Maginnes departed for California, Rosabella also departed – for a holiday in Switzerland, the staff were told. While Rosabella was away on 'holiday', she gave birth to a son whom she named Paul Bernard. When she eventually returned to Sutton Place, she discovered that Getty had bought a house in Sussex for a Czechoslovakian lady called Ann Hladka. Mrs Hladka met Getty years earlier when she was a reporter working for the state news agency in Prague, and they had kept in touch sporadically ever since. She escaped to England with her two sons shortly after the Russian invasion of Czechoslovakia and arrived at Victoria Station in London, knowing no one in England except Getty. She telephoned him from the station and said: 'I am here. What can I do? I have four pounds in my purse.' 'Come to Sutton Place,' he replied. 'I will take care of you.'

Getty gave Mrs Hladka a job as his art researcher, but Sutton Place was hardly a suitable place for her to bring up her two sons and he asked Albert Thurgood, his estate manager, to find her a modest house somewhere not too far away.

Rosabella, naturally, was insulted and outraged that a newcomer – a complete outsider – should waltz in and immediately finagle a house for herself. Rosabella determined she, too, would have a house. It did not take her long to persuade Getty that she needed a place of her own, although she was somewhat disgruntled by his insistence that it should not cost more than twenty-five thousand pounds. The luckless Thurgood was again detailed to handle the purchase and take Mrs Burch to view suitable properties. 'It was very difficult,' said Thurgood, 'because she always wanted much grander places than I was showing her. Mr Getty had told me the top limit was twenty-five thousand pounds and she got very angry when she couldn't have what she wanted. In the end I said to her, "If you carry on like this, you'll not get a house at all." Mr Getty told her the same and so she settled for a place in Cranleigh for exactly twenty-five thousand.'

Getty did not appear to be perturbed either by Rosabella's demands or by the birth of her son, being infinitely more interested in his business than anything that happened at Sutton Place. At the age of seventy-two he was still working long hours, still in complete control of an international conglomerate made up of nearly a hundred corporations. He had also found time to publish an autobiography, *My Life and Fortunes*, which he dedicated to Robina Lund (no doubt further upsetting members of the harem). It was a sober, straightforward account of his business career which rarely strayed into the minefield of his private life.

Towards the end of the book he made a brief, affectionate mention of his sons and how they often visited him at Sutton Place. 'This has been a source of tremendous pleasure and gratification for me,' he wrote. 'My boys and I have got to know each other much better than was possible in previous years. I have always loved my sons; now I can honestly say that I know them well enough to like and respect them as men.'

The timing was ironic, for the myth of the happy Getty family was about to crack.

PART FOUR

THE FAMILY
1965-85

16. 'Bad health, bad news and death'

In the summer of 1964, an astrologer called Peter Clark published an 'astrological assessment' of J. Paul Getty which was uncannily accurate and perceptive. Getty was astonished when he read it, the more so because he was sure he had never met Mr Clark. Normally he was nervous of fortune-tellers or individuals who claimed to have a sixth sense, but he could not help but be impressed by the astrologer's apparent insight. 'I'm tempted to ask him to give me a rundown on all the company's employees,' he said to Robina Lund. 'I think he'd be a great deal more accurate about people than some psychiatrists.'

A few weeks later, by one of those inexplicable coincidences that so often cause paths to cross at significant moments, Robina met Clark at a charity reception in London. Explaining that she was Getty's legal adviser, she complimented him on the accuracy of his article and casually asked if there was anything he had left out.

Clark hesitated before he replied. 'Astrologers have to be very careful not to upset people by what they write,' he said at last, 'and for that reason I left out quite a lot. However I will tell you, in confidence as you are his lawyer, and in case you are able to protect him, that he has a very serious time ahead of him in the next decade or so. I did not stress this in the article and you must not tell him because I know he is highly superstitious and almost neurotically frightened of bad health, bad news and death. I can tell you that all three are going to affect his life greatly.'

Robina said nothing to Getty because she knew he would be terrified by what Clark had said. But as the events of the next twelve years unfolded, she thought often of the astrologer's words.

Well into his seventies Getty kept up the ludicrous charade of pater-familias, always seeing himself as head of the Getty family, even though there was no family in any meaningful sense and never had been. Five wives and five sons, one tragically dead, could not be said to comprise a happy family, particularly when they were strangers to each other. 'I don't suppose,' says Gordon, referring to his brothers, 'there was ever a time when we were all in the same room together.'

Getty's view of his responsibilities as a father was myopic in the extreme; certainly he never considered he was under any obligation to devote his precious time to his sons while they were growing up. George was brought up by his mother in Los Angeles as an only child, occasionally visited by a man he knew was his father but whom he insisted on calling 'Mr Getty'. Ronnie was at school in Switzerland until he was nine and even when he moved to California with his mother, he saw little of his father and even less of his half-brothers except on rare occasions when he was driven to the cheerless house on South Kingsley Drive to visit the old, crippled woman he was told was his grandmother.

Paul and Gordon were close, but only to each other. Their mother remarried three times and they saw more of their maternal grandmother than anyone else when they were home from their various military academies. Paul's enduring memory of his father was of laboriously writing him a letter when he was twelve years old and having it returned with all the spelling mistakes corrected.

It seemed that Getty could only find space for his sons in his diary, not in his life. And for all the affectionate notes he jotted to himself about George, Ronnie, 'Pabby', 'Gordo' and little Timmy, none of them could have had any illusions as to their place in their father's list of priorities. Getty loved the oil business, art, money, women and sex: five passions that always took precedence over his five hapless sons, even at times of crisis. The saintly Timmy went to his grave with one of his most frequent prayers – to see his father again – unanswered, because Getty considered business to be more important than sitting in a hospital at the bedside of his ailing son.

Even after Getty had been declared the richest man in America, for George, Ronald, Paul and Gordon there was not much to be gained from being a Getty or from having such a man as a father. Indeed, the sons of the richest man in the world could claim with some justification that their father's fabulous wealth had brought them precious little joy.

In 1965 George was forty-one and president of the Tidewater Oil Company. He was the high-flier, his father's favourite son and natural successor. But he found the difficulty of living in his father's shadow near intolerable. His marriage was in trouble, he was drinking too much and suffered bouts of melancholia. One evening, during a visit to Sutton Place, he turned to Baroness von Alvensleben and said: 'You know, Marianne, my life is a disaster.' She was not sure what he meant but knew that whatever his troubles were, he could not take them to his father. 'Paul was not interested in the private lives of his sons,' she explained. 'They would never tell him if they were unhappy.'

Early in 1965, George and his father clashed openly about the future direction of the business. Getty wanted to sell Tidewater's West Coast marketing division, which included the Avon refinery, five tankers and four thousand gas stations, in order to reduce the company's long-term debt and facilitate an early merger with Getty Oil. George adamantly opposed the move, arguing that by selling the division Tidewater would virtually forfeit any chance of getting back into the California gasoline market.

Getty was not even an officer of Tidewater. George, as president, should have had no difficulty in thwarting his father's plans. But Getty had been working towards the consolidation of his business interests for years and he certainly did not intend to let his son stand in his way. Getty Oil was practically debt-free, while Tidewater owed about $330,000,000 as a result of its expansion programme. Tidewater was perfectly able to carry such a debt, but a merger with Getty Oil was not really feasible until it had been reduced.

In June 1965 George was summoned to Sutton Place for talks with his father. Rumours about the dispute between the two men had been circulating in the oil industry for months and there was a great deal of speculation about how it would turn out. For George it was an opportunity – at last – to demonstrate that he was his own man and that he was running Tidewater, not his father.

They met behind firmly-closed doors in the study at Sutton Place and remained closeted together for hours. Getty always liked to pretend that he never interfered in the running of Tidewater and that George was the boss. 'I went no further than to give him advice,' Getty said. 'It was for George to make the final decisions. Although he and I generally saw eye to eye, he never hesitated to speak and make his case when he disagreed with me or had views that differed from mine. As often as not, his logic and arguments prevailed.'

In the crucial case of whether or not to sell Tidewater's western division, George's views clearly did not prevail. In 1966, it was announced that the division had been sold to Phillips Petroleum. George knew then he would never be able to shake off the humiliation of being no more than 'Paul Getty's son' while his father was alive. He was put in charge of organising the Getty Oil/Tidewater merger in September 1967 and was promoted to executive vice-president and chief operating officer of the consolidated company. But the titles were meaningless while the old man sat in his Tudor mansion in England, pulling the strings – and everyone in the oil industry knew it.

In the same year as this blow to his pride, his sixteen-year marriage to Gloria broke up. Their three daughters – Anne, fifteen, Claire, thirteen, and Caroline, eleven – stayed with their mother and at first George hoped that there would not be a divorce, just a formal separation: both he and Gloria were Roman Catholics. It was not to be. In January 1968 Gloria won a divorce in Los Angeles on grounds of mental cruelty, complaining that her husband was 'very aloof, indifferent and distant'.

Getty's difference of opinion with his eldest son did not in any way

257

dilute his high opinion of George, whom he still considered to be a first-class businessman and worthy heir, an opinion widely shared. George was generally respected and admired, both in the oil business and by his father's friends. Not so his half-brother, Ronnie, who was arrogant, self-opinionated and almost universally disliked. 'There was something about him,' said George Money, managing director of Tide Water (UK), 'which put everyone's backs up. People were frightened that if they fell foul of him they would lose their jobs. The charitable view of Ronald was that he was "difficult", the less charitable view was that he was a right bastard.'

Even Getty made it clear that he had little time for his second son. The old man took a malicious pleasure in keeping Ronnie waiting whenever he visited Sutton Place for business discussions and he told anyone who cared to listen that he thought Ronnie was 'hopeless' as a businessman.

Getty more or less gave up on Ronnie when as president of Veedol Petroleum International he was arrested in France on a charge of 'improperly enticing' employees of another company, Labo-Industrie, to join Veedol-France. It was both a criminal and civil offence in France for one company to try and seduce executives from another. Getty was incensed that Ronnie should deliberately flout French laws and jeopardise Veedol's operations in France (he was a good deal less concerned that his son might end up in jail). In the event, Ronald was found guilty by a Paris court and given two suspended prison sentences, each of three months.

Not long after this debacle Ronald decided, at the age of thirty-four, to get married. His bride was a twenty-one-year-old language student, Karin Seibel. Getty was invited to the wedding, at Lübeck in Germany, in October 1964 but claimed he could not make it because of 'stomach flu'. He was also smarting about Ronnie's decision to take a three-month cruise around the world for his honeymoon. Getty did not consider a three-month holiday was either deserved or appropriate for any of his executives, least of all one with the name of Getty.

Over the next few years, Ronald showed less and less interest in the family business and in 1967 he decided to leave Hamburg and move to Los Angeles to set himself up in Hollywood as a movie producer. He conveyed this decision to his father during a sour little confrontation at Sutton Place. When Getty sarcastically inquired what qualifications Ronald thought he possessed to become a film producer, Ronnie airily replied that he had already hired people with the necessary 'know-how'.

'I see,' said the old man slowly. 'So you have the money and they have the know-how?' Ronald nodded. 'Hmm,' his father grunted. 'Well, I've no doubt they will soon have the know-how *and* the money.'

* * *

258

Gordon, still studying music at the conservatoire in San Francisco, was a rather more welcome visitor at Sutton Place during this period, until he suddenly took it upon himself to sue his father.

Everyone knew when Gordon was staying at Sutton Place because he spent hours every day singing scales at the top of his voice or practising on one of the Steinway grand pianos in the Long Gallery. One evening he staged a little concert of his own compositions, which his father sat through with reasonable good grace. Getty was perfectly resigned to Gordon never being an oilman and content he should follow what he described as 'artistic and intellectual pursuits', although Gordon had not entirely abandoned commerce: in his spare time, he wrote a book about new economic theories. He proudly showed a couple of chapters to his father. Getty read them, and confessed in his diary that he could not understand a word.

Relations only became strained between Gordon and his father when Gordon wanted a little more money out of the Sarah C. Getty Trust. It was not an unreasonable request for the son of the richest man in the world to make. Unlike his brothers Gordon was not on a salary and he had a paltry income for a Getty. Yet while he was having to count his pennies, he was aware that the assets of the trust established to provide for all the Gettys had grown to a staggering three hundred million dollars.

When he and his brother Paul were boys, they each received around fifteen thousand dollars a year from the trust, courtesy of their father, who was the principal beneficiary. This income abruptly ceased for a time in the mid-fifties when Getty, in his capacity as trustee, decided that the trust would no longer distribute dividends but simply amass capital. His reasons were entirely selfish – he did not want to pay huge sums in tax on the dividend, money he certainly did not need. In 1960 the trust resumed payments to George, Paul and Gordon of about $50,000 a year each.

As early as 1962 Gordon asked his father if the trust could pay him more, but the old man reacted so angrily to the suggestion that he did not dare ask again. He attempted to persuade his father, in a letter, that he was not questioning his authority. 'If a plow horse and a cow pony were pressed into each other's occupations,' he wrote, 'each might appear lazy, irresolute and unstable. Aptly employed, they won the west together. You are a cow pony, father, and it seems to me that I am too, though vastly less adept. That's a lot different from a bucking bronco.'

In December 1964 Gordon married Ann Gilbert, a ravishingly beautiful and ambitious young woman of twenty-three, born and raised on a peach farm in the San Joaquin Valley. Getty was advised, after the event, by telegram. 'Heck, he was living thousands of miles away,'

Gordon explained. 'Heck, I was thirty-one years old – I didn't have to ask his blessing.' Ann, who was twenty-three years old and selling clothes at Joseph Magnin at the time of the wedding, was credited with some responsibility for the events that followed; certainly her aspiration to a lifestyle befitting a Getty were never questioned.

Even more short of cash now that he was a married man, Gordon asked Bill Newsom – an old school friend who was a lawyer – to comb through the small print of the Sarah C. Getty Trust to see if he had any legal claim on the income. Newsom's opinion was that there was a good chance of making out a case that the trust was legally obliged to distribute annual cash dividends to its beneficiaries. In June 1966 at San Francisco Superior Court Gordon filed what was called a 'friendly' suit against his father, claiming $7,400,000 in unpaid dividends. He wrote to Sutton Place assuring his father that the litigation would not affect 'my confidence in you as trustee or my love for you as my father'. 'Nevertheless,' said Gordon, 'I think father was a little upset.'

Getty was not upset, he was boiling with rage. Asked by reporters for his reaction to the suit, he issued a statement saying he would 'await with interest the decision of the court'. But in private he fumed and ranted, dispatched word to San Francisco that Gordon was no longer welcome at Sutton Place and immediately instructed his lawyers to fight the case. 'Paul was absolutely furious,' said Robina Lund. 'He kept saying, "If he wants money why doesn't he go to a bank, like everyone else?"'

Neither was the old man's temper improved by the news from Rome, where it was reported that Gordon's brother Paul had 'dropped out' and become a long-haired 'hippie', affecting multi-coloured velvet pants and floral shirts in preference to the grey worsted befitting the boss of Getty Oil Italiana. Thanks to the tireless efforts of Rome's *paparazzi* who pursued Paul everywhere, his father was well-acquainted with what was going on from the dozens of tawdry magazines which were publishing photographs of 'the son and namesake of the world's richest man' in a variety of colourful outfits and in even more colourful company.

When Paul and Gail arrived in Rome with their two-year-old son in 1958, they were just another young expatriate family employed by an American corporation. Gail had three more children – Aileen, Mark and Ariadne – and perhaps had they not been Gettys and had they been in some other place, they might have remained just another nice young family. But J. Paul Getty II had not the slightest interest in Getty Oil Italiana: he liked parties, books, music and literature and hated the oil business. Parties there were in plenty in Rome in the sixties and that sweet, sinful, decadent city drew them inexorably into its wanton embrace. They took all there was on offer – highlife and lowlife, drink and drugs – wheeling round the city in their Rolls-Royce, hazily convinced they were where 'it' was 'at'.

By 1965 their marriage was over: Gail was living with a B-movie American actor called Lang Jeffries and Paul was pursuing an exotic Dutch actress by the name of Talitha Pol. As part of a divorce settlement, Paul agreed to pay fifteen per cent of his net income into a trust fund set up for the four children. Gail married Jeffries in a brief ceremony at Rome's city hall in August 1966 and shortly afterwards moved back to Los Angeles with her children and her new husband.

Paul remained in Rome, besotted with the dazzling Talitha. Born in Bali, the step granddaughter of the painter Augustus John, Talitha was twenty-five years old, tall and slim with long russet hair and fulgent brown eyes. In the summer of 1965 she had gone to a party in London hoping to meet Rudolf Nureyev, but he did not turn up and so she got talking instead to a dark-haired, rather intense young American by the name of Paul Getty. In December 1966 they were married in the same red-damask room at Rome's city hall where Gail had been married four months earlier. Talitha wore a hooded minidress in white velvet, trimmed with white mink; Paul sported a flame-coloured 'psychedelic' tie.

A few months later, Paul left his secretary to get on with running Getty Oil Italiana and moved with Talitha to a nineteenth-century Moorish palace within the ancient walled city of Marrakech, where they experimented with drugs and held open house for luminaries of the 'swinging sixties' – painters, freaks, writers and rock groups like the Rolling Stones. That they had joined the beautiful people was validated by the ultimate authority of *Vogue* magazine, for whom they were photographed in fetching kaftans by Patrick Lichfield, a cousin of the Queen of England.

The house, *Vogue* breathlessly reported, was a

stage setting for the way the Gettys live – a welcoming, fantastical, joyous life, at once sensible and sybaritic. With a small runner-boy to bargain and carry, Mrs Getty prowls the marketplace bringing back delights for the house and the table. Best, she brings back entertainers – dancers, acrobats, storytellers, geomancers and magicians. A day that began with a picnic, complete with a huge onion tart, on a great flat rock near a waterfall in the Atlas Mountains may end with dinner for a houseful of young Moroccan and European friends by the light of candles, among roses wound with mint. While *Salome* is playing in the background, snake charmers charm and tea boys dance, balancing on their feet trays freighted with mint tea and burning candles.

In his study at Sutton Place, Paul's father slowly turned the glossy pages

261

of *Vogue* with an expression on his face even more doleful than usual. He viewed the lifestyle described therein as not just utterly worthless, but offensive to all the values he held dear: the work ethic, loyalty, diligence and responsibility. He also had little doubt that his impressionable son had been corrupted by *la dolce vita*. Much earlier, the old man had noted in his diary that Paul was not exactly 'setting the world on fire' as a businessman and he recognised there was little point in hoping that Paul would return to Italy to take over the reins of Getty Oil Italiana. He issued instructions for the company to be sold, along with its refinery.

Paul and Talitha soon tired of the recherché delights of Marrakech and floated off on the hippie trail around the East, drifting aimlessly through Indonesia, Bali and Thailand, searching for the meaning of life and accumulating an extensive ethnic wardrobe. Early in 1968 Talitha discovered she was pregnant and they returned to Rome, to a huge rooftop apartment in the fashionable Piazza d'Aracoeli, next door to Carlo Ponti. They once again attracted the attention of the *paparazzi* and were even photographed out shopping, perhaps because the son of the world's richest man now wore beads, a beard and sunglasses and 'carried a handbag', a phenomenon unusual, even outrageous, for males at that time.

In July Talitha gave birth to a boy, whom they named Tara Gabriel Galaxy Gramaphone Getty, guaranteeing derision in newspaper gossip columns everywhere. Under the headline 'RICH KID WITH A SILLY NAME' in the *San Francisco Chronicle*, Talitha explained that each of the names had a precise significance – Gramaphone being chosen, for example, because the boy would 'undoubtedly be fond of music'.

The arrival of Tara did not in any way inhibit their vibrant social life and they plunged back into a round of extravagant revelry with Rome's wild and dangerous sleek set. Talitha's penchant for see-through dresses, then the latest fashion, ensured that their entrance at every party was marked by exploding flashbulbs, even if Paul's handbag failed to excite attention.

For a while they were happy. They divided their time between their apartment in Rome and the 'Posta Vecchia', a fifty-five room villa on the coast at Palo, twenty miles north of Rome, which Paul's father had bought a few years earlier from Prince Ladislao Odescalchi.

But by the end of the sixties, that swinging decade had claimed them among its victims. Both Paul and Talitha were heroin addicts.

Ronald Getty's move to Los Angeles in 1967 to begin a career in the motion-picture industry certainly caused a stir, although not quite of the kind he had anticipated. Not long after his arrival Ronnie and his mother were in court, fighting over the occupancy of a house on South Beverly Glen Boulevard at Westwood: each wanted the other kicked out.

Fini, Getty's third wife and Ronnie's mother, was fifty-seven and had lived at South Beverly Glen Boulevard ever since moving to California from Germany shortly before World War Two: Getty had bought the property in Ronnie's name, but with the apparent intention of providing her with a home for the rest of her life. For the fourteen years that Ronnie was abroad working for his father, Fini occupied the house alone, perfectly happily, welcoming her son back whenever he visited Los Angeles. But when he moved in permanently with his young wife, Karin, their son, Christopher Ronald, and baby daughter, Stefanie Marie, Fini began to resent their presence.

In September, Fini filed a suit at Los Angeles Superior Court to try and obtain exclusive possession of the house. She claimed she had been given a life estate in the property by her former husband, had been accustomed to living there alone for many years and had been unable to do so since her son's marriage.

Ronnie professed himself to be 'distressed that his mother had chosen to air family problems in public', but he resolved nevertheless to fight the case. In court, his counsel said that the suit forced him to choose between his mother and his own family and that he was 'amazed by his mother's action'. He alleged that although he and his mother had shared the house without incident for many years, since his marriage in 1964 she had failed to share the home with his family 'under tranquil conditions'.

The case was settled out of court, no doubt to the disappointment of the local newspapers, which were delighted to be privy to such a squabble. Ronald disappeared from public view for many months thereafter, seemingly determined to make himself unique in the film industry by maintaining the lowest possible profile. (He had never much liked publicity – at his wedding in Germany, he hid his face behind his top hat in order to avoid being photographed.)

He surfaced in the summer of 1969 to be 'introduced' to the industry at a cocktail party at The Bistro in Beverly Hills. Hollywood correspondents invited to be present were generally impressed – by his height (six feet four inches), his no-nonsense, businesslike approach to filmmaking, his resemblance to a bank manager and most of all by the fact that his father was a billionaire. As no reporters delved too deeply into the details of his business career, he was portrayed as being part of a significant trend towards the involvement of leading industrial and financial figures in motion-picture production.

I'm interested in any business that makes money [Ronnie told the

Los Angeles Times], and there's money to be made in movies. I'm going to be very much involved in the creative side; I've been an avid movie-goer for many years. So many movies have been ruined by bad casting because so many stars were cast simply because they were under contract or were somebody's friend. You can't have actors as friends and I don't actually know any. You've got to be ice-cold – the right person in the right part at the right price.

In partnership with veteran producer Leon Fromkess and businessman Richard McDonald, Ronnie set up a company called GMF Productions at 8730 Sunset Boulevard. His half-brother George had written to warn him against using any name that might cause confusion with Getty Oil and Ronnie had replied by saying that he would call his company whatever he liked; a typically cool exchange between them.

For all his tough talk, Ronnie did not turn out to be another Cecil B. De Mille. GMF's first production was a modest lady-in-distress thriller called *Flare-up* that played drive-ins and was chiefly notable for giving Raquel Welch a chance to prove she could act. This was followed by *Zeppelin*, an aerial spectacular starring Michael York and Elke Sommer and *Sheila*, a forgettable love story about a white high-school boy and a black girl. Thereafter the career of Ronald Getty, film producer, petered out.

Gordon's career as a singer and composer was no more successful, neither was his adventure as a litigant. In August 1970 Superior Court Judge Charles S. Peery rejected Gordon's claim for a greater share of the Sarah C. Getty Trust, ruling that such a distribution would not carry out the 'intention of the trustor', Gordon's grandmother. Getty's counsel, opposing the suit, had successfully argued that Sarah Getty was not interested in giving her grandchildren an income but in protecting the business. Much was made of the elderly lady's desire that her grandchildren should have to work for a living. After the judge's ruling, George dispatched a triumphant letter to Gordon warning him that he would 'discover what happens to people who take on J. Paul Getty and lose'.

In fact, Gordon quickly patched up his differences with his father. Even before the suit was settled his wife, Ann, had flown to England to meet her new father-in-law at Sutton Place and pave the way for a reconciliation. As she was young, attractive and utterly charming, she was guaranteed to please and she had the old man eating out of her hand in no time at all. 'All his life,' said Robina Lund, 'Paul could hardly ever say "no" to a woman or "yes" to a man.'

Thanks to Ann, Getty's view of the lawsuit was miraculously transformed. Instead of being a case of his venal ne'er-do-well son trying to squeeze more money from him, it became a matter of high principle – enabling the old man to save face and indicate a grudging respect for Gordon's willingness to fight for what he perceived to be his rights. 'The suit marked a real improvement in their relationship,' said Bill Newsom, Gordon's friend and lawyer. 'Getty was impressed by Gordon's stand and began to think of his son as a pretty tough guy who was not going to have his rights trifled with, rather than just someone sitting around reading poetry.'

Gordon followed Ann over to Sutton Place for a 'frank talk' with his father. Getty privately conceded that Gordon had not been treated fairly, agreed that he should receive a bigger income from the trust and offered to include him in the business. 'I became a kinda trouble-shooter,' said Gordon proudly. 'Father sent me wherever the ink was reddest. I didn't want to be a nose-to-the-grindstone line executive, but I was happy to be a consultant, going to various trouble spots and giving my two bits worth.' One of Gordon's first assignments was to make a report on how economies could be effected at the Hotel Pierre in New York. He discovered that the air-conditioning units could also provide heat and suggested removing the central-heating system.

There were perhaps moments when Getty might have suffered slight pangs of doubt about the ability of his new 'troubleshooter'. During lunch one day at Sutton Place, Gordon announced he was thinking of buying an amphibious jeep. 'How fast do you think it will go over water?' he asked the assembled company. 'A hundred miles an hour?' Getty, at the head of the table, choked over his plate. When a guest suggested gently that perhaps a hundred miles an hour was a mite optimistic, Gordon replied heatedly: 'Oh no, it'll do a hundred miles an hour *easily*.'

Gordon's older brother Paul did not attempt a similar rapprochement with his father. Getty made it clear that he disapproved of Paul's lifestyle and he was deeply disturbed by rumours that his son was involved with drugs. On the last occasion they met, when Getty made a brief visit to Rome, Paul indicated he had no intention of returning to the business. 'It doesn't take anything to be a businessman,' he snarled at his father, 'anyone can do it.' No jibe could have been more calculated to wound Getty: he went ashen and refused to speak to anyone for an hour afterwards.

After this incident, Getty did his best to pretend that Paul did not exist. He never wanted to see him or talk to him and would not allow Paul's name to be mentioned in his presence. Paul did not care, he had enough troubles of his own. What had started as an idyll with Talitha had become a bleary struggle to exist from one fix to the next. Talitha was injecting heroin, Paul was sniffing it, but both had the dreaded monkey on their backs and needed to score ever-increasing supplies from underworld drug dealers. Both were also drinking heavily.

Outwardly they were still a golden couple 'making the scene', living life to the full and at the wildest level Rome could offer. But Talitha suffered terrifying bouts of depression, there were disagreements between them, ever more serious, and they began spending more and more time apart. In February 1971 Talitha left Rome with two-year-old Tara to spend some time in London, away from Paul. They telephoned each other often, fumbling to discover if they wanted to be together or apart. Paul was as much in love with her as ever but could see little future for them as a couple and in May he instructed lawyers to begin divorce proceedings.

On Saturday 10 July Talitha flew back to Rome alone to discuss a reconciliation. She met Paul at their apartment in the Piazza d'Aracoeli, where they had once been so happy together. Paul did not know whether or not he wanted a reconciliation and they began to argue, bolstering their turbulent responses with drink and drugs. At three o'clock on Sunday morning, Talitha, confused and tired, fell into bed. Paul blundered about the kitchen making himself something to eat and followed her to bed half an hour later.

He woke at midday and was surprised to find Talitha still sound asleep. It was only when he tried to rouse her that he realised something was wrong. Talitha was not sleeping: she was in a coma. Paul telephoned his doctor, Professor Franzo Silvestri, who arrived at the apartment within a few minutes. After a brief examination, the doctor said Talitha was in a critical condition and needed to be got into hospital immediately; he thought she might have had a heart attack.

An ambulance whining through the narrow streets of Rome rushed Talitha to the Villa del Rosario Clinic, where heart massage was attempted to try and revive her. She died that evening without regaining consciousness.

Paul was devastated and choked with guilt. He had no doubt he was to blame and believed, fervently believed, he could have saved her had he not himself been comatose in a drug-induced stupor.

Doctors at the clinic ascribed the cause of death on the death certificate as 'intoxication by mixture of barbiturates and alcohol'. But Paul soon learned, from Doctor Bruno Farina, Rome's deputy public prosecutor, that a postmortem was to be carried out and he knew what would be revealed – that Talitha had died from a heroin overdose. He also knew that he could expect little sympathy from the police once they discovered, as they surely would, that he, too, was a junkie.

In a panic, Paul fled. Two days after being questioned by the deputy public prosecutor, he drove out to Rome's Fiumicino airport and caught the first flight to London. For many months he lived in terror that the Italian authorities would issue a warrant for his extradition: he heard that the Italian police were 'gunning' for him and wanted to charge him with manslaughter.

Paul went into a rapid decline after Talitha's death. Obsessed by remorse and guilt, he wanted only Talitha; she became the love, the lost love, of his life. He bought a gloomy double-fronted house overlooking the Thames at Cheyne Walk, Chelsea, and shut himself away with Talitha's ghost, seeing no one but a few 'friends' who kept him supplied with drugs. He had the garden planted with Talitha's favourite flowers and added a clause to his will asking to be buried alongside her grave in Holland.

In March 1972 an inquest in Rome revealed that Talitha had died from a massive overdose of heroin and the judge conducting the inquiry into her death issued a statement appealing for Paul to return. 'In the interests of everyone concerned,' the judge said, 'it would be a valuable contribution if he would come here voluntarily and give what help he can.'

Paul stayed resolutely in his house at Cheyne Walk, with the shutters closed – abandoning Tara Gabriel Galaxy Gramaphone to the care of his maternal grandparents in the south of France.

At Sutton Place, Getty had received the news of Paul's misfortune with compressed lips. He had no wish to become involved, no wish to see his son. When he heard that Paul was intending to make his home in London, Getty issued instructions to the staff at Sutton Place that his son was not to be allowed on to the estate under any circumstances.

In his seventy-ninth year Getty was thin, frail and somewhat shaky, suffering from the onset of Parkinson's disease. He was still working every day, but he was increasingly susceptible to the fears and phobias which had afflicted him all his life. In particular, he was beset by anxiety about his personal security and Sutton Place had been turned into a fortress with alarms and guards everywhere and attack dogs prowling the grounds. Visitors penetrating the security screen around the estate were advised not to approach the dogs. There were signs everywhere warning: 'Danger. Keep away. These dogs are trained to treat all strangers as enemies.'

When Getty took his regular half-hour stroll in the garden at lunch time, he insisted on being followed by a guard. Whenever he left the estate, his Cadillac was shadowed by a second car carrying two armed bodyguards and an Alsatian dog. At night all the gates were closed at ten o'clock, the lawns were floodlit and guards with dogs patrolled the house. Six locks were fitted to the old man's bedroom door, all the windows were barred and by his bedside was a sophisticated alarm system connecting directly to the police station at Guildford. A security man with another dog sat in the corridor outside his room all night.

Although he was increasingly reluctant to go out in the evenings, his friend Margaret, Duchess of Argyll, persuaded him to show up at the Orchid Suite at the Dorchester Hotel in London on 15 December 1972 for a party she had organised to celebrate his eightieth birthday. The duchess (who clung tenaciously to her title even though she had been divorced from the duke years earlier) invited one hundred guests – including ex-King Umberto of Italy, the Annenbergs and the Bunker Hunts – for dinner and a further two hundred friends to a dance afterwards. President Richard Nixon, soon to be engulfed by Watergate, telephoned to wish Getty a happy birthday and his daughter, Tricia, turned up later in the evening, explaining to reporters that she had been dining with the Prime Minister at 10 Downing Street but wanted to be at the party as 'I met Mr Getty when I stayed at his house with my daddy.' Tricia posed prettily for a photograph with the old man and pretended not to hear when one of the photographers loudly demanded of a colleague, 'Who's the bird? The old boy certainly likes 'em young, don't he?'

The duchess, in a silver organza dress by Harald of Curzon Street, had given strict instructions to the band to play nothing but pre-war dance music of a tempo unlikely to strain the constitution of an eighty-year-old and Getty, wearing a dinner jacket that appeared several sizes too big, obliged by shuffling round the floor both with Tricia and the duchess. At midnight, a huge cake with eighty candles was wheeled in and the band struck up Cole Porter's 'You're the Top', for which a special lyric – 'You're the top, you are J. Paul Getty' – had been written. One verse brought a big laugh:

> You're the top, you are like Jack Benny,
> You're the top, wouldn't waste a penny,
> I have an open cheque that I'd like to pop
> And if you'd kindly sign the bottom . . .
> You're the top.

The Duke of Bedford proposed an elegant toast, expressing the hope that Mr Getty would be around to enjoy his hundredth birthday and roguishly adding the wish that 'the many lovely and witty ladies around him grow wittier and lovelier'.

Gordon and Ann Getty, who had flown from San Francisco for the occasion, smiled broadly at this. Neither George, Ronald nor Paul were present at their father's eightieth birthday party.

In the spring of 1973, Gordon began to hear rumours that George was behaving strangely. George had remarried in 1971 and moved to a large château-style house in Bel Air with a spectacular view of downtown Los Angeles. The new Mrs George F. Getty was a wealthy thirty-nine-year-old widow whose first husband, a millionaire businessman, died in a horrific accident when a mudslide engulfed their hillside home during a rainstorm.

Gordon rarely visited Los Angeles but he had many friends there, some of whom knew George and frequently attended parties at his house. They began to relate worrying stories about 'scenes' involving George. It was said that he was taking amphetamines to try and lose weight and a doctor had prescribed barbiturates to help him sleep. The drugs, sometimes combined with alcohol, seemed to be inducing erratic behaviour. One night George's wife, Jacqueline, invited an old boy friend to a party and George, in a rage, brandished a gun at him. Another evening he fired a gun into the bushes at the back of their house and then tried to swallow a bottle of sleeping pills.

'I seriously thought about telling my father,' said Gordon, 'but decided not to. It was a damned close call, but I didn't want to look like a tittle-tattle trying to undermine George.'

On the evening of 6 June 1973 Getty had been invited to a dinner party at the Duchess of Argyll's house in Mayfair. Just as he arrived, there was a telephone call for him from Los Angeles. It was Stuart Evey, a vice-president of Getty Oil. He said that George had had a bad fall and was unconscious in hospital. Evey appeared not to know much more and so Getty told him to stay in touch and call again if he had further news. According to the duchess, Getty continued with the dinner party as though nothing was wrong.

At eleven o'clock, Evey called again. 'I think you'd better brace yourself, Mr Getty,' he said. 'George died a few minutes ago ...'

Numb with grief Getty was driven back to Sutton Place, where he sat up for hours, staring into space without speaking. Next day, he learned that an autopsy disclosed the cause of death as an overdose of barbiturates and alcohol and it was being said that George had committed suicide. Getty could not, would not, believe it.

There was much he could not understand about the whole tragic affair. It appeared that George had fallen over during a late-night poolside barbecue and hit his head. For a while he seemed all right, but later became unconscious and was driven to hospital by Stuart Evey. For some reason, however, Evey did not go to the hospital nearest George's home in Bel Air but drove instead to the Queen of Angels Hospital on the outskirts of Hollywood, passing en route much more distinguished medical centres at UCLA and Cedars-Sinai. George, still unconscious, was checked in at 2.40 a.m. under a false name – George Davis – allegedly to avoid 'notoriety'. At the hospital he was discovered to have superficial wounds in his chest and left leg, perhaps caused by a barbecue fork.

On 9 June Getty wrote in his diary: 'George's funeral was held in Malibu at 10 a.m. – 6 p.m. English time. At six, I walked to the church and said a prayer for my dearest son.'

Rumours about what had really happened at the party were soon circulating throughout the company. One popular story was that there had been a drunken brawl and that a woman guest had picked up a barbecue fork and run it deliberately into George Getty's chest. It was said the old man had paid out a great deal of money to gloss over the truth and 'protect the family name'.

In August the Los Angeles county coroner ruled that George's death was 'probable suicide', even though the alcohol content in his blood was not particularly high and the traces of barbiturates found in his body were not excessive. The wound in his chest had not penetrated the abdominal wall and could not have contributed to his death.

Getty refused to accept the verdict and asked Norris Bramlett to conduct his own investigation. After 'exhaustive inquiries' Bramlett told Getty what he wanted to hear – that George's death was an unfortunate accident.

> One question will continue to gnaw at me [he said later]. I know that all too many businessmen and executives rely on a few evening drinks – and barbiturates – as a means of easing the tensions and pressures created by their work. Is it possible that these were unduly greater for George because he strove too hard to live up to the images of his grandfather and me?

The old man did not have long to ponder this question. In July he learned his grandson, J. Paul Getty III, had been kidnapped.

17. 'Don't let me be killed'

On 17 July 1973, a few days after sixteen-year-old Paul Getty had apparently gone missing in Rome, a letter arrived by special delivery at the apartment on the Via della Scala he shared with his twenty-four-year-old German girlfriend, Martine, and her twin sister. It was addressed to his mother, Gail, and was in Paul's large, childish handwriting:

Dear Mummy,

Since Monday, I have fallen into the hands of kidnappers. Don't let me be killed. Arrange things so that police don't intervene. You must absolutely not take the thing as a joke.

Try and get in contact with the kidnappers in the manner and the way they tell you to.

Don't let the police know about the negotiations if you don't want me to be killed.

I want to live and to be free again. Arrange things so that police don't know I have written to this address.

Don't publicise my kidnapping.

Pay, I beg you, pay up as soon as possible if you wish me well.

This is all you have to know. If you delay, it is very dangerous for me. I love you.

Paul

Martine knew instantly it was not a joke. She had felt for several weeks that they were being watched; there always seemed to be two or three men hanging around outside their apartment. When she pointed them out to Paul, he got very angry and threw something at them through the open window. They did not go away, just moved further back into the shadows. Martine told the police, but they just shrugged their shoulders and said there was nothing they could do.

A few days before Paul disappeared, an attempt had been made to kidnap Martine and her sister, Jutta. 'We had been writing a television script together and we were told to take it to a certain office where there was someone who wanted to read it. When we got there, we were locked in. We were very scared. I really believed we were going to be killed. We were kept there all night and next day they bundled us into a car to take

271

us to some other place. But the car got stuck in a traffic jam and I managed to get the door open and we ran away.'

It was, then, not surprising that Martine took Paul's letter very seriously. She also knew Paul well enough to realise that he could never have organised such a hoax. 'He was just not capable of doing it,' she said, 'he would have been far too scared.'

Martine hurried round to Gail's apartment on the Via dei Monti Parioli with the letter, but Paul's mother was out so she took the letter to the police. They knew all about Paul Getty, the grandson of the richest man in the world; Italian newspapers called him the 'Golden Hippie'. Staging a fake kidnapping was just the kind of crazy stunt he would pull, probably to try and get some money from his grandfather. Everyone knew he was penniless and most days he could be seen with all the other hippies congregated in Rome that summer, hanging around the Spanish Steps trying to sell trinkets to the tourists.

Martine was frightened when the letter arrived from Paul. But she was even more frightened when she realised that the police did not really believe he had been kidnapped.

The 'bright, red-headed little rascal' who so charmed his grandfather in 1957 had grown into a striking, if somewhat unorthodox, teenager by 1973. Paul was almost six feet tall, gracile in stature and faintly androgynous in appearance, with a freckled face, pale blue eyes and a shaggy mane of long, red, curly hair.

He was also a rootless, disturbed and highly troublesome young man. His problems stemmed from the trauma of his parents' divorce and the loss of the father he idolised. When Paul II went off with Talitha, his son was nine years old and he was bitterly hurt that his father seemed to forget that he existed. He began to misbehave from that moment onwards.

Gail and her new husband, Lang Jeffries, set up home in the smart Los Angeles suburb of Brentwood and Jeffries did his best to establish a relationship with his stepchildren, but Paul was an unrewarding prospect – usually surly and difficult. He sneered at Jeffries behind his back, telling his younger brother, Mark, and his two sisters, Aileen and Ariadne, that Jeffries did nothing but play 'gladiator' roles. At the Paul Revere Junior High School, Paul won no friends by constantly drawing unfavourable comparisons between America and Italy; if he was reprimanded by a teacher, he would respond by sticking two fingers down his throat and vomiting over the desk.

After only a year together, Gail and Jeffries separated, and Gail returned to Rome, trailing her brood of unruly children. Paul was allowed to make a rare visit to his father and Talitha at their exotic retreat in Morocco and was thrilled to discover Mick Jagger staying there: he spent the whole time silently taking pictures of Jagger with his new miniature camera.

Back in Italy, Paul seemed determined to prove that no school could control him. He cut classes that did not interest him (most of them) and disrupted those he deigned to attend by trying to make the other kids laugh. When teachers lost their tempers with him, as they frequently did, Paul bellowed at them: 'I pay you to teach me, why are you screaming at me?' Once when a teacher rapped him with a ruler, Paul picked up another ruler and hit the teacher back with all his strength.

After he had been expelled from seven successive schools, the despairing Gail sent him to a boarding school run on the spartan lines of an English public school and with a reputation for discipline. Paul hated it and wrote to his mother that it was like being in the army. One evening, more out of boredom than anything else, he set fire to a blackboard with his Zippo lighter. As the classroom filled with smoke, he casually sought out a teacher and said innocently: 'Can you smell smoke? I think something might be burning.' After the fire was brought under control, teachers questioned Paul for four hours. Every time they tried to get him to admit responsibility, he shouted belligerently: 'I bloody well didn't do it.' But in the end he tired of the game and said: 'Yeah, what the fuck, I did it.' Next day, he was back home with his mother, his brother and his sisters.

Paul was then fourteen and his mother was ready to give up the struggle to educate him, although he was obviously intelligent and very creative – he liked to draw, paint and take photographs. Gail decided he should be encouraged to develop his artistic talents in his own way rather than be burdened by formal schooling. It was an arrangement that suited Paul very well because it meant, in effect, that he could do what he liked, and what he liked to do was hang out in the Piazza Navona, in his star-spangled pants and Grateful Dead T-shirt, with the hippies who lounged in the sun around the Bernini fountains and endlessly discussed the alternative society. Before he was fifteen Paul had sampled many of the pleasures of that fabled society, notably dope, cocaine and 'free love' or, as he preferred to put it, 'balling chicks'. Determined to deny his youth, he always tried to act much older: he wanted to be hip, cool, laid-back, *sophisticated*. And while he might not always have pulled it off, on the whole he made an excellent job of camouflaging the fear and uncertainty within.

Running wild in pursuit of thrills, he bought a motorcycle and a leather jacket and took to roaring through the crowded narrow streets around the Vatican, exulting in the danger and the speed, crashing more times than he could remember but always escaping injury. Once he lost control going down an underpass and somersaulted with his bike eight times, scraping most of the leather from his jacket. He picked himself up without a scratch and walked away.

At night he could often be found drunk in one or another of the open cafés around the Piazza Navona or in the discotheques where the rich and the louche and their groupies gathered. Because his name was Paul Getty he had a curiosity value which provided him with an instant entrée to the celebrity circuit and he could be seen at parties with the likes of Andy Warhol and Jack Nicholson and Roman Polanski. He even got bit parts in a couple of spaghetti westerns and called himself an actor.

In the summer of 1972 Paul moved into a small studio apartment on the Vicoli de Canale, in the old Latin quarter, with two friends, a painter called Marcello Crisi and a young Englishman, Philip Woollam.

Gail did not object to him leaving home [said Woollam], she thought it was a good idea for him to get out and about. He was great fun, had a very bright outlook and wanted to enjoy life. At that time he had not been burdened with the Getty name, as he was later.

Paul had a terrible time with money; he was literally penniless. I was doing some work as a translator and Marcello was trying to earn a living as a painter. Paul started painting too and tried to sell his paintings with Marcello on the Spanish Steps. Sometimes they exchanged a painting for a meal in a restaurant. He always wanted to be independent, but he talked about his father a lot. He wanted to be close to his father and he was unhappy that it was not possible. Sometimes I thought he was trying to outdo his father and make a mark that his father would notice.

In January 1973 Paul was arrested during a communist demonstration and accused of throwing a Molotov cocktail into the *carabinieri* barracks. Actually, he was nothing more than a spectator. The demonstrators marched by the front door of the apartment on the Vicoli de Canale and he went outside, with a cup of tea in his hand, to watch them go by. When he saw policemen in riot gear running towards him he was at first unconcerned as he had not done anything, but before he knew what was happening they started hitting him with rubber truncheons and he was pushed into a police van crammed with demonstrators and taken off to Rome's biggest jail. Frightened that he would be beaten up by other prisoners if he protested his innocence, he told them he had blown up a police station and consequently enjoyed considerable status. Two days later, the charges against him were dropped and he was released.

Paul's arrest made headlines, while his release hardly merited a mention. The event was, of course, solemnly noted by his disapproving grandfather in England. Not long afterwards, word of a further outrage concerning 'young Paul' was communicated to Sutton Place – he had posed in the nude for a pornographic magazine. He did it for the money, and for a laugh; his grandfather failed to share the joke.

Around this time, Paul met Martine Zacher. Nearly eight years his senior, Martine was a beautiful, unconventional and serious young woman working as an actress with an alternative theatre group. She was immediately attracted to the wild young American and within a few weeks of their first meeting they were living together. If anyone raised an eyebrow about a divorced woman of twenty-four with a twelve-month-old baby daughter living with a boy of sixteen, Martine certainly did not care.

In some ways Paul was quite immature, but on the whole he was much more advanced than most other people of his age. He had a pretty loose life style and had been through a lot and he was very cynical about life.

We had a lot of common interests, and we did lots of things together – painting, writing, taking pictures. We had a great group of friends and we would all meet at night in the Piazza Navona. There was a big drug scene going on, cocaine mostly, and we were involved. It was such common knowledge that it would be ridiculous to deny it. We never considered ourselves hippies, but at that time everyone was into alternative life styles.

I was acting and Paul was making money day by day, painting or photo gigs. He lived on almost nothing. He always thought nothing could ever happen to him, that someone would always bail him out, take care of him. He was kind of schizophrenic about being a Getty. He knew who he was, but felt inferior because the one thing he was supposed to have – money – he did not have.

He spoke often of his father and was very sad that they did not speak to each other. It affected him very deeply.

Paul never let the hurt show to the outside world. When people asked him, as they often did, about his relationship with his father, he had a standard, sarcastic reply. 'We have perfect communication,' he liked to say. 'We never talk. That way we don't fight, either.'

On the afternoon of 9 July, Paul telephoned Martine from a café in the Piazza Navona and asked her to meet him right away as he had something urgent to say to her. She hurried to the café and found him waiting to ask her to marry him. She was pleased and happy and accepted. 'We knew then,' she said, 'that we wanted to be together.' Paul was due to have dinner with Marcello and Philip that evening but Martine did not want to join them, so she kissed him goodbye and walked back to their apartment.

275

It was the last she was to see of him for five months.

Paul went to the movies after Martine left for home, then joined his friends for dinner. Philip Woollam thought he seemed perfectly normal and noticed nothing out of the ordinary about the evening. After dinner Paul went alone to a discotheque, hung out with the 'Warhol crowd' for a bit, then returned to the Piazza Navona around midnight, by which time he was a little unsteady on his feet from Bacardi and Coke. Finding none of his friends in the usual cafés, he went round the corner to a nightclub called Treetops where he ran into an old girlfriend, a go-go dancer called Danielle Devret. Thoroughly drunk an hour later and perhaps forgetting he had just become engaged, he asked Danielle to go with him to Gaeta – a seaside resort sixty miles to the south. Danielle laughed and refused, saying she was leaving next day for a holiday in Portugal with a boy friend. Paul became abusive and began swearing, shouting at her to 'fuck off'. She managed to get him out of the club and he staggered off down the street, still shouting.

At three o'clock in the morning he stopped at a newsstand in the Via de Mascerone and bought a Mickey Mouse comic book, then continued on his way home. In the Piazza Farnese, a large white car pulled up alongside him and three men jumped out. Paul turned blearily towards them and caught a glimpse of a pistol butt as it cracked down on his head. 'Oh please,' he whimpered, 'what have I done?' He was hit twice more then dragged into the back of the car, which drove off with a squeal of tyres. Paul thought he was probably in for a beating for balling someone else's chick, but he was too drunk and confused to care. Then a chloroform pad was clamped over his face and he felt himself falling before he lost consciousness.

When he came to, he realised he was still in the back of a fast-moving car, but he could see nothing as a thick cloth was tied over his eyes. His ankles and wrists were also tightly bound and he could feel blood running down the back of his neck from a wound on the top of his head. He was very, very frightened. A gruff voice suddenly spoke to him in Italian: 'Where are your documents?' He said he did not have any documents.

'What's your name?'

'Paul Getty.'

'All right. If you want something, ask for it. If the answer's yes, you'll hear one clap. If the answer's no, you'll hear two claps. Remember this because no one will speak to you again.'

Paul felt curiously comforted by this; he thought that if they were willing to communicate with him they would probably not kill him.

Although he was hung over and disoriented, he reckoned they were driving for about six hours. When the car eventually stopped, two men lifted him out. Paul felt they were somewhere very high up and for one dread moment he thought he was going to be thrown over a cliff. But instead, they put him on a blanket on the ground. It was very hot and he could feel a warm breeze against his cheeks; he imagined they were somewhere in the south of Italy.

After about an hour the ropes around his wrists and ankles were untied, but the blindfold remained over his eyes. He could hear people around him all the time, snatches of whispered conversations and a car door slamming in the distance. A few hours passed and then he was suddenly told to stand up. A hand grabbed him tightly around the arm and he was led across rough terrain, frequently stumbling, to another spot no more than one hundred yards distant, where he was told to lie down again. This happened three or four times.

He had to ask when he wanted to urinate and was not allowed to take his own trousers down or pull them up. One of his captors was nervous, for Paul discerned the hands that unfastened his trousers were clearly trembling.

Paul thought he was blindfolded for at least five days, perhaps longer. He was given one hot meal of pasta every day, frequent cups of coffee and a bottle of cognac which he swigged so quickly his head began to swirl.

On what he judged to be the sixth day, he was put in a car again and driven for about an hour. When it stopped, he was pulled out and led down a steep incline to where he could hear a waterfall splashing. He was made to bend forward so he could drink the water and then the blindfold, which had been fixed to his head with sticky tape, was suddenly ripped away. He yelped from the pain as the tape tore at his skin and someone snapped: 'Don't hurt him.'

It was dark. Paul looked around and saw five men in the gloom, all wearing woollen masks covering their faces. One of them said: 'Listen kid, you're going to be here a long time. Don't do anything stupid. Ask for whatever you want, we'll try and get it for you. Don't blame us, we're paid men.' Paul nodded. He was taken into a small hut with a corrugated-iron roof and shown where he could lie down for the night.

Next day, one of the men came into the hut with a pen and paper and dictated the letter that Paul was to write to his mother to tell her he had been kidnapped.

Martine did not particularly worry when Paul did not return home that first night. He often stayed out all night, or crashed at Philip's pad or sometimes stayed with his mother. But when she heard nothing from

277

him all the next day and he did not show up the following night, she began to fret and started telephoning their friends to find out where he was. Many of them teased her, saying that Paul must have taken fright and run away because she had agreed to marry him. At first it was funny but as the days passed with no word from Paul she became seriously alarmed, particularly when she noticed that the men who had been hanging around outside their apartment were no longer there. By the time the letter arrived, she was almost expecting it.

Before the letter Gail, too, was not particularly concerned by her son's disappearance. Living the way he did she thought it was entirely possible that he might have run off with some girl, although she was annoyed that he had not bothered to telephone to tell her where he was. After she read the letter, she did not know what to think. Next morning, the telephone rang in her apartment. When she picked it up, a gruff, muffled voice told her that Paul had been kidnapped and she was to wait for further instructions.

By then, the news was out that Paul Getty's grandson had been 'kidnapped' and a crowd of reporters and photographers were camped on her doorstep. Although she was still clinging to the hope that it might be a hoax, Gail decided to play safe: she called the reporters in and told them she was willing to pay a ransom for the safe release of her son. 'I hope to know, to have proof,' she said, 'that my son is well. I hope that it will all end as quickly as possible. We don't know how the next contact will be made. The important thing is that they be convinced we are willing to deal.'

It did not take long for reporters in England to track down Paul's father to the house in Cheyne Walk, Chelsea, but he would answer neither the door nor the telephone.

At Sutton Place, Getty also refused to take calls from the press and warned the staff not to allow reporters on to the estate. Still grieving over George's death, he asked Robina Lund to issue a brief, prepared statement in answer to all inquiries: 'Although I see my grandson infrequently and I am not particularly close to him, I love him nonetheless. However, I don't believe in paying kidnappers. I have fourteen other grandchildren and if I pay one penny now, then I will have fourteen kidnapped grandchildren.'

The news that the richest man in the world was not prepared to pay 'a penny' for the release of his kidnapped grandson made headlines around the world and provided an excuse for rerunning the riveting tales of Getty's legendary meanness. Most newspapers gave some prominence to doubts as to whether or not the kidnapping was genuine and there was no shortage of lurid material about the missing boy's degenerate lifestyle. None of the more salacious tabloids neglected to point out that sixteen-year-old Paul was 'living with beautiful twins',

Portrait of Marten Looten by Rembrandt, donated by J. Paul Getty I to the Los Angeles County Museum of Art.

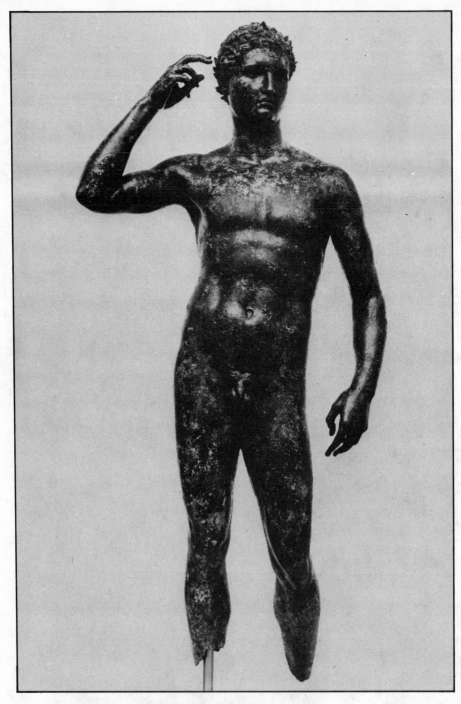

The controversial Getty Bronze
Statue of a Victorious Athlete, fourth-century BC, attributed to
Lysippos (possession of the J. Paul Getty Museum).

The Ardabil Carpet by Mazsud Kashani, Persian, Safavid Dynasty,
1540 AD, said to be 'too beautiful for Christian eyes to gaze upon'.

The benevolent billionaire
The old man saw little of his own grandchildren but Christmas parties for orphans were an annual event at Sutton Place.

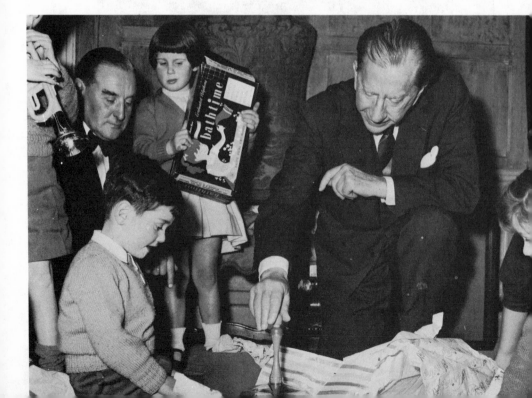

(*above*) Obsessive about security in his later years, the billionaire's world narrowed first to the spacious grounds of Sutton Place, then – at the last – to the confines of his study. (*below*) The seat of power from which he had for years administered his business empire and where he eventually died on 6 June 1976.

(*above*) J. Paul Getty I laid out in his coffin in the Great Hall at Sutton Place and (*below*) his daughter-in-law Anne *née* Gilbert, leaving the memorial service held in Los Angeles with two of her four sons and husband Gordon (in the background). (*opposite*) J. Paul Getty II after the memorial service in Mayfair, London, which he enlivened with his yellow shoes and choice of escort – Bianca Jagger.

(*above*) A scale model of the J. Paul Getty Museum in Malibu, California – the closest its creator ever came to seeing the real thing. (*below*) Replica of the Roman Villa dei Papyri, buried in lava 79 AD, the completed museum now stands a bizarre monument to the oil billionaire.

leaving readers to draw their own prurient conclusions from this shocking fact.

Aided by rumour and innuendo, the hoax theory gained credence over the ensuing weeks and unquestionably hampered the search for Paul: policemen who did not believe the boy had really been kidnapped could hardly be expected to show much interest in investigating his disappearance.

Every hippie on the Piazza Navona had a theory about where Paul had gone and none was averse to talking to the press. Reporters hoping to make their names invested extraordinary amounts of time and energy into trying to prove 'the boy had done it himself', even though kidnapping was hardly an unusual crime in Italy – there were more than 320 reported kidnappings in the country between 1960 and 1973 and probably a similar number went unreported. Italian newspapers even suggested that Paul's 'sexy' mother was a party to the plot, citing as evidence the fact that she was behind with her rent. To help the theory along, the police let it be known that under questioning Martine had confessed that Paul had told her – several weeks before he disappeared – that the only way he could raise any 'big money' would be to simulate his own kidnapping.

It was a lie. Paul had never mentioned kidnapping to Martine and she was frantic with worry. 'As the time passed I got really scared,' she said. 'I was afraid something would happen to him because no one was taking it seriously enough. We were harassed every day by the press and things got over our heads. We didn't know how to handle it.'

Paul's grandfather had been sceptical right from the start. On the day after he learned that Paul had been kidnapped, he was walking in the garden at Sutton Place with Norris Bramlett when he stopped suddenly and said: 'You don't suppose the boy and his mother have cooked this up to get money out of me, do you?' Bramlett murmured something about how awful it would be if members of the family had to resort to such tactics. 'You're right,' the old man said quietly, and continued his walk in silence.

The British newspapers inevitably increased Getty's initial scepticism by routinely referring to the 'kidnappers', using quotation marks to indicate the probability they did not exist. In an attempt to find out for himself what might have happened to the boy, Getty sent Fletcher Chase, a former CIA agent employed by Getty Oil, to Rome to compile a confidential report on whether or not Paul had really been kidnapped. Chase's report largely confirmed the old man's suspicions. It alleged that Paul had frequently been heard to joke about staging his own kidnapping in order to squeeze money out of his grandfather. He was said to be deeply in debt to drug pushers; a figure of twenty thousand dollars was mentioned. Most damning of all, a chauffeur formerly employed by Getty Oil Italiana swore he had seen Paul in the Trastevere section of the city *after* the kidnapping and said the boy ran away when he realised he had been spotted. Chase also noted that a film then showing in Rome, *Travels With My Aunt*, included a fake kidnapping scene and that Paul had been to see it three times.

Even the fact that there was continuing contact between the kidnappers and Gail's lawyer, Giovanni Jacavoni, did not shake confidence in the widespread belief that Paul Getty had engineered his own vanishing act. Jacavoni, a widely respected attorney in Rome, had taken over negotiations with the kidnappers after a second telephone call to Gail. On 25 July Jacavoni received a letter, postmarked Taranto, an industrial town in southeast Italy, informing him that the ransom for Paul's release would be a staggering ten billion lire – some seventeen million dollars.

Next day, Jacavoni got a telephone call. He kept detailed notes of all his conversations with the kidnappers:

'Did you get it?' a voice asked.

'What are you talking about?'

'The letter.'

'Yes, I got it.'

'We want to be paid in very small notes. You will be told later where the exchange will be done. Either we're paid or Paul is dead. Let us know on radio or TV if you agree to the terms.'

That evening, Jacavoni called a press conference and said the ransom demand was unreasonable and the kidnappers should ask for less. Four days later, there was another telephone call:

'What do you mean you can't pay that much? You want to find the boy dead somewhere?'

'There isn't that much money in the whole world.'

'How much can you pay?'

'The most kidnappers in Italy ever got was three hundred million lire.'

'That is a joke. We have spent that much on expenses.'

'I'll talk to the boy's mother but I know she doesn't have any money.'

'Tell her to get it from London.'

A week later, the kidnappers seemed ready to take three hundred million lire. Jacavoni offered them about a fifth of that amount – a hundred thousand dollars. Three weeks passed and the demand was up again, this time to three billion lire. Jacavoni again offered a hundred thousand dollars.

'For a hundred thousand dollars,' said the angry voice on the telephone ominously, 'we'll send you a photo of the boy missing an arm or a leg.'

Italian police quoted the wavering demands as further evidence that the kidnapping was a hoax, on the basis that no self-respecting kidnapper would first ask for ten billion lire, then three hundred million, then three billion. It did not make sense, they said. Even Jacavoni was beginning to have his doubts. 'I'm having serious perplexities,' he explained in his quaint English to the *New York Times*, 'about the genuineness of this kidnapping. And his mother is also probably having doubts.' At a crowded press conference a few days later, he said: 'It cannot be excluded that Paul planned the kidnapping either as a joke, or to get money, or for publicity.'

At the end of August, Bill Newsom, the lawyer who was at school with both Paul and Gordon Getty and who was also an old friend of Gail, arrived in Rome from San Francisco to act as an intermediary between the family and the kidnappers. He went around telling anyone who would listen that it was 'preposterous' to presume that either the boy or his mother was involved in staging such a crime.

'No one wanted to know,' he said.

While Newsom was trying to persuade the Italian authorities that the kidnapping was genuine, Paul was chained to a stake under a makeshift shelter high up in the scrub-covered mountains of Calabria, a rugged and sparsely-populated region in the 'toe' of Italy. His chain was ten feet long, just long enough for him to reach the rock where he made a scratch to mark each passing day. At the end of August, there were twenty scratches on the rock.

He was watched, day and night, by a changing series of armed men in cheap, flashy suits, down-at-heel shoes and holed socks. They wore masks all the time. He was given one meal a day, usually tinned sausages, and was taken to a cold running stream nearby to wash himself twice a week. His sole source of entertainment was a small transistor radio which they had given him and on which he listened to the news bulletins on his kidnapping. Chained up like a dog with no idea where he was, Paul heard people being interviewed in Rome and declaring their firm belief that he had not been kidnapped at all.

As the scratches on the rock multiplied, Paul felt himself losing control. He stared at his reflection in a spoon for hours, making faces at himself, just so that he could see a human expression. When his hands got dirty, he licked them clean like a cat licks its paws. He started collecting bitten-off pieces of fingernail in a matchbox, hoarding them and counting them as if they were some kind of treasure.

One day he heard on the news that the charred body of Paul Getty had been found in a ditch outside Rome. (Martine, in Rome, heard the same broadcast and nearly fainted. 'It was one of the worst moments,' she said, 'a moment of real panic. It was so long to hide somebody I began to think he must be dead.')

When there were fifty scratches on the rock, the guards became nervous that there were police in the area and Paul was blindfolded again and marched for six hours to another location higher up in the mountains. For a week he was shuttled from one place to another, finally settling in a small cave about three feet wide and six feet long. He had a foam mattress to sleep on and began touching certain rocks for good luck in a meaningless ritual about which he soon became paranoid, fretful that he might not touch the right rocks in the right order.

Not long after arriving in the cave, his guards began threatening to cut off one of his fingers unless his grandfather paid the ransom soon. 'We'll send them a piece each month,' one of them warned him viciously, 'until he pays. We'll cut you into little pieces for a whole year.'

Paul was terrified, more frightened than he had ever been in his life. He couldn't stop looking at his hands, wondering which finger they would cut off first, how they would do it, how much it would hurt, what his hand would look like with a finger missing.

One morning in mid-October, two men walked into the cave and said they were going to give Paul a haircut. He sat on a block of wood and one of them snipped away at his long hair, cutting it very short at the back and sides, then cleaning the exposed skin with alcohol. When they had finished, they said it looked very nice and told him to go back to bed.

Paul crawled on to his mattress and fingered his shorn hair, wondering what was going on. It came to him suddenly, in a moment of stark terror. They were not going to cut off one of his fingers – they were going to cut off his ear. And they were going to do it soon, before his scalp got dirty again.

They came for him about half an hour later, seven or eight of them. One man gave him some tough steak to eat, but he could barely swallow. Then they ordered him to put on his blindfold, sat him down on the wooden block and put a handkerchief in his mouth, telling him to bite on it. They held his legs, his arms and his head, clamping his entire body so that he was unable to move a muscle. He felt one of them pull on his right ear, then there was an intense, blinding pain as the razor sliced through his skin. He bit right through the wadded handkerchief in his mouth.

On 21 October Gail received a curt telephone call from the kidnappers at her apartment in Rome telling her that Paul's ear had been cut off and that it was being sent to her in the post by express mail. She very nearly passed out; the notion was so horrific she could hardly believe anyone could be capable of such an act.

At the beginning of October Jacavoni had noticed that the kidnappers had become markedly more threatening during their telephone calls, so much so that he wondered if he was dealing with different people. They began to talk about mutilating the boy unless the ransom was paid immediately but the police, who had been tapping both Gail's telephone and Jacavoni's, discounted this threat as they still suspected that the kidnapping was a put-up job.

Gail was distraught, yet when nothing appeared in the post after five days, she began to hope that it was no more than a macabre joke. Ten days passed, still nothing. On 7 November the kidnappers telephoned to ask if she had received the ear. When she said no, a voice at the other end snapped: 'Stop fooling with us.' Still she hoped it was not true. 'When fifteen days had gone and there was still no news,' she said, 'I had almost persuaded myself it was a hoax.'

She forgot that there was a postal strike in southern Italy. On 10 November an express package posted twenty days before in Naples was finally delivered to the offices of *Il Messaggero*, one of Rome's biggest daily newspapers. A secretary fainted when she opened it. Inside the package, sealed in a plastic bag, was a severed ear with a tuft of blood-encrusted hair and a typewritten note: 'We are the kidnappers of Paul Getty. We keep our promise and send the ear. Now find out whether it belongs to Paul. Unless you pay the ransom within ten days, we shall send you the other ear. And then other pieces of his anatomy.'

A reporter telephoned Jacavoni to tell him what had arrived. He immediately picked up Gail and drove to the offices of *Il Messaggero* in the centre of Rome. Gail, in a state of shock, gingerly picked up the partly-decomposed ear and tearfully confirmed that it was Paul's. It was still possible to see the freckles on the skin. Her son's face was covered with freckles, she said, and the lobe was exactly the same as her own ear lobe.

Martine was in Munich, visiting her family. She was sitting on a bench at Munich railway station, waiting to meet a friend, when she glanced at the front page of a newspaper being read by a man sitting opposite her. Most of the front page was filled with a gruesome blow-up of a severed ear in a plastic envelope. She saw the name Getty in the headlines and thought she was going to be sick. 'I couldn't really comprehend it, it was so cruel,' she said. 'I thought if something doesn't happen fast now, he will surely be killed.'

On 15 November Professor Silvio Merli, one of Italy's foremost forensic experts, confirmed that the ear had been cut from a living human being and that 'comparisons indicate it belonged to Paul Getty'. Next day, the kidnappers telephoned *Il Messaggero* and told a reporter he would find 'something interesting' at a certain point on a road outside Rome. It was an envelope containing Polaroid photographs of Paul, staring with dull, pain-filled eyes into the camera. His right ear was missing. In the envelope was a note threatening to cut off his foot next. His seventeenth birthday had passed only twelve days before.

The kidnappers did their best to bandage Paul's head, but he bled profusely for three days. He kept thinking that the pain would not be as bad next day, but it was.

For ten days he lay on his mattress in the cave, unable to move, vomiting frequently. He lost control of his bladder and was helpless to prevent himself urinating in his trousers. Someone came in every day and gave him an injection. They told him it would help relieve the pain but it did not.

After a while, it seemed the kidnappers became worried that he was not moving. They lifted him up and made him walk, slowly, around the cave. 'Your body is dying,' they told him, 'you have to move.' Paul thought, as they walked him around, that his heart was coming out of his head, so intense was the pain. He never said anything to them about what they had done, for fear that something worse would happen to him.

One day they came in and said they were going to move him to another place, closer to the road, because he would soon be going home. They drove him to another hide-out, but three days later he was back in the cave. Next day, they unwrapped his blood-caked bandages and made him pose for photographs. Then they took him to a huge barn, where he was hidden in a cavity hollowed out in the middle of a haystack.

He heard on his transistor radio that the photographs they had taken of him were on the front pages of all the Italian newspapers. By then, the worst of the pain had subsided and he could think about what had happened and wonder why his grandfather, with all his money, could not have paid a ransom before they sliced off his ear. He wondered if he would ever be able to wear sunglasses again; he loved sunglasses.

The grisly, decomposing missive sent to *Il Messaggero* belatedly convinced a doubting world that Paul Getty was in dire peril. The Italian police grudgingly admitted that they could no longer consider the kidnapping to be a hoax, a decision which Paul's grandfather also arrived at, with similar reluctance.

There was a strong suspicion at the beginning, certainly, that it was not a genuine kidnapping [said Norris Bramlett]. We thought the boy was probably sold and that whoever was originally involved passed him on to real kidnappers. Once the boy's ear was cut off it became clear to us that he was in ruthless hands and that arrangements would have to be made rapidly to pay the ransom.

Getty was obliged at this point to communicate directly with his estranged son, J. Paul Getty II, the father of the kidnapped boy. It was the first time they had spoken for years (Gordon had been acting as an intermediary since the start of the kidnapping) and their contact was icily formal. Both agreed a ransom would have to be paid. Getty was insistent that it should be paid by his son, for there was no knowing what the kidnappers would demand if they felt that 'the richest man in the world' was at last ready to pay a ransom.

It was decided they would offer a ransom of one million dollars. As Paul II did not have anything like that kind of money, his father agreed to lend him $850,000 at 4%, on the understanding it would be repaid in full by an annual deduction of 7.5% from the income Paul II received from the Sarah C. Getty Trust. Robina Lund drew up the formal agreement between father and son: 'For value received, I, Jean Paul Getty Junior, promise to pay Jean Paul Getty I ("Mr Getty") in respect of payment made on my behalf by Mr Getty in connection with the ransoming and safe return of my son, J. Paul Getty III, the sum of $850,000 by the following method . . .'

On 17 November lawyers acting for J. Paul Getty II issued a statement in London: 'Mr Getty has offered to pay a ransom to the kidnappers. The amount is the maximum that the father is able to raise for the return of the boy. Acting upon the advice of those familiar with such cases, he has required that the boy be released simultaneously with the payment of the ransom, since this is the only way in which the safety of the boy can be assured.'

At Sutton Place, Getty continued to insist that he would not pay any ransom. 'My position is still the same. I must consider the safety and welfare of all my grandchildren and the rest of the family. What has happened to my grandson, Paul, is heartbreaking and I pray he will be safely returned. But I know that for me to become involved in any ransom could only make things worse. It is a lonely decision, but I know it is the right one.'

In Rome, Gail issued an angry open letter to the kidnappers pleading with them to accept the ransom and release her son:

We have talked at length, you and I. Always I have felt that you were surprised because the grandfather and the father have not been moved for the future of young Paul. You have not believed me. Yet this is the truth. I have interceded with the grandfather and the father. The grandfather has remained firm. But the father has agreed to pay a ransom of one million dollars (more than that he cannot give you). I beg of you – accept the money that has been offered to you. It will be given to you within a few hours of your conditions. In this supreme moment of my life as a mother, decisive only for the life of my son, I feel only pity. Pity for my little Paul, so alone, his adorable face mutilated. Pity for you, who do not know what is good in life.

The letter was signed 'Gail Harris, mother of Paul Getty III.'

On 1 December Fletcher Chase arrived back in Rome with an authorisation from Getty to withdraw one million dollars in small-denomination notes from an Italian bank.

One night Paul peered out from his hideaway in the haystack and saw candles flickering against the wall of the barn. His captors were clearly celebrating, drinking wine, slapping each other on the back and dancing to music from a crackling radio. Paul prayed that it meant the ransom had been paid.

Over the next couple of days, they were much more friendly to him. They gave him better food, as much drink as he wanted and made him take exercise. On the afternoon of Friday 14 December Paul was told they had collected the money and he was going to be released. He was given a sweater and ordered to put on a blindfold, then he was taken out of the barn and guided, in pouring rain, to a car. He estimated they drove for between four and five hours before the car pulled off the road.

They helped him out of the back seat, still blindfolded, told him to sit down and wait. 'Don't move,' a voice warned him, 'because there is someone behind you. We will telephone your mother. *Ciao*.'

'Goodbye,' Paul replied. He heard car doors slamming and engines starting up, then there was no sound except the beating rain. He cautiously removed his blindfold and looked around. It was dark and there was no one about. Frightened that his captors might change their minds and come back for him, he started walking along the road hoping to hitch a lift. Wearing sneakers with no socks, baggy grey trousers and a sweater, with a crude bandage round his head and his hair plastered down in the rain, he looked a thoroughly unalluring prospect in the headlights of passing cars and no one would stop for him.

Eventually he reached a filling station, where he asked if he could use the telephone. 'No phone,' the attendant replied, looking Paul up and down suspiciously. 'Go away.'

He continued plodding along the road, trying unsuccessfully to wave down a car. At about five o'clock in the morning, close to exhaustion, he took shelter under the canopy of a filling station which was closed. A truck which came by a few minutes later slowed down when Paul stepped out into the road.

The driver wound down his window and heard this wild-looking boy shouting something about a kidnap in a foreign accent, but he thought it might be a hijack and drove on. Only when he was further up the road did it occur to him that the boy might be Paul Getty. He decided to stop at the police station in Lagonegro, the next town, a few miles up the road, to report what had happened.

Not long afterwards, Paul saw the flashing blue lights of several police cars approaching. They screeched to a stop where he was standing, shivering with cold and drenched to the skin. 'I'm Paul Getty,' he said wearily as the policemen jumped out of their cars like extras in a cops and robbers movie. 'Please give me a cigarette. Look, they've cut off my ear.'

At the police station in Lagonegro Paul was given coffee with milk and cake, which he wolfed down. Then someone produced a plate of spaghetti. More and more policemen were crowding into the room where he was being held, then *carabinieri* officers arrived and tried to interrogate him, firing one question after another. Paul burst into tears, sobbing that he did not know where he had been or who had taken him; he had not seen any of his captors' faces.

Soon after dawn his mother arrived with Fletcher Chase and Dr Ferdinando Masone, the head of Rome's flying squad. A furious argument developed between the *carabinieri* and the police, who wanted to take Paul back to Rome. The *carabinieri* refused to allow Paul to leave before they had finished their interrogation. Dr Masone said the boy was in no condition to be questioned. While everyone was arguing, more and more photographers were arriving at the police station and trying to take pictures through the windows or through a crack in the door every time it opened.

Paul sat in a daze throughout the brouhaha in the arms of his weeping mother. Fletcher Chase, who was tall, silver-haired and authoritative, finally stepped in, buttonholed the senior *carabiniere* officer and said menacingly: 'Let the boy go *now* or you can be sure there will be serious trouble.'

With Chase's trench coat over his shoulders, Paul was hustled out of the police station, through the hysterical mob of photographers and reporters and into a police car. During the five-hour drive along the *autostrada* to Rome, they were followed by thirty or forty press cars.

Every time they stopped at a tollbooth, photographers jumped out and surrounded their car, banging on the windows and asking Paul to show them where his ear had been cut off.

At Rome police headquarters, there was a scene of utter chaos, complete madness. Photographers were climbing over each other, screaming at him to look this way and that, while reporters bellowed questions. The police tried to get him into a lift, but so many newsmen crowded in after him that the lift doors would not shut.

After twenty minutes, Dr Masone gave up any attempt to question Paul and he was smuggled out of a side door with his mother and driven to a private clinic where he could rest and recover from his ordeal.

In London, his father made a brief statement to reporters. 'I intend,' he said, 'to devote the rest of my energies to teaching the Italians the meaning of the word "vendetta". I suggest those associated with the kidnapping would be well advised to sleep always with one eye open.'

At Sutton Place, a spokesman for the old man said it was his eighty-first birthday and the boy's release was the 'nicest present he could have'.

Some time later, Paul tried to telephone his grandfather to thank him for helping to organise his release. Marianne von Alvensleben answered the telephone at Sutton Place. 'It's young Paul calling from Rome,' she said to Getty. 'Do you want to speak to him?'

Getty did not look up from the papers he was reading. 'No,' he said.

18 'A lecher, a miser, a womaniser'

Throughout the kidnapping, Getty was subjected to a barrage of hostile publicity for his refusal to pay a ransom for the release of his grandson. 'Mr Getty was not the kind of man who showed his personal feelings very much,' said Norris Bramlett, 'but I do think he was deeply hurt by all the adverse press coverage.'

Paul's girlfriend, Martine, had no sympathy for the old man's predicament. 'I would give everything I had, every penny, if my child was kidnapped,' she said. 'Money would have no meaning for me.'

It was a viewpoint widely shared, particularly after the horror of the severed ear. But what really rankled, certainly with those sections of the media susceptible to outrage, was that while Getty was refusing to pay 'a penny' in ransom he was spending spectacular sums on his art collection and on the construction of a fanciful museum in California. Here was the richest man in the world laying out millions of dollars for works of art while his grandson was held prisoner in Italy for the want of a ransom.

On a single morning in London Getty spent six million dollars at Christie's, paying one million for an oil sketch of four Negro heads attributed to Rubens, another million for two paintings by François Boucher and four million for Titian's 'The Death of Actaeon'. There was an uproar in Britain when it was learned he planned to ship the Titian to California and he was subsequently denied an export licence: the British government put up the money so that the National Gallery could acquire it. Getty was indignant and acidly complained that he had been obliged to lend the picture to the National Gallery, interest-free, for a year. 'At six per cent,' he groused, 'my loss was more than a hundred thousand dollars.'

Young Paul's loss was an ear which might easily have been saved. The new J. Paul Getty Museum, built in the grounds of the ranch at Malibu at a cost of seventeen million dollars, opened in January 1974 – exactly four weeks after J. Paul Getty III was freed by his kidnappers. He was not invited to join the celebrations.

Getty had not set eyes on his ranch house for more than twenty years and he had never seen the museum wing added in 1957 to accommodate the Greek and Roman antiquities. But he knew from the photographs and reports sent to Sutton Place that his collection was rapidly outgrowing the space available and he had decided in 1968 to build a new museum, not just as a showcase for his treasures but to stand as a permanent monument to the Gettys.

Uncompromisingly opposed to modern architecture – 'I refuse to pay for one of those concrete-bunker-type structures, nor for some tinted-glass and stainless-steel monstrosity' – his first idea was to build a replica of Sutton Place, California's first and only Tudor manor house.

He then thought something in the Roman style might provide a more suitable setting and passed the problem to the Los Angeles architects who normally designed office blocks for Getty Oil. This did not prove to be fruitful, so Getty next considered an amazing hybrid – a building that looked like a Roman villa outside and Sutton Place inside. Fortunately, design problems proved insuperable.

Getty had employed a London architect by the name of Stephen Garrett as a consultant; it was Garrett who had struggled, unsuccessfully, at the old man's behest, to fit Tudor windows into a Roman villa. One night in November 1968 Getty summoned Garrett to Sutton Place and announced he had made a decision about the new museum. He wanted to build a replica of the Villa dei Papyri.

'I'd never heard of it,' said Garrett. 'I had to go and find a book to look it up.'

The Villa dei Papyri stood on the slopes of Mount Vesuvius in the first century. Overlooking the Bay of Naples to the south of Herculaneum, it was probably the home of Lucius Calpurnius Piso, the father-in-law of Julius Caesar and patron of the Epicurean philosopher Philodemus, who taught at the villa. When Vesuvius erupted in 79 AD, the house was engulfed by lava sweeping down the flanks of the mountain. Buried under tons of volcanic rock its existence was unknown until the middle of the eighteenth century, when it was discovered by archaeologists investigating Herculaneum. Karl Weber, a Swiss engineer, explored the villa in 1750 by digging a shaft sixty feet into the rock and then tunnelling horizontally underground. He brought out a fabulous collection of bronze and marble sculptures and an extensive library of papyrus scrolls, which gave the villa its name. A few years later, the tunnels filled with poisonous volcanic gases and the exploration was abandoned; the tunnels eventually collapsed and the villa was never excavated.

Getty had always been fascinated by Roman history: he could name every Roman emperor, recite speeches from Pliny and whole chapters of Caesar's *Gallic Wars*. He had visited the site of Herculaneum in 1913 and read extensively about the discovery and exploration of the Villa dei Papyri. Although the project was primarily a treasure hunt on behalf of the Bourbon King of Naples, Weber took the trouble to make a detailed plan of the villa and its gardens and it was this fact that convinced Getty the villa could be faithfully recreated in the twentieth century.

Garrett did not share the old man's enthusiasm for the idea and pleaded with him to change his mind. 'It was ridiculous,' he said. 'Here was this strange old man, sitting in rural Surrey, saying he wanted to recreate, in Malibu, on the borders of Hollywood, a Roman villa that no one had ever seen and was lying sixty feet under the ground in Italy. I wrote a long report advising him against it because I thought there was a serious risk both he and the building would be ridiculed.

'I did not want that to happen because I had come to like him very much. He was infinitely more interesting than people gave him credit for. It was a mistake to judge him by conventional standards. To see him sitting alone at night in that huge house reading a drilling report, one might have thought he was a lonely, miserable old man. But you have to understand he was quite happy – he *enjoyed* reading drilling reports.'

What Getty did not tell Garrett was that recreating the Villa dei Papyri was part of an elaborate, romantic and secret fantasy tied up with his belief that he might be a reincarnation of the Emperor Hadrian.

Only Getty's closest friends knew about the phantasmagorical facet of his character. To the world, he was a sober, tightfisted businessman. But behind that flinty facade was a man beset by irrational fears, capable of the wildest flights of fantasy, frightened of ghosts and deeply superstitious. To those few people who knew Getty well, it was not at all surprising that he believed in reincarnation or believed that he might be a second Hadrian.

Of all the Roman emperors, Getty most admired Hadrian, whose literary and architectural tastes set the tone for the cultural activity of his age. When, as a young man, Getty began to study Hadrian's life and times, he experienced repeated *déjà vus* which he found both puzzling and exciting. 'It was as if I knew everything about him already,' he told Robina Lund, 'and understood why he made the decisions he did.'

The old man believed he had a direct link with the great emperor through his ownership of the Lansdowne Herakles, a marble statue unearthed at Tivoli near the site of Hadrian's villa in 1790. He conjured up an ingenious history for the Herakles in which it was transported to Rome after the sacking of Corinth, then bought by Lucius Calpurnius Piso for the Villa dei Papyri, eventually ending up at Hadrian's villa where the 'dust of centuries settled on it'. After the statue was found in 1790, it was sold to an English nobleman, the Marquis of Lansdowne, before finally 'following the sun westward to the new world' at the urging of some irresistible destiny.

By rebuilding the Villa dei Papyri, Getty felt he was bringing his time-tripping fantasy to life and fulfilling the expectations of the great spirit he now incarnated. 'Hadrian liked things on a grand scale,' he explained to Robina Lund. 'Like me, he enjoyed palatial buildings with fine pictures, gold and silver plate and *objets d'art.*'

Despite his doubts, Garrett agreed to supervise the project and construction of the 'Roman' villa-museum began in December 1970, when bulldozers rumbled on to the site to excavate the huge underground car park which was perhaps the most incongruous feature of the whole venture. Apart from the car park, strenuous attempts were made to create an authentic replica of the Villa dei Papyri, even taking into account the fact that the museum needed modern office accommodation, washroom facilities, a restaurant and elevators connecting the car park with the floors above.

Roman builders did not, of course, have Californian safety codes to worry about. The long reflecting pool surrounded by colonnades and painted loggias in the front garden of the Villa dei Papyri was twelve-feet deep; in the Los Angeles version it could be no deeper than eighteen inches without having a lifeguard on duty at each end. However the museum gardens were planted with the varieties of trees, flowers, shrubs and herbs known in Roman times, bronze casts were made of the statues discovered in the original garden during Karl Weber's exploration and the trompe-l'oeil murals along the garden walls were based on frescoes found at Herculaneum.

The villa itself, a two-storey white-stucco building around a collonaded courtyard, comprised thirty-eight galleries. On the ground floor all the rooms were of Roman design with floors and walls of inlaid marble and ceilings of carved wood painted green, purple and yellow. There was an atrium, a columned basilica and a circular temple for the Herakles. On the upper floor, the galleries were planned to accommodate Getty's collection of paintings and decorative artefacts.

Getty followed the progress of the building from colour photographs, movie film and detailed reports sent to him every week at Sutton Place. He had a scale model made and spent many hours musing over it, but he never made any serious plans to see his new museum for himself. He was always talking about returning to California 'as soon as my work in Europe is done', but he had been talking about it for so long no one believed him any more. As the museum neared completion Getty expressed the hope, rather movingly, that it would be as 'beautiful as I imagine it to be'.

The founder of the new J. Paul Getty Museum was represented at the opening ceremony in January 1974 only by a film shown to the assembled guests, in which he made it clear that time-tripping was essential for proper appreciation of the museum he had never seen. 'The ideal visitor,' he said, 'should fancy himself back two thousand years ago, calling on Roman friends who live in the villa.'

All Garrett's worst fears were confirmed by the reaction of the critics, who greeted the new museum with ridicule even more poisonous than Garrett had anticipated. The old man's fantasy was dismissed as 'vulgar' and invariably compared with Disneyland or a Cecil B. De Mille set. The *New York Times* reported that it was 'gussied up like a Bel Air drawing-room', while the *Los Angeles Times* sneered 'Walt Disney would turn green with envy' and the *Economist* declared that art connoisseurs could not decide whether the museum was 'merely incongruous or actually ludicrous'. The mosaic floors were said to be 'garish', the murals 'back lot', the design 'inauthentic' and the concept '*nouveau riche*'.

'I think the old man was very hurt,' said Garrett, 'by the mocking.'

In his great cold and lonely house, with its threadbare carpets, prowling attack dogs and silent retinue of servants, Getty was still working every day, still in nominal control of a worldwide conglomerate of nearly two hundred companies with twelve thousand employees and annual profits in excess of $142,000,000 – but the dynamism and tenacity had gone. Now in his eighty-second year, he was leaving more and more decisions to line management and only wanted to be consulted on matters of major policy, like when Getty Oil invested $41,000,000 for a 23.5% stake in two exploration leases in the North Sea, or when the company acquired a 35% interest in a gold mine in Australia, where huge uranium deposits had recently been discovered.

Robina Lund thought that the death of his son George, which knocked the old man sideways, marked the beginning of his decline. 'He gave up hope of the family business continuing and began to lose interest in it,' she said. 'His memory and his judgement went; he no longer had the same capacity to make decisions. He would say "Do whatever you think is best".'

After George died, whenever he was asked who would take over the business from him, he usually expressed the hope that he would be 'represented' by his other two sons (J. Paul Getty II was never mentioned).

He had no such hopes in reality. Gordon was by no stretch of the imagination a businessman and Ronald's aspirations in that direction had signally failed to impress his father. Every now and again, Ronnie and Gordon would receive in the mail from their father a newspaper clipping about some young man who had made a sensational success in business. The old man did not need to add any comments.

Although he would never have admitted it, his estrangement from

Paul caused him considerable grief. During the brief time they spent together in Italy he had got to like Paul a lot, but it was an affection that could not possibly have withstood Paul's lifestyle after he went off with Talitha. There might, conceivably, have been a rapprochement some time after Paul came to live in London, except that he managed to exasperate his father further. Paul began collecting antiquarian books, but frequently neglected to pay for them. Because his name was Getty, dealers seeking settlement of their accounts sent the bills to Sutton Place. It infuriated the old man.

The routine of Getty's days at Sutton Place settled into an invariable pattern. He would stay in bed until mid-morning, nibble a light 'brunch' and read the newspapers before descending to his office suite on the ground floor. At midday, wrapped up in a scarf and a heavy overcoat and shadowed by a security guard, he would take a short walk. (He had a peculiar, plodding gait which the staff liked to imitate for a joke; they used to say he walked like a yeti.) He worked through the afternoon and most evenings he spent watching television – he enjoyed Westerns and old Laurel and Hardy movies – in a small, overheated room adjoining the study.

With the help of regular H3 'rejuvenation' injections, he maintained an active sex life and there were always 'girlfriends' about the place. The notorious promiscuity of the master of the house seemed to provide a licence for others to follow suit and there was much below-stairs gossip about unseemly scenes at Sutton Place as Getty got older and took less interest in what was going on. Von Block opened a door into a corridor one day and found the son of one of Getty's mistresses having inter-course with a secretary against the wall. On another occasion Bullimore discovered Raymonde, a chambermaid known as 'the Black Pearl', in a bathroom *flagrante delicto* with Norris Bramlett. When the horrified Bullimore remonstrated with Bramlett, pointing out that Raymonde should have been on duty, there was a shouting match which ended with Bramlett taking a swing at Bullimore and cracking two of his ribs. Not long afterwards John, the footman, collapsed with a heart attack and one of Getty's personal secretaries resigned with hypertension.

Getty turned a blind eye to most of what was happening under his roof. He had lost interest in Sutton Place and regretted buying it. Despite the constant presence of the ladies of 'the harem', he often felt lonely and unwanted in the great house and his vast wealth created a barrier which isolated him from normal social contact. 'A rich man must expect that many people are more interested in his money than anything else about him,' he said, turning down the corners of his mouth. 'It is something I have learned to live with.'

While he recognised that he was often surrounded by sycophants and spongers, he felt powerless to do anything about it. 'If I gave up seeing everyone who uses me or has taken advantage in some way,' he once glumly confessed to Robina Lund, 'I wouldn't have many friends left. And, in the end, one must have someone to talk to.'

Resentful and suspicious of being 'used', he had no qualms about manipulating others, shamelessly holding out a promise of inclusion in his will, or a threat of exclusion, to get his own way. He frequently assured women they would be rich, or 'looked after', without the slightest intention of adding them to his beneficiaries. But when he was crossed by someone already mentioned in the will he very often acted, signing a codicil reducing their share of the spoils or cutting them out altogether. 'I used to tell Paul,' said Robina Lund, 'that if he kept bringing up his will every time we had a disagreement I would rather not be in it.'

Mrs Kitson, his oldest friend, was threatened with exclusion when, in 1973, she told Getty that she was going to get married. He was incensed at what he considered to be her 'betrayal' and tried for weeks to talk her out of it, warning her that she was making a mistake and if she went through with it she would not get a penny in his will. But the forceful Mrs Kitson would not be dissuaded and went off to marry businessman Patrick de Laszlo, leaving Getty with her clutch of Norwich terrier lap dogs. He did not conceal his delight when the marriage rapidly broke up and he soon restored her to favour.

By November 1974 Getty's palsy had become so bad that the daily entries in his diary were virtually illegible and he had to give up writing it himself. The last entry was on Sunday 17 November – one and a half lines of indecipherable scrawl. As his diary was never much more than a roll call of who visited him and who he visited and what time he went to bed, he had no fears of revealing his innermost thoughts and continued to keep a journal by dictating to a secretary.

His hands might have been shaky, but his mind was still alert and he determinedly kept in touch with the outposts of the Getty empire. He was especially gratified to learn, in a message from Los Angeles at the beginning of 1975, that the museum was proving to be a huge success with the public despite the critics. During its first year, more than 360,000 people visited the replica of the Villa dei Papyri at Malibu to gawp at his treasures. Getty had provided the museum with a forty-million-dollar endowment and a two-million-dollar annual operating budget. It was a magnificent philanthropic gesture, but he could not resist counting the cost – minutely calculating that as there was no entrance fee his 'personal, out-of-pocket net cost' was around three dollars per visitor.

In April, he donated fifty thousand dollars to the World Wildlife

Fund and at a press conference at Sutton Place to announce the award he told reporters he did not want to spend another winter in England. He had suffered severe bouts of bronchitis during the past three winters, he said, and they were 'no picnic'. It was a constant worry for the resident ladies that Getty might one day carry out his oft-voiced resolution to return to California and leave them all in the lurch. To deter him, they made it their business to ensure he did not miss newspaper reports about the increasing crime rate in the United States. When von Block returned from a visit to America, one of the ladies earnestly encouraged him to talk to the old man about how violent America had become. 'What am I supposed to do,' he asked sarcastically, 'scare the pants off him? Would you like me to tell him a machine gun missed me by inches on the way to the airport?' 'Mmm, that's a good idea,' said the lady after a moment's thought.

That summer, Getty was visited by most of his grandchildren. Gail showed up with Aileen, who was fifteen, Mark, fourteen and Ariadne, thirteen. 'Always a delight to see my grandchildren,' he dictated for his diary. 'Mary Tessier also visiting.' Gail's eldest son, Paul, did not join the family visit, which was perhaps just as well since his grandfather was not a man to forgive easily; neither did Tara Gabriel Galaxy Gramaphone Getty.

George's first wife, Gloria, brought her three daughters, Anne, Claire and Caroline, who helped to show visitors round during an open day at Sutton Place and posed with their grandfather for the photographers. Gordon and Ann, who were regular visitors, also came with their four sons, Peter, Andrew, John and William. Even Ronnie and his wife, Karin, showed up with their children Christopher, Stefanie, Cecile and Christina.

Although even the fanatically loyal Norris Bramlett admitted that 'Mr Getty was not a family man', this sudden and unexpected influx gave the old man the opportunity to pretend the Gettys were a close family and warmly congratulate himself for their unity. 'It was a most reassuring summer,' he noted, 'for grandfather J. Paul Getty.'

It was a less reassuring summer for the ladies of the 'harem' and the tensions and jealousies always present at Sutton Place undoubtedly sharpened as the old man became more frail and it dawned on the interested parties that he was unlikely to live for much longer. During the absence of Penelope, temporarily banished as a punishment for daring to marry against Getty's wishes, Lady Ursula d'Abo had moved into No. 1 position. Still beautiful at fifty-eight, she sat at his right hand at dinner, took him for drives in the countryside in her silver Mercedes and entertained him overnight at her house in Kensington Square when he had business meetings in London.

Although she did her best to stay out of the newspapers, responding to impertinent questions from reporters with innocuous comments like: 'I am just one of Mr Getty's many lady friends', she was unable to avoid attracting the attention of the dreaded *National Enquirer*, which reported in June 1975: 'Getty has struck it rich in love – he's won the heart of a British aristocrat, Countess Ursula d'Abo . . . In a soft, tender voice she told the *Enquirer* "I love him very much. It's all very romantic".' The newspaper, if such it may be called, said marriage could not be ruled out and quoted an 'unidentified source' as saying 'Paul is fascinated by English aristocratic ladies. He seems to get a kick out of having a real-life countess cook for him.'

Neither Getty, nor the 'real-life countess', were particularly concerned by this nonsense, but Rosabella Burch was spitting tacks. Outraged that her chief rival should be publicly extolled as the old man's favourite, Rosabella gave an interview at Sutton Place to the *Daily Express*.

'I've thought about marrying him,' she simpered. 'Maybe he has thought about it too. If he asked me I would say "Of course." He's such a dear man and so amusing.

'My role in Paul's household? It's simple. I keep him company and act as hostess for him when he needs one. I've never wanted to be anywhere else. This is home for me.'

Rosabella was pleased that the newspaper made it clear that 'of all the ladies in attendance at Sutton Place, Rosabella is the one closest to bringing Getty to the altar.' She was perhaps less pleased by the comment of a spokesman for the old man, probably Norris Bramlett, who was usually available with a pithy quote at such times: 'Mrs Burch is just a friend. There is no romance. If Mr Getty was to walk down the street with Mrs Golda Meir someone would ask her if she was to be the sixth Mrs Getty.'

As well as fighting between themselves, the ladies of Sutton Place always had to suffer competition from outsiders, which undoubtedly heightened stress levels. Zsa Zsa Gabor, all blonde, bust and lipstick, swept in on one occasion, announcing to all and sundry that 'darling Paul' had paid her first-class air fare from Los Angeles. 'He's a dream,' she said to reporters at London Airport on her way back. 'I should love to be his hostess when he comes to California. I consider myself to be a *very* good friend now. All the other women were jealous.'

One evening in November 1975 tensions rose to such a point that Rosabella and Lady Ursula very nearly came to blows. It was the night of the Miss World contest on television, which Getty wanted to watch. Present at Sutton Place were Bramlett, Bela von Block and his friend Joan Zetka, Marianne von Alvensleben, Lady Ursula and Rosabella.

Bitchy sniping between the women began over dinner when Getty chose to put Miss Zetka at his right hand and Baroness von Alvensleben on his left, relegating Mrs Burch and Lady Ursula to humbler down-table positions. After dinner, everyone repaired to the television room to watch 'Miss World'. Getty, Bramlett and von Block sat on three chairs facing the screen passing mildly ribald remarks about the contestants, while the women sat behind on a sofa and two armchairs, eyeing each other.

'Watching the girls on television,' von Block recalled, 'the old man started to perk up and Ursula and Rosabella sensed it. They began jockeying to see who was going up to the bedroom with him, helping themselves to drinks from the bar and going at each other like cats. It was past the point of sheer bitchiness and reached genuine feminine rage – another couple of drinks and they would have been pulling each other's hair.'

When the programme finished, Mrs Burch (who was, said von Block, 'faster on her feet') walked across to Getty, leaned over his chair and put her arm round him possessively, bodily pressing her case. 'If you will excuse me, goodnight everyone,' said the old man, rising to his feet. 'Come along, my dear,' he added, patting Rosabella affectionately on her rear.

After their departure, Ursula let out a shriek of rage and began weeping pitifully. She insisted that Bramlett and von Block stay up drinking vodka with her. 'I'm the one who loves Paul,' she wailed while the two men tried to find somewhere to look. 'She's nothing but a little South American tart. All she wants is his money. I'm the one who loves Paul ...' It was three o'clock in the morning before von Block was able to get to bed.

A few days after this incident, Getty found himself alone at Sutton Place – a situation he hated – on Thanksgiving. None of the staff had remembered it was an American holiday and so he missed the traditional dinner of roast turkey and pumpkin pie. 'American friends residing in London,' he noted, 'had invited me to have a real Thanksgiving dinner with them. I was reluctantly forced to refuse their invitation for the same reason that I have (or have not) done so many things in life. Business required me to stay at Sutton for the day.'

A few days after his eighty-third birthday, Getty presided over the sixteenth annual Christmas party for orphans in the Long Gallery at Sutton Place. Forty-eight children from the British Rail Southern Region Home at Woking were invited for a tea of jelly, cakes and ice-cream. Mrs Burch's two children, Paul Bernard, ten, and Carolina, seven, home from their Swiss boarding school, were also present. Getty looked tired and wan, muffled in a striped woollen scarf, stooped and shrunken inside his grey suit. The children sang 'Jingle Bells' for him and he managed a thin smile.

At Christmas he complained of pains in his back, although by New Year's Eve he had apparently recovered sufficiently to make love to Mrs Burch, as she announced to everyone the following day. But with the onset of the New Year, the old man's health began to decline rapidly. On 22 January 1976 he was driven to London to attend a public offering of offshore leases in the North Sea; it was to be his last visit.

Thereafter Getty either cut himself off from the outside world, or he was deliberately cut off by the people around him. There were two versions of what was going on at Sutton Place during the old man's final days. Friends and lovers who were denied access to Getty before his death inevitably concluded there was some sinister plot afoot. Those people who controlled access, notably Bramlett and Mrs Kitson, claim the old man simply did not want to be bothered with a stream of visitors.

At the beginning of February Getty's private, unlisted telephone, Guildford 667639, was disconnected. To the outsiders this was an event of dark significance. For most of his working life, Getty had managed his affairs at the end of a telephone line. His private telephone was an essential tool, an umbilical link both with his business empire, his friends and the world outside Sutton Place. It was a link many friends found it hard to believe he would ever willingly break, no matter how ill he was.

Robina Lund was one of them. Miss Lund had not been able to visit Sutton Place for some months because both her parents were ill. She last saw Getty in May 1975 and thought that he had been 'grossly neglected' – she spent an hour cleaning patches of ingrained dirt off his face. Convinced that he was desperately ill, she tried to persuade him to see a doctor in London, but he refused. When she tried to enlist Penelope Kitson's support, Mrs Kitson dismissed her fears and said she could see no point 'pandering to his hypochondria'. Puzzled by finding Guildford 667639 unobtainable, in February Miss Lund telephoned Barbara Wallace, Getty's private secretary, who said she did not know the private line had been disconnected. Miss Lund then spoke to Bramlett, who told her that Mr Getty did not want to speak to anyone; he was not ill, just a 'little tired'. She telephoned four or five times a week for a month or more, without ever getting through to Getty. She also wrote several letters, but received no reply. Visitors to Sutton Place fared no better: the door was shut in their faces.

With suspicions already aroused, the timing of what happened next was unfortunate, to say the least. On 11 March Getty signed a final, twenty-first, codicil to his will, removing the Getty family from control of his vast fortune and handing it over to professional managers. It was an extraordinary volte-face. All his life Getty believed in the principle of family inheritance; he liked to boast of the family's 'clear-cut numerical control' of Getty Oil. Even at moments of maximum disaffection with his sons, none of the previous codicils ever envisaged anyone but a Getty being in control of Getty money.

In March, Getty gave up his daily walk in the garden and began taking his meals in his study. On 10 April he decided he wanted to take a ride out into the countryside in his Cadillac. He was wrapped up in a coat and scarf and helped out to the car with the usual entourage of ladies, aides and security guards. The Cadillac, followed by a second car packed with bodyguards and dogs, drove slowly out through the gates of the estate on to the A3 road. At the first roundabout, less than half a mile down the road, Getty became agitated and insisted on returning: the two cars turned round and drove back through the gates, which closed automatically behind them. It was the last time he would leave Sutton Place.

A few days later Getty was told by his doctor, Clive MacKenzie, that he had cancer of the prostate gland. He apparently took the news calmly. MacKenzie organised round-the-clock nursing for the old man, but he proved to be a somewhat irascible patient. When one of the nurses, Monica Cazeley, told Getty it was time for him to have a bath, he grunted something about not wanting a bath, but wanting Norris.

'You can't have Norris, whatever that is,' the nurse replied briskly. 'You must have your bath and if you go on like this I shall have to fetch Mr Bramlett.'

'Don't be a fool,' Getty snapped. 'Norris *is* Bramlett. Norris Bramlett is a wonderful man. I can rely on him. He is the only one who doesn't want anything from me.' The old man paused, then added malevolently, 'And that's more than I can say for some of the others.'

As Getty approached death, a bizarre procession of quacks, healers and medicine men with magic boxes were summoned to Sutton Place. He had been a hypochondriac all his life and now he was willing to try anything to stave off the end. A Chinese acupuncturist was flown in from Paris, a diapulse radiation machine arrived, a masseuse moved in and Tom Smith, a part-Cherokee Indian who Getty believed had 'healing hands', was hauled over from Florida.

Dr MacKenzie did his best to cope with the competition, as well as the ladies of the entourage who, he complained, were 'shouting, ranting and raving' as they battled for access to the dying man. A Getty Oil executive visiting Sutton Place at this time later reported to one of his colleagues that the ladies 'took to each other with short, blunt knives'. No one could have honestly disagreed with Barbara Wallace, who complained that Sutton Place had become 'a nuthouse'. 'I don't know what is going on,' she wrote to Robina Lund. 'Things are most peculiar.'

Lady Ursula was convinced she could save Getty with the power of prayer and wanted to take sole charge of the nursing. When Dr MacKenzie suggested she was perhaps a little too inexperienced, Lady Ursula's son, Henry, retorted: 'Nonsense! Mother nursed Americans during the war.' Ursula insisted that an elevator should be installed to help Getty get upstairs to bed, but as soon as it was functioning Getty asked for his bed to be moved into his ground-floor study so he did not have to use it.

When she failed to take over the nursing, she offered to help Paul with the business, pointedly mentioning to the old man that her son, Henry, would make a 'fine president of Getty Oil'.

In the end, Lady Ursula made such a nuisance of herself that Norris Bramlett and Tom Smith had to eject her forcibly from Getty's study and the security guards were told not to allow her back on to the estate. Undeterred, she returned the following day, crept round the outside of the house and tapped on the study window. 'She talked her way in through the gate,' said Albert Thurgood, the estate manager, 'and she was again asked to leave.' The old man was so alarmed by the rattling on his window that he insisted Bramlett and Smith sleep in the same room with him for the next few nights. He was beginning to have nightmares about a hidden staircase somewhere in the house and was only sleeping fitfully.

Through March and April Rosabella was allowed to wave at Getty from the door of the study, but then she, too, was barred from Sutton Place. She wept and wailed that Getty lived only for her and insisted that they were to be married, but doors remained firmly closed to her.

Bramlett fielded all other callers and visitors, repeating over and over again in a monotone that Mr Getty was 'not available'. Only Penelope Kitson was assured regular access to the dying man; she spent hours with him in the study, reading aloud his favourite G. A. Henty stories while he sat wrapped up in his favourite armchair, sipping rum and Coke. 'He was very weak towards the end,' she said, 'but he never complained. He was alert, but heavily drugged and slept a lot in his chair. He never wanted to get into bed and would say "All anyone wants to do is get me into bed so I can die".'

On 30 May, Gordon and Ann arrived from San Francisco. It was clear to both of them that the old man had only a short time to live. 'He was very enervated,' said Gordon. 'He couldn't walk much and was sleeping most of the time. But he was alert, knew who he was and where he was and the time of the day. He could understand questions and give answers.'

Aware that the old man had always expressed a wish to die in the United States, Gordon said: 'Father, do you want to go back to the ranch?' Getty nodded, but when Gordon said he would charter a plane, the old man mumbled 'Well, I'll think about it.'

Penelope Kitson had heard him say that a thousand times and knew it meant he would never do it.

On Wednesday 2 June Getty dictated his last diary entry: 'Had good night's sleep. Mrs Shaw [a masseuse] came for treatment and after morning treatment walked eight lengths of study. U. [Lady Ursula, allowed back to Sutton Place after a promise of good behaviour] here. Pen here.'

Rosabella, meanwhile, had given an interview to *Woman* magazine, talking frankly ('for the first time' the magazine noted hopefully) about her life with 'the richest man in the world' and as the 'mistress' of Sutton Place. 'I love him,' she said. 'I'd be lost in the world if anything happened to him. My life would be empty. I wouldn't know what to do. I worry every time he doesn't feel well.'

The magazine appeared on Saturday 5 June. The timing was unfortunate, to say the least. A few minutes after midnight on Sunday 6 June 1976 J. Paul Getty died, sitting in his favourite armchair in the study at Sutton Place. (Coincidentally, his eldest son, George, had died on the same day three years earlier.)

His body was laid out in the Great Hall and Rosabella was among those allowed in to pay their last respects. Sobbing dramatically, she leaned over the coffin, pinned a crucifix to Getty's lapel and placed a rosary in his hand. While she remained keening outside, a bitter argument developed around the coffin about whether Rosabella's trinket should be removed and, if so, who should do the deed.

'He was a true eccentric,' said Penelope Kitson. 'Only an eccentric could have achieved what he achieved. He was a genius in his way, but very naughty.'

A memorial service was held at the American Church in North Audley Street, Mayfair, on 22 June. J. Paul Getty II turned up late wearing yellow shoes, with Bianca Jagger on his arm. The assembled mourners did not know which they considered to be more shocking. In his address, the Duke of Bedford was unable to resist a reference to the billionaire's notorious libido. 'His love of beautiful women,' said the duke, 'as well as his appreciation of all beautiful things, was to continue and develop thoughout his life.'

Among the tributes to Getty's life and career, there was one sour note. Mark Goulden, whom Getty described in his autobiography as the 'noted English publisher' and a 'good and close friend', showed what kind of a friend he was.

I am one of the few people [he said] who could reveal the incredible facts about the late, unlamented multi-billionaire. He was a lecher, a miser, a womaniser whose private life was often bizarre beyond belief. He never conquered his fear of death and he tried in vain to stay the ravages of time by frequent face-lifts. He was secretly contemptuous of the sycophants who surrounded him, particularly the members of his 'harem' and it was his firm belief that anyone who approached him was simply trying to muscle in on his millions. This he actually said to me in his own words. He lacked affection yet he yearned to be loved. Throughout his adult life, love eluded him. To be loved, says Ovid, you must be lovable, but the gloomy, pathetic, remote Getty was totally and utterly unlovable. I doubt if he could have counted five faithful friends in all the world and I question whether anyone, anywhere, shed a tear of genuine grief when last month among his earthly trappings he quietly closed his chronicle of wasted time.

19. *'Money to fuel the legal engines forever'*

It was to be expected that the last will and testament of the richest man in the world would cause something of a stir. Getty did not disappoint.

The will was filed for probate in Los Angeles on 9 June 1976. To the astonishment of everyone, not least the staff of the J. Paul Getty Museum, Getty chose to leave almost his entire fortune – about four million shares of Getty Oil stock, then valued at around seven hundred million dollars – to his museum. The fake Roman villa overlooking the Pacific at Malibu, the target of so much derision, suddenly became the most richly-endowed museum in the world, wielding far more purchasing power than even the Metropolitan Museum of Art in New York.

Among the individual beneficiaries, prime candidates for attention were those the newspapers were pleased to describe as the 'Getty Girls' – a round dozen of them, ranging from Hildegard Kuhn, the girl he met at a dance in Berlin fifty years earlier, to his long-standing friend Penelope Kitson. Only one of his five wives was mentioned – Teddy Lynch, the mother of Timmy.

Less in the public eye, but no less numerous, were all the disaffected ladies who had been promised inclusion in the will and were destined to be disappointed. Lest any of them were tempted to step forward and press a suit for a legitimate claim, the wily billionaire inserted a clause stating that anyone claiming to be his wife or his child should receive, if the claim was upheld, 'ten dollars and no more'.

The will's twenty-one codicils provided a fascinating insight into Getty's character and the power he exercised over his loved ones, for they were a barometer of his capricious affections, precisely charting the movements of girlfriends and lovers in and out of favour and logging the various misdemeanours of his sons.

The original will, drawn up in September 1958 and signed in Italy, was a simple enough document, despite its seventeen typewritten pages. He directed that his clothes (most of which were well worn, since he hated to buy new clothes), jewellery and personal effects were to be shared between his four sons (Timmy had died a month previously), along with any art objects not considered suitable for exhibition in the museum.

George, Ronnie, Paul and Gordon were also left thirty-four thousand shares in Getty Oil between them. At first sight it might have appeared to be a niggardly bequest by a billionaire who professed to love all his sons deeply (none of them was yet in bad odour), but the fabulously rich Sarah C. Getty Trust existed to provide for Getty's lineal descendants and so there was no real need for the old man to make separate provision. Of the block of shares allocated, Ronnie was to receive ten thousand and the other three eight thousand each. Ronald was presumably favoured with a few more as he was not a full beneficiary of the Sarah C. Getty Trust.

There were personal bequests to his cousin, Hal Seymour, who got five thousand dollars; to Louise Lynch Getty, who was to receive thirty-five thousand dollars a year for life 'in full discharge of the terms of our separation agreement'; to his friend Ethel Le Vane, who got five hundred dollars a month for life; and to two old girlfriends from Berlin – Margarete Feuersaenger ($125 a month for life) and Hildegard Kuhn (seventy-five dollars a month for life).

Getty had a horror of cremation and set aside a sum of fifty thousand dollars to build a small, marble mausoleum at the ranch for 'myself and those of my sons and their wives as shall choose' to join him therein. A further hundred thousand dollars was to be invested to maintain it.

The remainder of his estate – his personal fortune, all his property and his multi-million-dollar art collection – was bequeathed to the museum. It was a move clearly designed to avoid saddling the family with massive inheritance taxes, while perpetuating family control of the business. Control of Getty Oil was vested in the Sarah C. Getty Trust which held about forty-two per cent of the stock, combined with the old man's personal shareholding of about twenty per cent. Getty envisaged that his four sons would succeed him as co-trustees both of the Sarah C. Getty Trust and the museum. By donating his Getty Oil shares to a museum controlled by his sons, he not only avoided tax but ensured the family remained dominant in Getty Oil. It was neat and looked, in 1958, as if it would work beautifully. How could Getty have foreseen that his oldest son would die before him and he would fall out with the other three?

In an attempt to avoid any dispute over the will, Getty inserted a final clause warning that anyone contesting probate would automatically forfeit any bequest. This was a provision which was to prove toothless.

In the first codicil, signed on 18 June 1960, Mrs Kitson made her debut in the will with a useful 2500 shares. This was a few days before the house-warming party at Sutton Place, to which she made such a vital contribution. Mary Tessier, an early rival of Mrs Kitson, was rewarded for her friendship with a thousand shares and four hundred dollars a month in the second codicil, dated November 1960. But

305

Penelope also got an additional five hundred dollars a month to keep her place at the top of the pecking order.

Gordon Getty, who in 1962 suggested to his father that he might perhaps receive a little more money from the trust, was punished for his insolence in the third codicil, signed on his twenty-ninth birthday in December 1962, by being dismissed as an executor. At the same time, Getty remembered three girlfriends from California for whom he presumably harboured a lingering affection – Mary Maginnes, Gloria Bigelow and Belene Clifford, the sister of his second wife, Allene. Each got five hundred oil shares. Another German girlfriend, Karin Mannhardt of Lübeck, was given two hundred shares and Getty's personal legal adviser, Robina Lund, was put down for a thousand shares.

Gordon was soon in further trouble and in March 1963 Getty signed a fifth codicil almost entirely devoted to nailing his youngest son. Gordon was no longer to share in his father's personal effects or jewellery and his eight thousand shares were taken away. Instead, he was to receive from his billionaire father 'five hundred dollars and nothing else'. George and Paul, on the other hand, were very much in favour – their shares were doubled. George was at this time confidently climbing the corporate ladder and Paul, in Italy, had not yet embarked on the Bohemian life style that was to cause his father such anguish. Ronald's bequest was unchanged.

In September 1965 the sixth codicil upped the ante for all the ladies in rough proportion to their status, ranging from Hildegard Kuhn's modest one hundred dollars a month at the bottom of the ladder to Mrs Kitson's $1167 a month and five thousand shares at the top.

In the light of later events the most important of the first twenty codicils was the ninth, added in November 1967, in which Getty opted for a permanent hereditary structure to ensure that the family remained in control of the Getty fortune. A 'testamentary trust' to be controlled by members of the family was to be set up to receive and administer the museum's legacy. George, Ronald and Paul were appointed as trustees, each to be succeeded on death or retirement, by the next oldest lineal descendant over the age of twenty-one. At the same time, George was appointed to succeed Getty as trustee of the Sarah C. Getty Trust. Gordon, who had recently filed a lawsuit against his father, was not included as a testamentary trustee and still languished with 'five hundred dollars and nothing else'.

In February 1969 Mrs Kitson caused some offence, for her bequest was reduced to only a thousand shares and two hundred dollars a month. Whatever Mrs Kitson did, it must have really angered the old man – her inheritance was effectively reduced from more than one million to less than two hundred thousand dollars, but she remained only briefly in disfavour and her 7500 shares and $1167 a month were reinstated the following month.

Baroness Marianne von Alvensleben made an appearence in March 1971 with one thousand dollars a month, in the thirteenth codicil. Some of the staff at Sutton Place – notably the indispensable Bullimore, John the footman, Lee the chauffeur and Kathrine the cook – were also included, largely at the instigation of Mrs Kitson who had been pressing Getty for months to mention long-serving staff in his will. Getty, who cared nothing for *noblesse oblige*, at first argued that they were corporate employees of Getty Oil and as such adequately rewarded. But in the end he wilted under Mrs Kitson's nagging and agreed to six or three months' pay for fourteen of the staff at Sutton Place. Norris Bramlett was also awarded six months' salary.

Less than three weeks after the death of Talitha Getty from a heroin overdose in Rome, Paul Getty II joined his brother in the wilderness. In the fourteenth codicil on 29 July 1971, he was dismissed as an executor and testamentary trustee, barred from a share of his father's personal effects and left, like Gordon, with 'five hundred dollars and nothing else'.

Two years later, when George died, only Ronald remained as an executor and testamentary trustee. Although Gordon was not reinstated in the will at this time, he was back on speaking terms with his father and was appointed to replace his late half-brother, George, as trustee designate of the Sarah C. Getty Trust. Getty planned that Gordon would be a co-trustee with the Security Pacific National Bank and C. Lansing Hays, a New York attorney who was a close friend of the old man and whose law firm had acted for Getty Oil for many years.

When Mrs Kitson married in 1973 against Getty's wishes, the old man rapped her over the knuckles by reducing her legacy from 7500 shares to 5000, although he never cut her out of the will entirely as he had threatened. He actually showed her a draft codicil abolishing her inheritance, but he apparently could not bring himself to sign it.

Arch rivals Lady Ursula d'Abo and Mrs Rosabella Burch made a joint debut in the seventeenth codicil, signed in October 1973. Lady Ursula was bequeathed a thousand Getty Oil shares and Rosabella got five hundred, a somewhat ungenerous amount for a lady who proclaimed herself to be the mistress of Sutton Place, the love of Getty's life and the principal contender for the title of the sixth Mrs Getty. Fortunately none of the ladies was aware of their wildly-fluctuating fortunes in the old man's will, or of the different amounts he judged each of them to be worth, otherwise the atmosphere at Sutton Place might have been even more highly charged than it was ordinarily.

In the same codicil, Robina Lund's remaining one thousand shares were withdrawn. Miss Lund's crime was to announce to Getty, a trifle tactlessly, that she did not want to be lumped in his will with all his mistresses since she was not one, had never been one and had no intention of being one. Getty was not pleased.

The nineteenth codicil in January 1975 marked Gordon's triumphant reinstatement as executor and testamentary trustee, thus moving from the rear of the filial field into an undisputed position as the most favoured of Getty's three surviving sons. His brother Paul was still *persona non grata*, due to receive 'five hundred dollars and nothing else', which was no more or less than a nicely-calculated slap in the face from the richest man in the world. Ronnie was also an executor and testamentary trustee, but he was still excluded from the Sarah C. Getty Trust, font of the family's wealth.

In the twentieth codicil of August 1975, the last one signed while the old man was unequivocally sound in mind and body, the final disposition of the ladies was established. Teddy Lynch, whose endowment had remained unchanged from codicil to codicil, was to receive $35,000 a year for life. Mrs Kitson got 5000 shares and a life income of $1167 a month. For Mary Tessier there were 2500 shares and $750 a month. Gloria Bigelow and Mary Maginnes each got 625 shares and $400 a month. Belene Clifford also received 625 shares but only $300 a month and Karen Mannhardt was given 250 shares and $200 a month.

Monthly incomes without shares went to Marianne von Alvensleben ($1000), Robina Lund ($209) and Hildegard Kuhn ($100). Lady Ursula d'Abo and Rosabella Burch received only shares – 1000 for Lady Ursula, half that number for Rosabella. At 1976 values, Rosabella's inheritance was worth about $87,500.

Getty's state of health when he signed the final, twenty-first codicil in March 1976 was to be the subject of bitter dispute. Those people excluded from Sutton Place at that time tended to believe the codicil was evidence of some sinister plot to manipulate a dying man who had become so enfeebled that he no longer knew what he was doing. 'Insiders' viewed it as no more than a device to streamline the museum's access to its legacy.

Whatever the truth, the twenty-first codicil fundamentally shifted the direction of the will. If Getty's mind was functioning, it indicated he had at last faced up to the unreality of his dynastic dreams for it revoked the provisions of the ninth codicil, which would have ensured the family retained control of Getty's fortune. With the twenty-first codicil, the 'testamentary trust' was abandoned and control of the museum's assets was handed directly to the board of six museum trustees, only two of whom – Ronnie and Gordon – were Gettys. The other four members of the board were Norris Bramlett; Harold Berg, executive vice-president of Getty Oil; Stuart Peeler, an executive of the Santa Fe International Oil Company and son of a senior partner in the old man's personal law firm; and Federico Zeri, a former director of the Spada Gallery in Rome, who had been advising Getty on paintings acquisitions since 1963. Outnumbered on the board of trustees, the Gettys not only lost control of the museum under the provisions of the twenty-first codicil, they also lost partial control of Getty Oil.

As a footnote the twenty-first codicil also contained a final kick in the teeth for J. Paul Getty II and his son, Paul Getty III. The old man decreed that neither of them should ever serve as trustees of the museum.

Norris Bramlett insisted that there were no ulterior motives to the twenty-first codicil and that Getty was perfectly aware of what he was doing when he signed it. 'It was essentially designed,' he said, 'to make the running of the museum easier. The original plan, with Mr Getty's lineal descendants succeeding each other, would have meant that in fifty years time the people running the museum would all be elderly and they would be succeeded, as they died, by more elderly people. My recommendation, which Mr Getty accepted, was that businessmen should be put in charge of the museum.'

It was a perfectly plausible explanation. Nevertheless, a number of questions remained unanswered. Firstly, why had Getty, with his brilliant analytical brain, not considered the problem of aging hereditary trustees before he signed the ninth codicil? Secondly, as he grew older himself, he judged age and experience to be a distinct advantage rather than a drawback. What made him change his views at the age of eighty-three? Thirdly, the twenty-first codicil handed control of his fortune to professional managers, a species he held in poor esteem. ('Some of my executives wouldn't know when to come in out of the rain,' he used to growl, pulling down the corners of his mouth and shaking his head.) Why would he suddenly decide to hand over his vast fortune to the very managers he had formerly despised? Fourthly, although his relationship with his sons was unquestionably cold and remote, it was no worse in 1976 than it had been for years; certainly none of them did anything to make him suddenly despair of the idea of primogeniture. Why did he abandon a principle he had cherished all his life?

There was one other oddity about the whole affair. Getty was careful to cancel small bequests to members of staff who had either left his employment or died. At least four people mentioned in the will had left Sutton Place before he signed the twenty-first codicil; none was omitted. He had also meticulously recorded the signing of previous codicils in his diary. Although by March 1976 he was no longer able to write, he was still dictating a daily journal to a secretary. The entry for 11 March *makes no mention of signing a codicil.*

*   *   *

One immediate effect of Getty's death was to release a torrent of money from the Sarah C. Getty Trust to the next generation. While he was alive, Getty was the sole beneficiary and he parcelled out relatively frugal amounts to his sons and their children. None of the younger Gettys could claim to be particularly rich while J. Paul Getty was alive; it was just not in his nature to hand out money to his family, even though the annual income from the trust's forty-two per cent stake in Getty Oil ran into millions of dollars.

The moment their father died J. Paul Getty II and his brother, Gordon, became millionaires overnight as each of them was immediately entitled to a third of the trust's income – about eleven million dollars a year, give or take a million depending on stock-market fluctuations. The remaining third was divided equally between the three daughters of the late George F. Getty II.

Suddenly awash with funds the Getty family found there were many scores to settle and no end of lawyers willing, not to say eager, to help settle them.

The eldest of George's daughters – twenty-four-year-old Anne – was the first to invest some of her new-found riches in litigation. In November 1976, Anne Getty filed a suit at Los Angeles Superior Court contesting her grandfather's will and seeking to have the twenty-first codicil revoked.

This action, seen as the first round in a protracted struggle for control of the Getty fortune with explosive ramifications for both the J. Paul Getty Museum and the Getty Oil Company, launched a bonanza for lawyers around the world. (Lawyers also did rather well out of the will – probate fees, shared between three law firms, totalled $13,224,851.) 'The Gettys have enough money to fuel the legal engines forever,' said William Newsom, longtime friend of the family and a justice in the Court of Appeal in San Francisco. 'Lawyers centuries hence will be sending their sons to college because of the Gettys. It's sick.'

Anne Getty seemed an unlikely litigant at first sight. Quiet and intensely shy she lived in a small chalet with peeling paint on the beach at Corona del Mar, a yachting resort south of Los Angeles. Like her two younger sisters, she was a keen environmentalist, with few interests beyond the gentle pursuits of surfing and whale-watching. But all three of George's daughters – known collectively in the family as 'the Georgettes' – were fiercely loyal and possessive, with their grand-father's blood flowing strongly in their veins. They viewed themselves very much as the Getty girls of Getty Oil, the company their great-grandfather founded, their grandfather built into an empire and their father should have inherited. It was an inheritance they did not intend to see squandered.

Anne's younger sister, Claire, had visited Sutton Place unexpectedly three months before her grandfather died. She was shocked by his condition and told Anne later that she did not think he was able to understand what was going on. It was this that prompted Anne to take up the cudgels on behalf of the family to get the twenty-first codicil thrown out. She alleged that Norris Bramlett and C. Lansing Hays had conspired to influence her grandfather against the interests of the family at a time when he was too ill to know what he was doing and that they had devised the twenty-first codicil to obtain a voice for themselves in Getty Oil operations. Her grandfather, she claimed, would never have signed it if he had been in his right mind.

The petition asserted that Bramlett 'isolated the decedent from most of his ordinary and normal friends, companions and acquaintances, provided for his emotional needs, catered to his whims, offered attentions and flatteries to the decedent and by his [Bramlett's] acts and deeds did create a situation in which decedent relied on said respondent for his daily needs.'

A harrowing picture was painted of Getty's dying days. It was said he was suffering from cancer, palsy, Parkinson's disease and a chronic disorder of the central nervous system, resulting in 'limited mobility, slowness, weakness, tremors, muscular rigidity, forgetfulness, hearing and seeing afflictions, delusions and fears ... the decedent's physical and mental faculties had become so impaired that he was easily influenced by those in whom he had confidence.'

Bramlett vigorously denied the accusations, but never had to contest them in court because Miss Getty's suit was doomed from the start. Probate law in California requires people who contest a will to have a pecuniary interest in it. Anne Getty had no such interest, indeed was nowhere mentioned in the will's final twenty-three pages. Since her financial position would be unaffected by the outcome, her suit was dismissed in December 1976. She appealed the decision both to the Californian Court of Appeal and the California Supreme Court, without success.

'Annie was badly advised,' said Gordon Getty. 'She became convinced there was some dark plot to manipulate Father. It just wasn't true. I think it was true that some of his girlfriends would have been delighted to keep other girlfriends away, but that was limited to the girlfriends. There was certainly no conspiracy and no one except Annie argued that my father's faculties were in question. When I got to Sutton Place shortly before he died, he was perfectly capable of understanding an argument and still competent to sign a document, even then.'

While Miss Anne Getty was occupied challenging the will, the comely Mrs Rosabella Burch was pursuing a claim of her own in Los Angeles for a somewhat bigger share of the estate, submitting that Getty not only promised to support her for the rest of her life, but also agreed to

311

pay for the education of her two children. Instead of the five hundred shares allotted to her in the will she suggested six times that number, plus one thousand dollars a month for life, would be more acceptable. When the action began to look less promising she settled out of court for around a hundred and fifty thousand dollars, which included an award of seventy-five thousand dollars for her son, Paul Bernard and a hundred dollars for her daughter, Carolina. Lawyers refused to say why Carolina received so little, but there was no shortage of predictable gossip.

Rosabella announced afterwards that she planned to write a sensational book about what went on at Sutton Place, promising it would upset a lot of people. 'Perhaps certain persons, afraid of what I know, will try to stop me but I am determined to tell the true story. All sides of life at Sutton Place will be revealed – the intrigues, the sadness, the infighting between members of his staff and other women competing for his favour. Sometimes it was like war. I used to sit with him for hours, telling him stories just to amuse him. His eyes would sparkle because he loved my company so much.' Mrs Burch's book never appeared, neither did Mrs Burch. The garden of her little house near Sutton Place became overgrown and neighbours said they thought she had gone back to South America.

Other Gettys, as well as Anne, were busy filing suits. Gail Getty sued her former husband, J. Paul Getty II, for non-payment of one hundred and sixty thousand dollars owed to their children's trust fund, which was set up at the time of their divorce, and Gordon Getty petitioned San Francisco Superior Court, claiming that his father had improperly removed him as a trustee of the museum back in 1966, alleging 'vindictiveness and retaliation'.

Next into court was 'film producer' Ronald Getty, whose absence at his father's deathbed and at the memorial services held in London and Los Angeles had not gone unnoticed. Ronald brought a civil suit against the J. Paul Getty Museum for $28,522,041. He claimed 'ancient documents' discovered among his father's personal effects revealed that in May or June of 1940 his grandmother had intended to rescind the Sarah C. Getty Trust and set up a new one in which Ronnie would have been an equal beneficiary with his brothers. The documents showed that his father had dissuaded Sarah from making the change by promising he would make special provision for Ronnie in his will. As the old man had failed to do so, Ronald was claiming from the museum's inheritance the amount he would have received at that date had Getty kept his promise.

Ronald's suit attracted the attention of the US Internal Revenue Service, which was looking for every opportunity to raise taxes on Getty's estate. The IRS claimed that because the suit made it impossible to calculate precisely how much the museum would receive, it could not be considered a charitable contribution since such contributions must be capable, under law, of precise calculation. If it was not a charitable contribution, clearly tax would have to be paid – the IRS slapped in a bill for $628,631,523 and 81 cents.

After some initial panic, lawyers acting for all three parties reached an agreement. The museum settled Ronald's suit with a payoff of ten million dollars and agreed to pay the IRS forty-five per cent of the payoff in settlement of their claim.

Flushed with this success, Ronald then sued his half-brothers and his three nieces to try and force them to cut him in on the Sarah C. Getty Trust. There was a certain amount of drawing in of breath in Los Angeles Superior Court when the extent of the imbalance between them was revealed. While Paul and Gordon were each receiving in excess of eleven million dollars a year from the trust, Ronald's share, it was pointed out, was fixed at three thousand dollars a year.

In any other family but the Gettys, it would probably have been considered entirely reasonable for Ronald to ask Paul, Gordon and the Georgettes to share their good fortune by chipping in a quarter of everything they received from the trust and thus making Ronnie an equal beneficiary. But neither Paul nor Gordon, nor any of the Georgettes showed the slightest inclination to accede to Ronald's request. Their attitude, discreetly couched in legal terminology in the accumulating files at Los Angeles Superior Court, was that Ronnie's situation was Ronnie's bad luck and nothing to do with them.

Once again Ronald's case rested on the legal significance of Sarah Getty's intentions, so far as they could be ascertained. The court learned that in her initial decision to effectively exclude Ronnie from the trust, his grandmother had been guided by purely egalitarian motives. It was not that she had had anything in particular against Ronnie, but simply a question of his expectations. When the trust was being drafted in 1934 it was believed that Ronnie would eventually inherit a substantial fortune from his maternal grandfather, Dr Otto Helmle, who was a wealthy German industrialist. As none of her other grandsons had similarly rich maternal relations, it was agreed that Ronnie would receive nothing from the trust except a nominal stipend.

But the situation of the Helmle family in Germany changed dramatically with the rise of Hitler. Dr Helmle was an outspoken opponent of the Nazis and went the way of all such courageous men: in 1937 his assets were confiscated by the German government and he was sent to a concentration camp. Getty claimed to be unaware of what was happening to Dr Helmle (curious, considering the number of trips he made to Germany in the thirties), but Sarah – then in her eighties – began to fret that no provision was made for Ronnie in the event that he did not

313

inherit the Helmle fortune. Getty told her not to worry and promised her that he would make sure Ronnie got an equal share of the trust with his brothers. Nevertheless, the old lady left Ronnie two-hundred-thousand-dollars worth of Getty Oil shares in her will, perhaps not entirely trusting her son's good intentions.

After the war, when Helmle's attempts to recover his property or win compensation failed, Getty constantly assured both Ronnie and his mother, Fini, that he would make arrangements to include the boy in the trust. He never did and Ronald Getty only discovered the awful truth after his father had died.

The consequence of Getty's failure to carry out his promise, an affidavit explained, was that the defendants in the case were being 'unjustly enriched by receiving from the Family Trust one third more than they are entitled to receive . . . one fourth of all sums received or to be received by said Defendants rightfully belongs to Plaintiff and said Defendants have no other or better right thereto.'

It was not an argument the judges felt they could accept. After dragging through the courts for years, Ronald's suit was eventually dismissed in January 1984, by which time his three thousand dollars a year looked even sillier against the incomes of the other beneficiaries — Paul and Gordon were then each receiving in excess of a hundred and twenty million dollars a year.

The judge sympathised with Ronald but found that no enforceable promissory agreement had ever been made to equalise his share, neither was there evidence of misrepresentation by Getty to his mother. In any event the action was barred by the Statute of Limitations, since Ronnie and his mother had had many opportunities to sue to redress the balance while the old man was alive.

Gordon, too, was sympathetic. 'I think my father should have treated the four of us alike,' he said. 'It is a mystery to me why Ronnie was never included. I personally would have been happy to cut him into the trust, but it was enormously complicated because of tax reasons. It is not as if he is *in want*. My grandmother did seek to redress things in her will by leaving him some Getty Oil shares. If he had held on to them they would be worth fifty million dollars now, and on top of that there is the ten-million-dollar tax-free settlement he got from the museum. They are big enough sums to make Ronnie's claim more to do with prestige and one-upmanship than any tangible use. I hardly ever see him now; I haven't set eyes on him for about a year. The last I heard he was in the real-estate business.'

At the J. Paul Getty Museum at Malibu, the founder's money was causing rather different agonies. Frightened of death and unwilling to be reminded of his own mortality, Getty never told the staff at the museum that they would be receiving something of a windfall after he had gone; indeed, in 1972 he intimated that no further funds would be forthcoming. Thus they were both flabbergasted and totally unprepared when the will was read and they learned that the Getty had become the most richly-endowed museum in the world.

By the time the estate was distributed, high interest rates, a stock split and booming share prices had increased the museum's endowment from $700,000,000 to a staggering $1,260,000,000. Federal tax laws require such institutions to spend a percentage of their income annually and in the case of the J. Paul Getty Museum it meant spending nearly fifty-four million dollars every year.

The news set alarm bells ringing in the art world and there was much worried speculation that the Getty's monster chequebook would drive up prices and cause chaos in the market. The legacy effectively meant that a small, rather eccentric provincial museum was suddenly in a position to outbid every conceivable rival for the few remaining privately-owned masterpieces likely to come on the market in the foreseeable future. The Getty's *need* to spend more than a million dollars a week was laconically contrasted to the acquisition fund of the prestigious National Gallery in London, which stood at rather less than six million dollars for the whole year.

Curators at the Getty did their best to dispel suspicions that the museum would plunder the art treasures of Europe, but they were unable to dispel the view that it was a museum with too much money. In the rarified milieu of top auction rooms in London and New York, dealers and collectors talked gloomily of prices being artificially inflated by what became known as 'the Getty factor'.

The museum's first major acquisitions did nothing to convince the art world its fears were unjustified. In 1977 it paid $3,900,000 for a life-size bronze statue of a young athlete dating from the fourth century BC and believed to be the only surviving work by Lysippus, court sculptor to Alexander the Great. This hauntingly beautiful piece, soon to be known as 'The Getty Bronze', embroiled the museum in an international art scandal.

Originally discovered, encrusted with barnacles, on the sea bed near the Italian port of Fano in 1964, the statue was bought by an antiquities dealer and hidden in the home of a local priest while negotiations were opened with possible purchasers in Europe. Police, acting on a tip that an archaeological treasure was about to be smuggled out of the country, raided the priest's house. They were too late: the bronze was gone. It disappeared for some years, then turned up in South America where it was acquired by Artemis, a Luxembourg-based art consortium.

When it was revealed that the J. Paul Getty Museum had bought the bronze there was an uproar in Italy and the museum was accused of buying an illegally-exported treasure. Undoubtedly, this furore fuelled fears of the Gettys' potential to pillage the European art market, fears that were further exacerbated when the museum set an auction record in 1979 by paying two million dollars for a Louis XV rococo corner cabinet designed by Nicolas Pineau and crafted by Jacques Dubois. A flood of record-breaking bids soon followed — $3,200,000 for a marble statue by Giovanni da Bologna, $4,000,000 for a Goya, $2,000,000 for two Louis XV silver soup tureens, $2,700,000 for a late Renaissance masterpiece by Dosso Dossi, $3,000,000 for a Gauguin, $5,500,000 for four Gobelin tapestries...

'The world art market will never be quite the same,' the *Economist* declared. 'Though the Getty museum promises to use its riches responsibly, the fact remains that when it really wants something, not even the mighty Metropolitan Museum of Art in New York, which sits on an endowment fund only one sixth as large, will be able to outbid it. Art connoisseurs shudder.'

The old man would have been horrified at being commemorated by 'the Getty factor', an epithet synonymous with avarice and obscene wealth. 'I don't think there is any glory in being remembered as old moneybags,' he once said. 'I suppose I'll be a footnote in history as a businessman, but I'd rather be remembered as an art collector, not a money-laden businessman.'

While the benighted Getty family squabbled over the will and the art world came to terms with 'the Getty factor', the late billionaire lay in refrigeration at the Forest Lawn Memorial Park in Glendale. His body had been flown to Los Angeles within a week of his death at Sutton Place, but when the coffin arrived in California it was discovered that no one had obtained the necessary permits for him to be buried, as he had requested, in the grounds of the ranch. Nearly three years of bureaucratic wrangling were to pass before he could be interred in the marble mausoleum behind the museum, along with George and Timmy who were moved from other cemeteries in Los Angeles.

But at least, in the end, one of his dearest wishes was granted. He returned to California.

20. 'Not all the Gettys are interested in becoming billionaires'

Unlike his grandfather, Paul Getty III cared nothing for money. When the old man's will was made public, Paul was in London and he told reporters that he 'didn't give a damn' that he had been left nothing. 'Not all the Gettys are interested in becoming billionaires,' he said.

His own billionaire prospects looked distinctly unpromising. He had disqualified himself from inheriting a share of the trust set up when his parents divorced by marrying his girlfriend, Martine, when he was only seventeen. (Under the terms of the trust, any of the children who married before the age of twenty-two forfeited their allotment.) A few months later, a Los Angeles court appointed his maternal grandfather to be his 'financial guardian' because of his inability to handle money. No, Paul Getty III did not look set to become a billionaire.

Paul emerged from the ordeal of the kidnapping in December 1973 severely traumatised, even more disturbed than formerly and with his nerves in shreds. Beset by paranoid fears, he saw kidnappers all about him and the slightest incident – real or imagined – would arouse his suspicions. He would fidget unhappily in a restaurant if someone was standing in one place too long or looked towards him too frequently. Sudden noise, sometimes no more than the jangle of the telephone or a tap at the door, frightened him. A stranger approaching him in the street with the innocent purpose of asking directions brought him out in a sweat. And whereas he had once exulted in speed, it now terrified him; he was always asking taxi drivers to slow down.

Nights were worst. 'He was afraid to go to sleep,' said Martine, 'and he had terrible, terrible nightmares. He would scream and toss around in bed. He started to drink heavily just so that he could get to sleep. I remember sitting with him in the evenings while he drank one beer after another. He was not like an alcoholic; all he wanted was to sleep.'

What most worried Martine and Paul's mother, Gail, was that he absolutely refused to talk about what had happened. Both women believed that it would be therapeutic for him to re-examine the whole appalling experience rather than keep it bottled up inside him; but Paul would not be drawn. Every time Gail gently prompted him to tell her about it, he shrugged and shook his head in despair. 'What's the use?'

he always said. 'What's the fucking use?' He never once asked why it had taken so long to pay the ransom.

Paul was in a private clinic in Rome for two weeks, then his mother took him to the Austrian ski resort of Igls, near Innsbruck, to recuperate. His brother, Mark, and his sisters, Aileen and Ariadne, went along too, as did Martine and one or two of Paul's friends from Rome. Gail wanted to give him time to relax, rebuild his strength and try to forget.

While they were enjoying the snow and the mountains the *carabiniere* colonel in Lagonegro, where Paul was first interrogated after his release, claimed to have discovered new evidence that there had been 'two kidnappings'. In a report to the public prosecutor the colonel dredged up the old allegation that Paul had been seen 'on more than one occasion' in the Trastevere section of Rome after his disappearance. The report concluded that the first kidnapping had been a hoax – probably organised by Paul himself – and when it failed to produce a ransom, real kidnappers somehow took over.

Paul learned of this development in an Italian newspaper. He read the story in silence, then angrily tossed the paper aside, refusing to discuss it with either family or friends – not even with Martine. The 'two kidnappings' theory was to haunt him for years, for it meant, effectively, that he could never be exonerated from collusion in the crime. Even when the Italian police finally began making arrests and a number of the kidnappers were sent to jail for long periods, a question mark remained over his involvement.

After two months in the Alps, skiing nearly every day, they all returned to Rome. Paul and Martine moved into a small, anonymous hotel as he did not want to return to their old apartment on the Via della Scala – it was too close to where he had been abducted. 'We were very reclusive,' Martine said. 'We hardly ever went out.'

Paul's post-kidnapping neuroses were not in any way soothed by the amount of attention he began to attract. His case had become something of a *cause célèbre* and he found himself inundated with fan mail – some of it addressed simply to 'Paul Getty, The Golden Hippie', a title that now seemed cruelly inappropriate. Everywhere he went in the city he was recognised, to his considerable discomfort. Girls flocked round him as if he were a rock star, pestering him for his autograph, none of them able to resist trying to catch a glimpse of the stump of his ear through his long unkempt hair. The worldwide publicity had turned the kidnapping and its aftermath into a macabre circus – in the Piazza Navona, where Paul used to hang out with his hippie friends, gypsies were selling stick-on 'Paul Getty ears' made of plastic.

In May 1974 Martine discovered she was pregnant and they began to think once more about getting married. Paul was still only seventeen and knew he would lose his inheritance from the divorce trust if he married before he was twenty-two. He did not hesitate for a moment. It seemed that money had brought nothing but misery to the Getty family; he loved Martine and wanted to marry her – why should he wait five years?

They planned a quiet wedding in Tuscany, where Gail had rented a house in the small town of Sovicille, near Siena. The date was set for 12 August, but there was a last-minute hitch when Paul's birth certificate could not be found and the ceremony had to be postponed for a month. This contretemps alerted the world's press and on Thursday 12 September, the day of the wedding, more than 120 reporters and photographers were in Sovicille to cover the event and sightseers were arriving by the busload.

When Martine and Paul arrived at the town hall for the ceremony, they were at first unable to get into the building because of the crowd. Photographers were everywhere – some had even clambered up trees and were leaning out of the branches, clicking furiously. Perspiring *carabinieri* reinforcements toting sub-machine-guns struggled unsuccessfully to keep order while the bride, in a black dress, and the groom, in a cotton Mao suit and white tennis shoes, pushed through the noisy crowd, followed by Gail, her three other children, Martine's twin sister, Jutta, and two friends who were to be witnesses.

Inside at last, still surrounded by scuffling photographers, Gail pleaded with Mayor Roberto Coverti to exclude the press; they all wanted the ceremony to be 'totally private', she said. But the mayor, thoroughly enjoying the unaccustomed limelight, insisted that the town hall was public property and he had no right to bar the public from entry. Martine was nervously watching Paul who, she could see, was becoming more and more tense.

With the mayor adamant that nothing could be done about the presence of the uninvited media, the sombre little wedding party elbowed its way through the jostling mass and into the room where the ceremony was to be held. Paul stood sullenly with his hands in his pockets and mumbled his responses so quietly that the mayor kept asking the witnesses 'Did you hear that?' Once they had been proclaimed man and wife, photographers began shouting at Paul to kiss the bride, but he shook his head and held tightly on to Martine's arm.

'I had imagined it so differently,' said Martine. 'We did not want all the publicity and we were hoping that if we got married in a small village we could do it privately. The day was ruined by all the photographers; the crowds made Paul very, very unhappy and nervous.'

They got away from Sovicille as soon as they could after the wedding and went to Munich, Martine's home town, for a few weeks. Neither of them was sure what they wanted to do with their lives, although they had often discussed writing film scripts or music together. Martine thought they could probably both get work as actors, and they dreamed about writing their own film, directing and acting in it. If that didn't work out, they could perhaps be photographers or painters. Both of them were creative and full of hope and ideas, although Paul was still having terrible nightmares, still drinking heavily.

Towards the end of 1974, they decided they would set up home in Los Angeles and try to break into the film business. They rented a small house on the beach at Malibu and Paul enrolled at the nearby Pepperdine University to study art, paying frequent visits to his grandfather's museum, just along the coast, where he was soon well liked by the curators, who enjoyed having a Getty show an active interest. On 24 January 1975, Martine gave birth to a son whom they named Paul Balthazar Getty. 'Paul was very happy about the baby,' she said. 'After the baby things were good for a while and he seemed to be getting better. He was very affectionate, very dedicated to the children.'

For a while it seemed they had a chance of being just another young couple with two small children, that Paul had outdistanced his demons at last, but he was soon in trouble again – firstly, with money. They were living off a thousand-dollars-a-month allowance from Paul's mother, but Paul had no idea how to budget for his family. Because he was a Getty, he had access to unlimited credit in restaurants and shops and seemed unable to avoid running up debts. Gail asked her father, a judge in San Francisco, what she should do and they decided between them to ask for a court order to supervise Paul's finances.

In April, a Los Angeles court appointed Judge George B. Harris to be Paul's 'financial guardian'. Gail's lawyer told the court that Paul was financially improvident, easily victimised and no more knew how to keep a chequebook or put deposits in a bank than a thirteen-year-old. 'There are a great many people only too willing to take advantage of him,' he added. 'He can go into a store and once he satisfies them who he is, he can walk out with anything.'

The fact that the grandson of the richest man in the world was unable to manage his own modest finances naturally attracted the attention of newspapers, both in the United States and Europe. Paul pretended not to be bothered by the fuss and continued very much as he had before. Three months later, he was arrested on a ludicrous charge of grand larceny.

Driving home late one night in his battered Volkswagen, he skidded on a bend and crashed into a guard rail. He abandoned the car and had made up his mind to hitch a lift when he spotted a truck parked in the driveway of a house with the keys in the ignition. He decided he would 'borrow' it to get home and return it the following morning. Barely a mile down the road, he was overtaken by a Highway Patrol car with its siren wailing. He pulled into the side of the road expecting the worst and to his relief was only given a ticket for speeding.

He was not as lucky as he imagined. The truck he had so calmly appropriated belonged to the son of a local judge. It was reported stolen early next morning and was traced to Paul through the speeding ticket. He was arrested at his home later that day. After much wrangling by lawyers, the grand larceny charge was dropped and Paul eventually pleaded guilty to the minor charge of failing to report an accident. He was fined $150 and placed on probation for two years.

Martine did not worry overmuch about such mishaps since she could see sharper rocks ahead. 'Paul had started to study and tried, really tried, to get work as an actor. But a lot of people in Los Angeles were interested in Paul and he started going out alone while I stayed home with the children. I don't really know who he was seeing, but I do know he got involved in drugs again.'

As she watched Paul spin helplessly out of control, Martine conceived a deep loathing for Los Angeles. It seemed to her that there was no limit to the number of people in and around the movie community who were not just willing, but eager, to push Paul off the rails. There appeared to be no limit to the range of drugs he could obtain and certainly he had no inhibitions about recklessly experimenting with them. It was almost inevitable that he would soon become hooked. Less than twelve months after arriving in California, Paul was a heroin addict.

Martine, who was trying to get work as a photographer as well as look after the children, did her best to provide a stable home for Paul but he flitted in and out of their lives, sometimes disappearing for weeks on end. He always stayed in contact with Martine by telephone, but she often had no idea where he was. In the summer of 1976, Paul suggested they should leave Los Angeles and live in London for a while. Martine was happy to go, hoping that Paul might find it easier to settle down in London away from the insidious temptations of LA.

They flew to England with the children and found a small apartment in Notting Hill Gate. A few days later, Paul learned from the newspapers that his grandfather had died. To Martine's distress, reporters soon ferreted them out and she took to climbing over a wall at the back of their apartment whenever she had to go out, so as to avoid the posse of newshounds waiting outside their front door.

Six days after the memorial service for J. Paul Getty I at the American Church in Mayfair, a policeman on late-night patrol through Hyde Park discovered a couple engaged in oral intercourse on the bandstand and arrested them both for 'offensive behaviour'. The young man gave his name as Paul Getty. Next morning, Paul and the girl, whom he had met at a party earlier the previous evening, were each fined ten pounds at Bow Street Magistrates Court. Martine found she was again obliged to enter and leave their apartment over the back wall.

In July, Paul was back in America and was photographed at a party at Regine's in New York with Liz Taylor, Shirley MacLaine, Halston, Diana Vreeland and Huntington Hartford. From New York, he drifted on to Los Angeles where he was given a small part in an avant-garde film being made by Wim Wenders.

Martine said she could no longer stomach Los Angeles and that the children needed some stability: they could not just trail around after Paul for the rest of their lives, particularly as they would soon be starting school. Paul agreed, but felt that with a role in the new Wim Wenders film he was at last on the verge of a big break and he wanted to stay in LA. In the end, Martine decided to move with the children to San Francisco, which was a city she liked and which was close enough for them all to stay in contact.

It seemed they had attained a measure of peace – a solution of sorts to the logistical problem of staying together. Martine found a job as a teacher in San Francisco and made a proper home for herself and the children. Paul was a frequent visitor and when he could not come up to San Francisco, she sometimes flew down to Los Angeles to spend weekends with him. They talked constantly on the telephone and Martine felt reasonably encouraged that it would be all right in the end. 'I kept thinking,' she said, 'there's a chance, a good chance.'

But Paul remained chronically unstable, vacillating between sunshine and darkness. Sometimes he seemed determined to overcome his problems, put the past behind him, make a career for himself and re-establish his relationship with Martine and the children. He was in and out of hospitals and clinics looking for a cure to his drug addiction and drinking; he even entered into psychotherapy with Martine as a last-ditch attempt to rescue their marriage.

Friends who saw the sunny side of Paul during this period found him charming, funny, very bright and interested in everything around him. Bill Newsom, Paul's godfather, remembered going out with him one day and briefing his own small son not to mention the kidnapping. 'We were all sitting in the car,' he said, 'and I became uncomfortably aware that my son was staring at Paul's head, trying to see where his ear was severed. In the end he suddenly said "Paul, how many ears have you got?" Paul nearly fell out of the car laughing. "I used to have two," he said, "but now I've only got one." It was wonderful to hear him laugh like that.'

But there were the black times, too, when it appeared that Paul was intent on self-destruction. He abused his body with a plethora of drugs and alcohol, seeking escape from the periods of fear, confusion and unhappiness to which he was still so vulnerable. The heavy drinking he claimed was necessary to send him to sleep escalated to the point where he was drinking a quart of Wild Turkey whisky every day. As for drugs, he tried everything, in every possible permutation of oblivion-inducing cocktail.

At the beginning of 1978 Doctor Burt Brent, a plastic surgeon at Stanford University Medical Center in San Francisco, fashioned a new ear for Paul from flexible cartilage cut from two of his ribs. Two operations were required to remove the cartilage and then graft it into place. The surgery was reported to be a success, both cosmetically and psychologically.

Not long afterwards, Paul was given a much bigger role – ironically as a young alcoholic – in another movie directed by Wim Wenders, entitled *The State of Things*. Paul admired Wenders enormously and was very excited to get the part, but Martine became more worried every time she saw him. 'He had been away, filming, in Portugal and he looked ill when he came back. He was having liver and kidney problems and I thought he was in very poor shape.

'He came to see us in San Francisco and we spent some time together working every day on a film script. At that time he was drinking a bit, although he was not on heroin. He was trying to get off it with methadone, but he didn't look good. I was very worried.'

A few days after Paul returned to Los Angeles, his mother telephoned Martine and broke the shocking news that Paul had had a stroke. It was very serious, she said. Martine had better get down there straight away.

Paul had been sharing a house in Westwood, Los Angeles, with an Italian girl, Emmanuella Stuzzhi, and a young Englishman. On the afternoon of 5 April 1981 Paul had gone to bed, complaining that he did not feel well. In the early evening he got up, still saying he did not feel too good, and went to lie down on a sofa in the sitting-room.

Neither of the other two people in the house took much notice of him for some time. It was not in the least unusual for Paul to pass out from drink or drugs or both. Several hours passed before Emmanuella tried to rouse him. She shook him gently on the shoulder, then tapped his cheek. When he did not respond, she shook him by both shoulders, harder and harder, the fear rising as Paul failed to wake. By now thoroughly frightened, she slapped his face repeatedly, crying 'Wake up, Paul. *Wake up!*'

But Paul did not stir and eventually Emmanuella phoned for help. Within a few minutes, the apparently lifeless body of Paul Getty was being carried out on a stretcher and slipped into the back of an ambulance which howled through the night streets of Los Angeles to the Cedars-Sinai Medical Center.

At the centre a call was put through to Gail, who now lived not far away, in Brentwood. She arrived by car shortly after and waited anxiously while doctors examined her son. They were not able to say much at first, except that Paul had had a severe stroke and was in a coma. To what extent his brain had been damaged, no one could yet tell.

Gail called Martine, who hurriedly made arrangements for the children to be looked after, then caught the first flight from San Francisco. Together the two women kept watch at Paul's bedside, waiting and praying for him to regain consciousness.

The following day Bill Newsom also came down from San Francisco, to try to reconstruct the events leading up to Paul's seizure: the doctors were anxious to know what drugs he might have taken immediately before he fell into the coma. He questioned Emmanuella at length and talked to as many of Paul's friends as he could find. All of them agreed that his godson had probably been on nothing more than methadone and tranquillisers and that he had not even been drinking much in the previous few weeks.

Paul's younger brother Mark, then twenty-one and a student at Oxford, flew home to visit Paul with his sisters, Aileen and Ariadne. They talked to him for hours, hoping their voices would stir a response, and brought in tapes of his favourite records.

Paul remained in a coma for six weeks. When he regained consciousness, the terrible extent of the damage was at last revealed. He was blind, unable to speak and paralysed. 'Everything was gone,' said Newsom, 'except his mind.' He was twenty-four years old.

None of the doctors offered much hope that he would ever recover sufficiently to lead a normal life but Gail, gathering courage from she knew not where, refused to accept the gloomy prognosis. She was determined that Paul was going to get better and resolved to find the best treatment in the world for her son. She did not care how much it cost: her son was Paul Getty and the Gettys had more money than they knew what to do with.

There was no shortage of people claiming they could help the young man: Gail put them all on the payroll.

The dingy, double-fronted house in Cheyne Walk, where Paul Getty II had lived as a recluse ever since the death of Talitha, was once owned by the painter and poet Dante Gabriel Rossetti. His wife died there of an overdose of laudanum in 1862 and the melancholy Rossetti grieved for her behind the shutters at 16 Cheyne Walk. After Rossetti's death in 1882 his friend Algernon Swinburne, the poet and critic, moved into the house and suffered a collapse brought on by drinking and masochism.

Along with the ghosts of Rossetti and Swinburne, Getty shared the place with a single manservant and a secretary, Mrs Joan Gadsdon. 'He was highly intelligent, brilliant,' said Mrs Gadsdon. 'He tried to keep me away from the bad things, didn't want me to get involved, but I knew the pushers were the problem; all the lovely people gradually left and he did not have many friends. He never mentioned Talitha, but there were photographs of her all over the place.'

By the opulent standards of Cheyne Walk – the best address in Chelsea – the house was shabby and neglected. Behind the iron railings, the white paintwork of the windows was peeling and the brown front door was flaked. In contrast the gardens at front and rear were meticulously tended, planted and replanted throughout the year so that Talitha's favourite flowers were always in bloom.

Very thin and pale, Getty rarely stepped outside the front door of 16 Cheyne Walk except sometimes at night when he would leave the house at around one o'clock in the morning in his red Mercedes and return shortly before dawn. He was said to spend most of his days poring over antiquarian book catalogues, sucking cream caramels and worrying about his phlebitis, which caused his legs to swell unpleasantly. One of his few regular visitors was his doctor, who arrived in a chauffeur-driven Bentley each morning and stayed for around half an hour.

Closed-circuit television security systems guarded both front and back of the house to provide some protection for his antiquarian books, perhaps the most valuable collection in the world in private hands and reputed to include one of the oldest copies of the Koran. Getty was no dilettante and his knowledge of seventeenth- and eighteenth-century books, particularly fine bindings, was profound: he could take any volume from the hundreds on his shelves and minutely describe its provenance.

His collection grew rapidly after the death of his father in 1976, when he became a beneficiary of the Sarah C. Getty Trust, with an income of around twenty million dollars a year. As well as buying books he also began making substantial donations to charities and appeals, becoming a major benefactor of the National Film Archives. He gave randomly, often prompted by something he had seen on television. In June 1978, after watching a report on the television news of fighting in Eritrea, he telephoned Independent Television News and offered a £7500 donation to the hospital featured in the bulletin. Not long afterwards, he responded to a BBC appeal to send five stranded orphan seals back to sea; a few days after that, he was writing out a large cheque for medical aid for Poland.

Friends speculated that he wanted to give his money away to spite his dead father. The old man would never have approved of the income from the Sarah C. Getty Trust, which was supposed to preserve the family fortune for the Gettys, being frittered away left, right and centre to any cause that took his son's fancy while he sat watching television, drinking white rum and sniffing heroin. The certain knowledge of his father's disapproval made the giving even more pleasurable.

But Getty's generosity stopped short when it came to his own son. After the kidnapping, Getty contemptuously referred to him as 'the earless wonder': he viewed him as a hopeless layabout who caused trouble wherever he went. Nevertheless, when he heard about Paul's stroke in April 1981, he was appalled and at first gave his lawyers "carte blanche" to pay his medical bills.

Difficulties soon arose when bills from many different doctors began arriving at Cheyne Walk in astonishing numbers, demanding ever increasing sums. Getty and Gail argued frequently on the telephone. Their relationship was always prickly and they could rarely agree on anything; now they were in serious dispute. He accused her of trying to expurgate her guilt at not bringing up her son properly and said he thought the American doctors were trying to save 'a vegetable' – he wasn't going to spend money on a vegetable. He would pay proper and necessary bills, but not bills from whole lists of doctors. The more Getty thought about what was going on, the more he became convinced he was being exploited and the less inclined he was to pay up.

While this argument was going on, Getty learned that the beautiful Jessica Kitson, 'Pen's' daughter and godchild to Paul I, had been found dead from a heroin overdose on the kitchen floor in a small terraced house in seedy Shepherd's Bush, with her infant son, Wolf, asleep on a sofa nearby. She was only thirty-four years old. It was a sordid end for a young woman who was Debutante of the Year when she was seventeen and whose coming-out ball at Sutton Place was the highlight of the season. An inquest recorded a verdict of misadventure and noted the cause of death was heroin and alcohol poisoning.

In August 1981, Gail apparently tired of arguing with her former husband and shocked the family by filing a suit at Los Angeles Superior Court claiming that Getty had 'failed and refused' to pay for the care of his 'incapacitated adult child who is blind, paralysed and unable to speak articulately'. She asked for twenty-five thousand dollars a month to meet bills for 'the frequent services of doctors in various specialties, including neurology, psychiatry and internal medicine . . . and the regular services of qualified speech, physical and occupational therapists.'

The suit caused a sensation: even for the Getty family, it was almost beyond belief that a man as rich as Paul Getty could refuse to pay for the treatment which held out the only faint hope for improvement in his son's pathetic condition. It was the first the world knew of the tragedy that had befallen young Paul Getty, the 'Golden Hippie'. Most newspapers came to the conclusion, in the light of the young man's record, that the stroke occurred after 'a night of alcohol and drug abuse'.

Paul's twenty-two-year-old sister Aileen, who had some experience of the media having married Elizabeth Taylor's son, Michael Wilding, only a month previously, leapt to her brother's defence. 'The newspapers made it sound like he'd had a night on the town and that he had been taking illegal drugs,' she said. 'People just assumed, because of his reputation, that that was the case. It wasn't like that at all. He had been ill for two weeks before the stroke happened and was only taking prescription drugs. He hadn't had any alcohol in his body for eight days.'

Aileen's protests did little good and a further untruth quickly became enshrined in newspaper libraries everywhere: the boy widely believed by the media to have engineered his own kidnapping was now similarly believed to have orchestrated his own appalling fate.

Paul's brother and both his sisters pleaded with their father not to fight Gail's suit. Bill Newsom also tried to use his influence to persuade his old schoolfriend to change his mind; even Getty's own lawyers advised him to settle the case.

Getty first instructed his lawyers to fight a subpoena for him to appear in court in Los Angeles. He said he was unable to travel because of 'circulatory problems' and argued that the case should be dismissed on the grounds that he was a British resident and therefore not subject to the jurisdiction of Californian courts.

'By this motion,' Ed Stadum, the lawyer representing Paul and his mother told the court, 'one of the world's richest men is attempting to defeat his blind, paralysed son's actions for support by raising technical and insubstantial objections. It seems beyond comprehension that a man with the kind of resources he has would hesitate for one minute to do everything medically possible for his son.'

At a hearing in Los Angeles on 30 November, Judge Bruce Geernaert rejected the arguments submitted by Getty's lawyers and delivered a stinging rebuke to their client. 'Mr Getty should be ashamed of himself,' the judge said. 'He is spending far more on court obligations than living up to his moral duties. It is shameful he is spending money on all these legal gymnastics, this is not what our courts are for.'

In London Getty issued a written statement to *The Times*, the only comment he would ever make on the affair: 'Anyone who believes I am unmoved by my son's tragedy, or willing to see him become a public charge, simply does not know me. I have never failed to meet my obligations towards my children under the legal settlements as agreed or my paternal responsibilities as I saw them.'

It was not a good enough explanation for Bill Newsom, his class-mate at St Ignatius High School, a witness at his wedding to Gail and godfather to Paul.

The lawsuit was preposterous, absolutely grotesque. What was going on in his mind I have no idea. I told him on the telephone I was appalled by what he was doing.

His actions were despicable and I could only attribute them to some kind of emotional disfigurement that had occurred over the years. My reading of the situation was that Paul somehow thought he was being taken advantage of; perhaps he believed the sums of money being expended were excessive. But the amounts were minuscule relative to his income, considerably less than one per cent. He had books in his library that cost more, much more, than it would have cost to look after his son for years.

The tragedy of young Paul was that he had had a hell of a hard time getting things together after the trauma of the kidnapping and the emotional damage done earlier in his life at the time of the divorce. His father never spent much time with him and when a ten-year-old boy who loves his father never gets to see him, it hurts.

Paul never spent much time with his own father and sometimes I wondered if subconsciously Paul was doing to his son what his father did to him.

When Getty's claim that Californian courts had no jurisdiction over him was dismissed, his lawyers changed tack, serving a notice of intention to arrange for their own medical examination. Getty wanted only to ensure that the boy was being properly cared for, but the move engendered deep suspicion in California.

'He was actually questioning the legitimacy of his son's condition,' said Newsom in disgust. 'He wanted to send over doctors from England to see if they could find some less severe impediment, while the boy was lying there, blind and paralysed. Any reasonable person would say there was nothing to discuss. To describe the boy as crippled was an understatement. He was as profoundly afflicted as it was possible to be and still be alive.'

While the legal wrangles continued, Paul's Uncle Gordon uncomplainingly paid all the medical bills and made sure that Martine and the children were looked after in San Francisco.

At his mother's house in Brentwood, therapists worked with Paul for up to twelve hours a day, six days a week. A nurse was on duty round the clock to feed and dress him and keep him clean. Twice a day, usually, he was carried to the heated swimming pool for exercises designed to coax life and movement back into his nerveless body. Encouraged by his mother, he worked at his exercises with extraordinary dedication and determination and if he brooded over what had happened, he rarely showed it. When he was not involved in therapy, he sat in the garden in his wheelchair, feeling the warmth of the Californian sun through his cotton pyjamas, listening to rock music or novels for the blind on recorded cassettes.

Although his spirits were usually good, unquestionably some days were better than others. Some days he could make out broad shapes and vague colours through the dark curtain of his blindness. He tried desperately to articulate and there were times when he could form almost-recognisable words. After six months nurses could stand him up, although his limbs were still grotesquely twisted; nevertheless Gail began to hope that one day he might perhaps walk again with sticks, maybe even see a little.

He liked to be taken to the beach to listen to the surf and on his twenty-fifth birthday the whole family took him out to his favourite Italian restaurant. He was able to indicate which dish he wanted by making a gurgling noise when the menu was read out to him.

Most weekends his brother Mark, then twenty-two and a political-science graduate at the University of California, spent hours sitting with Paul, joshing, reading to him or pretending to arm wrestle. Aileen, who was running a dress shop in Santa Barbara with her new husband, telephoned every day and twenty-year-old Ariadne, a student at Bennington College in Vermont, spent all her vacations at Brentwood to be with Paul.

Martine remained steadfastly loyal, visiting as often as she could afford the trip from San Francisco where she had had to give up her teaching job but had found part-time work in a bookshop. The children, Anna aged ten, and Paul Balthazar, six, telephoned Paul regularly. Little Paul Balthazar Getty was really too young to understand what had happened to his father, but he chattered away happily into the telephone, making what he could of Paul's strangled and largely unintelligible replies.

'Paul could understand what the children said to him,' Martine said. 'They telephoned him all the time and we tried to see as much of him as we could. It was impossible to say if he would ever get better; no one really knew what was going to happen. All we could do was hope.'

In February 1983, after nearly eighteen months of ferociously expensive litigation, J. Paul Getty II finally agreed to a settlement which provided 'fully and adequately' for his son's support. In Cheyne Walk, where Getty learned the medical bills now totalled almost $1 million a year, the perspective was different.

'It was the single greatest example of parental default in history,' said Ed Stadum after the settlement. 'How could a man as wealthy as Paul Getty turn his back on his son? All he had to do was reach for his chequebook.'

21. 'A curse on the family'

After the tragic loss of his son George, J.Paul Getty used to mutter gloomily that he could never be considered a good businessman: 'A good businessman always grooms a successor and there is no one to step into my shoes.' It was true: there was no one to replace him and Getty Oil remained in a state of limbo for some years following his death in 1976. It was as if the life had gone out of the company, just as it had flickered out in the old man's tired, withered and cancerous body.

During the twenty-odd years he had run Getty Oil from the anachronistic Tudor splendour of Sutton Place, Getty seemed not to be interested in further expansion (his last significant acquisition was Tidewater, in 1951) and Harold E. Berg, the new chairman, followed the same policy. Berg, a veteran oilman from Kansas who had started with Tidewater in 1937 and was one of Getty's closest confidants, was determined to perpetuate the old man's style of cautious, tough and stubborn management. Getty Oil made reasonable, but unspectacular, profits year by year until 1979 when decontrol of crude oil prices suddenly boosted earnings by eighty-three per cent to $604,400,000 on sales of $5,200,000,000.

By the summer of 1980 when Berg retired, Getty Oil had more than one billion dollars in cash in its coffers and was the target of considerable criticism in Wall Street for its conservatism. Berg's replacement, and the first chairman from outside the oil patch, was Sidney R.Petersen, a bespectacled, dapper, corporate and financial planner who had joined the company twenty-five years earlier straight from business school. Petersen was an ambitious and aggressive businessman and immediately embarked on a major programme of expansion and diversification, digging deeply into the cash box for acquisition funds.

Within a year of Petersen taking over as chairman, Getty Oil purchased fifteen offshore leases in Texas and Louisiana for $267,000,000, bought the Reserve Oil and Gas Company for $631,000,000 and then moved into the insurance and communication fields, prompted by a study of investment options commissioned by Petersen. The company's first important diversification outside natural resources was the acquisition of the ERC Corporation, an insurance company based in Kansas City, for $570,000,000, followed by a $10,000,000 bid for a cable-television sports network – Entertainment and Sports Programming Network Inc. Not long afterwards, Getty Oil entered into a joint venture with four major Hollywood studios to set up a pay-TV movie network called Premiere.

Petersen claimed that the company would not stray too far from the course mapped out by J. Paul Getty, although Getty never approved of diversification. 'I buy only my own stocks,' he said in 1967. 'I know that goes against one of the principles of good business, that you should be diversified – that you shouldn't own eighty per cent of one company, you should own one per cent of eighty companies. But I'd still rather have eighty per cent of one company.'

Getty Oil's rapid growth under Petersen left the stock considerably undervalued, selling for about one third of the company's underlying asset value. When executors of the J. Paul Getty Museum sold twenty-five per cent of the museum's shareholding in Getty Oil to comply with the tax laws, some analysts recommended that the company should purchase the museum's shares to boost the stock price but it chose instead to press forward with its expansion programme.

J. Paul Getty I had always hoped that whoever succeeded him as head of the company would move into Sutton Place, but neither Berg nor Petersen were inclined to move from Los Angeles to the English countryside. It was costing more than a million dollars a year to run the estate and while Getty Oil was heavily committed to exploration and development in the North Sea and other areas of Europe, planning restrictions prevented Sutton Place being converted into a practical regional office. In 1981, Getty Oil sold Sutton Place for seventeen million dollars to another American millionaire – Stanley J. Seeger Junior, a fifty-year-old art collector who had inherited a fortune from family interests in oil, lumber, railroads and land in the American southwest.

None of the Getty family showed an interest in buying Sutton Place, indeed none of them showed much interest in Getty Oil and for more than five years after the old man's death, the directors were able to run the company free from interference by any scion of the founder. But in 1982, a tall, curly-haired man often described as living 'in another world' appeared more and more frequently in the boardroom. He could hardly have been less welcome, for his name was Gordon Getty.

At the age of forty-eight Gordon was a rumpled, shy, self-effacing man. He occasionally sang with the Marin Opera Company, while cheerfully admitting he was 'the world's funniest singer', but it was as a serious composer that he still longed for recognition, cherishing a secret fantasy that one day J. Paul Getty would be remembered as the father of

Gordon Getty, the composer, rather than as an oil billionaire.

Although he had had his first composition (a piece for chorus, written while he was in the Neutral Zone) published in the early sixties, success had eluded him. 'I have had around twenty criticisms,' he said, reviewing the sum of his musical career with his usual endearing candour. 'Several were good, fifteen-odd were warm and two were *stinkers*.' He was a generous benefactor of the San Francisco Symphony Orchestra and the San Francisco Opera, which often staged the first public performances of his compositions. In 1982 he was working on a difficult and ambitious song cycle set to the poems of Emily Dickinson.

Gordon readily admitted that his reputation for being absent-minded and unworldly was deserved. 'I'm a bit of a scatterbrain,' he confessed, 'more capable than other people, I suppose, of forgetting where I have parked my car.' Once he drove to a local restaurant to collect some hamburgers for lunch, forgot he had brought his own car and waited outside for an hour to be picked up, happily humming Schubert and munching the hamburgers.

Not all multimillionaires would enjoy hamburgers for lunch, but then Gordon did not in any way aspire to a lifestyle befitting his exalted financial status. 'The poet says a book of verse underneath the bough, a loaf of bread, a jug of wine and thou. Well, instead of bread I might want something a little better, but otherwise I think that's pretty close.' He had not the slightest interest in the traditional trappings of great wealth – yachts, helicopters, diamonds, fast cars and islands in the Caribbean, et cetera. He had to park his car – a modest Buick Electra – outside his house because he did not have a garage, he enjoyed playing ping pong and kicking a football in the street and spent part of the summer vacation in a rented house at Lake Tahoe.

He was very involved with his sons – Bill, John, Andrew and Peter, aged from thirteen to eighteen – who were at private schools in New England and was thrilled when Peter, the eldest, won a national competition for young playwrights. 'He had his play performed at the Circle in the Square Theater in New York and got very good reviews, even from *Clive Barnes*.'

Apart from music, he was also interested in anthropology – he was a hard-working chairman of the Leakey Foundation which researched into human origins, and was president of the Jane Goodall Institute, named after the first person to study chimpanzees in the wild. He could be found at either place licking envelopes, when necessary. Both he and his wife, Ann, gave generously to charities and favourite causes, including different political campaign funds – Ann was a Republican, Gordon a Democrat.

The Gettys lived in the fashionable Pacific Heights area of San Francisco in a neoclassical mansion designed in the thirties by the San

Francisco architect Willis Polk, 'a name to conjure with', said Gordon, 'in these parts'. A New York decorator, Sister Parish, was responsible for the lavishly rococo interior of gilt antiques and crystal chandeliers. Callers were usually greeted at the door either by the imperious Bullimore, the butler formerly at Sutton Place, or by John, the footman, both of whom had joined the Gettys' domestic staff in San Francisco after the death of Gordon's father.

While Gordon resolutely preferred the quiet life, his wife, Ann, was one of the leading hostesses in San Francisco. She had featured on the cover of *Town and Country*, her name was a fixture on the best-dressed list (she was rumoured to be the biggest-spending private customer at Saks Fifth Avenue) and she drove around San Francisco's switchback streets in a turbo-charged Porsche. The car was the subject of a family joke: when a friend asked her what Gordon thought of it, she waspishly replied: 'I don't think he's noticed it yet.'

Willowy, elegant and beautiful, Ann was generally credited with being the driving force behind Gordon and revelled in the social whirl in San Francisco and New York, where they kept an apartment on Fifth Avenue. Gordon was perfectly happy to let Ann dazzle: he was not in the least offended when, at Manhattan's fashionable Le Cirque restaurant, he was escorted, dishevelled and unrecognised, to a table at the back by the kitchen while Ann awaited him at the best table in the house.

In San Francisco, Ann thought nothing of giving a candle-lit dinner party for 120 people; indeed, she had had the open courtyard of their home covered with a glass roof for just such occasions. The guest list was usually heavily laden with celebrities – Princess Margaret, Placido Domingo, Rudolf Nureyev and Prince Saud al Faisal of Saudi Arabia had all dined at the Gettys. Her parties were invariably described as 'fabulous' and were tirelessly chronicled in the society columns.

It was not unusual for Gordon to absent himself from such events and, while Ann was busy entertaining the glitterati, to seclude himself in his soundproof music room overlooking the bay, listening to records. Only if there were singers or musicians among the guests could his presence be guaranteed. The Gettys usually gave a party for the cast of the San Francisco Opera after the opening night of a new production and Gordon could sometimes be persuaded to sing, in a faintly uncertain baritone, closing his eyes in concentration and clasping his hands as he reached for the difficult notes.

Although he never claimed to have much of a voice ('It is a good job Gordon Getty doesn't have to earn his living as a singer' a critic sourly noted after Gordon had performed with the Marin Opera), he loved to be in the company of singers and he was always ready to offer the use of his house for rehearsals. Once, during a rehearsal for a choral concert, he asked the cast during a break if they would like some beer. He disappeared and returned ten minutes later to confess, somewhat shamefacedly, that he could not find where it was kept.

Up until the spring of 1982, Gordon did not concern himself overmuch with Getty Oil. His music, his responsibilities as a trustee of the J. Paul Getty Museum and his other interests kept him busy. He was also a trustee of the Sarah C. Getty Trust, but he largely left the running of it to his domineering and curmudgeonly co-trustee, C. Lansing Hays, a New York attorney who had been a close friend of his father. (Paul Getty I had also appointed a bank as a corporate co-trustee, but in the event the bank declined to serve because it feared – presciently – becoming involved in lawsuits.)

In May 1982 Hays died, leaving Gordon in sole charge of one of the biggest family fortunes in the world. 'As sole trustee,' he said, 'I realised I would have to be more assertive than before to safeguard the interests of the trust.' As the trust owned 40.2% of Getty Oil, Gordon viewed it as his personal responsibility to take an interest in the management of Getty Oil.

This legitimate and apparently harmless resolve was to stir up a hornet's nest of jealousy, malice and corporate intrigue which would overshadow any soap opera, *Dallas* and *Dynasty* included.

It came as a very nasty surprise to the directors of Getty Oil when Gordon Getty not only began to take an active interest in the company's affairs, but also began asking penetrating questions about its lacklustre performance. Under Petersen's chairmanship, Getty Oil's net income had fallen to $691,000,000 on sales of $12,300,000,000 in 1982, compared to earnings of $856,000,000 on sales of $13,200,000,000 the year before. The company also had a poor record for finding oil – the key to future profitability – and had sunk $100,000,000 into the Entertainment and Sports Network without seeing a cent of profit. Gordon was vigorously opposed to diversification. 'I had always thought that the company should stick to the oil business,' he said. 'Diversification was for the birds. But I was mainly concerned that the asset value of the company was nearly three times higher than the stock-market quotation. I kept urging upon them the need to restructure the company and bring the stock price up.'

Gordon's suggestions were deeply resented, perhaps with some justification. Gordon neither looked, acted nor talked like a business-man and was widely viewed as something of an eccentric. Although he liked to claim status as a consultant and troubleshooter while his father was alive, the details of his business career were all too well-known and signally failed to impress. Nevertheless, as sole trustee of the Sarah C. Getty Trust, he could not be ignored.

The directors of Getty Oil adopted a thoroughly patronising attitude towards Gordon, wearily affecting to listen to his nutty ideas, humouring him as an important stockholder, before getting on with the serious business of running Getty Oil. Gordon did not help his own cause by canvassing opinions from other businessmen and enthusiastically taking up almost every suggestion. One week he was in favour of spinning off the company's assets into royalty trusts, the next week he thought 'disincorporation' was the solution. The directors claimed they did not know what Gordon wanted and hinted that they suspected Gordon did not know what he wanted, either.

He was soon the victim of malicious tittle-tattle circulating in those bars and clubs of Los Angeles and San Francisco where businessmen gathered. It was whispered that Sid Petersen frequently had to help Gordon find his car after board meetings – not because he had forgotten where it was parked, but because he had forgotten what make and colour it was. That story always raised a smile as did the canard that he often closed his eyes during board meetings in order to run through opera scores in his head. The consensus of opinion was that Gordon was belatedly trying to be taken seriously as a businessman after a lifetime of derision from his family.

Blithely unaware of what was being said behind his back, Gordon continued to put forward his ideas and Petersen, supported by all the other directors, continued to reject them. None of them seemed worried about so lightly dismissing the views of a man who controlled forty per cent of the company: Gordon was largely viewed as a harmless irritant and because his usual demeanour was amiable and easy-going, it was easy to underestimate him, easy to forget that his name was Getty.

Frustrated at his apparent failure to make any progress with his fellow directors, Gordon discussed his problems with his old school chum, Bill Newsom. 'Gordon's one weakness is that he can't see evil,' said Newsom. 'I am convinced that the Getty board was trying to destroy him. They didn't like this guy with a strong artistic streak in his personality encroaching on to their terrain and coming up with some good ideas. I kept telling him that Petersen was going to cut his throat and he'd better do something about it. But he wouldn't believe it.'

The relationship between Gordon and Petersen only became strained after an incident involving Mark Getty, Gordon's nephew. While he was a student at Oxford, Mark was involved in a project to build a replica of the Globe Theatre in London and when he returned to California he asked Gordon if it would be all right to solicit a contribution from Getty Oil. Gordon told Mark to see Petersen and provided him with a polite letter of introduction; he was upset when he learned later that Petersen had been rude to Mark, snapping 'What do you want? I'm a busy person.' Mark told his uncle that he thought Petersen had deliberately humiliated him. Gordon was not pleased.

By January 1983 the board was beginning to tire of listening to Gordon going over and over the same ground and during an acrimonious meeting at the Bonaventure Hotel in Los Angeles, Petersen accused him of 'disrupting' the smooth running of the company and leaking inside information by discussing company affairs with outsiders. Gordon indignantly refuted the accusation.

With boardroom tension rising all the time, Gordon kept up relentless pressure for a restructuring of the company, calling for an end to the diversification strategy and greater efforts to increase the company's oil reserves. He now strongly favoured a buy-back of shares as the best option – a course rigorously opposed by the other directors since it would inevitably result in the Sarah C. Getty Trust becoming the majority shareholder, the very last thing they wanted to happen.

Gordon denied that he was promoting the buy-back option as a means of taking control of Getty Oil, claiming that he was acting in what he believed to be the company's best interests. Nevertheless, he was increasingly attracted to the idea of running the company. 'Management was worried that I wanted to take over,' he said, 'and in a sense I did – not going down to the office and solving problems on a day-to-day basis the way my father had done in his time, but being in a position to call the balls and strikes.'

The single concession the board made to Gordon was to hire the investment bankers Goldman, Sachs and Company to investigate alternatives for the company – and then only after Gordon had declared his intention to retain Goldman, Sachs on his own account. Petersen thought that if a forty-per-cent shareholder was seen running off to New York to hire an investment banker to study the company's future, the board might just as well hang up a 'For Sale' sign.

Goldman, Sachs reported in July and, to Gordon's unmitigated delight, came down in favour of a stock-repurchase plan as the best course of action. Gordon imagined that he had won, but the board still refused to act. In the end, Petersen offered Gordon a deal: the company would approve the stock purchase plan if Gordon would agree to the trust being limited to forty per cent of the shareholder votes, even though its stock would actually increase to fifty-one per cent. Gordon, still enamoured of the prospect of taking control, bitterly rejected the proposal.

Around this time, a third party entered into the dispute – Harold Williams, a former chairman of the Securities and Exchange Commission. Widely respected as a businessman, Williams had been appointed chairman of the J. Paul Getty Museum Trust in 1981 and had been following the boardroom battle at Getty Oil with mounting concern. The museum trust owned 11.8% of Getty Oil stock and as such held the balance of power, a premium position Williams was anxious to maintain.

Unattracted by the prospect of becoming minority shareholder in a company controlled by Gordon Getty and equally worried that any restructuring of the company would endanger the museum's position, Williams retained a New York attorney, Martin Lipton, to look out for the museum's interests. Lipton, a seasoned mergers and acquisitions specialist, would play a central role in the forthcoming events.

In September *Forbes* magazine put Gordon at the top of their annual list of the four hundred richest people in America, much to his distress and that of his mother, the former starlet Ann Rork. Gordon's mother married three more times after her divorce from Getty and eventually settled in an apartment in Palm Beach, Florida, from where she ventured a single opinion: 'I think the *Forbes* list is just disgusting. Why zero in on poor old Gordo?' The reason was simple: the list was compiled on the basis of how much money individuals controlled and Gordon inherited his father's title as the Richest Man in America because he controlled the Sarah C. Getty Trust, then valued at around $2,200,000,000.

Towards the end of September, Petersen and his colleagues became convinced that Gordon and the museum were intending to join forces to take control of Getty Oil. They heard that he was going to make the museum 'an offer it could not refuse' and they decided the time had come to 'neutralise' Gordon. For several months, attorneys hired by the Getty Oil management had been secretly exploring ways of either ousting him from his position as sole trustee of the Sarah C. Getty Trust, or curtailing his power by getting a corporate co-trustee appointed. Gordon, of course, knew nothing of this.

With Gordon away in London at a meeting of museum trustees, Petersen called a special board meeting at twenty-four-hours' notice, to be held in Philadelphia on Sunday 2 October. All the members of the board were alerted by telephone, with the exception of Gordon, who was sent a telegram, delivered to his home in San Francisco, on Saturday afternoon. When the board assembled in a hotel suite in Philadelphia on Sunday, Gordon Getty's absence was noted and a proposal was put forward to issue an additional nine million shares in Getty Oil to an employee stock-ownership programme, thereby diluting the percentage held by the combined shares of the Sarah C. Getty Trust and the J. Paul Getty Museum to less than fifty per cent.

The board unanimously authorised the extra share issue and went on to discuss what to do about Gordon. Barton Winokur, a Philadelphia lawyer retained by Getty Oil, reported to the meeting that 'contact' had been made with numerous Getty heirs to encourage them to file a suit seeking the appointment of a co-trustee on the grounds that Gordon's interference in the company's affairs was not in the best interests of the trust. (Among those contacted was Claire Getty, one of George's daughters, who had a six-year-old illegitimate son, Beau Maurizio George Getty-Mazzota. Lawyers suggested he would be a good candidate to bring the suit; Claire disagreed.)

Winokur said that J. Paul Getty II, Gordon's brother, had agreed to allow a suit to be filed in the name of his fifteen-year-old son, Tara Gabriel Galaxy Gramaphone Getty. Ever helpful, the company had lined up a distinguished Los Angeles attorney, Seth Hufstedler, to act as Tara's guardian *ad litem*. (Another law firm, Gibson, Dunn and Crutcher, was originally approached, but chose not to become involved in an action so curiously originated.)

The board agreed to encourage the suit and, in the event of its not being filed by Tara or any of the other Getty grandchildren, authorised Getty Oil to bring the suit itself. That evening, Petersen and Winokur left for London in the hope of making a last-minute deal with Gordon. They were aware that authorising the new share issue was tantamount to throwing down the gauntlet in front of him and they were anxious to prevent details of the boardrom strife leaking out – in the jargon of Wall Street, it would put Getty Oil 'in play' and make it vulnerable to outsiders attempting a takeover.

Monday 3 October found the principal players closeted in different hotel suites in London, attended by lawyers in ever-increasing numbers. Petersen had with him Winokur, Herbert Galant, a New York attorney who had been hired as special counsel, and Geoffrey Boisi, head of the mergers and acquisitions department at Goldman, Sachs which was still retained by Getty Oil. Harold Williams had Martin Lipton and Patricia Vlahakis, an associate hurriedly flown over to help with the negotiations. Gordon was accompanied by Charles Cohler and Thomas Woodhouse from Lasky, Haas, Cohler and Munter, Gordon's personal attorneys in San Francisco.

Despite this impressive gathering of legal talent, nothing was achieved that day. Gordon's hope of making a deal with the museum in order to take control of Getty Oil came to nothing. He suggested joining forces, kicking out the board and forging ahead with the stock repurchase plan. Williams turned him down flat. With this power play thus thwarted, Gordon was not of a mind to kiss and make up with Sid Petersen, whom he perceived to be his main antagonist. 'I was willing to negotiate,' Gordon said, 'but it seemed the more I agreed to, the more demands came back.' Talks ended late Monday night in Gordon's suite at Claridge's with tempers frayed all round.

Next day, the resourceful Lipton came up with a new idea. He proposed a tripartite 'standstill agreement' to allow time for passions to cool and the warring factions to resolve their differences. He suggested all hostilities should cease for eighteen months, and that no changes should be made to the stock position of the company during that period while discussions continued to formulate a constructive and agreed strategy for the future of Getty Oil. Petersen and his team were warm to the idea; Gordon was cool, but said he would think about it. Lipton delivered a handwritten draft of a standstill agreement to attorneys on each side and left it at that.

Two weeks later, all the parties convened at the cluttered offices of Lasky, Haas, Cohler and Munter in San Francisco. Petersen and his lawyers were put in one room and Gordon and his lawyers were in another, while Lipton shuttled back and forth between them trying to get the standstill agreement signed. In the process, he managed to antagonise quite a few of his legal brethren: 'He thought of himself as some kind of goddamn Henry Kissinger' said one.

Lipton's two-page handwritten draft agreement had been transformed by Petersen's lawyer into a closely-typed contract of sixteen pages. Gordon obstinately refused to discuss it, insisting he was only prepared to consider signing the draft and nothing else. He also wanted the agreement to be in force for twelve months only, instead of the eighteen months Lipton had originally proposed. Lipton secured the other side's approval for Gordon to appoint four directors of his own choosing to the Getty Oil board and, with this concession to sweeten the pill, Gordon finally signed the draft amended to cover a twelve-month period. Lipton took it in to Petersen and presented it as a 'take-it-or-leave-it' deal. Petersen signed.

The announcement of a cease-fire at Getty Oil did nothing to calm the fears of other members of the family as to what Gordon might, or might not, do. The Georgettes, in particular, displayed little confidence in their uncle's business abilities and were extremely unhappy that he was in sole charge of the family fortune and their money. By 1983 Anne and Claire were married, both to former Peace Corps volunteers. Anne, who had two children, lived in Seattle and Claire was in Connecticut, where her husband was at Yale. The youngest of the Georgettes, Caroline, lived in a small town to the south of San Francisco. All three of them were quiet and reserved and intent on trying to live ordinary lives, despite their great wealth.

In October, the Georgettes met Uncle Gordon in San Francisco to find out what was going on. After he had carefully explained why he thought it was necessary to close the 'value gap' and push up the price of Getty Oil stock, one of the young women posed a pertinent question that had been uppermost in all their minds. 'Since the trust has so much money already,' she asked, 'why are we trying to get more?'

Gordon was taken aback. 'A very interesting philosophical question,' he said after a moment. The best he could do by way of reply was to put forward the proposition that it was his 'fiduciary duty' to maximise the trust's wealth. The Georgettes left, unconvinced. The old man would have been turning in his grave had he known that his grandchildren were questioning the morality of acquisitive wealth.

Paul II also expressed concern about what was happening at Getty Oil. As brothers they had always been close, although Paul's drug addiction put a strain on their relationship. 'I get along with him as well as you can get on with a drug addict,' said Gordon. 'I maintain contact with him by letter because he has no set waking hours and you never know what his condition will be if you reach him by telephone. He's very bright, you know, and we have a lot of similar interests.'

Somewhat to Gordon's surprise, Paul telephoned one day to try and persuade him to accept a co-trustee. During the course of the conversation, Paul burst into tears. 'I don't think he realised what was going on,' said Gordon. 'He just thought that as there were so many seasoned people in the company against me, I must be wrong.'

Paul followed up with a glowering letter: 'It was Father's clear intention that there should be a corporate co-trustee . . . I don't want to threaten you, or even appear to, but I am afraid that litigation will be inevitable if you don't quickly agree to another trustee and I'm sad to think that I, too, would be sucked into it.'

On the morning of Friday 11 November, the full board of Getty Oil met in Houston to formally ratify the truce. After a brief preliminary discussion, Gordon was asked if he would step outside the room for a moment while the other directors voted on the agreement; it was explained that they would like to confer without him present. Gordon thought it was rather odd, but shrugged his shoulders and pushed back his chair.

As he walked out of one door, Winokur and Galant were ushered in through another. While Gordon kicked his heels outside imagining the board was debating the details of the truce, Winokur and Galant were explaining their view that the standstill agreement need not deter the company from joining the suit against Gordon, due to be filed the following Monday. Such litigation, they advised, would not violate the terms of the agreement. The two lawyers were politely thanked, then shown out. The board approved a motion to support the suit. Gordon was called back into the room and told only that the board agreed to the truce.

On Monday 14 November Seth Hufstedler, acting as guardian *ad litem* for Tara Gabriel Galaxy Gramaphone Getty, petitioned Los Angeles Superior Court for the appointment of the Bank of America as a corporate co-trustee to the Sarah C. Getty Trust. Next day the Getty Oil Company petitioned to intervene, seeking to have a 'disinterested' co-trustee appointed to protect the company and its shareholders from the 'trustee's follies'.

Both Gordon Getty and Harold Williams were completely taken by surprise and were outraged at the company's action. 'The fact that they had stirred it up behind my back,' said Gordon, 'while pretending to negotiate with me in good faith, shocked everyone to a man.'

Martin Lipton, the man largely responsible for getting the standstill agreement signed, felt 'utterly betrayed'. He telephoned Galant and spluttered 'You snookered me!' Galant was surprised at Lipton's reaction. 'If anyone should feel snookered, Marty,' Galant calmly replied, 'it's Gordon.'

On Monday 21 November, five directors of Getty Oil demanded an urgent meeting of the board. They were Gordon Getty, Harold Williams and three of Gordon's appointees – Laurence Tisch, chairman of the Loews Corporation, Alfred Taubman, a multimillionaire industrialist and owner of Sotheby Parke Bernet, and Graham Allison, dean of the Kennedy School of Government at Harvard University. (All three were close friends of Ann – she had been instrumental in helping her husband choose the new directors.)

Petersen refused to call a meeting, asserting that the upcoming holiday season – it was Thanksgiving that week – made it impossible. On Friday, the *New York Times* reported 'intense speculation' in Wall Street about a possible break-up or takeover of the company; the price of Getty Oil stock was climbing rapidly in anticipation.

In the midst of all this bruising turmoil and Byzantine feuding, Ann Getty flew forty friends from San Francisco to New York to join 160 other guests at Gordon's fiftieth birthday party in the Metropolitan Museum's Temple of Dendur. Isaac Stern played the violin and Luciano Pavarotti sang 'Happy Birthday'. Ann paid the travel and hotel bills for all the guests, some sixty-five thousand dollars. A few days later Gordon's song cycle, setting to music the poems of Emily Dickinson, was performed at the Alice Tully Hall in New York and received the usual drubbing from the critics.

By the beginning of December it became clear to Petersen and his associates that in their anxiety to neutralise Gordon they had made a fatal misjudgement by counting on the continuing support of the Museum. What in fact happened was that the company's duplicitous behaviour convinced Harold Williams he could no longer work with the board; Lipton's advice was that Getty Oil had violated both the letter and the spirit of the standstill agreement and that it could no longer be considered in force.

On 5 December the board's manoeuvring backfired and the coalition it had been striving so hard to prevent, took place: Gordon and Harold Williams joined forces and signed a 'consent to action by majority shareholders' (a convenient Delaware corporate law that allowed a majority of shareholders to change the company's bye-laws) enabling them to assume legal control of Getty Oil and order the withdrawal of the motion to intervene in the trustee litigation. 'We were of the opinion,' said Gordon, 'that the directors were so wound up emotionally that we could no longer rely on them to behave rationally.'

Getty Oil issued a brief press release stating it was 'shocked and alarmed' by the move. There was now no question in Wall Street that Getty Oil was 'in play', riven by dissent and ripe for takeover.

The first hopeful customer was J. Hugh Liedtke, chairman of Houston-based Pennzoil and coincidentally an old friend of Gordon's father. Liedtke telephoned Gordon and said he thought they could 'work together'. Three days after Christmas, Pennzoil made a $1,600,000,000 bid for a twenty per cent stake in Getty Oil, offering a hundred dollars a share – twenty dollars over the market price. The board considered the price was too low and turned down the offer. But with takeover rumours now rife Martin Lipton, acting on behalf of the museum, put forward an alternative strategy based on the Pennzoil offer which would buy the beleaguered board precious time to sort out its problems. He suggested the company should make its own tender for twenty per cent of the shares at $110 a share, thereby acceding to Gordon's principal demand and making the trust the majority shareholder. In return, Gordon would refrain from exercising control for ninety days while the company sought a buyer at a higher price or some other solution. On Saturday 31 December, this proposal was agreed in principle by both sides.

Lipton thought he had every reason to congratulate himself – until the next day. He held a New Year's Day party at his apartment in New York the following evening and among the guests were Laurence Tisch and Martin Siegel, Gordon Getty's investment banker from Kidder, Peabody and Co. They had some astounding news for their host. Gordon had changed his mind about signing the self-tender agreement because he had decided he could no longer trust Sid Petersen. Liedtke and Gordon had got together earlier in the day at the Hotel Pierre – the first time they had ever met – and struck a deal for a leveraged buy-out of all the museum and publicly-held stock at $110 a share. A new Getty oil company would emerge from the deal, four sevenths owned by Gordon and the remainder by Pennzoil. Gordon would be chairman and Liedtke the chief executive. If at the end of a year they were not in accord over how the company should be run, the assets would be divided into two new companies – one owned by Gordon, the other by Pennzoil.

A meeting of the Getty board had already been convened for six o'clock on the evening of 2 January at the Hotel Inter-Continental in New York, to discuss the self-tender proposal. Instead Gordon and Pennzoil presented their new joint offer, to the undisguised fury of most of the directors, who believed they were being railroaded by Gordon. A noisy, disorderly and hostile discussion followed, with any number of rancorous arguments going on at the same time. Harold Williams declared the museum to be 'a seller at $110 a share', but some of the other directors, led by Tisch, still believed the price was too low. Lipton and Siegel kept slipping out of the meeting to confer with Pennzoil lawyers, posted outside, to try and 'sweeten' the offer, but to no avail. As the museum was in favour of selling, Pennzoil kept promoting the idea that Williams should push the deal through by simply signing another majority consent with Gordon. Williams demurred; he thought it was unfair for the museum to impose its will on the board. The meeting finally broke up at 2.30 a.m., with the Pennzoil deal still hanging in the balance.

The directors reconvened twelve hours later, by which time Pennzoil lawyers were ready to put forward a new, convoluted offer involving an extended pay-out from the planned sale of a Getty insurance subsidiary which would be an add-on, they called it 'a stub', worth $1.50. By 6.30 p.m. Pennzoil had increased the value of the stub to $2.50, making its offer worth $8,700,000,000. Williams proposed a motion accepting this; it was carried by fourteen votes to one, with Chauncey J. Medberry III, a retired chairman of the Bank of America, as the only dissenter.

Gordon Getty, after exchanging a few handshakes, returned to his suite at the Hotel Pierre to celebrate with a bottle of champagne. He had achieved his ambition – he was chairman of his own oil company. He thought his father would have been proud of him.

While Gordon was contentedly sipping his celebratory champagne, the lawyers were engaged in a muddled and caustic altercation. Getty Oil directors, having spent the best part of twenty-four turbulent hours negotiating the Pennzoil deal, left it to their luckless lawyers to sort out the details. There were, by that stage, no less than seventeen lawyers and bankers involved and most of them were utterly confused about the precise nature of the deal that had just been agreed. No one quite knew who was paying what to whom, when and how. Ralph Copley, a Getty Oil counsel who had been trying to take minutes during the rumpus, offered the opinion that it was impossible for anyone to 'accurately state what had happened'.

At midnight the lights were still burning in the Park Avenue offices of Paul, Weiss, Rifkind, Wharton and Garrison, the firm representing

Pennzoil, where the lawyers had all gathered. Some of the participants reported scenes of total chaos, with raucous argument and occasional shouting matches as the various factions tried to agree how the transaction should be effected.

They might have saved their breath. Poor Gordon barely had time to savour his new-found corporate prominence before bad news arrived from the West Coast, where the Georgettes had conferred and decided they did not like what was going on. At four o'clock on the afternoon of Wednesday 4 January Gordon's niece, Claire Getty, successfully petitioned a judge in California to sign a temporary restraining order preventing the Pennzoil deal from going ahead, pending disclosure of the terms to the beneficiaries of the Sarah C. Getty Trust.

It was the Georgettes's fervent ambition to save Getty Oil. Ironically their action guaranteed its demise, for the delay allowed a new contender to enter into the battle.

At the age of thirty-six, Bruce Wasserstein, ebullient co-director of the mergers and acquisitions team at First Boston Corporation, was known in Wall Street as the 'merger maestro'. A friend of both Martin Lipton and Laurence Tisch, he had built up a dossier of information about Getty Oil and had been following the tangled boardroom drama for some months, patiently waiting for an opportunity to make a move. As early as October he had made contact with Texaco, offering his services to broker a deal if an opening presented itself.

The opportunity arrived on Wednesday 4 January. First Getty Oil unwisely issued a press release announcing that the deal with Pennzoil was 'subject to execution of a definitive agreement', alerting Wasserstein to the possibility that the deal might be resting on a weak foundation. Then Claire Getty filed her suit and gave him the time he needed to make a bid. He telephoned John K. McKinley, chairman of Texaco, warning him to be ready to act within twenty-four hours and telling him it was the 'perfect set-up for Texaco'. McKinley called Petersen to ask if the Pennzoil deal was final. No it was not, said Petersen, 'the fat lady has not sung.' (The only sure sign an opera was over; a quip Gordon would have appreciated.)

Wasserstein worked all night at Texaco's headquarters at White Plains, New York, preparing his strategy. He knew that Standard Oil of California and at least one other overseas oil company were also planning to bid and he decided that the fastest way into Getty Oil would be to 'lock up' the museum.

On the morning of Thursday 5 January, Wasserstein telephoned Lipton to tell him that a better offer for Getty Oil was coming down the pipeline. At noon, Texaco's executive board authorised Wasserstein to offer $122.50 a share for Getty Oil and by seven o'clock that evening Wasserstein, McKinley and Texaco lawyers were in Lipton's office in Manhattan putting forward their offer. (Harold Williams, chairman of the museum, was celebrating his fifty-sixth birthday with his children and had delegated all negotiating to Lipton.)

Lipton said the museum wanted $125 a share to make a deal with Texaco. McKinley said it might be possible, if he could get Gordon to sign an agreement that night before anyone else could jump in. By midnight, Wasserstein and McKinley were huddled with Gordon at the Hotel Pierre, trying to persuade him to give up his dream of running the company and become a seller at $125 a share, rather than a buyer at $112.50. As the trustee of the Sarah C. Getty Trust, Gordon believed he could not turn down an offer that would vastly increase the trust's wealth and at three o'clock in the morning he sadly signed an agreement to sell out to Texaco.

'It all moved rather quickly and somewhat out of control,' Gordon confessed. 'These takeover battles do go fast. It's amazing how dinosaurs of corporations who can take years to fire somebody can buy a company in a day if they want to. I would have preferred the company to survive with myself in control, but selling was always one of the acceptable outcomes, although it was never my first choice.'

When the surprise announcement was made later that morning that Texaco had acquired Getty Oil, another challenge was mounted by perhaps the least-known branch of the Getty family. The four children of the reclusive Ronald Getty stepped into court with their own guardian *ad litem*, claiming that Uncle Gordon had no right to sell the stock that they would one day inherit.

Ronald Getty was then chairman of the Getty Financial Corporation, a private investment company in Los Angeles which backed Don the Beachcomber restaurants. He avoided publicity so successfully that the existence of his children – Christopher, Stefanie, Cecile and Christina – came as a complete surprise to many Getty watchers. Their lawsuit was sufficiently alarming to prompt Texaco to raise its bid to $128 a share, making it – at $10,100,000,000 – the largest corporate takeover in history. At this figure, the family settled.

In these thoroughly unhappy circumstances, the Getty Oil Company disappeared into the maw of the Texaco giant. It was a brave and extraordinary company, founded when George F. Getty stepped off a train in Bartlesville, Oklahoma in 1903. His son, J. Paul Getty, laboured long, sacrificing five marriages and five sons along the way, to build Getty Oil into a corporation that would endure into the next century. In the event, it survived without him for rather less than eight years.

* * *

The Gettys, of course, continued to sue each other. Indeed the small print of the Texaco deal included a clause, inserted at the insistence of the family, banning Gordon from using their agreement to the sale of the company as a defence in any legal action they might want to take against him.

The Georgettes, not in the least grateful that the takeover had increased their annual incomes to about forty million dollars each, tirelessly pursued Uncle Gordon through the courts in the hope of having him removed as trustee.

When Gordon made an ill-advised attempt to appoint his wife as his successor trustee to serve in the event of his removal the Georgettes, according to one lawyer, 'went bananas' and added a claim for substantial damages to their suit.

Tara Gabriel Galaxy Gramaphone Getty's suit to clip Uncle Gordon's wings by getting a corporate co-trustee appointed plodded on in Los Angeles Superior Court, prompting smirks every time the plaintiff's exotic name was read out.

Ronnie's attempt to force his brothers to cut him in on the Sarah C. Getty Trust went to appeal, doubtless spurred on by the fact that the value of the trust had increased to around four billion dollars. Gordon's income, after the takeover, soared to about $150,000,000 a year, making Ronnie's $3000 look even sillier than formerly.

In April 1984 lawyers acting on behalf of the wretched Paul Getty III filed a malpractice suit in San Francisco Superior Court claiming that doctors negligently prescribed methadone for him and thus contributed to the stroke that left him blind, paralysed and unable to speak.

That same month, young Paul's father demonstrated his affection for the family by contributing five hundred thousand dollars to an appeal in Britain to prevent a fourteenth-century painting by the Italian master, Duccio di Buoninsegna, from being exported to the United States. It had been bought, for $2,360,000, by the J. Paul Getty Museum. Paul was sulking because he believed his children were siding with his brother and he warned his son, Mark, then a trainee stockbroker in New York, not to expect to inherit his book collection. 'That's OK Dad,' said Mark, 'I've joined the Book-of-the-Month Club.'

None of the animosity mattered to Gordon after Wednesday 13 March 1985, for on that momentous night he achieved his heart's desire – *rapturous* reviews for his latest composition, 'Plump Jack', a twelve-minute cantata inspired by Falstaff's speeches in *Henry IV* and played by the San Francisco Symphony Orchestra. Byron Belt, the WNBC-TV critic, described Gordon as a 'welcome major force in the cultural life of America'. Gordon wondered if he had died and woken up in heaven.

While the Gettys were enthusiastically suing each other, a judge ordered the assets of the Sarah C. Getty Trust to be held in Treasury bills, creating an embarrassing problem. Treasury rules prohibited one buyer from taking more than thirty-five per cent of the bills sold at each weekly auction and the Getty Trust was so immense that it took many weeks to comply with the judge's direction. But it turned out to be a profitable move: when the transfer had finally been effected, the trust began piling up interest at the rate of a million dollars every twenty-four hours. In June, the two dozen lawyers representing different feuding factions of the family reached an agreement to break up the Sarah C. Getty Trust into four smaller trusts of $750 million each. All twenty-six of J. Paul Getty's living heirs were required to sign the agreement, which was likened by a lawyer to 'an elaborate treaty negotiation among warring nations'.

'The money is the root of the problem with the Gettys,' said Justice William Newsom. 'It is a ludicrous, preposterous amount of money, enough to make you wonder if anybody in the world should have that much. It taints everything. When you consider what has happened to the Gettys, it is not unreasonable to conclude that the money has been a curse on the family.'

Epilogue

The courage of Martine

Martine Getty sits in a coffee shop in San Francisco. She did not want to meet me at home because, well, it is 'a little difficult'.

In a crumpled cotton flying suit and boots, she is casually beautiful, with curly auburn hair, glowing brown eyes, clear skin and very white teeth. Today she wears a bright red lipstick that makes her look younger than her thirty-five years.

She has never talked before about her life with Paul and she does not find it easy. I ask her how she felt about him when they first met in Rome and she blushes and giggles and shakes her head. 'I think it's too private,' she says.

There is little to uplift the heart in the unhappy machinations of the Getty family: the devotion of Martine to Paul is the shining exception. She has nothing in her life but her two children and her tragically afflicted young husband and she wants for nothing more.

Not long after the stroke, there was talk of a divorce and outsiders assumed that Martine was unable to face surrendering her life to the care of a helpless cripple. But Martine never wanted a divorce, not then, not now.

What happened was just another bizarre twist in the anguished family chronicles: one of Paul's nurses formed 'an attachment' to him. A divorce and a remarriage under such circumstances was more than even the Gettys could stomach and Paul was returned to Martine's welcoming arms.

They live in a rented house in San Francisco, not far from Gordon, who often visits. Paul still needs round-the-clock nursing – he is too heavy for Martine to lift – but she spends almost all her time with him.

'At the moment, I am concentrating on Paul,' she says. 'I really believe he is making progress, although it is very slow. He is very close to the children. They have always been around him, even when he was in hospital. Children have very direct communication and they can understand what he says. They don't even seem worried about it now. They cuddle up with him in bed and talk to him all the time and tell him what they have been doing. Now they have him all the time and they are happy about that.'

348

Epilogue

Doctors have told Martine that there is little hope of any real improvement in Paul's condition. He will never walk again, never see again, never speak again. She will not accept it.

She has bought a small synthesiser keyboard in the hope that they might be able to compose music together and combine their interests like they did before. He cannot move his fingers to play it yet, but she is hoping – one day – he will be able to play a little. 'It might be good practice for later on if we can get some communication devices, you know, computer things.

'He has faced a lot and changed very much. Mentally he is very alert and intuitive. He senses everything and emanates a wonderful friendliness. People like to be in his company. Friends come by quite often and we go out to the theatre or the movies, or for walks in the park in his wheelchair. We are hoping to get a special car, so we can get the wheelchair in it.

'He went through some periods of depression, but coped with it. Generally his spirits are good, pretty good.'

I ask her how her own spirits are and she seems surprised by the question. 'Me? I think the only sin one can commit is to give up. I feel one has always to strive and hope. Even if you don't see things come right straight away, you have to keep on hoping. What I hope is that he can find some way to realise himself and find some sense in his life.

'I think if someone is so physically impaired and can't do anything on the outside, it raises very deep, very essential, questions about what life is about. It hits you very profoundly and it is something you have to struggle with.

'I'm pretty optimistic really. We're actually quite happy. In a way, we are happier than we were before. At least he is home.'

Index

Getty, Gertrude Lois (J. Paul Getty
I's sister), 15, 16, 199
Getty, Gloria (George's first wife), 188,
257, 296
Getty, Gordon (J. Paul Getty I's
son), 1, 4, 209, 255, 268; birth, 97;
relations with his father, 138, 145,
225-6, 259, 264-5, 293; education,
168; in oil business, 225-6; arrested
in Saudi Arabia, 229-31; musical
interests, 231, 264, 331-2, 333-4,
341, 346; visits Sutton Place, 248,
259, 296; and the Getty Trust,
259-60, 264-5, 307, 310, 313-14, 334-7,
345; financial position, 2, 259, 346;
marriage, 259-60; and George's
death, 268-9; and Paul's kidnapping,
285; and his father's death, 301;
and Getty's will, 305-8, 311; sues
Getty museum, 312; and Paul's
stroke, 328; and Getty Oil, 331,
334-46; lifestyle, 3, 332-3; family,
332; and the Getty Museum, 334,
336-8
Getty, Jacqueline (George's wife),
269
Getty, James (cousin of John), 12
Getty, James (John's son), 12-13
Getty, Jean Paul I
private life: birth, 16; education,
19, 26, 27, 28, 31, 32; European
trips, 28, 33-6, 74-5, 78, 93, 114,
127-30, 132-4, 137-41, 189-202;
clandestine social life, 28-30;
relations with his father, 29-30, 37-8,
63, 67, 74, 80; builds car, 30;
at Oxford University, 32-3; Far
Eastern tour, 32; liking for Cadillacs,
45; playboy lifestyle, 47-50, 52; in
World War I, 50; and his father's
stroke, 62-3; relations with his
mother, 67, 74, 87-8, 95-6; first
marriage, 63, 67-9; Jeanette divorces,
69, 74, 82, 86; second marriage, 71-2,
74; disinherited by his father, 72,
86; marriage to Fini, 78-81, 82;
and Ann Rork, 89, 90, 91, 93-4,
97, 100; Fini wants to divorce, 2-3,
83-4, 93, 102; and his father's
death, 84-5, 86-8; Ann Rork divorces,
113-14; lifestyle, 113-14, 125, 198-201,
208, 218; marriage to Teddy, 115,
124-5, 127-8, 137, 138-41; obsession

Getty, Jean Paul I – *Contd*
with his health, 129-30, 194-5, 200,
300; parsimony, 129, 130, 208,
218-19, 237, 245-7; art collection, 32,
130-2, 135, 138-9, 170, 191-3, 197-8,
199, 289; pursuit of women, 144-5,
198-9; relations with his sons, 137-8,
145, 168, 223-6, 252, 255-62, 264-5,
267, 293-4; *Europe in the Eighteenth
Century*, 148; and his mother's
death, 151-2; and Joan Barry, 159-60,
161-3; and his son Timothy, 167-8;
Malibu ranch house, 166, 169-71;
leaves America, 196-7; buys three
Elgin Marbles, 201-2; and Penelope
Kitson, 206, 207-12, 242, 295; Teddy
divorces, 207; and Timmy's ill-health,
223-3, 226; and Timmy's death,
227-9; buys Sutton Place, 232,
233-52, 294; mistresses, 241-5, 294,
296-8; *My Life and Fortunes*, 4, 252;
Gordon sues, 260; paranoia, 267-8;
and George's death, 270, 293; and
J. Paul Getty III's kidnapping, 4,
270, 278-88, 289; museum, 1-2,
289-93, 295, 304, 305, 308-9;
admiration for Emperor Hadrian,
291-2; last years, 294-302, 311;
cancer, 300-2; death, 302-3, 316, 321;
will, 2-3, 295, 299, 304-12;
mausoleum, 1, 305, 316
business life: introduction to oil
business, 19-24; moves to California,
26; *The History of the Oil Business
of George F. and J. Paul Getty*,
135-6; goes into oil business, 27-8,
31, 37-8, 39-47; ambitions, 37;
returns to oil business, 50-1, 52-3;
oil prices slump, 56-7; and the
California oil industry, 60-3, 69-70,
72-3, 76-8; boycotted, 73-4; and
George F. Getty Inc., 80, 81-2,
94-102; Wall Street crash, 83;
becomes president of George F.
Getty Inc., 88-92; and Tide Water,
104-13, 115-23, 146, 169, 196;
consolidates Getty interests, 125-6;
in World War II, 140-1, 148-50,
152-64; and the Spartan Aircraft
Factory, 153-8, 159-61, 163-5; goes
into the trailer business, 164-6, 167,
168-9; Middle Eastern oil, 178-88,
202-4, 205, 209-13; worldwide

Index

357